AFC

Also available at all good book stores

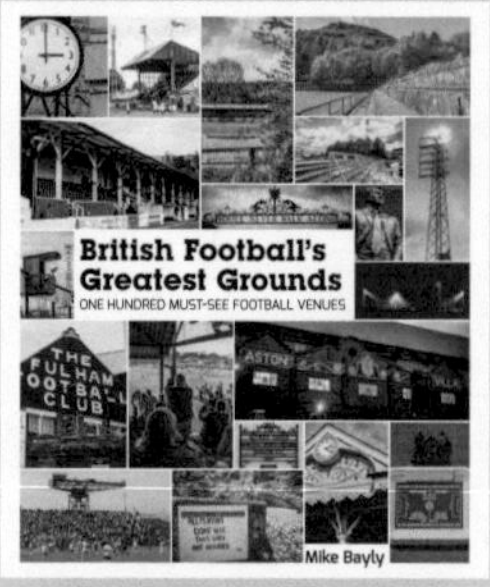

9781785316470

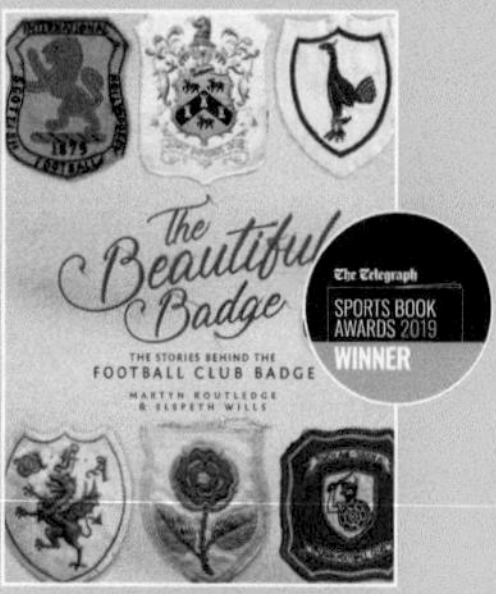

9781785313929

9781785315466

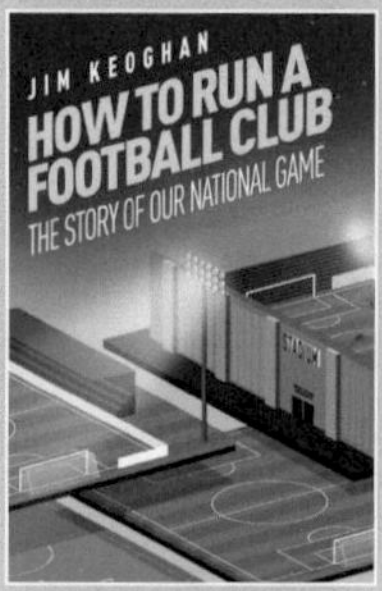

9781785316449

9781785311918

9781785316463

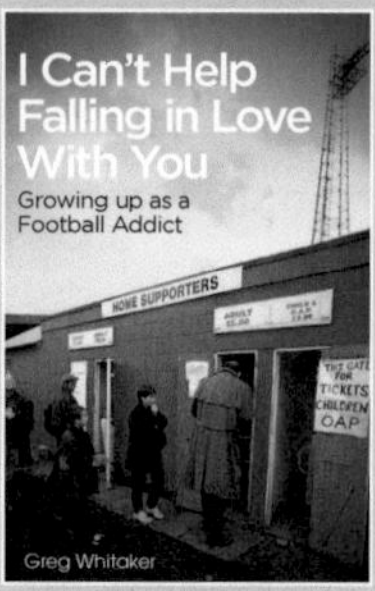

9781785315305

9781785318009

9781785316791

All Together Now

Best wishes,
Erik Samuelson

All Together Now

How Wimbledon Fans Brought Their Club Back Home

ERIK SAMUELSON

pitch

First published by Pitch Publishing, 2021

Pitch Publishing
A2 Yeoman Gate
Yeoman Way
Worthing
Sussex
BN13 3QZ
www.pitchpublishing.co.uk
info@pitchpublishing.co.uk

A CIP catalogue record is available for this book
from the British Library.

ISBN 978 1 78531 850 4

Typesetting and origination by Pitch Publishing

Printed and bound in Great Britain by TJ Books Ltd

CONTENTS

To Eileen

1

INTRODUCTION

'Never doubt that a small group of thoughtful, committed citizens can change the world; indeed, it's the only thing that ever has.' Margaret Mead

THIS BOOK is set inside the world of football but it is really about a group of very resilient, determined people and how they reacted to and overcame adversity. It starts with a travesty of natural justice and the uprooting of a community football club as the justification for a new hypermarket in a bland, anonymous town in Buckinghamshire. It ends with the re-formed club, AFC Wimbledon, moving to its brand new stadium a mere 200 metres from the site of their old home in Plough Lane. And throughout this extraordinary journey the club was owned and run by its fans.

I am from Sunderland. I grew up watching 'The Lads' from the Fulwell End terrace at Roker Park and have great memories of the promotion-winning team in 1964 through to the glory of the 1973 FA Cup Final win.

My career took me to London and in the late 1980s I started taking our sons, Pieter and John, to support their local football team, Wimbledon FC. After following the Dons around the country for a few years I realised that they were now my team – a switch that amounts to heresy where I come from. Fast forward a few years and I'd become known to chat site users for financial analysis and criticism of the WFC announcements that sought to justify a move to Milton Keynes. As a result I got to know the people leading the protests against the move and drafted a plan to take over the club when, as I thought would happen, it fell into administration. Instead, four fans founded a new club and I was fortunate enough to be alongside them and able to help from the beginning.

Having explained how I got involved, that is enough about me; this is not an autobiography. Instead I see myself as the narrator of this fantastic story, drawing upon my memories, the thousands of documents I've trawled through to inform that story, and the 96 conversations I've conducted with the extraordinary people who've contributed to this great journey.

All Together Now[1] starts with a decision to allow WFC to relocate to Milton Keynes and the fans' decision not to accept this nonsense and instead start again at the bottom of the football pyramid. Working to an almost impossible timescale, the four founders created and registered a club and found a stadium in which to play. Rebuffed at the first attempt, they found a league to take the fledgling club, a manager to oversee the team and, following open trials on Wimbledon Common, players to play for that team.

Within a year the club had acquired its own stadium; within nine years it had won five promotions and regained a place in the Football League. I say 'regained' because there is no doubt in my mind that this club is the true continuation of football history and heritage in Wimbledon. Five years later the club was promoted to the third tier of English football and briefly above the club which tried to usurp its history. A further four years later our new stadium opened in Plough Lane, Wimbledon. And all of this was achieved while remaining a fans-owned club.

This book isn't about football matches, goals and saves. It is about the people in football, their resilience, their determination to right a wrong and their incredible commitment, all set to a backdrop of the game we love. It talks about the heroes who played major parts in where we are today. Plus a few villains, of course. It also includes some insights into areas that fans don't often hear about, such as agents and transfer tribunals. But it is primarily about how a group of football fans turned on its head the FA Commission's pompous proclamation that, following the move to Milton

---

1 As a diversion from writing this book I tried to think of song titles, lyrics or other sources from popular culture as chapter titles. *All Together Now* was a natural choice for the book because it reflects the cooperative way we build our club. It is serendipitous but pleasing that the song, by The Farm, was inspired by the famous Christmas Day football match in no man's land in World War 1.

Keynes, for fans to form a new club in Wimbledon 'would not be in the wider interests of football'. As Craig Slater of Sky Sports News said on the day of our debut in the Football League, 'If this isn't in the wider interests of football, I don't know what is.'

A few things about the book. If you are looking for detailed match reports then you will be disappointed. Instead of, for example, describing how hard Danny Kedwell hit his decisive penalty in the play-off final and how high the net billowed, it will tell you what he was thinking as he stepped forward to take it.

And finally, this isn't a history; it's a story. Nonetheless, I've gone to great lengths to verify dates and places. Quotes have been sourced either to a specific publication or an individual. But different people have different recollections of the same event and, as I have found, those memories have changed and in some cases been distorted over the years. Where there are inconsistencies I've gone with the version that fits best with my memories or, failing that, the one that sounds most credible. Douglas Adams said at the start of his wonderful creation, *The Hitchhiker's Guide to the Galaxy*, that it 'contains much that is apocryphal, or at least wildly inaccurate'. I hope I've done a little bit better than that.

2
WE ARE WIMBLEDON

'WE'VE LOST.'

That was the stark message lifelong Wimbledon FC supporter Ivor Heller received from an insider at the FA. It was Monday, 27 May 2002. The football club he'd followed from boyhood was to be uprooted from its community and moved 60 miles north, to Milton Keynes. There was to be no review, no right of appeal, no second chance. The decision would be announced publicly the next day.

A local man, Wimbledon born and bred, Ivor is five foot nothing. But he is the one people remember; a non-stop bundle of energy with a never-give-up attitude, even in the face of great adversity. So his immediate reaction to the call seemed totally out of character; he decided that it was time to close the book on protesting. Instead, with three other fans he would form a new club. More exactly, they would re-form Wimbledon FC in its home community. We would get back into the Football League – and wave two fingers at that Milton Keynes lot and their pirated football club.

There was a precedent for such ambition. In its long and colourful history WFC was renowned for ignoring conventions and confounding expectations. For 88 years the club had played in one or other of the leagues below the top four divisions that are collectively known as the Football League. In 1977 WFC was elected to the Football League and after an astonishing rise through the divisions, the club was promoted into the top tier of English football (later to be rebranded the Premier League) for the 1986/87 season.

In 1988 this success was sealed when WFC won the FA Cup, beating the newly crowned league champions, Liverpool, then one of the top two or three teams in Europe. But then came the Hillsborough disaster in 1989 when 96 Liverpool fans died as a result of a crush in an ill-equipped stadium at a badly managed FA Cup semi-final. The Taylor Report, instituted in the wake of the tragedy, introduced new safety regulations and a requirement for all-seater stadiums in the top two leagues. Wimbledon's ramshackle, albeit much-loved, Plough Lane ground couldn't meet the new safety regulations and in 1991 WFC decamped to Selhurst Park, to ground-share with Crystal Palace on a temporary basis.

There followed years of bitter wrangling between the club's owner, Sam Hammam, and Merton, the local council, about a site for a new stadium. Each blamed the other for the lack of progress. During this time there was much talk about a new home at various mooted sites outside the borough. In particular, news leaked out about an astonishing and barely believable proposal to relocate to Dublin, in Ireland. The idea won the enthusiastic support of Premier League teams and was very close to success before being scuppered by opposition from League of Ireland clubs, fearful of competition for players and fans from a Premier League club based in Dublin.

In 1997 Hammam pocketed a reported £28m by selling an 80 per cent interest in the football club, but not the stadium, to two Norwegian multi-millionaires. They reputedly believed that the Dublin move was a done deal, but quickly realised they'd been sold a pup. They had bought a team with a small fan base, no stadium of its own and limited income.

In 1998, having persuaded the council to remove a restrictive covenant, Hammam sold the old Plough Lane stadium to a supermarket chain for £8m. Within a couple of years, WFC had been relegated to what is now called the Championship.

Along came Peter Winkelman, former music producer and property developer. He was desperate to bring a league club to Milton Keynes, in part because planning permission for an out-of-town hypermarket could not go ahead without 'enabling development' – a stadium would do just nicely for that purpose. But he needed a club to play there and had no interest in bringing a local club up through the divisions. He needed a ready-made club. He wasn't fussy which one. Luton, Barnet, Queens Park Rangers and Wycombe rejected his advances but WFC was vulnerable and a deal was done. Wimbledon FC was going to up sticks and move, lock stock and barrel, to Milton Keynes.

Fans, led by the Wimbledon Independent Supporters Association (WISA), had protested strongly against the proposed Dublin move. Now they swung into action again. A sophisticated press campaign was supplemented by lobbying MPs and councillors, protest marches, boycotting the club's merchandise, and even lying down in front of an opposition team coach to prevent it leaving.

Hopes rose when the Milton Keynes proposal was rejected by the Football League. Then, in the light of a threatened legal challenge, the Football Association (the guardian of football in England) chickened out and appointed an 'independent commission' to resolve the dispute. There was to be no appeal. And the call that Ivor took meant all the protests had come to nothing.

It was over.

Ivor leapt into action. Immediately he called Kris Stewart, the WISA chairman. They agreed that Kris should stay with the group of protesters outside the FA's headquarters in Soho Square for the formal announcement the next day, Tuesday, 28 May 2002. In the meantime Ivor would get things in motion from his office at his print works, just around the corner from the now dilapidated stadium in Plough Lane. Kris would join him the next day.

Next, Ivor called Trevor Williams. Trev loves football, any football at any level. For years he'd been watching non-league games so he was the automatic choice as the expert advisor on forming a new club – something he cheerfully admitted he knew nothing about. He and Ivor arranged to meet the next morning where they would later be joined by fellow Dons fan and leading protester Marc Jones. And so Marc, Ivor, Trevor and Kris became the founders of a new club.

Many action films start with the bringing together of a band of stroppy, idiosyncratic individuals who go on to achieve great things against all the odds. Marc, Ivor, Kris and Trev would never dream of describing themselves as heroes but what they started turned into one of the greatest ever stories in football.

To paraphrase an old saying, great ideas have many parents. No one knows who first suggested forming a new club (or, as many prefer, re-forming the old one) but the idea had been bandied around for months, with Marc one of the most energetic and persuasive proponents. It didn't need a genius to brainstorm the main elements. They needed to register a club with the Football Association, find a league to play in, find somewhere to play, and recruit a manager to bring in some players. They would make up everything else as they went along.

Ivor's print factory was to be their headquarters. Their designated office was narrow and drab with no external light. Imagine a corridor with a couple of tables in it; if anyone sat down they had to stand up again to let people past.

They worked quickly, interspersed with much animated debate about details; what to call the new club, where they would prefer the ground to be, who could be the manager? Very soon the faded paint on the walls was obscured by dozens of Post-It notes of actions to be taken, people to be called, e-mails to be written. Some of the Post-It notes lost their urgency long before they lost their adhesiveness.

By mid-morning on Tuesday, even before the official announcement of the decision, Ivor had contacted David Fowkes, the chief executive of the London FA. By the time David arrived at the print factory on the Wednesday morning, Ivor, Trev and Kris had agreed what they wanted to say.

David recalled events later in a book about the Wimbledon and District League,[2] 'While the former Wimbledon FC was registering with the Berks & Bucks FA as Milton Keynes Dons FC, any attempt to register Wimbledon FC back in London should have been doomed to failure. Normal FA policy was for newly formed clubs to begin life at the lowest level of Saturday football, in other words below the National League System (commonly known as "the pyramid")'.

What Ivor and Kris didn't know was that David was delighted to have the opportunity to correct a decision that he regarded as a travesty. His philosophy was simple, 'Wimbledon fans want to watch Wimbledon in Wimbledon.' He had watched WFC as a boy and for 32 years had been involved in one way or another in the Wimbledon and District Football League, so he saw this as 'an opportunity for the WDFL to give something back to the club that had given so much to the league for so many years in earlier times'. No wonder that, years later, Ivor led David on to the pitch

2 From *A History of the Wimbledon and District Football League.*

and introduced him to the fans by saying, 'We wouldn't be here today if it wasn't for this man.'

Huddled together in the cramped little office, David completed the form on a question-and-answer basis. He dismissed 'Real Wimbledon' as the club's name because, 'While nicely ironic, it would raise eyebrows at the London FA,' and he didn't want anything to stand in the way of the application. After 'FC Wimbledon' and 'Wimbledon AFC' had been rejected as being likely to cause objections, they settled on 'AFC Wimbledon'.[3] In most clubs, 'AFC' stands for 'Association Football Club' but in this case it was just a means of getting as close as possible to calling the club Wimbledon FC, and no more than that.

Next on the form came 'date of formation'. To their delight, 'David didn't even look up when Ivor said 1889 [the date that WFC was formed]. He just wrote it down and moved on.' Next came the question about where the team would play and Ivor winged it, 'We're close to an agreement to play at Kingsmeadow.'

The application needed approval by the London FA Council. David moved quickly. He knew that the LFA could well regard us as a newly formed club and consequently insist that we start at the bottom of the ladder. And that would have meant playing games on public pitches. To avoid that, we needed to be awarded senior status.

Not for the first time, good fortune intervened. A meeting of the LFA board was scheduled for that evening. David takes up the story, 'I was absolutely not going to take this to the LFA cups committee who do the status because there were one or two on the committee who I knew wouldn't support it.' He was right because for the next ten years one member of the cups committee could be heard muttering into his beer, 'They're not really the true Wimbledon.'

Instead David went direct to Norman Moss, the LFA chairman, and collared him at the Guildhall. With the full-on zeal of a convert, David explained to Norman that this would be the real Wimbledon, 'The fans

---

3 Thanks in part to the club's success, the 'AFC' prefix became increasingly popular. Ten years later, when Croydon Athletic applied for re-registration to the FA Leagues Committee following the demise of their original club due to fraud, they asked to reform as AFC Croydon Athletic. The Leagues Committee accepted the application but decided that it was the last 'AFC' they would accept because, in an un-minuted remark, 'The use of AFC in the name buggers up the alphabetical order for cup draws and league tables.'

aren't going to travel up to Milton Keynes, they are going to go and watch this team, and we can't have them playing on Tooting Bec Common in Division Four of the WDL. They are going to be massive from the word go.' Norman didn't hesitate and they quickly agreed that AFC Wimbledon must be allocated senior status. David called Ivor with the good news the next morning.

The next step was to find a stadium in which to play. Terry Eames was a former WFC player who had taken part in the protests against Milton Keynes and had got to know Ivor, Marc, Trev and Kris while doing so. He joined them at the office. Ivor takes up the story, 'Terry had managed a couple of non-league clubs fairly recently. He knew Dulwich would have us and also he had a mate at Leatherhead who would help. I said that was too far and there's closer grounds.'

After the meeting, thoughts returned to Ivor's comment about non-league Kingstonian's ground, Kingsmeadow, on the outskirts of Kingston upon Thames. Among its attractions was a link to Wimbledon FC because the reserves and ladies teams had played there for some years. The other obvious candidate was Tooting and Mitcham's new ground at Bishop's Road, not least because it was in Wimbledon's home borough of Merton. That was discarded because, in Ivor's words, 'It didn't feel right.' I have never understood why Ivor was set against Tooting but, as I realised some years later, the feeling was deep-rooted and he was against most suggestions that had anything to do with Tooting! So Kingsmeadow was the target.

It was desperately urgent. They had set their sights on joining the Isthmian League, commonly known by its then sponsor's name as the Ryman League.[4] It was 29 May and to comply with the rules, the new club had to have a three-year ground-share agreement signed before the Ryman League AGM on 17 June, or the application would founder. So Ivor phoned Kingsmeadow and got through to Anup Khosla, the stadium owner's son. After a brief conversation, Anup spoke to his father, Rajesh Khosla, a businessman who had bought the stadium and Kingstonian FC a year earlier. He saw the stadium as a group of lounges and bars he could hire out for Indian weddings; it just happened to have a football club attached.

—

4 The Isthmian League has new sponsors nowadays but it was known as the Ryman League all the time we played in it, and that's still what most of our fans call it. So I've used that name throughout this book.

Within an hour, Ivor took a call from Rajesh and they agreed to meet the next day. It was still less than 48 hours since the commission's announcement.

Kingsmeadow is a nicely laid-out non-league ground, which had been built as recently as 1989. It comprised one stand with seats for just over 1,000 fans and three terraces, two of them partially covered, with space for a further 3,500 or so. There were over 200 parking spaces and three bars which were capable of accommodating about 700 people in total. And, importantly, while it wasn't in Wimbledon's home borough of Merton, it was only just over five miles from Plough Lane. After a quick tour, Kris and Ivor concluded that it would do nicely!

Good fortune shone on us yet again because it was clear from the beginning that Rajesh Khosla wasn't 'a football man' but he was definitely a money man. 'That,' said Ivor, 'was obvious as soon as we met him.'

There were already three teams playing on the poorly maintained pitch and adding another would make it almost unplayable. For that reason alone, a football man would have dismissed our approach out of hand. But Old Man Khosla (OMK), as we came to call him, clearly wanted us – or at least our money – especially after Ivor told him we expected crowds of 1,000. So the need for a stadium, which had looked like it could derail the club even before it started, was sorted almost immediately. It was perfectly situated. A sizeable number of fans already lived in the area and for others the journey was only one bus or one train ride. AFC Wimbledon had somewhere to play.

Ryman League Division Two had 16 teams. The contract with OMK rather eccentrically provided for us to play 16 league games, plus one pre-season friendly. The annual fee was £20,000 with extra games at £1,200 each. In return we got a prepared pitch, goalposts, etc., and the promise that bars and concession stalls would be open – although all the profits from those would go to OMK. The deal was for the Ryman-stipulated minimum of three years but OMK had the right to terminate it after only one season if Brentford FC took up an existing option to use the stadium.

All that was needed now was the £20,000 licence fee for year one, but there were already plans in hand for that. By then Ivor had been in touch with Nick Robinson, a lawyer by profession who was the secretary at the Ryman League. Nick was already on the case. The league's chairman was Alan Turvey, coincidentally a member of the three-man FA Commission which had voted 2-1 to allow the move to Milton Keynes. Alan died in 2018 but Nick remembers their conversations vividly, 'Alan felt that the commission had made a very bad decision and he was furious about it. He kept saying "it shouldn't have been allowed", but he was barred from speaking publicly about it. So he was very frustrated that he couldn't say anything or be on the record – but he made sure it was known that it was a majority decision and that he voted against!'

As soon as Turvey heard about the new club he told Robinson, 'We must get involved. We will offer them a home [in our league].' Robinson pointed out that there needed to be a vacancy in the division but Turvey was adamant, saying, 'Just make it happen, get them in.' This determination to help was reflected in a letter from Nick to Kris Stewart, in which he said that 'in the particular circumstances' he was prepared to recommend that the Ryman Management Committee accept our application, despite the possibility that our lease might be terminated after only one year.

As it turned out there was a vacancy and the application was submitted – but there was a problem. The Ryman League is a limited company and as such is bound by its rules, known as the Articles of Association. The problem was that any resolution to be voted on at an annual general meeting had to be circulated 21 days in advance. Since there were only 20 days between the commission's decision and the Ryman League AGM it was impossible to comply. The papers had already gone to members and AFC Wimbledon wasn't on the agenda.

Searching for a way around the problem, Robinson sought legal advice. He was told that if 95 per cent of the votes at the AGM were in favour, then the 21-day rule could be set aside and the club could be admitted. Ivor and Kris completed the forms, submitted them and marked 17 June in their diaries.

Aware that time was of the essence and confident that fans would support the idea of a new club, the founders hadn't sought support for their actions. However, not everyone was as quick to see things their way, as they found at the WISA AGM on the Thursday night, two days after the announcement of the commission's decision.

The timing of the meeting was fortuitous. Having heard the news and the possibility of a new club being formed, the attendance rocketed. Instead of the usual 50 or 60 committed members, 1,000 fans crowded in to the community centre in the middle of Wimbledon with an overspill outside, listening to the proceedings on loudspeakers perched precariously on window sills.

Everyone was impatient to debate whether to form a new club. The formal agenda items were dispatched with almost indecent haste and the meeting turned to three resolutions. Resolutions to boycott 'franchise' (as they were already being called) games at Selhurst Park and to continue to fight the plans for Milton Keynes were quickly passed and the meeting moved on to debate forming a new club. The AGM minutes reported a lengthy and impassioned debate on the merits of these strategies.

The debate swung backwards and forwards. Some fans wanted to continue protesting and thought a new club would be a diversion. Could we seek a judicial review of the decision? Should we take the protest campaign to Milton Keynes and put pressure on local politicians?

A few fans wanted to wait for a year before deciding to form a new club, hoping that an acceptable solution could be negotiated within that time frame. Those in favour of forming a new club argued that we had very little time and we should get on with it. And if we didn't form a club we'd have no team to watch in the following season. We needed to do something positive rather than protesting.

Listening to the debate, I wasn't sure which way the decision would go. And then two things happened. First, Trevor Williams, who isn't one for pushing himself forward, was pressed to repeat what he'd been muttering throughout the meeting. So, for what was possibly the first, and almost definitely the last, time in his life Trev spoke at a public meeting. His message was simple, 'If everyone here tonight turns up and watches us, we'll be one of the biggest non-league clubs around.' The tide started to turn.

Then came a watershed moment in the development of AFC Wimbledon. Kris Stewart recognised that the meeting had reached a crucial point. As chair of WISA he was required to be neutral so he temporarily handed over to vice-chair Nicole Hammond and took up the microphone.

He spoke with a passion and energy that would have been the envy of many an evangelical preacher, 'I've had enough of protesting, of trying to talk sense to owners who will never listen. I just want to watch some football.'

There was the briefest of pauses and then a roar of approval. The debate was settled, just like that. There was enough time to add a fourth resolution, that WISA should fight specifically for the name, badge, history and colours of WFC. The minutes record that both resolutions were 'resoundingly carried', including overwhelming support for creating a new club. That was just as well since that was all Kris, Ivor, Trev and Marc had been doing from the moment Ivor had taken that late-evening call, 72 hours earlier.

The meeting ended with Ivor asking for a show of hands from people who would be willing to pay £200 for a season ticket for the new club. He explained that to secure a ground-share agreement for next season, we needed to be able to commit £20,000 within two weeks. In his full-on salesman mode, Ivor urged supporters to please send cheques for £200 as soon as possible.

Trevor Williams continues the story, 'When Ivor made the season ticket request I went from "all this is exciting and a good idea" to "it scares the shit out of me". I suddenly felt a massive responsibility that this now had to work. The standard of football didn't worry me, or the fact that we might lose every game, but people had emotionally invested in the football club and suddenly I felt that we mustn't screw this up.'

The already frenetic pace increased, as Trev explains, 'I had a key to Ivor's place. I got there at silly o'clock on the Friday morning, only a few hours after the WISA meeting had ended. There was a queue of people already there, "Papers"[5] being at the front. That is when I first went "bloody hell". It was 7am and if you were at the meeting you'd only have found out about it at 10pm the previous day.'

It was becoming obvious that we had something very substantial on our hands. It was also becoming clear, although perhaps not to him yet, that Trevor was acting as club secretary, a role that was to be thrust upon him soon afterwards.

My life changed as a direct result of that evening. The WISA meeting transformed my commitment from behind-the-goal supporter and chat-site commentator to full-time finance man plus anything else I thought I could do to help.

Originally my involvement had been limited to posts on the WISA chat site, critically analysing WFC's financial pronouncements. That led

---

5 'Papers', so called because he is never seen without a sheaf of papers under his arm, is a well-known and much-liked fan of the club. He scarcely misses a game, first team, ladies, youth matches, and was well known for counting the crowd at our games and announcing, via one of the chat sites, what he declared the actual attendance to be.

to me meeting Kris and Ivor. The WFC chairman, Charles Koppel, had threatened to put the club into administration if the move was rejected, so I had volunteered to write a business plan for taking the club out of administration. That idea was redundant; now we needed a business plan for a new club.

Despite my normal reluctance to be pushy this was something I was desperate to do, so I told Kris and Ivor that they needed a proper business plan and a finance director – and it should be me. I was astonished when, without pause for breath, they agreed. As Ivor said later, 'We knew we needed someone with your sort of background and credibility and we weren't going to hang around to see if we could get permission to appoint you.'

I went away to find anyone who could help me think through what you need to run a football club while the four founders continued making sure everything was in place for us to start the 2002/03 season in the Ryman League Division Two. AFC Wimbledon was on its way.

3

GOOD VIBRATIONS

WIMBLEDON FOOTBALL Club Supporters Society, universally known as the Dons Trust, was formed in February 2002 with the objective of winning a place on the WFC board and thereby influencing the club's strategy. But just over three months later the FA Commission's decision had made that strategy redundant and suddenly the Dons Trust was going to be the owner of a football club. The board needed to get its act together, and quickly.

After a hastily convened meeting on the Friday evening, three days after the decision, the Dons Trust Board (DTB) decided they needed to call a members' special general meeting (SGM) to get formal approval to spend money on forming AFC Wimbledon. By 11.30pm they'd issued a letter calling a meeting on 13 June. In the meantime, recognising what the outcome was certain to be, the DTB also announced it had agreed to help the founders to collect advances for season tickets.

Unlike the DTB, the founders had no constraints on their actions and their decision-making, so everything proceeded at pace. Some things needed doing urgently and the four founders were the people who just got on with it. As a result, the SGM became, in reality, a platform for Kris and Ivor to update everyone on their progress.

Before the meeting started, Dan Norris, a long-term fan and a real estate lawyer, brought the Kingsmeadow ground-share agreement for signing. We couldn't find anywhere quiet in the meeting room so, on a miserable, damp, drizzly evening, a small group of us congregated under the shelter of the community centre fire escape. Kris and Ivor then officially convened a board meeting of the football club. The minutes recorded that Kris and Ivor had been authorised by the board (which comprised Kris and Ivor!) to sign the agreement and they duly did so. Then all it needed was for Dan to phone Rajesh Khosla (OMK), the owner of Kingsmeadow, to complete the deal. He went off to do that and we went into the meeting.

By now the press were on the case and CNN, Sky Sports and BBC radio were all covering the meeting.

Everything was falling into place. Kris and Ivor kicked off the meeting by announcing that the London FA had formally confirmed that we had been awarded senior club status. They went on to say that a company, AFC Wimbledon Limited, had been formed and it was their intention to transfer the ownership of that company, and with it the football club, to the Dons Trust. Further announcements followed. Our application to the Ryman League was to be considered the following Monday and Terry Eames had been appointed the club's director of football.

Terry took the microphone to a rapturous reception and chants of 'Terry Eames's yellow and blue army'. Stoking the general sense of euphoria, he announced that he had already approached a dozen or so players and then, after a suitably theatrical pause, he promised promotion in our first season.

While the others had been seeking league entry and somewhere to play, Marc Jones decided the club needed a badge and a kit, so he went off and worked on them. The idea was to make the new club credible.

At the meeting Marc unveiled his retro design for the team strip and the new badge, the design for which borrowed heavily from the old Merton double-headed eagle to emphasise that the fans and the newly formed club were the true inheritors of the club's traditions and history. The shirt was based on the one used for the Wimbledon–Leeds games in 1975, with a big yellow stripe down the sides. The colour reverted to the blue from the period before WFC was owned by Sam Hammam.

It went down well and the good news continued. We'd received nearly £70,000 in season ticket advances, many times more than was needed to pay the £20,000 cost of a ground-share. And then Kris topped off the evening by announcing that OMK had signed his copy of the ground-share agreement. We had somewhere to play!

With nothing but good news to declare, the meeting closed at about 10pm and everyone left, fired up about our club, a fans-owned club. Next was the small matter of securing that place in the Ryman League.

4

ONE MORE TRY

THE FOX and Grapes on Wimbledon Common is the pub of choice for WFC fans and indeed players – the team slipped out for a few beers there the night before winning the FA Cup in 1988. So it was the natural place for fans to congregate and wait to hear the good news from Kris and Ivor that the Ryman League had accepted us. But in an eerie echo of that first phone call only three weeks earlier, Marc Jones took a call from Kris to say we'd lost again.

Everything had been going so well. We had a club with senior status, the ground-share was assured, the cash was rolling in, and the press coverage was increasing exponentially. The excitement increased when Terry Eames announced that there were to be open trials on Wimbledon Common. The mood of euphoria continued when on 16 June, the day before the Ryman League AGM, the *Non-League Paper* trumpeted Terry's boast that 'we're going to win Ryman League Division Two'.

In the late afternoon, Kris and Ivor travelled to Le Meridien Hotel (now the Hilton) at Gatwick Airport for the Ryman Annual General Meeting. Their confidence bolstered by assurances from chairman Alan Turvey and secretary Nick Robinson that they were fully behind our election into Division Two, they were asked to sit outside and wait to be called in.

The Ryman League comprised 72 senior clubs, each with one vote, and 16 associate clubs in Division Two, with four votes between them. After a pre-meeting in which the associate clubs appointed their voting representatives, the meeting started. The room was laid out with a top table of Ryman League Management Committee members, resplendent in blazers, on a raised stage, while club representatives sat at long tables, classroom-style. They were organised by division and then alphabetical order to make it easy for Turvey and Robinson to identify speakers. To avoid the embarrassment of not recognising a speaker they had plans of the layout on crib sheets discreetly placed in front of them.

Almost without exception, AGMs are deeply boring affairs which run through a prescribed format of routine matters. Beforehand there had been much talk among the clubs about the last-minute introduction of a Special Resolution to allow AFC Wimbledon to join the league. After about 45 minutes of standard agenda items, Turvey opened the discussion. The resolution was proposed by Harlow Town and, not surprisingly given their financial interest, seconded by Kingstonian. Turvey explained the requirement that 95 per cent of the members needed to vote in favour for the resolution to succeed and that he, Robinson and the Management Committee all recommended approval.

Turvey argued strongly that the Ryman League had the chance to make some amends for what had happened to us. As Robinson put it, 'We were virtually pleading with clubs. Alan made the point that as football people we owed something and we wanted to show that we didn't support the decision that had been made and we wanted to help the newly formed club.'

There is no detailed record of the debate, but Turvey was surprised by the amount of resistance to the proposal, especially from the more senior clubs. In the classic tradition of football politics, this resistance was partly due to some general ill-feeling towards the top table and they used the issue to bloody the Management Committee members' noses (the issues were generally accepted to be a reflection of the rather authoritarian way that Turvey ran the Ryman League at the time). After a short debate the meeting went to a vote. The AGM minutes report it starkly, 'All clubs who wished spoke on the matter and on a vote the matter failed to reach the required majority.'

Ivor and Kris had been waiting in an anteroom with an ominous feeling gradually overtaking them as the evening went on with no word. Then Robinson emerged to tell them that only 87 per cent of the clubs had voted in favour and so we hadn't been successful. Ivor later told the *Non-League Paper*, 'Only 11 voted against us. We got 67 out of 78 votes and still didn't get in.' While the numbers don't stack up (there were only 76 votes available) the message was clear. We were screwed.

However, as we were soon to find, in many ways it worked out for the best.

Alan Constable was at the meeting as the club representative for Ashford Town (Middlesex) FC. Alan is a widely respected football man. He'd been involved with Ashford for nearly 40 years, first as a player of over 500 games and then as club secretary. But, crucially for us, he was the fixtures secretary of the Seagrave Haulage Combined Counties League.

Bemused by the outcome of a meeting which he describes as 'ending noisily', Constable thought that if we weren't going to be accepted into the Ryman League, we would be a huge boost for the CCL and its clubs. So while the fans at the Dog and Fox were assimilating the bad news, he spoke to Robinson and suggested that the CCL should approach us. Robinson immediately saw this as a solution to the embarrassing and unwanted outcome to the meeting and encouraged Constable to press ahead.

Trevor Williams takes up the story, 'In retrospect I don't know why I was so disappointed since I knew there were other leagues, but we'd all fixated so much on the Ryman League that we set aside any logical sideways thinking to say there must be somewhere else. Some people said "let's play a season of pre-season friendlies", but that wouldn't have worked.

'When I got back home from the news of the Ryman meeting, Alan Constable had left a message on my voicemail, presumably because my name was down on the form as secretary.'

Robinson also called Kris and Ivor that night with news of this potential alternative. Greatly encouraged by this turn of events, they urged the departing Dons fans not to be despondent. The next morning Kris spoke to Constable, who recalls, 'I spoke to Kris the very next morning, without actually speaking to John Bennett, the chairman, although he was always supportive, and suggested the possibility of AFC Wimbledon joining the CCL. John was slightly more tentative but he was happy to meet them.' By the time they met, Constable had won Bennett over.

The best chairmen arrive at meetings with votes in their pockets and the decision already agreed; Bennett quickly spoke to a couple of the committee and they agreed to call a meeting on the Friday night. Once again, speed was of the essence because the league's AGM was less than a week away.

Meanwhile, the Dons Trust had set up several working groups. They met on the Thursday night, again at the community centre, and Ivor and

Kris took the opportunity to update everyone. They explained that there was a lifeline and they were meeting the CCL's management committee on the Friday. All the signs were good and we only needed a simple majority to get in – 'We're not counting any chickens, but there is a back-up plan.'

That Friday, Kris and Ivor and the league committee members met, to quote Constable, 'crowded in to Ashford's little boardroom'. In this intimate environment the committee agreed to recommend the proposal to the clubs at their AGM the following Monday, 24 June. Their only reservation was the likely size of the crowds for clubs whose average attendances were around 60. That's 1,380 paying spectators for an entire season; we might be bringing that many to a single game. While looking forward to an entire season's gate money in one fell swoop, clubs were understandably worried about crowd safety. So Kris and Ivor promised that we would provide stewards.

A revised AGM agenda was sent out and the CCL clubs met at Old Woking & District Recreation Club, which Trevor described as a 'Surrey-posh version of a working men's club'. This time Trevor attended along with Kris and Ivor. The meeting room was large, with a bar open at the back. Much like the Ryman AGM, the management committee sat at a raised table while club representatives sat in classroom style.

The CCL is a smaller and more informal organisation than the Ryman League and so Kris, Ivor and Trev were introduced to the clubs beforehand, along with the other applicants, Frimley Green and North Greenford United. The applicants were then despatched to an anteroom while the other AGM business was completed. While they waited, John Bivens, the North Greenford chairman, regaled them with his experiences of non-league football and exactly why he hated footballers. And then everyone was invited into the meeting to present themselves.

We were on last. Trevor says, 'We'd been rehearsing questions – "what do we say if they ask that…?" and we repeated our offer to help with stewarding. We were expecting to be grilled. But the only question we were asked was, "How many fans will you bring?"'

Withdean 2000 proposed and Hartley Wintney seconded a motion that we be elected. With only a couple of votes against, we were in.

All Kris, Ivor and Trev wanted to do was get back to the Fox and Grapes but first they called ahead. Marc Jones took the call and this time announced to the gathered fans, 'We're in!' Not wishing to be rude to their new-found fellow clubs, the trio lingered for a quick drink. They stayed long enough to hear, repeatedly, that no one could believe that the Ryman clubs had rejected us. And then they rushed back to the Fox and Grapes to join celebrations that went on well into the night.

5

LOVELY DAY

THE PACE was unrelenting. Terry Eames had been announced as director of football at the Dons Trust meeting on 13 June. There wasn't time to advertise the role and he was an obvious choice. Terry's credentials were perfect; he was a former WFC player, he'd been a non-league coach and he'd taken part in the protests against the move to Milton Keynes. Also, time was short and he was in the right place at the right time.

Terry was clear. With all the publicity, we would be the team everyone wanted to beat. So the friendly games needed to be against clubs from higher leagues; we would need to get used to playing under pressure. It was now apparent that we would bring sizeable support (and very welcome funds) to games, so offers of pre-season friendlies came pouring in. It was left to Terry to select the opposition and Trevor Williams to arrange the details. But we wanted a showpiece first game to maximise the publicity that we were already attracting.

The obvious choice was Sutton United. Sutton were WFC's long-term rivals and beaten opponents in the 1963 Amateur Cup Final.[6] Time was short so we didn't wait until we'd been accepted into the CCL before contacting Sutton's chairman, Bruce Elliott. Very soon, he and Ivor were talking terms.

Ivor wanted Sutton to be our first game to reinforce the message that we were the continuation of WFC, so he sought to tempt Bruce into

—

6 Wimbledon FC are the only club to have won both the FA Amateur Cup and the FA Cup.

agreeing by telling him that we would bring at least 1,000 fans to the game. In a world where a pre-season friendly did well to draw a crowd of 300, this was a very attractive proposition. Desperate to do a deal, Ivor upped the forecast to 'at least 2,000'.

In fact, Bruce was already keen to stage the game for several reasons. First, he wanted to upstage Sutton's local rivals, Carshalton Athletic, by being the first club to play us. As he puts it, 'I made it a bit of a mission to get us to be your first game. Why did I do that? Perhaps I thought that it might be a little bit of history for us as well as you. And being totally honest I thought it would raise a little bit of money for us both.'

The game was scheduled for 10 July, sufficiently early to allow us to arrange the extensive series of other pre-season friendlies we'd need to bed in a totally new team. But that date was also chosen with at least one eye on the fact that on the same night Carshalton were due to be hosting the franchised club in a friendly, less than three miles away. If we got a bigger attendance they would find that very embarrassing, not least because their chairman had told the *South London Press* (on 31 May 2002) that he expected 50 per cent of the WFC fan base to follow them to Milton Keynes.

Bruce's hesitation wasn't about getting a sufficiently large attendance. Sutton's big challenge was getting the pitch ready in time. Groundsmen have an incredibly difficult task getting and then keeping their pitches in good condition, so they tend to have a reputation for defending their sanctity. Sometimes it feels as if they'd prefer it if no one ever played on the pitch at all. And now the annual pitch renewal programme was being accelerated with scarcely any notice. The other problem that Sutton faced was that, like most non-league clubs, they are heavily dependent on volunteers who would be on holiday in the summer. With pressure on resources, Bruce was delighted when we offered to produce the programme.

A deal was quickly done. Sutton would get the gate money and retain the profits from the bars and food outlets. Out of this they would give us £1 a head for paying spectators and all the proceeds from programme sales. The match was announced in a press release dated 19 June, a mere three weeks after the FA Commission's decision and only two days after we had been welcomed as members of the CCL.

We had our first game arranged but we needed players quickly. So, in what turned out to be an inspired piece of PR, Terry announced that we would hold open trials on Wimbledon Common on 29 June.

The pressure on Trev and the volunteer admin team was ferocious. He was responsible for much of the detail of the Sutton game, while also arranging the other nine pre-season matches Terry wanted. And now he had to collate and analyse the applications to attend the trial. Meanwhile, other hard-working volunteers were dealing with non-stop phone enquiries and, while processing a deluge of season ticket applications, chatting to curious fans who dropped in just to see what was happening. And this started even before we knew we had a league to play in. All of this was being done in the airless, windowless sweat box that constituted our office space.

The level of interest in the trials was incredibly high. Trevor remembers, 'We had loads of applications, filling folder upon folder. Some were very good players who'd played at a higher level.' We were being overwhelmed. Ivor recalls, 'On the day of the trial I asked Trev how many we were expecting and he replied, "It's completely out of control. I don't know. I can't count all the bloody e-mails, never mind anything else."'

The trials were not, as many people assume, held in a jumpers-for-goalposts session on Wimbledon Common but at Wimbledon Common Extension, adjacent to the busy A3 trunk road. The council-owned facility is extensive, comprising nine full-sized pitches. The pitches are heavily used and maintained on a shoestring budget so they are, to put it politely, of variable quality.

On a scorching hot day, Trev and his fellow volunteers set up a gazebo near the entrance while Terry and several coaches designated various areas for player assessments. Footballers in general, and non-league footballers in particular, are not well known for following instructions. As a result, the administration was a nightmare. Although Trev ticked players off against his master list as they arrived, many more simply turned up, the extra numbers broadly matching the no-shows.

As Trev put it, 'We had hundreds of players and it was impossible to assess them properly. I am sure we missed so many good players who went on to play at a higher level than us – it was an impossible task. I'm not sure how many turned up [published estimates varied from 230 up to in excess of 300] but there were so many people there that we could have had Pelé turn up for a trial and not notice him.'

One man who did turn up was Joe Sheerin. Joe was a former Chelsea player, albeit only for a few minutes as a substitute for Gianfranco Zola. In one of life's quirky coincidences Joe's one first-team appearance was against WFC. Injuries made him drop out of football but Joe knew his worth. He played in a 20-minute game, one of several arranged to get a quick look at the trialists. That was enough for him, 'I could see it was a total circus so I wasn't going to hang around. Instead I asked who was the manager and went to see him. I told him my background and left him my contact details if he was interested. A couple of days later he called me to say he wanted me to be his captain.'

With an almost impossible job, Terry, supported by a group of coaches (some of whom he'd never met before), whittled the numbers down to about 60. That was roughly the number he'd initially expected to turn up on the day. The select 60 were invited back for further trials.

Media interest in our fledging club continued. Sky TV and BBC London were there to film the proceedings, along with all the local and some national press. They were excited to see Terry Burton, a much-loved former WFC manager, turn up to give his support, along with David Barnard, the respected former WFC chief executive. Both are men of principle and both had been sacked by Charles Koppel (the chairman appointed by the Norwegian owners) for resisting his plans. On Tuesday, 2 July, only eight days before the Sutton friendly was due to be played, the *London Evening Standard* ran a full-page feature on the first trial. It included a photo of the applicants setting off on a warm-up run. It looked more like the start of the London Marathon than a football trial.

After two more trials the squad had been whittled down to a manageable number. By then the Sutton game was nearly upon us. Trev was, 'Working my nuts off in the build-up to the game, insane long hours. It took ages to organise, while still processing season tickets, and answering calls and drop-ins from fans and volunteers.

'The night before the Sutton game Marc Jones [who had designed the match programme] and I left at about 2am. I had to be back at 6am to let a volunteer in to install a computer; the only time he could do it was on his way to work. After that it was a full-on day.'

Trev had recently left Barclays Bank ('it wasn't for me') and made it clear to anyone who would listen that he really needed to get a job. However, Kris and Ivor weren't listening and Trev found he had been appointed as club secretary. Managing the demands from the media for access to the press conference and the associated interviews would have been a complex and time-consuming task at a large club with substantial resources. Here we were, seven levels below the Premier League, with no previous experience of football administration and what felt like the world and its uncle clamouring for access.

By the time the press conference started there were 55 accredited attendees and quite a few others who simply blagged their way into the room. For a club that had not yet played a game it was astonishing to see BBC radio and TV, ITV, Channel 5, Sky Sports, Thames TV, the *Daily Mirror*, *Express*, *Guardian*, *Observer*, *Telegraph*, *Times*, Reuters, all the local press and a host of other media people crowded into the Sutton Vice Presidents' Lounge.

The conference was chaired by Kris, with Ivor and Terry flanking him. The unannounced person on the top table was Miles Jacobson of Sports Interactive, makers of the hugely successful computer game, *Football Manager*. Miles is a Watford fan who loves all football. He had been aware of the discussions about a move to Milton Keynes and the fans' protests. When he heard that the move would go ahead he was horrified. It was our good fortune that shortly afterwards he heard first Kris and then Ivor being interviewed on BBC Radio 5 Live.

He picks up the story, 'I tried to persuade our parent company, Eidos, that we should sponsor the club as part of our marketing of the new game we were bringing out. They refused, saying they no longer did football sponsorship.'

Miles is another one of those invaluable people who regard setbacks as just another challenge so he contacted the two founders of Sports Interactive and told them of his idea. 'They were as opposed to the Milton Keynes decision as I was, so it was agreed that I'd fax across our offer to Ivor, by now officially the club's commercial director.'

From our point of view, the deal was stunning. It was rather coyly described as a six-figure sponsorship and indeed it was, over a three-year period, starting at £40,000 followed by two years at £30,000. This was in a league where a club with average attendances would have total gate receipts for a season of about £10,000.[7]

Trev says, 'The sponsorship deal had to be kept secret until the press conference. We didn't have a kit so Sports Interactive gave us their own

—

7 Sports Interactive are still the club's shirt sponsors today. It is the longest-running shirt sponsorship deal in British football.

team's kit. When we got the shirts out of the box on the afternoon of the game there were no numbers on them but we had to return them after the game so we weren't allowed to do anything about it.'

That's why our players had no numbers on their backs in our first game.

There were interminable interviews before the game. Bruce Elliott recalls, 'I was supposed to be saying a few words from the announcer's box at the back of the stand. But the size of the crowd meant that at the last minute I was dragged out on to the middle of the pitch to present an inscribed memento and say a few words about how delighted we were to be staging the first ever AFC Wimbledon game and wishing you well.' Kris also spoke and then 200 yellow and blue balloons, blown up by Ivor's wife Claire over the previous couple of days, were released and the game could finally start.

But it couldn't. Ivor's guarantee of 'at least 2,000 fans' was a massive under-estimate. The interest was massive, partially stoked by the *Daily Telegraph* and *The Times* previewing the match. The queue snaked down the narrow road leading into Sutton's Gander Green Lane ground and a further couple of hundred yards down the street. Mindful of spectator safety, the referee was asked to delay the kick-off to avoid a rush of impatient fans thinking they might miss the start. Kick-off was put back 15 minutes to 7.45pm and then, with the queues still stretching down Gander Green Lane, another 15 minutes to 8pm.

Looking back on it, Bruce says, 'It wasn't just a game about AFC Wimbledon – it was about football. A lot of people were saying "this shouldn't happen, this isn't right" and a lot of people who came to the game did so because of that aspect of it. They wanted to express their support.'

Released at last from his pre-match duties and absolutely exhausted, Trev had time to look around, 'The Sutton game was nuts. The crowd just kept coming in. The place was rammed and there were people sitting in the trees. When the teams finally walked out that was when I felt the football club formed. I couldn't find anywhere to sit so I went over to the cinder track that circled the pitch, plonked myself down and watched the game. At half-time I went in to sort out the players for the second half.'

There was a carnival atmosphere, fortified by the arrival of an open-top bus organised by Dons fans. In line with a long tradition of fans' attitudes to authority, the bus had circled Soho Square (the home of the FA) before setting off for the game. For complicated reasons I was unable to attend this momentous occasion, which is a matter of enormous regret to me, so long before the days of sat-nav my wife Eileen set off alone with an A-Z and little idea where Gander Green Lane was. Catching sight of a bus draped in blue and yellow with Dons fans hanging off the upper deck was a godsend to her and she followed it, nose to bumper, all the way to the ground.

The result was almost incidental to the evening's proceedings. After a goalless first half Sutton took control in the second half and won 4-0,[8] but no one seemed to care. As Kris put it at the time, 'How often, if ever, have you seen a joyous post-match pitch invasion after a team has lost 4-0?' Everyone was in a state of euphoria, except the Sutton groundsman who had put so much effort into getting the pitch pristine and then had to watch a couple of thousand people trample all over it.

The football world seemed stunned by the attendance. It was officially announced as 4,657 but there is a widely held view that as kick-off approached the turnstiles were overwhelmed and many more fans simply walked in.

The media loved it. TV footage and articles of varying length showed unanimous enthusiasm across the major nationals, and there were two-page spreads, or more, in all the local press. Meanwhile, the *Sutton Comet* had quietly announced that the franchised club's game at Carshalton, due to be played on the same night, had been postponed. It was left to the Carshalton manager to offer the rather plaintive excuse that his players weren't yet fit enough.

Our first match was over, the momentum was growing and the focus now shifted to the forthcoming friendlies and the start of the competitive season.

---

8 According to the club's website, 18 players played a part for us in the Sutton game. Of them, Joe Sheerin started 32 league or cup matches for us and came on as a substitute three other times. Of the other 17 players, seven made it on to the pitch in a league or cup game; between them they made a total of 22 starts and 22 substitute appearances in the 54 matches we played in our first season. Such is the shelf life of a non-league player.

One other player that night went on to make 97 starts and nine substitute appearances for AFC Wimbledon, scoring 107 goals. He was Kevin Cooper. The two goals he scored in the game were for Sutton.

6

SEASON IN THE SUN

FIVE WEEKS after the Sutton match we had played nine more friendlies. As time went on the momentum and publicity continued to grow and more and better players started to emerge. Terry was always open to approaches and recommendations. As a result, 28 players are recorded as playing a part in one of more of those friendlies without ever going on to feature for us in a competitive match in the league or cup.

Some came, went and barely touched the sides. Club secretary Trevor Williams recalls, 'I signed players that we literally never saw again. They'd come to training on a Thursday night, they'd fill out a form and then you'd never see them again. They'd never make the first team, never play a reserve game, they would disappear after a week. Other clubs would enquire and I'd go back to Eamo and he'd say, "No, he left two weeks ago."'

At this level of the game, players are part-time and train on Tuesday and Thursday evenings, after their day jobs are finished. They almost invariably sign to be registered for a club. This means that the player and the club may each give the other seven days' notice; only players who might be sold to a higher level club are offered contracts, tying them to the club in return for guaranteed regular wages.

Across the four Ryman League divisions and the CCL there were about 2,000 players and only a very small proportion would be contracted for the following season. The remainder, as registered players, were free to go elsewhere. There were times when it felt like they'd all applied for trials with us.

The remaining nine friendlies were largely unexceptional, although a few milestones were passed. Our first goal was scored by Glenn 'Trigger' Mulcaire, who was to go on to be famous for non-football reasons.[9] Fans, who were used to segregation, found they could change ends at half-time so as to be behind the goal we were attacking; drinks were allowed in sight of the pitch. For many, especially those who followed the club through the WFC non-league days, this was simply heaven.

There was one other 'first', but more would follow. After we lost 2-0 away in a pre-season friendly at Leatherhead, Ivor recalls what happened next: 'Terry resigned. He lost the plot completely and stomped off and sat in his car.

'My attitude was "so now Terry's resigned, let's accept it". I always think that if someone has resigned you're best off accepting that resignation. He'd shown some signs of erratic behaviour by then so this was probably a good time to do this. But nobody else agreed. So he just carried on.'

This pattern was to repeat itself. As DT board member Luke Mackenzie says in *This is our Time*, 'Terry had threatened to resign several times. In the early days after games we had lost he would storm in and threaten to quit. Each time we had to spend ages talking him out of it. It was ridiculous.'

Personally I have no recollection of discussing whether or not to change managers and we soldiered on. Gradually, Terry added some more experienced players to the squad and in our last game before the competitive season was due to start, we finally won, beating Enfield Town 3-2. Played ten, won one, lost nine, scored seven goals, conceded 25. But I wasn't down because we'd been playing teams from a higher level. And now the season was upon us.

Terry had finalised his starting squad for the season and we were starting to look more like a team. We were to begin at Sandhurst Town where a record attendance was confidently expected for our first competitive match. Alan Constable, the CCL fixtures secretary and a pragmatist, explained the reason they were chosen. AFC Wallingford, near Oxford, was the longest away journey in the league. Most CCL clubs were bunched around the A3 and they all had players with day jobs, so none of them wanted to travel to Wallingford for a midweek away game. Sandhurst had volunteered to go

---

9 Some years later, Glenn became better known for his part in the phone-tapping scandal that rocked News International.

there in midweek the previous season, so Alan felt he owed them a favour. As a secondary reason, Sandhurst were judged to be one of the best-run clubs in the league and more than able to deal with the large crowds that the pre-season friendlies had led clubs to expect. As Alan said later, 'I knew they would do it properly and they turned out to be a good choice.'

As part of our application to the CCL we had undertaken to help steward our fans at away games. A couple of days after the decision, Ivor called Luke Mackenzie. Luke was well-known in the fan community. He was a member of the WISA Committee, one of the steering group that set the Dons Trust on its way and a regular participant in the protests outside the FA in Soho Square.

Luke recalls that Ivor got straight to the point. 'He said, "We're applying to the London FA and you're a big lump so we've put you down as head of security, chief steward and all that." I said "fine" and that was pretty much it.'

The Sunday after being voted into the CCL, Lou Carton-Kelly, chair of the Dons Trust and the club's newly appointed operations director, Trev and Luke drove around half a dozen away grounds to get a feel for what might be involved. A few clubs were open and showed them round. Some were clearly not going to be capable of hosting a lot of visiting fans at their grounds but the CCL had anticipated that and they were allowed to move their games to more suitable local venues.

Some clubs were in small villages I'd never heard of, such as Hartley Wintney (population about 5,000), where our intrepid researchers found the clubhouse open but looking like there'd been a riot. There'd been a big party the previous night for the manager's birthday. The man sleeping on the pool table was the centre-forward who'd got very drunk so they'd just laid him down there and left him. As Luke put it, 'We could see this season was going to be different.'

The day of the first game dawned, with blue skies. Ivor says, 'It was going to be a hot one. Early that day Steve Elson phoned to say it was all "brilliant, brilliant, fantastic, what a wonderful day". I said, "Where are you?" and he said, "We're here, we're in the Batsford Arms, in the middle of a field and we've named it the Batsford Arms."[10] I said, "So are you there

—

10 Allen Batsford was the revered manager who took WFC into the Football League in the 1970s.

on your own?" and an almighty cheer went up because there were loads of people there already. Later that day he tried to sell the mayor of Sandhurst a caravan.' He doesn't own a caravan.

The walk to Sandhurst's ground was alongside a stream, shaded by overhanging trees. It was the loveliest and the least likely approach to a football match I'd ever had. I was never very keen on the pre-match formalities in the boardroom (which, in the CCL, was sometimes simply a roped-off area of the bar) and I didn't like accepting freebies from clubs with limited income, so I queued alongside everyone else and paid to get in. Once inside it opened out into a wide expanse of grass, with a football pitch in the middle and, set back a little, the changing rooms and clubhouse.

A single crush barrier surrounded the pitch with a narrow strip of concrete just in front of it to allow standing. Everywhere was on the same level. The crowd limit had been set at 2,500 and we'd controlled the numbers by pre-selling vouchers for the game, to reduce the numbers paying at the turnstiles on the day. With so many spectators the crowd was nine or ten deep behind the goal we were attacking and many fans found it almost impossible to see. But with a carnival atmosphere prevailing, it didn't seem to bother them and no one complained when some supporters sat underneath the crush barrier along the sides of the pitch. The cameraman was perched precariously on top of the dugouts – the only vantage point around – and some fans tried vainly to improve their view by standing on nearby hay bales. To me it didn't feel like the start of a great adventure, it felt more like a village fete, but with a bit of tension thrown in, as I pondered how this adventure would all turn out.

The teams emerged with Wimbledon wearing our new kit for the first time. Ivor had found a local company which would manufacture the shirts in time for the first day of the season. However, they were new to the sports business and so for some reason the shirts were made of a hessian-like material and incredibly heavy for a summer's day. As Joe Sheerin said, 'It felt like wearing pyjamas – and they were itchy. But it was a small price to pay to be playing.' And then during the warm-up he pulled out of the game because he'd not fully recovered from an injury.

The crowd was a blaze of yellow. Everything had moved too quickly to be able to produce replica shirts for sale. Instead many fans wore Dons Trust yellow t-shirts with the ten pre-season games listed on the back, rather like the shirts that rock groups sell for their tours. Others wore old WFC replica kit as a way of emphasising that fans, not owners in suits, define what a club is.

Early in the game Kevin Cooper went into the record books for scoring our first goal in a competitive game. When Keith Ward made it 2-0 he went to celebrate with fans behind the goal and the crush barrier collapsed under the pressure of people pouring forward. No one was hurt but it was a sobering reminder of how quickly excitement might turn into calamity. The game ended with a nail-biting finish as we held on, just, to a 2-1 win and after some post-match chanting and singing, and more drinking, everyone went home, tired but very happy.

Now attention turned to our first home game of the season, which was to be against Chipstead on the following Wednesday.

The theoretical capacity of Kingsmeadow was 6,299. However, Kingston Council, our licensing authority, had restricted the operating capacity to 4,215, limiting the numbers in the light of the physical condition and layout of the stadium and the experience, or lack of it, of the stewards. We had already sold 1,200 season tickets and after allowing for demand from the press, sponsors and complimentary tickets for management and players, there was only room for about 2,700 'walk-ups' on the night.

Having seen the size of the crowds at Sutton and Sandhurst we realised that we were likely to sell out. It was too late to make the game all-ticket so we started a campaign to get fans to arrive early. That was probably counter-productive and the publicity probably increased the demand for places.

The queues started before 5pm and by 6pm the car park was full to overflowing. By about 7.30pm it was clear that there would be substantial numbers locked out when the game was due to start so, as at Sutton, it was delayed.

It was also clear that we couldn't fit everyone into the stadium so, after talking to the police, Kris had the painful task of counting his way down the queue and then telling everyone else that, no matter how far they had travelled, we were sorry they couldn't come in. Post-match analysis showed that we could, at least theoretically, have accommodated another couple of hundred fans before closing the gates. Given that we'd turned people away we thought it prudent to announce a gate of 4,142, a smidgeon below our official capacity.

One decision we made at an early stage was to honour WFC players from the non-league days, something that hadn't happened under the old WFC regime. Just before the scheduled kick-off Ivor led Tommy McCready and Ian Cooke, stars of WFC's Southern League days, on to the pitch and introduced them to the crowd. Shortly afterwards, in a show of solidarity for the new club, three stars of WFC's Premier League days, Marcus Gayle, Jason Euell and Neal Ardley, were welcomed to a standing ovation. As Neal put it, 'I saw this as a continuation of the club I'd played for and I wanted to show my support.' At one time or another over the next 15 years all three of them would play for, or manage, AFC Wimbledon. Former WFC manager Terry Burton and chief executive David Barnard, by then a director at Chelsea, also turned out to show their support for our fledgling club.

After a further delay to let everyone in, the teams entered the pitch just before 8.15pm. The mascot that day, ten-month-old Elliott Bolton, was carried on to the pitch by Joe Sheerin. Nineteen years later Elliott is an academy player for the club.

Unfortunately, Chipstead hadn't read the script and scored late in the game to win 2-1. We were all terribly deflated and Terry declared himself unavailable to talk to the press. To rub salt into the wounds, Chipstead then went on a long run before winning another league game.

As the season went on we experienced the joys and quirks of non-league football and relearned the sheer pleasure of watching a team when football is all that matters. We rediscovered the cathartic release of tension and the undiluted joy of a last-minute winner against Cove, followed by the despair of a last-minute defeat at Ash United. Clearly, a late winner is totally deserved while a late defeat is just, well, plain unfair.

Almost every club was friendly and welcoming. Some provided memorable, if rather idiosyncratic experiences. Southall away was the first game I've ever been to where there was a concern that the kick-off might need to be delayed because of the number of our fans queueing at the curry stalls, some of them going round for the second time. And if you mention Merstham to any Dons fan of that era they will immediately grin and say 'cheese rolls'. From 6.30am on the day of the game a small army of Merstham volunteers had slaved away producing rolls filled with cheese, cheese and onion, cheese and pickle, cheese and more cheese, while a rebellious breakaway faction made ham and pickle rolls – no cheese? –

ready for the afternoon's event. Mountains of rolls were presented for sale in a specially erected marquee.

At half-time Ted Hickman, the avuncular and hugely likeable Merstham chairman, walked round inside the crush barrier gamely attempting to shake hands with each and every one of the Dons fans who had turned up. As the supporters left the ground, unsold cheese rolls were thrust at them. It was a lovely day, organised and hosted by lovely people. But we still won 2-0.

Meanwhile, another chairman, John Bivens at North Greenford United, stood on a bar table after his team had endured a thumping 6-2 home defeat and proclaimed to the Dons fans, 'You lot are welcome here any time you like.'

The away grounds were very different from what we'd been used to in the Premier League. At Farnham, along with many others, I stood on a steep grassy bank behind the goal. Running along the top of the bank, just beyond the stadium's perimeter wall, was a pedestrian pavement where some of the meaner members of the local community were able to watch the game for no charge. At Guildford and Godalming a ball booted into touch was likely to find itself on a green of the adjacent golf course.

At Feltham the roof of the large main stand had been removed for safety reasons, leaving only the cantilever steel roof trusses in place. They made a stark metallic skeleton against a dull grey sky. With planes flying low as they came in to land at nearby Heathrow it made for a depressing sight, matched only for grimness by the Reading Town stadium's breeze block walls, topped with barbed wire. Meanwhile, Cobham's Leg O'Mutton Field is easily the best-named ground I've visited and will remain so until I finally manage to visit The Dripping Pan of Lewes FC.

The playing surfaces were of highly variable quality but it would be harsh to criticise others when Kingsmeadow resembled more of a sandpit than a football pitch. Nonetheless, Chessington and Hook's sea of mud deserves a special mention because, foolishly, that was where we chose to give our all-white strip its debut. It never recovered and might have been better described as a delicate shade of umber for the remainder of its useable life.

Modern footballers, especially those in the Premier League, lead highly restricted lives where their eating and drinking habits are tightly controlled and their social lives are monitored by the press and fans alike. To this outsider it looks like they are left with little to spend their money on except ever-larger SUVs, tattoos and increasingly elaborate hairstyles. But when it comes to tonsorial magnificence, non-league footballers got there long before them as Gordon Law, a sports reporter for the *South London Press*, noticed.[11]

Struggling with the challenge of writing copy about a small non-league club for two editions each week, Gordon started to spread his gaze more widely, hence this piece, 'The Combined Counties League never ceases to amaze me. I don't think I've seen so many teams in one league with at least one player sporting the most ridiculous haircut known to man. And Saturday's match at home to Feltham was no different. Step forward Will Storey, who was the spitting image of Jesus of Nazareth Himself, complete with long hair and beard… Only last week we had James Musu from Farnham Town with a ridiculous blond mullet, plus awful fringe. Then there was Gwynn Berry's ginger perm at Chipstead, Frank Baronski the Polish porn star lookalike with '70s mullet playing for North Greenford, Chipstead's Beckham wannabe Michael Corbett… the list goes on. Luckily, the Dons don't have any scarecuts, unless you count Danny Oakins's controversial new style, a wonky blond streak on the back of his head [Danny later explained that his girlfriend had done it when he was drunk].'

The size of, and frequent abuse from, the crowds affected some opposition players more than others. At one game the opposition goalkeeper became so aerated by being mocked that he offered to take on the entire terrace full of fans. Meanwhile the goalkeeper who reacted to the chant 'where were you when we scored?' by pointing to the ground and then diving headlong back into the mud won a couple of thousand admirers immediately. But my favourite was the Woodford Town player who, on being sent off at Kingsmeadow, tore off his shirt and walked the length of our main stand giving the wanker sign to the crowd. Ah, bless.

Another difference that took some getting used to was the strange new world of player sanctions. At WFC we were used to seeing, for example, a three-match ban for a player who had been sent off. At our new level of football, players' bans were for a specified number of days. The reason was that quite a lot of players turned out for more than one club and a

—

11 My thanks to the *South London Press* for permission to reproduce the article.

three-match ban could easily be served by playing Saturday, Sunday and Tuesday.

There was also quite a delay between an offence, the announcement of the punishment, and the ban actually taking effect. One consequence of all this was that Sean Daly, who was sent off for a foul in a defeat against Withdean 2000 on 22 February, was given a 112-day ban (in case you think that's a typo, that's 16 weeks). The ban was announced on 18 March and was to take effect from 7 April. The sanctions committee appeared to have shown some compassion, or common sense, since the majority of it would be served during the close-season and Sean would miss a maximum of six league games. The Withdean match was significant in one other respect, in that it was the last defeat we suffered in the league for the best part of two seasons.

There was a dark side to the publicity we were receiving, as we had found earlier in the season when we went to play table-topping AFC Wallingford in late November. The day had started well. Despite 48 hours of torrential rain the pitch was declared playable and, determined to treat the day as a celebration, nearly 2,000 Dons fans set off for the game. Supporters liked to turn these days into an event, as they had done when a group, some dressed as sailors, had taken a boat ride up the Thames to our friendly at Walton & Hersham. Despite Wallingford also being on the Thames, a boat ride wasn't an option. Instead, about 200 fans jumped on the 12.20pm heritage railway train from Cholsey to Wallingford, turning it into an unofficial football special. The train creaked and clanked its way along the three miles of track at a top speed of 15 miles per hour and spilled the travellers out close to the stadium in good time.

Despite the pre-match high spirits and optimism, it turned out to be a low point in the season. On a soaking wet, muddy pitch captain Joe Sheerin was sent off and although we played some of our best football of the campaign we tumbled to a 3-0 defeat. That was bad enough, but off the pitch we encountered a problem that was to become an intermittent feature of the first three or four years. Attracted by the likely size of the crowd and the pre-match publicity, a group of youths, reported by the local press as 20 to 30 Oxford fans, turned up looking for someone to fight. Anyone to fight.

At half-time they got what they wanted and violence erupted in the bar. By chance Kris was in there at the time and witnessed bottles, glasses and stools being hurled around the room. It was his first experience of being close to such violence and he did what he could, joined by Ivor, to calm it down. The police arrived very quickly and before long several men were sitting handcuffed on the floor in an adjacent room.

I had been standing in my preferred position behind the Dons' goal and, like most of the fans in the stadium, I was oblivious to these events. So when a police helicopter appeared overhead a group of fans, blissfully unaware of what was happening in the bar, waved a club banner at them, thinking it was Sky Sports covering our game yet again. As we left through the car park we saw a large number of Thames Valley police milling around and it began to dawn on us that something serious had happened. We were learning that the publicity and the size of our crowds had a major downside.

Security and safety had a different feel to them at some of our home games. Three or four times a season the local fire brigade would make a surprise visit. They'd arrive just before half-time, park their fire engine and walk along the front of the main stand. Immediately, my wife Eileen would disappear into the President's Lounge to give them cups of tea. Later they would stand in a corner of the ground steadfastly scrutinising the pitch for signs of possible spontaneous combustion (of which there was no chance unless Crawley manager Steve Evans was in the opposition dugout) before deciding all was well with the world and leaving ten minutes before the final whistle.

The police took their cups of tea (with sandwiches and biscuits) before the game. Once sated they would disappear into the car park to keep an eye on the relatively small numbers of visiting fans. The rule with the police was that if they were inside the ground we had to pay for their services, but outside they were dealing with public order, so there was no charge. Nonetheless, we'd often see them quietly slipping unannounced (and therefore unrecorded and, mercifully, uninvoiced) into a corner of the stadium partway through the game; no doubt a public order issue had lured them in.

One of the pleasures for me was to be able to stand behind a goal again. After half-time I'd filch leftovers from the boardroom, wander along the front of the main stand and distribute various buns and cakes among my sons and their friends in the Tempest End.

For many of our fans the biggest and most popular change was the amount of access to the players after the game. Many of our squad had played non-league football for years for £50 a week or maybe £100, watched by the mythical two men and a dog in a morgue-like atmosphere, where every spectator comment could be heard. Now they had been pitchforked into a world where crowds of over 3,000 regularly watched them, chanted their names and, in the days before selfies become the memento of choice, sought their autographs. Players went into the bar after the game, as they always had at previous clubs, only now they would be surrounded by adoring fans who wouldn't dream of letting them buy their own drinks. And, depending on how outgoing you might be, you might enjoy or endure being the object of Ivor's man of the match presentation in a bar filled with five or six times the number of people who used to watch you play. We were proud to be a club which eschewed making such presentations in a small, exclusive, sponsors' room. If the mood took you, and so long as you could squeeze in, all fans were welcome to witness Ivor's innuendo-peppered interrogations of that day's victim.

Not surprisingly it wasn't difficult to attract players. They came from a range of backgrounds. Some, like Gareth Graham, had made it into a league club's first team (in his case, Brentford) and international recognition at under-21 level, only to have his hopes of a professional career ended by serious injury. Others, like the hugely talented Paul Scott, had been unlucky with contract offers falling away as a club got into financial difficulties. And some others who are best left unnamed (but I bet Dons fans could name them all) were easily talented enough to make the grade but lacked the drive or the discipline to apply themselves.

Simon Bassey, who was to play a pivotal role in the club for the next 17 years, had played three levels higher in the Football Conference (one step below the Football League). Attracted by the opportunity to play in front of big crowds again, he dropped down to play at AFC Wimbledon. He had more reason to do so than most because he had been on WFC's books until he was released at age 16, being told he was too small. He describes what it was like being at AFC Wimbledon, 'You'd have a drink in the bar after a game and we'd always won. The bar was packed and then we'd end up in one of the bars down in Wimbledon, nine or ten players and loads of fans. Your wages would be spent by the time you got home. You'd got a team full of Herberts who were so happy to be playing for a club like Wimbledon at this level and they're thinking, "I can't believe it – I'm making the most of it. Every week people buy me drinks. Fans have got shirts with my name on the back. It is unbelievable and I'm going to enjoy this for as long as it lasts." Do you wonder that they wanted to be here?'

As the season progressed, Terry strengthened the team until every player was good enough to play at least one level higher. And we didn't have to pay them top-whack wages; after all, where else would they get the experience they were getting with us?

With most players being registered and not under contract they were very mobile and could quickly be free to move elsewhere. Strictly speaking, clubs were supposed to give seven days' notice to another club before being allowed to approach their player. However, it wasn't difficult to let a player know of interest without anyone being able to trace the approach back to them. So the rule was universally ignored.

One player who joined via an unusual route was Matt Everard. Matt is a dominating centre-half who scores goals, as we had found to our cost earlier in the season when we lost to Ash United. Like a lot of players who were curious about this new club, he used to frequent Weird and Wonderful World, then the fans' online guest book of choice. He explains, 'I went on the site because there wasn't a lot else to do sometimes in the office where I worked. My tag name was Mattaufc, so people knew who I was. Someone asked for my phone number to give to Terry.' Shortly afterwards, Terry called Matt and so it is arguable that he was the first ever player to be recruited via a fans' chat site.

There were goals and yet more goals, 125 of them in 46 league games. Kevin Cooper had joined from Sutton United after scoring twice against us in that first friendly. In 45 league appearances that season he scored 37 times. Like all strikers he had an insatiable appetite for scoring goals. Even the most modest of strikers, and not even Kevin would call himself that, have an arrogance about them that screams 'give me the ball and I will score'. And he did, time after time.

It didn't take fans long to notice that none of Kevin's goals were headers and it became a theme that he didn't head the ball because he didn't want to disturb his carefully gelled-down hair. Eventually, a group of supporters came together and announced that they would pay £1,500 to the club if Kevin scored a goal with his head during the season. Come the final game his hair remained undisturbed so he sportingly accepted a challenge from Ivor to score a headed goal in the pre-match warm-up. Andy Sullivan was dispatched to the wing to send a series of his trademark pinpoint crosses and, to ease Kevin's path to success, Ivor went in goal. He sought advice about being a goalkeeper from Dave Beasant, the former WFC custodian who was the first man to save a penalty in an FA Cup Final. Dave's response to five-foot-tall Ivor was 'grow'. With that advice ringing in his ears, and determined to secure the money for the club, Ivor dived this way and that to get out of the way of the ball. Even then it took Kevin four or five attempts to head the ball into the back of the net amid much celebratory noise and affectionate mockery from the crowd.

By the time we reached the end of the season the team had won 15 and drawn one of the games since the defeat to Withdean. It was all too easy and the players were having fun. Gareth Graham says, 'After the final away game of the season at Reading Town the players were, as usual, in the bar when someone said "on your head". Very soon Reading's portacabin [which doubled as a bar] was about three inches deep in beer.' Simon Bassey picks up the story, 'Someone nicked the hoover and took it on the coach. Just "why not?"'

In the final game of that first season, with nothing at stake, the players played 'pass the coin'. The rules are quite simple: it's a bit like tag. One player starts the game holding a coin and if he comes to you, you must take it from him. The players with the coin at half-time and full time each have to buy a round of drinks for the squad. This led to the ludicrous situation where players were actively running away from each other as half-time approached to make sure the coin wasn't passed to them. Then it all started again in the second half. No one in the crowd noticed and we still won 5-1. This sort of thing was fairly common in non-league football. At other clubs the manager might put all the team names in a hat for the last game of the season. The first name to be drawn from the hat went in goal, the second had to play right-back, and so on. Our crowd would have noticed if they'd done that!

From following a club that had battled to win games, the fans were now seeing their team victorious almost every week – and usually comfortably. Across the whole season we played 46 league games, won 36, drew three and lost seven. That gave us 111 points, with a positive goal difference of 79. With that total we'd have romped away with the league title almost anywhere else. But it was only enough to finish third, so we were going to have to stay in the CCL for at least one more season. It was doubly frustrating because neither of the teams which finished above us were eligible for promotion because their grounds fell short of the Ryman League entry criteria. But only the top team or, if the top team's ground didn't qualify, the runners-up could be promoted.

In some ways this was no bad thing. It gave us time to assess our progress and to understand better what would be needed to secure promotion the following season. But first there was a summer of substantial off-the-field activity to attend to.

7
HELP! (1)

BY THE end of our first season we were getting used to running a football club despite several stumbles on the way.

We had started a club with no players, no manager and no stadium, not even a name, but we also had no one to sell tickets, operate turnstiles, steward games and all the other roles we needed to be able to open the stadium. But help was at hand. In fact help was everywhere and very soon, through advertising, word of mouth, friends of friends and people approaching us directly, we had a massive group of people asking, 'How can I help?' There was so much excitement, energy and goodwill that I struggled to take it all in.

When we were arranging our first pre-season friendlies we had boldly promised that we would provide stewards for these games. So we needed to find some, fast. In Chapter 6 I described how Luke Mackenzie, our chief steward, was recruited by a call from Ivor Heller ('you're a big lump, so we've put you down as chief steward'). I asked Luke if he had any background or qualifications in stewarding, and he told me, 'No, not at all. I'd never done security, I'd never done door staff, I'd never done anything like it.' But one of the Dons Trust working groups was for stewarding, as Luke explains, 'We sort of just got together and a few random people came in and sort of sat with me.' That's how you form a stewarding group!

By the time we played our first competitive game, at Sandhurst Town, the number of stewards had grown. The crowd limit for that game had been set at 2,500 and we sent 'seven or eight' stewards. Some of them, such as Geraldine Messenbird, met Luke and some of her new colleagues for the first time when they collected her from a roundabout on the A3 en route to the game. Geraldine's training comprised a chat as they drove to the ground.

Looking back it was naïve, indeed reckless, to put a handful of untrained volunteers in charge of a crowd of 2,500 people. But it was more like a carnival atmosphere than a football match and there weren't going to be any crowd problems; everyone was so happy just to have a team. There was no issue if everybody needed to be evacuated in the event of problems – we were, in effect, standing around a single crush barrier in a very large open area and everyone could easily disperse rapidly.

Things were different for our first home game, the following Wednesday night. Kingsmeadow is a 'designated ground' and as such is subject to specific rules and regulations about how it must be operated. Fortunately for us, Kingstonian had an established team of paid stewards who had experienced larger crowds when they were in the Conference National division. They also had Phil Clarke, the safety officer, who had overall responsibility for safety in the ground on matchdays. With an expected capacity crowd of over 4,000 we were guided by him and his team. Furthermore, the police planned to have a visible presence, not because any trouble was expected (there would be only a handful of away fans) but to assess how well we ran a game and decide what regular involvement, if any, they needed.

The police were very supportive, offering sage advice in a quiet, unassertive way, for example, 'Please ask your steward not to run up and down in a hi-vis jacket with his arms out, like he's an aeroplane, every time you score.'

In addition to stewards we needed turnstile operators, cash counters and 'sweepers' whose job was to collect money from the turnstiles and programme sellers. I was grateful and relieved when, early in the season, Neil Messenbird volunteered to take over the recruitment and management of that team as well as reporting attendances and cash collections.

Neil and Varney Constantinou were the mainstays of the team. They usually missed half an hour of the first half while they totted up the ticket and programme sales and matched them to the takings. After half-time they'd collect the late turnstile ticket sales and rush back to finalise the cash count and attendance. This meant they missed at least the first 15 minutes of the second half. During the game they would listen to the club's internet commentary, which was always a couple of seconds behind the live action, from which they could hear the roar when a goal went in. Thanks to the roof void the other noise they could hear was the half-time team talk, especially during Dave Anderson's era; he always had the volume turned up to 11. Neil takes up the story, 'We could hear Dave and his sidekicks and the swearing. We used to sit there and try to work out which player was answering back. And you'd then hear other noises and you'd know something was being thrown across the room.' At least it wasn't someone being thrown.

I asked Neil why they were willing to miss so much of the game when supporting the team was everyone's reason for being involved. He said, 'Well, it was good fun and good camaraderie. And we were doing things for the club. That was a big part of it.'

The turnstile and cash office team was drawn from a pool of about 30 volunteers. They were from a range of backgrounds, including a District Judge and the chief cashier of a City of London bank. The one thing they had in common was a love of the club and a desire to help. New friendships were made and new relationships struck up, with Sandy Lawrence and Helen Beckett becoming the first couple to meet and marry as a result of volunteering.

Neil quickly had everything well under control and the finance director (me) started to relax. In the early days my matchday role reduced to collecting cash and tickets from the late turnstile, about 15 minutes in to the game. I didn't like doing that because it meant missing some of the action but that was nothing compared to the amount the cash office team missed. Nonetheless, I was pleased when the late turnstile started opening until half-time and I wasn't needed any longer.

For Neil and, in his absence, me, the work didn't stop after the final whistle. We decided we needed to improve our tickets, which were initially little more than cloakroom stubs, and with the help of a thermal printer we designed and printed our own. Neil recalls, 'A couple of weeks before every game our house would echo to the clicking and buzzing of the printer for hours on end. On the day of an FA Cup draw I would anxiously watch the TV; if we had a home draw I'd need to start printing tickets immediately.'

In our first season we were tenants so many of our activities were tucked away in cramped cubby holes. For the first few games we counted the entrance money in the tiny stewards' cloakroom. Dave Chan, who went on to be a steward throughout our time at Kingsmeadow, vividly recalls having to kneel on the floor to count the cash while fans walked past, staring into the room and no doubt wondering what on earth was going on. This was unbelievably insecure and very soon, for an additional rental charge of course, we created a cash office in a tiny room off the main bar, big enough for a desk and two people.

A matchday internet commentary, Radio WDON, sprang up, with the commentators and the PA announcer sharing the tiny press box at the back of the main stand. From an early stage the senior commentator was Michael Taliadoros, universally known as Mikey T. Mikey has had nearly as many assistants as Doctor Who but his voice has remained a constant and reassuring presence, home and away, ladling out arcane statistics about games from long ago, interspersed with a series of appalling puns. His regular summariser is now Rob Cornell but guest commentators have included former managers and players, plus John Motson, shortly after he retired from *Match of the Day*.

Just in front of Mikey, but definitely within earshot, in fact within most people's earshot, sat Laurence Lowne. Assisted by his sister Sandra, when she wasn't stewarding the car park, Laurence played host to visiting media, plying them with half-time biscuits, tea, coffee and opinions. The quality and warmth of his welcome was much appreciated by the press. However, immediately in front of the press sat the visiting directors who were treated to Laurence's stentorian voice bemoaning the iniquities visited upon our team by the referee and their players. From time to time I had to take him aside and brandish a metaphorical yellow card.

On the matchday catering side, we had inherited the burger bar staff. They were used to taking their wages in cash from the day's takings. When I insisted that we processed their wages on the payroll their reaction was immediate – they walked away. And, until we could find new staff to run the burger bar, commercial director Ivor Heller and his wife Claire flipped burgers while chairman Kris Stewart and volunteer Tim Hillyer took the cash and handed out the orders. Beginners or not, they were clearly efficient because the takings doubled.

Behind the scenes on a matchday you'd find Trevor Williams, who was one of the four founders and for some time acted as club secretary. Trev has been one of the constants about the club since day one. One of his current roles is to work with Robin 'Rocket' Bedford with the kit and indeed anything that makes the organisation go more smoothly. His partner, Clare McDonagh, is usually to be found managing the ticket distribution at the complimentary tickets window; they travel to every game together.

That's how it was when we started and, by and large, it's how it still is. There is no standing on ceremony. We are a fans-owned club and everyone pitches in to help wherever it is needed.

8

THERE'S A PLACE FOR US

EVEN BEFORE we started our first season in the CCL, we knew we were facing a threat to our future and possibly our existence. This was because our lease at Kingsmeadow contained a clause that allowed Old Man Khosla to terminate the deal after a year. He had insisted on this because Brentford FC had an option to move in at the end of our first season; if they did, we would have to move out. Although we were happy to stay at Kingsmeadow we desperately needed to find some alternatives.

In one of life's ironies, the option was owned by Ron Noades, who had been the owner of WFC and the driving force behind the club being voted into the Football League in 1977. Noades sold WFC in 1981 and bought Crystal Palace, where he oversaw some of the most successful seasons in their history. Ever restless, he sold Palace in 1998 and bought Brentford instead.

Noades was a property developer turned football club owner, with an eye on the development value of the grounds he owned. As part of his attempts to get out of Brentford's Griffin Park he had secured an option to ground-share at Kingsmeadow. He had until midnight on 28 February 2003 to take that up. Alternatively he was entitled to pay for a year's extension to the option; failure to meet that cut-off date would mean he lost the right forever.

There was a further problem. To be eligible for promotion to the Ryman League we had to send them details of an acceptable ground-share by early February 2003. So we faced the possibility of submitting our proposal and having our feet cut out from underneath us if Noades took up his option.

The Ryman League would be unlikely to accept such uncertainty so we urgently needed at least one other suitable ground.

The Dons Trust, as the owners of AFC Wimbledon, had set up various working groups. One of these was the Stadium Working Group (SWG), chaired by Tom Adam. The SWG's role was to look at the long-term strategic options for procuring a new stadium back in our home borough of Merton – ideally in Wimbledon itself. We added a second, urgent objective, which was to advise the board on the pros and cons of the various short-term options we identified. The latter role quickly became the SWG's priority.

There were three main ground-share possibilities: continue at Kingsmeadow; share with Tooting and Mitcham in our home borough of Merton; or share with Sutton United, WFC's historical, but friendly, rivals.

Another, and much more radical, possibility also emerged, which was to buy Kingsmeadow. A few weeks into our first season I started saying that we needed to buy Kingsmeadow. A stadium in Merton was years away and we needed somewhere secure until then. If we continued to ground-share we would be over a barrel when trying to negotiate a rent as we became more successful. Also, as we progressed up the leagues we'd have to pay for ground improvements to a stadium that wasn't ours. In my view the best option was to buy Kingsmeadow and give ourselves a temporary home until we could return to Merton.

In normal circumstances buying Kingsmeadow would have proved impossible but we were pretty sure OMK would sell if the price was right. It was only a year since he had bought Kingsmeadow from an administrator for £395,000 and Kingstonian FC (usually referred to as 'Ks') for £1. He'd been able to do this because Ks had seriously over-reached themselves financially and been forced into administration.

We knew that OMK had no interest in the football side of the business and seemed to see it as a money pit. He bought Kingsmeadow because his background was in running hotels and catering and he thought he could sell out the stadium's spacious bars with Asian weddings all year round. So, unlike most club owners, we knew he had no emotional attachment to the stadium and would probably sell if the price was right.

However, nothing was simple. We didn't know if we could agree a purchase price with OMK or whether we could raise the money. Also, the threat of the Noades option remained. If we bought Kingsmeadow we might end up owning a stadium where the option was still valid, so it was possible that we, Brentford and Ks would all want to play. The idea of simply kicking Ks out was something we couldn't countenance. Finally, there was the possibility that Noades would outbid us. As an insurance policy we needed to pursue other ground-share options.

In the early autumn of 2002 Kris, Ivor and I met Bruce Elliott, the Sutton United chairman, at an Italian restaurant just by Sutton station. Like many chairmen of similar clubs, Bruce had been involved with Sutton since his father had taken him to games in his early teens. He'd progressed via the supporters' club to the management committee and then chairman.

Bruce liked the idea of a ground-share and saw it as an opportunity to bring in more cash. From a strategic point of view he proposed that we create a joint fund to update their traditional but rather outdated stadium for the benefit of both clubs. But even if we agreed terms, he expected opposition from local residents with concerns about traffic congestion caused by our larger crowds. Getting Sutton Council's support would be an uphill struggle. Nonetheless, we agreed to pursue a possible deal and Bruce went off to talk to the council.

Meanwhile, Kris, accompanied by our volunteer planning expert, Hugh Scanlon, had opened up discussions with Tooting & Mitcham FC ('Tooting'), whose Bishopsford Road stadium had opened in 2002 with a capacity of 3,500. While Tooting were keen to make a deal, there were significant obstacles to overcome. Their planning permission imposed substantial restrictions on the site, including specifying that only Tooting could play there; that Merton Council permission had to be sought for any game likely to attract over 400 spectators; a limit on the number of parking spaces; and restrictions on the hours of use.

To resolve these issues, Tooting agreed to submit a planning application seeking amendments to existing restrictions. Given the size of our attendances, the application included 1,000 additional seats in the main stand, improved road access and parking, and extending the existing roof cover behind each goal.

The changes were extensive but we were very optimistic, buoyed by substantial support and encouragement from Merton Council. However, we made it clear that this was a temporary solution. This was partly to assuage local concerns but also to ensure that if we did agree a ground-share, Merton would not feel it was 'job done' and end their support for us to move to a new stadium in the borough.

At the same time as we were approaching Sutton and Tooting, we sought a new three-year deal with OMK. Our main priority had to be to get a ground-share deal that would meet the Ryman League's requirements before the deadline date. Otherwise we could kiss promotion goodbye.

So while Kris and Ivor led three sets of ground-share negotiations I led a volunteer group looking at financing the purchase of Kingsmeadow. We were at full stretch doing all this while running the day-to-day business of the club and, at that time, like all the other volunteers I was still in a full-time job. Time was getting short.

We kept our negotiations confidential because we felt that public knowledge of our activities would weaken our negotiating positions. This approach is always difficult in a fans-owned club where some members feel they are entitled to know everything, irrespective of commercial confidentiality. But nothing stays quiet forever, and in January news of the possible deal at Tooting leaked out.

We quickly issued a press release confirming we were in detailed talks. Kris made a suitably upbeat statement saying we were still looking for a permanent home in Merton but adding, 'Tooting would be a first-class base in the meantime.' This was true but the football club board members were agreed that Kingsmeadow was a better medium-term option if the right deal could be done. And, as I've said before, Ivor has never been keen on Tooting.

It was time to brief the Dons Trust members in detail; they are, after all, the owners of the club. A Special General Meeting (SGM) of the DT was called for 11.30am on a matchday in mid-January. By the time of the SGM we had only a couple of weeks until the Ryman League application deadline and we still had no agreed deal at any of the possible sites. But it was essential to retain the support of the members so we did our best to ooze confidence and look completely in control.

It was standing room only in the Kingsmeadow bar. Kris started by explaining the urgency of the timetable, which was now further complicated because the Tooting planning application wouldn't be heard until early March, after the Ryman League deadline. That was a body blow because if we pursued that option we would be homeless if the application failed.

AFC Wimbledon fans are always well briefed and the questions were thoughtful and challenging. Kris dealt with them openly and honestly and announced a formal meeting to be held in a few weeks' time at which members would be fully briefed and asked to vote for their preferred option.

The meeting closed just before 2pm. It had to finish then, since the stadium couldn't open for the game until the volunteer turnstile operators and stewards had left the meeting to take up their positions.

From that point things developed quickly and not for the best. First, Sutton Council wrote formally to Bruce setting out their concerns about traffic congestion; they wanted a consultation process. The consequence was that a go/no go decision wouldn't be given until May's council meeting at the earliest. That effectively killed the deal.

With the Ryman League deadline imminent we maintained the pressure on both OMK and Tooting and by early February we'd agreed ground-share deals with both of them. The basic rent for Kingsmeadow was about 50 per cent higher than the existing deal and there were added extras too. OMK was in a strong position and he knew it. Encouragingly, however, we had gained some breathing space by persuading the Ryman League to accept two alternative deals in our application.

Both had significant drawbacks. Kingsmeadow was only for three years and it was becoming apparent that we were unlikely to achieve promotion in the current season. As a result, to maintain the three-year tenure the new deal would need renegotiating in a year's time. The price was hardly likely to go down. To add to the complexity, the shadow of Noades's option still loomed over us and we were very aware that even if we did a deal with OMK, he might sell Kingsmeadow to another party and our long-term security would be jeopardised. And eventually, to gain entry to the Football League we'd need a ten-year lease. Owning the stadium would remove all those problems and leave us able to look for a permanent site in Merton while secure in our temporary home.

The Tooting deal was for six years but it also brought problems. Even if the planning application was successful we were far from sure that we could increase the capacity to meet Football League requirements. And we'd still be paying for improvements to a stadium that wasn't ours.

In the light of these uncertainties we had taken the plunge and opened up discussions with OMK about buying Kingsmeadow. First, we prepared the ground in a confidential meeting with Kingston Council to establish their attitude to a change of ownership. That meeting was led by Tom Adam, with his background in big projects at BT, supported by Terry Raggett, a fan and a stadium architect, plus me. It was quickly apparent that the council would be supportive so long as we ensured that Ks would not be made homeless. Also, and critically, they confirmed that Kingsmeadow already had planning permission to expand to over 6,000 capacity, which easily met the Football League membership criteria.

A few days later, Ivor and Dan Norris, a fan and the real estate lawyer who had worked on our existing licence to play at Kingsmeadow, talked terms with OMK and his son. Worryingly, the meeting had been interrupted by a call to OMK from Noades, apparently to arrange a meeting for the following week.

Dan was gloomy about Noades's intentions. He suspected that he would make an offer for the stadium and could easily outbid us. At that point we didn't know what funds we could raise or what price we could afford. The football club board met to discuss our position. When we talked about Noades's intentions, I was amused that for once in my long relationship with Ivor, he was the one who was downbeat whereas I was very confident that Noades wouldn't take up the option. In practice, it didn't matter. Whatever we thought Noades might do, our approach had to be the same; we would hold our nerve and proceed as if he wasn't going to bid. We agreed a target price for the stadium.

We were on tenterhooks on 27 February, a day before the option expired, until we heard that Noades hadn't met OMK. By 5 March it was clear that Noades hadn't spoken to OMK about buying the stadium and we could now proceed.

Dan wrote to the board summarising the negotiations. Ivor had made an initial offer of £1m and then upped it to £1.5m. Both of these had been 'dismissed out of hand' by OMK. He was asking £2.75m for the stadium and, as Dan put it, 'He was not very talkative and pretty intransigent.' Ivor upped the offer again and when he reached £2m OMK finally proposed a counter price of £2.5m.

Further attempts to lower that number were unsuccessful. OMK made it clear this was the only price at which he was prepared to proceed. However, in a sign that he was really serious about the deal, he suggested that if we didn't raise all of the cash by the end of 2003 he would lend us the balance with interest at one per cent per month.

The instant I heard this offer I knew we were going to buy Kingsmeadow. Okay, we weren't 100 per cent certain that we could raise the cash to buy it outright. But I was very, very confident that the club's profits could cover the interest on, say, a debt of £1m. So the challenge was to raise around £1.5m, do the deal and then seek replacement finance for the balance of £1m. The sceptic in me suspected that OMK made the offer of a loan because he thought we might not be able to make the payments, in which case he would be able to reclaim the property. But I never doubted we'd succeed. We ignored OMK's assertion that Noades had offered to buy the stadium as an attempt to keep up the pressure on us.

The scene was now set for a second Dons Trust SGM and at this one members would be asked to vote for their preferred option. We knew the attendance would be very high so we booked Wimbledon Theatre.

First there was a flurry of meetings to review the options with the DT board. The Stadium Working Group had circulated a report which drew heavily on the experience of Hugh Scanlon, our volunteer planning specialist. The report reviewed all 13 sites which the SWG had identified and assessed the chances of each site achieving a successful planning application for expansion to Football League standards. The SWG concluded that buying Kingsmeadow was the best option available at that time. They also pointed out that the old stadium site in Plough Lane had now been classified for residential development which made its likely cost well beyond our reach.

We drafted a briefing paper to send to members before the meeting but even as it was being finalised word came through that Tooting's planning application had been rejected. There had been a well-orchestrated series of objections by residents and despite the Merton planning officers recommending approval the application was rejected by the planning committee in what was described as a boisterous meeting. We were down to only two options – rent or buy Kingsmeadow.

The DT membership at the time was just under 3,000, of whom about 2,400 were adult members, entitled to vote. Of these, nearly 1,000 of them turned up at Wimbledon Theatre for the SGM. After a brief introduction from Lou, Kris took the stage. He summarised the problems at Tooting and the likelihood that an appeal against the planning rejection would fail. Furthermore, the timescale for an appeal was just too long to be practicable. The Tooting option was, in effect, dead in the water.

He summarised the pros and cons of extending the ground-share or buying Kingsmeadow. If we decided to buy we needed to pay £270,000 (which we already had available from our first year's profits) on exchange of contracts and the balance by the end of 2003. He announced that after taking other costs into account we would need about £3m to make the deal happen.

Kris was followed by Tom Adam who summarised the work of the SWG and confirmed their support for the Kingsmeadow purchase option. Then I ran through the financial benefits of owning Kingsmeadow, let alone the security it would bring. But it wouldn't be easy. To put the cost into context, every person in the theatre that night would need to commit £3,000 to raise the necessary funds. I then asked everyone to complete a pledge form to indicate what amount they would be willing to contribute.

Keen as I was to go ahead, I stressed that the proposed purchase was very high-risk because if we paid the deposit and then couldn't raise the additional funds we would lose the £270,000 we'd paid and the ownership of the stadium. It was a gamble and the downsides were potentially crippling, but we'd assessed the risks and decided they were worth taking. Although I stressed the risks I am not sure how many of those present in the theatre understood that we were arguably betting our new club that we could raise the money.[12] Personally I was sure we could do so and, in any event, the alternative was to continue as we were. But a club that doesn't own its own stadium can't prosper in the long term.

Members' questions focused on the price we were proposing to pay and the level of risk. There are always people who think they could have done a better deal and maybe they could. But the board's view, supported by Dan who had been with Ivor throughout the negotiations, was that this was the best deal we could get and we should proceed. Where else within the M25 could we acquire a stadium that could be made Football League-compliant for a price like this?

We moved to a vote. Over 95 per cent voted for the purchase to go ahead. Now all we had to do was complete the detailed negotiations and raise the finance.

---

12 At a later stage, Dan Norris invited the DT and football boards to his offices where he ran through what we were committing to, what we were getting, and the substantial risks we were taking if we couldn't complete the deal. It was only after that briefing that I was convinced that the boards fully understood the risks. Indeed, they were sufficiently concerned that they sought advice on the consequences on individual board members of an insolvency.

9

MONEY, MONEY, MONEY

WHILE THE football club and DT boards were edging towards a recommendation that we buy Kingsmeadow, there was a problem; the only money we had was the profit from our first season. So I was asked to lead a Finance Working Group to work on how we could fund such a deal.

The FWG comprised a group of volunteers, all with a finance or risk capital background, to evaluate the different ways we might raise the funds. After a couple of meetings where we brainstormed possible approaches, we broke into sub-groups, each charged with advocating one specific financing method. Each of us took it in turns to present 'our' approach to the FWG and after much debate we presented our conclusions to a DT board meeting in March 2003.

The problem was that commercial lenders wouldn't touch us. We were a brand new company with no track record, operating in a high-risk business sector, in the eighth tier of football and yet asking people to put their money at risk by investing in us. High net worth (i.e. rich) individuals who might invest would want a degree of control which we weren't willing to offer. So the FWG concluded that for practical purposes a share issue was the best way to raise finance for a new stadium. After a long discussion the DT board voted to support the FWG's recommendation.

Our proposal was to offer shares in a new company (eventually to be called AFCW PLC) which would own the football club and the stadium. However, the Dons Trust would retain over 75 per cent of the votes. The reason for this was 75 per cent is the percentage of votes needed to pass a Special Resolution. Such resolutions are required by law for certain decisions, generally those that are most important or sensitive. In effect, we were saying that even though we were issuing shares, the DT would retain effective control over AFCW PLC and through it the football club and stadium.

After a short tender process we appointed John East and Co. to help us to launch the share issue. John is himself a football fan and has followed Dagenham & Redbridge for many years, most of which were spent in non-league football. In 2003 the regulations relating to share issues were much more restrictive than they are now and required a substantial amount of work by professional advisors. However, John liked our story so he proposed a fee of £5,000 if the share issue was unsuccessful and £50,000 only if we achieved our minimum target of £1m.

Throughout the negotiations the football club board was meeting almost daily and there were regular briefing meetings with the DT board. A DT members' meeting was held to obtain approval to go ahead and buy the stadium. Then, with John East attending to answer questions, the FWG held a briefing session to explain the risks and the financial implications to members.

By the end of May, everything was in place ready for the launch – except the final detailed agreement with OMK. Our target had been to take ownership of the stadium on 1 June 2003 but the detailed negotiations were long and protracted with many sticking points. It was essential that we launch the share issue before the July holiday period but June was slipping away and we had still not struck a final deal as OMK tried to eke out the last drop of advantage from the negotiations.

Massively frustrated, we drafted an announcement that we'd been unable to agree final terms. I then 'inadvertently' let OMK overhear me saying that we'd done so. Whether or not that influenced him we will never know but the issues started to be resolved. Now that we finally had their attention, Dan Norris spent a very long evening finalising the contract with Anup Khosla, OMK's son, and at midnight on Friday, 20 June we were able to announce that we'd resolved all the issues and expected to sign the deal the next week. Five days later, that happened. The share issue was launched the next day accompanied by a promotional video presenting Kingsmeadow as 'The Fans' Stadium' to encourage wider investment in the issue.

The final, very substantial, hurdle was that the share issue had to raise more than £1m. If it failed then all the money would have to be returned.

In that case the stadium would revert to OMK and we'd lose the £270,000 deposit we'd paid. We were awaiting each day's returns anxiously as we crept ever closer to the £1m target. John East had assured us that much of the money in share issues came in close to the deadline, but this was our club at stake and the tensions were high.

We were agonisingly close to the target and I was desperate to see it reached before Eileen and I went on holiday in July to travel into the Arctic Circle where we'd have very limited access to a mobile phone signal. While I was sure we'd done the right thing I was also sure that I'd never enjoy our holiday if we set off without knowing that the target had been reached. And then, as we stood in a queue to board our plane to Svalbard I took a call from John telling me that the magic figure of £1m had been exceeded. The stadium was ours and I switched my phone off for the next ten days.

We kept the share issue open until late in the year and after deducting expenses and adding in other funds from our profitable first year we were able to pay £1.45m to OMK against a reduced purchase price of £2.4m.

OMK paid £395,000 for Ks and the stadium, so within 12 months he had made a profit of over 500 per cent on the purchase and sale of Kingsmeadow. Sometimes to be successful in business you need luck and our arrival on the scene proved to be very lucky for him. But I think we were even luckier that it was OMK who bought Kingsmeadow because a football man would never have agreed to us ground-sharing in the first place. And a football man would never have agreed to sell us the stadium.

OMK was unpopular with Ks fans because he didn't seem to care about their team and he wasn't an easy person to deal with. But in my view, were it not for him selling us the stadium we could not have achieved the success of our early years and the foundation on which we built our longer-term ambitions.

Because OMK's profit was widely known, quite a few of our fans felt we'd overpaid. We saw it differently. Where else could we have bought a stadium capable of meeting the Football League's admission criteria within the M25, let alone a few miles from Plough Lane?

From a financial point of view Kingsmeadow was a very profitable deal for us. When we sold it to Chelsea 16 years later the sale price was comfortably more than treble what we paid for it.

10

HELP! (2)

NOW THAT we owned the stadium we could make some much-needed changes. First it needed to be made ready for the new season. The weekend after we took possession a large group of fans answered a call for help to smarten the place up. This was the first of the summer volunteer work weekends. On a Saturday and Sunday about 120 fans would arrive at the stadium to re-paint parking areas, trim the bushes, and weed the car park. Inside the stadium painting and maintenance work went on throughout both of the weekend sessions we ran every year.

Initially these events were organised by Margaret and Tom Adam and lunch was provided by my wife, Eileen. To our delight we were the beneficiaries of some unexpected volunteers who came to help, including a family in full Spurs kit, and Dave and Simon Peacey, Bristol Rovers and Cheltenham supporters respectively, who for many years travelled miles to help because they liked what our club represented and the camaraderie of the event. That more than made up for the volunteers who arrived 15 minutes before lunch and left 15 minutes afterwards!

Tom and Margaret had a long list of tasks to dole out. I never missed a work weekend – partly because I thought I should be there and be seen to be there but partly because they were good fun and a relaxed chance to chat to fans. The only hassle was from the advocates of 'paint Kingsmeadow blue' who wanted to cover up the red of Kingstonian. The board thought that was disrespectful to Ks and adopted a policy that anything new should be blue and anything that was replaced or freshened up was done in the original stadium colours. That didn't stop some guerrilla painting and sometimes I'd wander around the stadium and find a blue wall, which hadn't needed painting at all, or freshly painted blue safety barriers.

The stadium had been poorly maintained for several years and was a nightmare to run. There were mice in the kitchens and when it rained hard, sewage backed up through the toilets. Fixing all of these problems fell to the Stadium Working Group, also led by Tom who commissioned a video of the drains to pin down the sewage problem. He's very proud of that piece of work and offered the video to our heritage museum.

Margaret also organised a large team of volunteers to clean the stadium after games. Meanwhile, Eileen didn't just want to tag along behind me. Never afraid to get her hands dirty, she joined up with Margaret to help clean the stadium before each game. Among other things this involved dealing with the consequences of the ill-maintained anti-pigeon protection in the main stand; in short, aided by Sandra Lowne she spent a considerable time before each game scrubbing pigeon shit off the seats, while Ray Armfield and Mike Harris swept the entire stadium clean.

One of the blue wheelie bins that Margaret introduced was immediately commandeered by Dean Parsons, who is 'Haydon', our Womble mascot. Dean/Haydon wheels his bin around with him during games, initiating chants by rhythmically banging its lid. Haydon can frequently be seen in the local community, visiting children in hospital, adult learning centres and anywhere else where we feel he can make a difference.

The summer work was supplemented by three volunteers, Roy Bacon, Alan Williams and Derek Goodhew, who turned up every Thursday, rain or shine, to put in a long day's work maintaining the stadium.

Now that we owned the stadium we could do our own catering on matchdays. So Eileen, Margaret and Sandra, along with Claire Heller and Charlotte Chalke, took over providing and serving hot drinks and a buffet for sponsors and guests in the President's Lounge, as well as sandwiches for the players, referees, managers, police, St John Ambulance and individually tailored rolls for volunteers. Eileen[13] prepared most of the catering at home, which meant I could eat my dinner knowing that our

---

13 Eileen squeezed this in alongside volunteering to be the club's first welfare officer, a forerunner of the safeguarding role that all clubs must have. A former special educational needs teacher, she helped to develop policies and procedures to fulfil the FA safeguarding requirements, including Criminal Record Bureau checks to ensure that everyone working with young people was cleared to do so.

kitchen had been inspected and certified by our local borough hygiene officials!

This group of volunteers served tea and coffee before the game, at half-time and after the final whistle. Like the cash office team, they missed so much of the game that they sometimes didn't know who'd won, but they loved the camaraderie. Meanwhile, Claire, along with Aideen Rochford, Zoe Linkson and Alison Perrone, made sure that visiting officials were made to feel very welcome in our tiny little boardroom.

One volunteer who didn't fit easily into any category was Clive Yelf. As 'Fleydon' he created a huge array of hand-painted flags which he hung up behind the goal at the athletics stadium end of the ground. They covered a range of subjects, from an AFC Wimbledon version of the raising of the flag at Iwo Jima, to Da Vinci's Vetruvian Man of Math, but in a Dons shirt and shorts. It wasn't all highbrow and included flags based on the opening credits to *Dad's Army* and The Ministry of Silly Walks, all with an AFC Wimbledon flavour.

Clive took his flag-making into sessions at local schools and held exhibitions at various sites across the borough, enabling the club to win a community award from Merton Council. Sadly he seems to have retired from flag-making but they can all be seen on the fleydon-flags blog, with a gentle parody of a *Guardian* arts page review for each flag, plus an AFC Wimbledon version of Wink Martindale's song, 'Deck of Cards'.

Things like Fleydon's flags helped Kingsmeadow to feel like home, at least for the time being.

11

CHANGES

IT'S TIME to explain how AFC Wimbledon went from being created and incorporated by a small group of fans to being owned by all Wimbledon fans, or at least the ones who pay the Dons Trust membership fee.

Long before the idea of Milton Keynes surfaced, there had been talk of relocating to Dublin and other possible moves. In response to this threat to our club, the Wimbledon Independent Supporters Association (WISA) developed and led a sophisticated, highly professional campaign of opposition. But they understood that it wasn't enough to be against something, they needed to create something positive to represent the views of all Dons fans – a supporters' trust.

The supporters' trust movement came into being largely thanks to one man, Brian Lomax, who chaired the first trust at Northampton Town FC. The idea spread by word of mouth until in 1999 the government decided to fund Supporters Direct to encourage fans to get involved in their clubs. The WISA committee picked up on the idea and Lou Carton-Kelly, Luke Mackenzie, Nicole Hammond and Mags Hutchinson came away from the Supporters Direct conference in September 2001 determined to set up our own trust.

A month later they held a public meeting at the Wimbledon Community Centre. The place was rammed. Brian Lomax spoke and our assigned case worker, Dave Boyle, talked us through how to create a trust. Working groups were created and on 10 February 2002 the Wimbledon Football Club Supporters Society Limited[14] (hereafter referred to as the Dons Trust

---

14 No attempt has ever been made to change the name to AFC Wimbledon Supporters Society Limited.

or DT) was launched in a packed Wimbledon Theatre. Lou Carton-Kelly[15] was the DT's first chair and the newly elected board set about seeking influence on the WFC board; at that time, the FA Commission hadn't been created.

Just under four months later the Dons Trust found itself the owner of AFC Wimbledon. As a change from the usual 'room above a pub' venue, the board meeting was held in a room opposite the Houses of Parliament (thanks to DT board member Lord Faulkner). It was at this meeting that Ivor and Kris, having formed the club and worked their guts out to get it going, sold it to the Dons Trust for £2, which is still the total issued share capital of AFC Wimbledon Limited. Lou recalls, 'I paid Kris and Ivor £2 using the 20p coins which I carried around for parking meters.'

By then, Ivor and I had been co-opted on to the DT board. He doesn't recall being paid and thinks he is still owed £1. It was never Kris's or Ivor's intention to own the football club. It was more a case of, 'Someone's got to set it up, let's get on and do it.' And they did and then passed it across to enable the club to be owned by all its fans.

We were now in a position where a board that had been elected to seek influence at WFC was suddenly responsible for overseeing a nascent football club. Kris had been appointed chairman of the club and after more than a year's debate the DT board agreed that he should be paid. (I never understood what alternatives the reluctant DT board members had in mind. It was our good fortune that Kris was made redundant the day before the FA Commission's decision was announced. I don't know his personal circumstances but with no income at all for such a prolonged period he must have come close to bankruptcy. Nonetheless, he kept working hard throughout all that time.)

As a paid executive Kris couldn't be a DT board member but he nonetheless was 'in attendance' at DT board meetings. This gave the bizarre situation where he was reporting to a board which included two members (Ivor and I) who reported to him in our roles as football club directors. Furthermore, Lou, the chair of the DT board, was also operations director of the football club. As such she reported to Kris, who reported

---

15 Lou Carton-Kelly flew to Japan for the 2002 World Cup the day after the watershed meeting at the community centre, when it was agreed to form AFC Wimbledon. As she remarked, 'If not in Japan I would have been an obvious choice to chair the club.' A *Sliding Doors* moment indeed.

to the DT board – chaired by Lou. It was ridiculous but a shared sense of purpose meant that we ignored these formalities and just made it work.

Before we took over Kingsmeadow we used to meet in an ill-lit room above a pub where your feet stuck to the linoleum floor and the chairs didn't feel much cleaner. At first the DT board didn't have a clear view of its changed role and when that happens people gravitate to topics where they feel comfortable. As a result, the meetings seemed interminable and focused on relatively minor details. Eileen remembers, 'You'd come home spitting feathers and deeply frustrated by those meetings.'

When I trained as an accountant there was a maxim that said, 'Good people can make awful systems work and awful people can ruin the best systems.' In our case this translated into Kris and the football club board, while keeping the DT board informed, simply getting on with matters. But it was clear that things needed to change.

After an intense session of introspection, the DT board recommended that all its members should stand down and fresh elections be held in November 2003, 18 months after we'd re-formed our club. The board's published reasons were:

- There have been such major changes in our circumstances since the current board was elected that it needs a new mandate
- We need to overhaul the constitution and this should be led by a board with the authority that comes from being elected by the current membership[16]

There were 20 candidates for the ten board places, which were decided using a single transferable vote system. An Electoral Steering Group (ESG) was formed and was called into action when some candidates introduced mischief into their campaigns. Luke Mackenzie, volunteer chief steward and a veteran campaigner of the protest era, plastered 'vote Luke' posters

16 The constitution is much changed now. Some years later the football club board instigated a rule change to prevent its members from serving on the DT board and terms were shortened to two years, meaning 50 per cent of the board is up for re-election each year. This is all for the good. The changes also removed a limit on the time members could serve from four terms (12 years in those early days). In my view that was a mistake. The AFC Wimbledon Foundation (in effect the charitable arm of the club) requires its chair to stand down after nine years and, as the incumbent, I plan to do so in the summer of 2021, a year early. Fresh blood is a very good thing.

on every spare inch of the walls all the way along the stadium's narrow approach road. He also put them behind the goal at one end of the ground and asked fans' hero Matt Everard to point at them if he scored. Luke laments, 'He did score but didn't do it.' Matt was too shrewd to get drawn into politics.

Luke's careful reading of the rules had identified that a ban on campaigning inside the stadium didn't stop him from fly-posting adverts. However, matchday club PA announcer and board candidate Chris Philips was censured for ending one of his announcements with a cry of 'vote Philo'. The ESG had a job to do but it was hard for it to avoid looking po-faced when most people took the breaches as harmless fun.

All candidates were required to produce a manifesto with a maximum of 450 words. Another piece of the ESG's heavy-handed application of the rules meant that Anne Eames (manager Terry Eames's wife) saw her manifesto terminated in mid-sentence for breaching the limit.

The nature of an election for a supporters' trust is that by and large the well-known names get elected. So it was no surprise that Lou Carton-Kelly, the chair of the DT board, Ivor Heller, the club's commercial director, and I, as finance director, ended up topping the polls. Among the others who were elected were Anne Eames, club founder Marc Jones, and rogue campaigners Luke and Chris.

The first meeting of the newly constituted DT board was held at Kingsmeadow and Tom Adam was elected as chair to succeed Lou. Shortly afterwards, Anne Eames resigned from her role. She and a couple of friends had all stood for the board but only she had been elected.

We entered 2004 with a new chair and a new board which had no idea of the turmoil it was to face within a few weeks.

12

RUNAWAY

FOLLOWING THE February defeat against Withdean 2000, we won 15 and, perhaps a little carelessly, drew one of our remaining fixtures in our first season. During that run we scored 52 goals and conceded 11 but it was too late to secure promotion.

At the start of our first season Terry had presented me with a spreadsheet setting out the squad's wages. The total weekly wages for a squad of 22 was £700, with Bassey, Sheerin and Cooper the top earners at £60 per week (we always regarded players' wages as a private matter but at 19 years' distance and given the sums involved I think it is okay to make an exception).

Every player was capable of playing one or two levels higher and they knew it. As Northern Ireland under-21 international midfielder Gareth Graham put it, 'We didn't need coaching. We were too good for that level but if you look at it from the other side we were probably all playing at that level because of something missing from our game, like attitude.'

At this level non-league footballers were typically paid for the playing season alone, i.e. from the first competitive game to the last, and no more. However, during the first campaign Terry had pressed for various players to be given contracts and paid for the next pre-season weeks. To be honest, at this stage the board didn't know any different so we just accepted it.

By the start of the second season, 2003/04, we had ten players under contract. With the possible exceptions of Joe Sheerin and Matt Everard, this was unnecessary. No other club at this level could offer the experience and excitement of playing in front of such large crowds and most of our players weren't going to leave voluntarily.

In the first season we'd been caught out by big spenders AFC Wallingford and Withdean 2000. By the time we realised what was happening it was too late. We were determined not to let that happen again so Terry was encouraged to strengthen an already very strong squad. Over the summer he released several of the recruits from late in the first season and by mid-July had signed 12 new players. Not all proved to be successes – eight of them made only 11 league starts between them. Joe Sheerin was now the only first team regular who remained of the 19 who had played in that first game against Sutton only a year earlier.

The players' weekly wage bill was now nearly double what it was when we started. Even then we were pretty sure that Wallingford were spending more. However, Withdean 2000 had cut their budget dramatically. After they failed to meet the stadium criteria for promotion to the Ryman League their backer upped and offed to Worthing FC, taking several of their best players with him. At the end of the 2003/04 season they were disbanded, the fate of many such clubs which are built on one man's money. In effect we now had only Wallingford as a competitor for the league title.

There was also a new competition to look forward to – the FA Vase. The Vase is, in broad terms, the successor competition to the FA Amateur Cup. The notion of amateur footballers was no longer believable with 'boot money' (so named because that was where you'd find your tax-free 'expenses' after a game) reaching silly levels. So the FA bowed to realism and started the Vase in the 1970s. It was open to all senior clubs in their second or subsequent seasons, at CCL level and below. We fancied ourselves to do well.

The team started where they left off the previous season, with 21 straight league wins. In practice they were finding it too easy and often turned to mischief, such as stripping off to compete with the pole dancers at the local pub. There were strong characters in the dressing room and a drinking culture. So when access to alcohol was cut off, the team reacted.

On the way home from a pre-season game at Dorchester the team coach pulled up at a supermarket. Using the players' kitty they bought a trolley full of drink. Then Terry told them they couldn't drink on the coach – it was illegal and they'd have to put the alcohol in the luggage area underneath the coach. Sitting on the coach for the long journey back, the players decided to stage a naked protest. In fact they'd smuggled some drink on to the coach and by the time they got back to Kingsmeadow they were dressed again and, let's say, relaxed. They unloaded the alcohol and sat in the car park drinking and listening to Noel Frankum's stereo.

It was no different during the season. As Paul Scott says, 'The dressing room was non-stop mucking about. Like being with all your mates and relaxed.' In December we played away at Ash. We'd won the game but with a fairly ordinary performance and Terry started to let rip at the players in the dressing room. He was interrupted by a low, moaning noise. He stopped and everyone looked around. He started again. So did the moaning. By now players were studying their boots – it's not a good idea to let your manager see you laughing when he's giving you a bollocking. Suddenly a cupboard door flew open and there was Noel Frankum, joker-in-chief, with Simon Bassey lurking in the shadows just behind him. Terry knew when to give in and joined in laughing with everyone else.

When the manager tears into you all you can do is sit and take it. An exception was when we played at Horley on a freezing cold night just before Christmas. Although we were winning at half-time, Terry was tearing a strip off the players for a lacklustre performance. Or at least he was trying to.

The piped music from the bar was being relayed into the dressing room, so while Terry was letting rip, he had to compete with 'Frosty The Snow Man' permeating the dressing room. Trevor Williams was despatched to sort it out. He recalls, 'This poor geezer was by the control panel at the end of the corridor and I said, "Mate, can you turn the music off in the dressing room?" He looked at me helplessly and said, "I don't know how to." I said, "Well then, turn everything off" – but he had no idea how to.'

Trev returned to the dressing room and broke the bad news to Terry. Trev says, 'Eamo shouted "I can't have all this" and threw a bag of balls at the speaker; they bounced back and spilled everywhere. By that stage I'd lost it completely and had to fake a coughing fit to cover me laughing. The players were half in shock and half trying not to laugh because he was the manager and they listened when he shouted at him. But when the substitutes went out to warm up they just kept singing Christmas carols and booting the balls at each other.'

In those early days the training facilities were very basic with poor pitches. In the first couple of years we moved around several different venues, looking for somewhere better. Trevor adds, 'The grounds didn't have any real storage so we had to lug all the gear and stuff like that to and from training.' It was all very primitive.

Training was on a Tuesday, if there was no midweek game, and a Thursday. Drinking was an important part of the team culture and, for example, after Thursday training up to a dozen of the players would go to a local pub for three or four pints. After a game they'd sometimes go on to Lee Harwood's pub (Lee was Terry's assistant in the early days) in South Wimbledon for a lock-in. Simon Bassey says, 'We used to go to his pub and he'd go to bed, lock it up, and leave a note with a pen saying "just write down what you had and shut the door on your way out". Sometimes we'd leave at 4am – it was mental.'

The training itself usually comprised small-sided games, played in tight areas to sharpen up close control. Players like this sort of training and as a result they generally work harder. They hate any training that doesn't involve a ball, so when they were told to run 400 metres Bassey once said, 'I've never run that far with a ball and I ain't doing it now.' He was dropped.

Paul Scott explains, 'Training wasn't as structured as I was used to at other places but it didn't need to be because the players were so much above the level we were playing at. We did lots of keep-ball games but very little pattern of play [where players rehearse formations and their respective roles in them].' Gareth Graham adds, 'The quality of players we had meant we could all play 4-4-2. We were long enough in the tooth to be able to do that without needing pattern of play.' But that backfired when Terry introduced a 3-5-2 formation for a home game against Walton Casuals. Within half an hour we were losing 3-0 at which point we reverted to 4-4-2 and with a more familiar formation, scored three goals in the last 11 minutes to run out 5-4 winners. It was hardly surprising it didn't work; Terry said, 'I decided to try three at the back without so much as a training session.'

Terry had successfully recruited good enough players that it was January before we dropped points with a 2-2 draw at Sandhurst. While lots of fans lapped up the success, I found it boring, with the result of every game a foregone conclusion. I wasn't alone. Gordon Law of the *South London Press* was struggling to find something different to say in his twice-weekly columns.[17] Eventually he gave vent to his feelings in his

17 My thanks to the *South London Press* for permission to reproduce this article

column, 'AFC Wimbledon have won again and again and again… I'm so bored about writing the same thing every week… Can't we just stop the season now and hand the trophy to them?

'At the moment I'm just sick of it. Win, win, bloody win. In an open message to the manager and all the AFC Wimbledon players – please, please lose the next match because I really want something different to write about… How can you savour all these victories when they come as often as Jordan appearing on the front page of the *Daily Star*?'

He had a suggestion, 'If there are any wannabe streakers out there, don't be shy. Make it to an AFC Wimbledon game before the end of the season. It will give me something different to write about.' Nobody obliged.

Perhaps things would be different in the FA Vase, where we had been drawn away at Pagham in the second qualifying round.

Cup competitions are very welcome because they provide new opposition and different grounds to visit. To be prudent I always budgeted to lose our first cup game. Therefore a win provided unbudgeted prize money – in this case it was £500 – and a promise of income from the next round because the net gate receipts from cup games are shared.

We took an early lead and looked comfortable in a scrappy game on a bone-dry pitch. I spent much of the afternoon fretting about our fans' safety, given the bottlenecks in the exits should they need to leave quickly. As a result, I only started to pay attention when Simon Bassey was sent off.

The thought of losing out on the prize money, as well as a share of the gate money from the next round, clearly got to me. Apparently it showed, as unflatteringly observed in Herbie Knott's unpublished book about that season,[18] 'Simon Bassey's dismissal for fighting on 67 minutes had Erik Samuelson dragging the thinning hair from his head in sheaves. With the Dons hanging on to a slender one-goal lead the club's number-crunching financial director was twitching. "If that costs us the FA Vase…you make good money in this competition…Bassey… *!*??**!!!… getting to the final is worth £30,000…Bassey…!!!" Erik watched from behind the Pagham goal as the minutes ticked down and the ten men fought on, sometimes literally. Erik had never quite bought the horrible totality of football, and certainly not the idea of player-misbehaviour [on his budget].'

—

18 My thanks to Herbie Knott for permission to reproduce this extract.

That's not quite how I see myself but it is true that I was furious with Simon for being sent off and putting welcome funds at risk.

Over 1,500 Dons fans travelled to the seaside for the next round of the Vase at Herne Bay. There is little more enjoyable than a late winner in a cup game and Matt Everard's 93rd-minute header was a classic of its kind. The day was marred, yet again, by off-the-pitch violence which was following us at the more high-profile games and would erupt again later in the season. The Herne Bay victory was followed by two more wins, putting us into the last 32 of the Vase. Until then the draw had been regional but now the competition went national. We were drawn to play Lancashire club Colne FC at Kingsmeadow.

The Saturday before the Colne game we'd dropped our first league points of the season. Nonetheless, we had every reason to be confident. Indeed, we were dreaming of a Wembley final.

We lost. As centre-back Matt Everard put it, 'We weren't good enough at our level. We had better players than all of the other sides but we couldn't do it against them… we were the better team but not on that day. If it hadn't been them we'd have got beaten by someone else and we'd not have got to the final.'

As I think of it, when you are so used to being easily the better team each week, you don't necessarily know how to raise your game when things go against you. It was an important lesson but, as the old cliché goes, it allowed us to concentrate on the league.

Another problem surfaced at the end of the match. Some weeks earlier Terry had introduced a bit of glamour into the side by recruiting Michael 'Junior' Harvey, a member of chart-topping So Solid Crew. At the end of the game Harvey complained that he had been racially abused. The whole team pitched in and a mass brawl started as they left the pitch. In the middle of it all, with a wildly misplaced punch, club captain Joe Sheerin landed a right cross on our manager's jaw!

Striker Paul Scott and fitness coach Paul Braham said they had also been racially abused. A war of words broke out between the two managers and the respective local press. It was a very sour end to our cup run. The FA investigated but nothing came of it and Colne announced themselves vindicated while we all seethed.

But if that was traumatic it was nothing compared to the events that followed a few weeks later.

13

HELP! (3)

BY NOW our merchandising had settled into a smooth-running operation. Until we owned the stadium, we had no permanent base and were restricted to matchday sales. Before every game the back bar was transformed by volunteers delivering a host of fundraising activities. Much of it was more akin to a church fete, with cupcakes and home-knitted Wombles on sale. Just before the kick-off there was a frantic flurry of activity as all the tables and displays were dismantled and loaded into the backs of cars. Once again, Old Man Khosla was happy to help by offering storage space under the main stand in return for extra matchday rent.

I asked Tim Hillyer, who had a retail background, to bring some order into things and consolidate all our merchandising activities under one person – him. This involved managing a range of activities which had sprung up, the most visible being a converted ambulance. Known as the Wombulance, it sat in the car park before home games and frequently turned up at away matches, selling a range of goods. In some ways it was typical of our early days. I didn't know whose idea it was, it just suddenly appeared. At the end of the first season it disappeared.

As is often the case with such ad-hoc ventures there was a lack of control. When I asked for records I was told, 'I'm no good at that, I'm only really interested in selling.' Tim recalls, 'There was no commercial nous. They were buying Dons Trust-branded umbrellas for £24 and selling them for £25. I also took a dim view of them holding money back from the takings to buy stuff with cash. There was no suggestion of dishonesty, but it was impossible to tell how much cash they were taking and what, if any, profit they were making. We also had the crazy situation of Dons Trust and AFC Wimbledon selling similar products.'

Tim held meetings and agreed actions and we started to become more organised. It was towards the end of the first season before he'd gained everyone's confidence. Slowly we were becoming more professional.

Soon after we bought Kingsmeadow we discovered that a garage built in to the stadium was only full of junk. Tim and his team set about converting it into a permanent shop using fittings scavenged from a local supermarket. A volunteer fitted the lighting for us and we were ready to move in.

The shop was staffed and supported completely by volunteers. Mike Arrowsmith wrote a bespoke online shop and others, led by Gerry Hever and Mags Hutchinson, came in to fulfil online orders. The shop was open only on matchdays except for the two weeks before Christmas, when the merchandise team pulled out all the stops and opened every day.

Everything we sold was designed and commissioned by a merchandise group, led by Tim who reported to commercial director Ivor Heller. Tim explained, 'We'd gather input from team members as to what they thought about pricing as well as design. I'd aim to get a consensus because I knew from experience how difficult it is to get people to sell things that they haven't had any involvement in selecting.'

The area where Ivor was most actively involved was the replica kit. He had done a deal with Tempest, a local company, to manufacture it. They had no experience with sports kit and, as Tim explained, this created problems: 'The cut of the early shirts was very square, but footballers tend to be lean – it's the supporters who are squarer in shape. So the kit was too short to get the right chest size and it was stopping at their belly button. So it looked terrible on the players.'

The big benefit of a local manufacturer was that we could have a unique design. Every other season we would issue a new home and away kit and in the intervening year we would issue a new third strip. In the 'two-kit years' we held an open competition to design the first-team colours. Almost without fail, club founder Marc Jones's design would win, even when he entered under an assumed name to quell grumbles about favouritism. Although some fans seemed to prefer conspiracy theories to explain his success, there was no favouritism; he is just a very good designer.

The launch of new home and away kits was a big event and was often held at Centre Court in Wimbledon. The merchandise team would build a shop in the main area of the mall and first-team members and, in the case of Neal Ardley, the manager, came along to model the new matchday kit, training kit and tracksuits. Neal in particular threw himself into it. 'If you're going to do this sort of thing you've really got to give it the full treatment,' he commented after camping his way up and down the makeshift catwalk.

When we reached Wembley in 2016 for the play-off final, Ivor Heller persuaded the Centre Court shopping mall in Wimbledon town centre to let us set up a pop-up shop for a week. Tim took part of his annual holiday to oversee a pool of volunteers selling tickets and merchandise to fans and every evening I'd arrive to collect the sales analysis for the day and check the cash banking.

As time went on and we went up the leagues, some of the roles became too onerous to be fulfilled by volunteers. After 15 years of running the shop, managing the merchandise team and engendering a great team spirit, Tim stood down and former volunteer Mat Haylock was appointed as our full-time, paid, merchandise and shop manager.

In the days of the protests against the move to Milton Keynes a group of fans got together to write, edit, produce, print and sell an alternative matchday programme, *Yellow and Blue*. Thanks to a combination of good writing, frank opinion and fans' distaste for anything produced and sold by WFC, it outsold the official publication two or three times over. So it was natural that most of the AFC Wimbledon programme would be written, designed and sold by the same volunteers. For many years Stephen Crabtree and Ray Armfield provided a great deal of the content, overseen by club secretary David Charles.

By now we'd pretty much got our act together. Fans arriving at Kingsmeadow would be met by stewards, they could drop in to the shop to buy club merchandise and they'd be invited to buy Golden Goal tickets before entering the ground. Once inside they would be able to buy a high-quality programme. Wherever you went or whatever you did, you would almost certainly be dealing with volunteers. Volunteers are the heartbeat of almost all non-league clubs but the scale of what ours were doing and the fact that most of them continued right up to our final game at Kingsmeadow in 2020 is a testament to the commitment they all showed.

14

END OF THE LINE

ON 18 February 2004, in a season where he had overseen 24 wins and one draw out of 25 games, Terry Eames was dismissed as manager following a disciplinary hearing.

At the beginning of the hearing we agreed that the proceedings would remain confidential. A recording of the hearing and all the written statements still exist and are in our archive. However, although the agreement was not in writing and it was 17 years ago, I believe it should be honoured. So this chapter deals only with the aftermath.

Terry had been suspended on Friday, 13 February, pending a hearing. We had agreed beforehand that if necessary we would ask Nicky English, the assistant manager, to step in. So, Kris rang Nicky, gave him a short update on what was happening and asked him to take over 'for now'. It can't have been an easy decision for Nicky. On the one hand Terry had brought him into the club and been good to him; on the other hand, this might be the only chance he'd ever get to manage a club of our scale. We were relieved when he agreed. We immediately called all the players into the club for a meeting that night. The bar was always closed on a Friday night so we gathered there; Nicky, Kris, Ivor, Trev and me, plus the players.

Kris took to the stage and addressed the players. He explained that Terry had been suspended, emphasising 'not sacked', and that Nicky had agreed to take the team until matters were resolved. Then Nicky spoke. He was in his early 40s, only medium height but with a ramrod-straight back. If he was nervous he didn't show it. He spoke quietly, but it didn't need to be loud. Everyone was listening closely, even the banter-meisters. He kept it simple. The team was going well and we were going to win the league. 'But if anyone doesn't want to continue then feel free to walk away – and if you're just concerned then come and talk to me.' It was hardly Churchillian but it was blunt and clear. Players prefer it that way.

Ivor had been worried that there might be a players' strike – there had been speculation about the possibility on the Weird and Wonderful World site. I wasn't concerned because I was convinced that the players' main concern would simply be about themselves and whether or not Nicky would 'fancy them', as the football jargon has it, and keep them in the team. (You see this phenomenon almost every time a club appoints a caretaker manager. Players appear in the press saying, 'We think he should get the job permanently.' That is code for, 'He's picking me for the team and a new guy might not, so please appoint him'.)

Several of the players in the room had been brought to the club by Nicky and he knew they'd be fine. It was the others he was worried about. After the meeting, he and Joe Sheerin, the captain, sought each other out. Nicky says, 'We had a chat and I urged him to enjoy it while we were all here. Later I spoke separately to all the players I'd brought and said to tell me if there was any dressing-room unrest – but there was none.'

When Nicky had finished, Kris asked if there were any questions. Ivor was still fretting until, as he recalls, 'One of the players said "the players want to know what about the bonuses" and I remember thinking straight away "now we're ok" and that completely turned everything. The big thing was, how were we going to get out of the PR disaster? I was very worried about it because we couldn't say anything before any disciplinary hearing but [when I heard them asking about their bonuses] I knew there would be no strike.'

After the meeting we opened up the bar to let the players chat and absorb what had happened. If you put a group of footballers together with drinks they will soon move on to their banter. By the time they drifted off into the night I felt that the tension had dissipated.

The players' reaction varied wildly. Simon Bassey was to the point, 'I remember thinking am I not getting my money [the bonus]!'

Gavin Bolger spoke to me with concerns about whether he would continue to be picked. Paul Scott was downbeat. He says, 'Nicky told me to do certain things as a forward but it was contrary to what I'd been told by [more experienced managers such as] Alan Devonshire and didn't make sense. So I basically ignored him.' This soon came to a head and Paul left the club just before the transfer deadline in March with Nicky telling the local press, 'There is no place at AFC Wimbledon for players who sulk.'

Rock-solid centre-half and fans' hero Matt Everard sums up his view in his usual pragmatic way, 'I don't think [Terry leaving] mattered. I think you could have appointed anyone, or no one. There was loyalty for Terry but we would never, ever get the chance to play in front of that number of people ever again. Most of us were mid-to-late 20s and the younger ones weren't going to go on to play professionally. It was a once in a lifetime opportunity to play for a big club – what it is like to play as a pro. But it would never have crossed my mind to leave because Terry went.

'If I was Terry's son and he got the sack I would still have stayed. Playing for Wimbledon was the golden ticket for players like us. It was just a case of keeping the motor running – by then we didn't even need to train.'

The next day, a matchday, dawned and with it a deep sense of foreboding. If Friday the 13th had been an awful day for Terry then Valentine's Day was a horrendous one for Kris and Ivor.

Chessington United had chosen to move their home game against us to Leatherhead's ground. I went to the game with my elder son. I'm not a great fan of wearing ties to games so I would quite often forswear the boardroom to stand. I'd also made it a point to pay to get in because it seemed a bit cheap to expect a freebie when we were playing clubs which were scratching along on a shoestring.

Once inside the ground we walked past the Dons fans amassed on the terrace behind the goal. At the time I was very much 'the other one' on the board; Kris and Ivor were the public faces of the club to many fans, although most people recognised me. Unusually, no one said 'hello' but I was simply pleased to get to the end of the stand without being abused. We made our way along the long grassy bank that constituted one of the terraces, picked a spot and watched the game. A couple of fans approached me and said something along the lines of 'I hope you know what you are doing' but that seemed perfectly fair to me.

I was praying that we would not lose. If we did, the conspiracy theorists would say it was because the team had gone on strike and the pressure on us and Nicky would have grown enormously. As it was, the tension lasted only a few minutes before Ryan Gray scored our first goal. By the half-hour we were three up and with a late flurry, we ran out with our record win, 9-0. Cue enormous relief.

Meanwhile, on the other side of the stadium things were very unpleasant. Kris and Ivor had carried out their duties and spent time with Chessington officials for a pre-match drink and snacks. Ivor says, 'It was the worst day I've faced at AFC Wimbledon; the atmosphere, things that happened that day, Kris being jostled by our own fans.'

Very aware that Terry was in the crowd, surrounded by family, friends and some fans, they had walked along the main stand to go behind the goal with the Dons fans. Ivor was lagging slightly behind and saw Kris being harassed by two or three supporters. Ivor is never afraid to go where angels fear to tread and he's very loyal to his friends so he went to join Kris to argue the board's case. The problem was that it wouldn't be right to Terry, or indeed any employee, to talk about their personal issues in public. So they couldn't tell fans what they wanted to know, which was why had Terry been suspended. It soon degenerated into angry, shouted accusations. Ivor and Kris decided it would be wise to watch from the almost deserted terrace behind the goal at the other end of the pitch.

At the end of the game, they decided they mustn't be deterred from acting normally, however uncomfortable it might be for them. So they joined the Chessington officials for a post-match drink and then drifted into the bar.

By and large, Wimbledon fans are reasonable, thoughtful people, not inclined to show open hostility towards those they know. But that day was different. It was horrible. People had divided into groups. Most fans were quiet and looked uncomfortable with the atmosphere. But a significant number of others felt sufficiently emboldened to criticise Kris and Ivor very loudly. Facts don't count for a lot when people feel aggrieved and a lot of it was about sacking Terry, even though we hadn't actually done so. The fact that we hadn't managed to get a longer press release on to the club's website before the game started made things doubly difficult for them.

It got worse. Deciding it was time to leave, Ivor and Kris split up and went to their respective cars. As Ivor made his way across the car park a car drove past with the windows open. One of the occupants leaned out and sang the Koppel song,[19] with Ivor's name in place of Koppel. Ivor says,

---

19 The Koppel song was sung at Charles Koppel, WFC chairman and regarded with contempt for his collaboration in the move to Milton Keynes. The song is sung to the tune of Bruce Chanel's 'Hey Baby', but with changed words – 'Hey, Char-arles Koppel. I want to know-whoa-whoa, why you're such a ****.' On repeat.

'That was my lowest point at the club. I've still not forgiven the man who sang the Koppel song at me. He was in a car being driven by another fan who came to me a long time later and said it was nothing to do with him. I said he should have thrown him out of the car.'

By then many of the players had joined Terry in the bar, which wasn't a pleasant place to go if you were a member of the DT board.

All this was meat and drink to the press, especially the *Non-League Paper* and the *South London Press*. There were extensive quotes from Terry and Anne while the football club and Dons Trust boards felt unable to expand on their statement. It was, after all, a personal issue relating to one of our employees.

Meanwhile, yet another DT board meeting had been called for the Tuesday night. Despite the short notice all board members except Lou Carton-Kelly were able to attend. Kris took members through events since the previous meeting only five days earlier. He explained the process for the next day's hearing and, once again, the possible outcomes. Most of the DT board had been at the Chessington game and those who weren't had been made aware of the abuse they were likely to receive from fans if Terry were to be sacked.

After a thorough questioning the football club board was asked to leave the room while the DT board members discussed the situation. After what felt an eternity we were called back in to be told that they felt we were acting in a fair and appropriate manner with regard to the actions taken already, and to be taken.

The board also noted that we had asked Steven Powell (a member of the Arsenal Independent Supporters' Association) to act as an independent observer and adviser. This was at the suggestion of WISA's chair, Nicole Hammond. Steven had nearly 15 years' experience as a trade union official and five as a human resources adviser in the voluntary sector. We welcomed this proposal because it dealt with possible objections that we were prosecution and judges of the same case and that any appeal could only be to the Dons Trust board, who had already heard our view of the issues. Steven's involvement was absolutely essential to the credibility of the proceedings.

After Terry left the hearing it was several hours before we arrived at our decision, having challenged ourselves repeatedly about whether we'd taken everything into account. We also sought assurance from Steven that in his independent opinion we'd done a thorough job and come to an objective decision. Looking back on it, Steven remembers thinking, 'Part of the reason I was there was to consider whether the decision taken was within the band of "reasonable responses" [which has a specific meaning as regards such hearings] and that [the panel] had no problem with falling within that range.'

Now we needed to write a press release explaining the decision. We spent an age over this and were still struggling over it when Charlie Talbot arrived mid-afternoon. Charlie was the club's journalist but with an excellent sense for the wider PR issues. There was a home game that night and staff and fans were starting to arrive. But we hadn't finished drafting the announcement so we had to close the President's Lounge to guests. My wife Eileen and Charlotte, her assistant, who were preparing the sponsors' food, were allowed into the pokey little kitchen in the corner of the lounge but told they couldn't come out until we were done.

We finished the statement just as the game kicked off and by then, the news had leaked out. The match was a fairly forgettable CCL League Cup tie against Raynes Park Vale. We won 5-0 and would meet Coney Hall FC in the semi-final. That was for another night – and what a horrendous night that would turn out to be. But right now most people's minds were elsewhere.

At the end of the game Kris went to the front of the press area and read the statement in a very clear and remarkably steady voice, given the heckling he was getting from some of the crowd. Kris detests any form of confrontation and he would normally go to great lengths to avoid it. I watched him knowing he was in his own personal Room 101. In my opinion it was, without doubt, his finest moment.

The discontent continued outside. Kris was confronted in front of the players' entrance by a small group of fans boiling over with anger about what we'd done. Gavin Fotheringham, another Eames family friend, his face bright red with anger, was up close to Kris and shouting 'what did he do?' repeatedly. And not waiting to hear the answer before starting again. Kris stood firm but it was obvious to me that we needed to get him out of there as soon as possible.

Only ten days had passed from realising there was a problem to concluding that there was only one course of action we could take. During that time enormous stresses were put upon members of the two boards and on Kris in particular. Our governance was tested and so was our resolve. And of course, this was a massively traumatic time for Terry. But it was done and we could start to think about moving on.

Through intermediaries I tried to engage Terry when I was writing this book, but he didn't respond. Despite the way it ended I hope that the club invites him to be there at the official formal opening of the new stadium. It is right that he should be there. He played a significant part in our story and his contribution should be acknowledged.

15

TUESDAY NIGHT'S ALL RIGHT FOR FIGHTING

LESS THAN a month after his appointment as caretaker manager, Nicky English was standing in the away dugout with warm piss running down the back of his neck. He could hear the sound of fighting behind him and, unknown to him, our commercial director Ivor Heller was lying semi-conscious on the terrace.

One of my roles was overall responsibility for matchday operations, specifically safety, at Kingsmeadow. This had opened my eyes to the many and varied risks we manage on a matchday to keep fans safe. It had also made me much more alert to how other clubs dealt with stewarding our games when the attendance could be over 20 times their usual gate. By now we'd been to quite a few games where we felt the stewarding was inadequate, but this one was to be the most extreme.

We had been drawn to play Coney Hall in the semi-final of the Combined Counties Premier Challenge Cup. This was their first season in the CCL in a newly formed division below us. Nonetheless, they had beaten three clubs from the CCL top division to get to the semi-final and needed to be taken seriously.

Coney Hall didn't have floodlights at their stadium so they couldn't host the tie. Instead they approached nearby Bromley FC, who had a ground and facilities that were more than capable of hosting the large crowd that was expected.

Bromley asked for help so our chief steward Luke Mackenzie arranged to provide five volunteers to act as marshals, taking on low-key roles such as telling fans which turnstiles to use, etc. They were led by Paul Fischer, universally known as 'Pooh Bear', who had substantial experience of working at Kingsmeadow.

By mid-afternoon rumours were circulating that there was likely to be trouble at the game and shortly after arriving, Pooh discovered that Bromley were allowing alcohol to be consumed pitchside. At senior grounds, known as 'designated stadiums', drinking alcohol within sight of the pitch is banned but at many non-league clubs it was allowed. We didn't allow it at Kingsmeadow.

When I arrived at about 6.30pm there were perhaps three Bromley stewards visible inside the stadium and one in the car park. From the numbers already inside the ground, the attendance was heading towards well over 2,000 (the final attendance was 2,700). Alcohol was being sold to youths who looked no more than 15 and they were standing on the terraces necking it down. My heart sank.

Before the match started a group of youths who were supporting Coney Hall positioned themselves behind the dugouts. There was no segregation or, if there was meant to be, there was no one to enforce it so some of our fans were right next to them. Ivor Heller was as troubled as I was by the atmosphere and the widespread under-age drinking, so he decided to stand with our fans to try to keep the temperature down.

Shortly after I got there, Luke arrived. After a brief conversation we agreed we were very worried that there would be violence, so I called our police contact to ask for help. However, his authority was restricted to Kingston and he had no remit. He knew us well enough to know we weren't over-reacting so he called his counterpart in Sutton. About an hour later a chief inspector from Bromley returned my call. I told him about the absence of stewards, no segregation, drink-fuelled youths, a very aggressive environment and that violence was pretty much certain. He promised to speak to his desk sergeant. That was the last I heard from them.

Meanwhile, the players had arrived and warmed up. Simon Bassey was in the squad that night, and recalls, 'You get a feel for stuff and when I turned up it felt edgy – the whole place. They were selling booze and there was a lot of people there who fancied it. I was playing left-back and I remember stuff being thrown on the pitch – it didn't bother me really – and I was thinking "this is lively!"'

My sense of foreboding was growing. The pity of it was that the game was fast and exciting and in any other circumstances I'd have loved it. Matt Everard had given us an early lead, only for Coney Hall to equalise. Just before half-time we scored again and led 2-1 at the break.

Almost immediately after our second goal the referee halted the match and made his way towards the players' tunnel. He was looking for some stewards to deal with missiles being thrown from behind the Wimbledon goal but, finding no one available to help, he turned round and re-started the game.

I've always loved fixtures played under floodlights where the lights intensify the focus on the pitch. Somehow they make the stadium feel smaller and the atmosphere more oppressive. But this night the shadows on the terraces simply added to the tension – by half-time it was palpable. The groups of fans were now standing only a couple of yards apart behind the dugouts and mouthing off at each other. Visibly drunk youths were clearly up for trouble and some of our fans had made their way over to the hotspot.

Luke and I were now so worried that we grabbed the referee as he left the pitch and asked permission to talk to him. At any other game we'd have been sent packing but he was genuinely relieved that someone was trying to do something about the obvious danger of violence breaking out. After we'd explained the situation he consulted privately with his linesmen and then summoned us back, along with the two managers. The referee demanded an announcement be made over the PA to warn spectators that the game would be abandoned if there were any more problems. Luke went to the PA box to pass on the message but it was deserted; it transpired that the PA had packed up and no announcements were possible.

Desperate to reduce the risk of violence, we cautioned the AFC Wimbledon bench not to do or say anything provocative and Kris and I went behind the goal to ask our fans to avoid any such behaviour, however minor. And not to react to any provocation.

The combination of events on the pitch and a looming sense of violence off it made for an electric atmosphere. Normally I'd sit in the stand with Eileen, but on this night I was too busy. She remembers, 'You could feel the intense hostility from their fans, even in the seats. I remember feeling quite frightened, sitting alone when you and Kris went off to talk to our fans.'

As the game drew towards its close we began to hope we were going to get away without any incidents. Then, from a safety point of view, came another blow – Coney Hall equalised again. This was making for a cracking game of football but it led to even more tension behind the dugouts. The full-time whistle blew with the teams still level and we moved into extra time, which was the last thing we wanted.

Nicky English takes up the story, 'They were from the league below. Their players were proper Addington [a suburb of Bromley] lads, much more spirited than we were. They played well and the pitch was awful, which didn't suit us. There was nothing between us in the game. As I remember it the bunch behind the dugouts called themselves "the naughty 40 from Palace".[20]

'I was standing there and I felt this liquid hitting my back and I thought they're flicking my coat with Coke. As I pulled up my hood I thought "it's warm" and I realised it was piss, so I turned round and called them sad bastards.'

Shortly after extra time began, with no obvious trigger, it started. Watching the video, later, I'm ashamed to say that the first punch seems to have been thrown by one of our fans. It wasn't a mass fight, with maybe 20 to 30 individuals directly involved one way or another, but a few people went down. And at that time there was no way of knowing whether it would spread more widely or how it would stop.

Not everybody got involved. Centre-back Matt Everard saw the fighting break out and the game came to a halt. He remembers, 'My old man used to come to nearly every game. It was all kicking off on the terrace, behind the dugout, a big fight and he's just standing there in the middle of it all, just watching. I shouted, "What are you doing up there?" and he shrugged his shoulders and slowly moseyed out of there while it was all going off in the crowd.

'If the game hadn't been abandoned I think we'd have lost that day. We were the better team throughout but we just couldn't score and the longer the game went on, the more they were getting into it.'

Nicky English had come to the same conclusion, 'In my mind we were going to lose that game – I could see it was rolling that way. We were tired, they were on us and we just wanted to be out of there. We'd given up the fight and there was nothing I could do, no one I could bring on to change

—

20 According to Wikipedia, 'the naughty 40' is a Stoke City firm, not Crystal Palace. So this seems like an early and unusual example of cultural appropriation.

the game. As soon as the fighting came on to the pitch and people came over the barrier I thought this is my opportunity. So I walked straight on to the pitch and said, "Ref, abandon this game. I can't stand here for another 20 minutes while this is going on, I want this game cancelled. They're fighting, they're on the pitch, there's no police and no stewards," and he went "all right" and off we came.'

Luke immediately strode on to the pitch to make sure our players didn't linger and to escort the referee back to the tunnel. His ankle-length coat was flapping like a cape as he marched the officials to safety and for a moment I thought, 'Jesus, he looks like Batman.' It was only years later when I watched it back on the security video that I realised how weird it was that someone with no obvious status, not even a hi-vis jacket, could just stride on to the pitch and march the referee to safety.

I was now able to call the police and demand a response. As soon as I'd done that I joined Luke, the match officials and both managers back in the referee's changing room where he formally abandoned the game on safety grounds.

Meanwhile, Ivor had been sent tumbling when the fighting broke out. He hit his head on the concrete terrace, knocking him unconscious. Around him the fighting died down and the crowd milled about for a while because there was no PA to tell them what was happening. Eventually the 'match abandoned' message sank in and they dispersed into the night. Ivor was carried back to the dressing rooms on a broken advertising hoarding and the club's physio tended to him. He was dazed but okay and was more concerned that he'd lost his phone in the melee.

As always happens after an incident like this, the blame game started immediately. We published a brief holding statement and then Bromley published a longer statement pointing fingers at us. We responded forcefully but eventually it all died down.

As a postscript, the abandoned game was replayed at Sutton United's ground. This time Coney Hall's problems were on the pitch. After nearly half an hour their left-back was sent off, harshly I thought, for a foul that gave us a penalty which we converted. Just before half-time their manager was sent off for 'his voluble protests to the referee' while our website reported, 'In the second half his deputy walked the same path for rugby-tackling the linesman.' In the last minute another Coney Hall player was dismissed for handling the ball on the goal line to prevent a goal. We were 5-0 up and so, not having scored for the club all season, or indeed ever, Simon Bassey was given the opportunity to take the resultant penalty.

The almost final word is from Nicky English, 'We played them off the park and should have won by more. After the game he [the Coney Hall manager] wouldn't shake my hand, saying, "You knew we'd beat you and you got it abandoned." I said, "Look, we beat you with a proper game of football on a proper pitch not a ploughed field," and turned away. Then someone went for me and Paul Braham [our fitness coach] grabbed them and there was a scuffle and he was on the floor in the tunnel and it was finished.'

So both games ended with violence, albeit the second time around it was on a different scale and there were people to quell it quickly.

After that night we decided that our stewards would never again work at away games and a small number of our fans were banned for violent conduct. Ivor Heller never found his phone and Simon Bassey's penalty went so far over the bar that, as footballers say, it is still in orbit. He never did score for AFC Wimbledon.

16

SIMPLY THE BEST

OUR SECOND season ended with Nicky English having presided over 21 league games, with 18 wins and three draws.

On the pitch the results helped to maintain the positive momentum; Nicky's first three games were won with 22 goals scored and none conceded. The league title and with it promotion were settled on Easter Monday at Walton Casuals where a 3-0 win killed off AFC Wallingford's challenge. Nicky was chaired off the pitch by ecstatic fans.

We seemed to play Walton more often than any other CCL club and their welcome was always warm and friendly. This particular visit is etched into many of our fans' memories, not just because it was when we sealed promotion, but also because a supplier failure meant that the usual portaloos weren't available. At the last minute a ditch had been dug and covered by a marquee. Many of our fans ended up wishing they'd not had quite so much beer in the preceding lunchtime. But at least no one fell in.

The season ended with us having played 46, won 42, drawn four and lost none. Our total of 130 points left Wallingford 23 points adrift in second place. We scored 180 league goals and conceded 30. By the end of the season we had gone 62 league games without defeat and were closing in on the English record.

Kevin Cooper had scored 53 of those goals. His figures for the club were astonishing. In 78 starts and eight appearances off the bench he scored 90 league goals in our first two seasons and a further 17 in cup competitions. He scored 11 league and two cup hat-tricks and beat WFC legend Eddie Reynolds's long-standing record for goals in a season.

Like all good strikers, he had a streak of arrogance and self-absorption that made him certain that he would score if he got the ball anywhere near the opponents' goal. But this same need to be the centre of attention led to the extraordinary sight of him leading his girlfriend on to the pitch and proposing marriage to her before the final game of the second season, while the crowd sang the anthem normally reserved for referees, 'You don't know what you're doing.'

The difference in quality between our squad and other clubs was illustrated at Chessington & Hook in late April. The game had featured a rare goal from the boot of centre-back Matt Everard, he of the salmon-like leaps and power headers. Unfortunately, his crisp drive into the bottom corner of the net was scored in our goal and left us two down within three minutes. By the time the second half started we'd also had a player, the manager and, bizarrely, our physio and club secretary sent off.

Midfielder Gareth Graham had given the referee some instant feedback as he left the pitch at half-time with, 'I'm having a mare ref but you're awful.' Cue a red card. By then Nicky had been sent off for expressing forthright views about the referee not seeing an 'obvious' penalty. As was the way in such games, being sent off merely meant Nicky had to stand behind the crush barrier adjacent to the dugout, about two yards further back than his pre-dismissal position.

Then John Harris, our physio, was dismissed for explaining the laws of the game to the referee while he treated Everard for a 'fist-to-head' injury. John said at the time, 'You can't send me off, I'm the physio. What happens if one of our players is injured?' Nonetheless, off he went. He joined Nicky to form the Chessington Two, standing behind the dugout but with his medicine bag at the ready.

As the officials stepped out for the second half, Trevor Williams was punished for arguing with the referee that he couldn't send our physio off. He recalls, 'He said, "Your physio can't come on the pitch," and I said, "If there is a nasty or dangerous injury I'm going to tell my physio to come on the pitch." He said, "No you're not," and I said, "I'm going to do it, I don't care, I'm not going to have their medical guy with a rusty bucket and a sponge coming on if we get a bad injury." And then he booked me. "Name?" "Ref, you know me, it's Trev."' And so Trevor became the first club secretary ever, so far as I'm aware, to be red-carded. It was now the Chessington Three behind the dugout. Meanwhile, Shane Small-King was booked for asking Simon Bassey if the referee was on drugs – not a good idea when he was within earshot.

With 15 minutes to go we were 3-1 down with only ten men. But even then I felt like I was watching one of those films where the hero is trapped in an impossible situation and you wonder how he will get out of it – then 'with one bound he was free'.

And so it was with us. Ryan Gray and Kevin Cooper scored to make it 3-3. Then Shane was sent off. Shane had been signed from AFC Wallingford by Nicky because, 'I thought if we signed their best player that would make it certain they couldn't catch us.' Alongside him went Chessington's Duffell who the referee said had been involved in a fracas with Shane as they made their way back to the halfway line following the equalising goal (the *South London Press* said Duffell appeared to be blameless). It was now ten men versus nine. Then Chessington suffered another red card for deliberate handball on the goal line. That gave us a penalty from which Cooper scored again. Now it was nine v nine and 4-3 to us. Our fifth goal was a formality.

We had two players sent off, two others yellow-carded, three of the management team dismissed and still won. In a masterpiece of understatement in his post-match press interview, Nicky observed, 'The referee had a poor game.' But what it really showed was that the players were much too good for the league. If we didn't win, or we got into trouble, it was because they'd taken their foot off the gas.

The aftermath of all these dismissals was that the players and staff were charged. As is the norm for such things, the players pleaded guilty by letter but the staff turned up for the hearing. Trevor takes up the tale, 'We were all sitting in the World Centre. I'd written extensive briefs for everyone and the referee walked in. "Hello, Trevor, how are you? Nice to see you," and he'd gone from being incredibly difficult and unmoving to being all friendly. He went in to the hearing for about 15 minutes but two of his linesmen didn't turn up. So basically he went in there and they went "well, yea, there's no evidence so all cases are dismissed". And nobody got banned for anything – which actually they should have done.'

The following week we played North Greenford United twice. The first time was during an almost biblical downpour when we eased to a 2-1 win on a Tuesday night in front of 492 fans. Three days later we met again in the final of the League Cup, at Woking's ground. The splendid

Leslie Gosden Stand behind the goal was awash with the yellow and blue flags, balloons and banners of the Dons fans. The attendance that night was 3,700 and I'd say 3,500 of them were ours.

North Greenford took the lead early on, which must have perturbed Hans-Petter Bakke, a Norwegian fan who'd travelled across especially for the game. In anticipation of success he'd already acquired a 'double winners' tattoo. Fortunately for him we went on to win by a rather flattering 4-1 margin. North Greenford, described on our website as 'possibly the nicest and friendliest team in the league', had made the game a genuine competition until very late in the day. Hans-Petter's tattoo didn't need to be surgically removed. We did, however, retain the sword he'd brought with him on the plane and put it in our trophy cabinet.

The league season ran out with two wins and a draw and then it was all over.

There was one other significant change in that campaign; at least it was significant for me. I had been spending more and more time on the club while nominally still full time at PwC. As a partner I could pretty much determine my own use of time, within quite wide limits, but it had got to the stage where it felt dishonest to continue sitting in Embankment Place while working on AFC Wimbledon matters. So at the end of 2003 I retired and made my wife Eileen two promises. The first was that I wouldn't spend all my time at the club – I comprehensively failed to live up to that one. The second was that I wouldn't spend my pension on the club – I did manage to keep to that.

It was time to turn our attention to appointing a permanent manager.

17

HELP! (4)

WE NEEDED to raise money.

In late 2003 four volunteers, Niall Couper, Bert Dale, Paul Jeater and Ian Pollock, championed by DT board member Brian Goodwin, put forward a proposal for a monthly lottery, the Dons Draw. They were inspired by Charlton Athletic's Valley Gold scheme, which had been set up to help end their club's exile from The Valley. The proposition was that tickets would be £2 each and could only be bought by committing to a monthly direct debit.

The first draw was made in September 2004. It made a slow start but by 2009 it was raising over £60,000 a year for the DT. Profits later rose to over £80,000 annually and now, 16 years after it was launched, the Dons Draw is still going strong having raised approaching £1m in total. For about the last ten years the profits have been used to contribute towards the cost of bringing young players through the club's academy.

Other initiatives quickly sprung up. Roger Dennis[21] and his wife Linda, stalwarts of the protest campaigns, volunteered to organise and sell Golden Goal tickets on matchdays. As Roger recalls, 'It arose from one of the Dons

---

21 Roger's remit didn't stop with the Golden Goals. Another Dons Trust working group 'volunteered him' to run the Junior Dons membership scheme. The most visible parts of this were stadium tours and birthday cards, signed by all the squad. The Junior Dons met the players after a home game and then went on a behind-the-scenes tour of the stadium. Roger recalls, 'There were always a few players who just wanted to get away. But when we did corral them they were very good, signing autographs and posing for photos.' The players might not have realised it, but Roger was very aware these experiences can bond a young person into their team for life.

Trust working groups. [We were] discussing what pre-match activities we could offer supporters and I came up with the idea of Golden Goals. I don't think I was alone with that idea but I was alone in actually taking it forward.' Linda designed the tickets and Roger drafted the wording. They printed them at home and then guillotined them into individual tickets.

In 2018 Roger and Linda retired from their oversight and organisational roles and Roger reverted to selling. In their time in charge they raised a total of just over £200,000 for the Dons Trust. Some of the first sellers are still volunteering in other capacities and, indeed, Roger and Linda have been succeeded by three volunteers from the early days, Jim and Maria Potter and Paddy Peel-Barnard.

Others were hard at work raising money. Mark Davis ran the fundraising group for some years. Among other things he organised the annual 'minithon' (a sponsored run, walk or crawl 5km event which, among other things, proved that I can no longer run much more than 200 metres) and highly successful dinners with guest speakers drawn from Wimbledon FC and, as we progressed, our own former players and managers. Ivor would preside over a post-dinner auction and some dedicated fans would buy yet another signed shirt. These events not only raised welcome funds for the DT, they were also a way of reinforcing our history and culture.

Volunteers ran silent auctions, a buy-a-brick scheme and invited season ticket holders to pay to have their name embossed on their seat. Making a positive out of our shortage of seats, my rather nerdy contribution to raising funds was to circulate an e-mail to fans before every game asking them to confirm that if they weren't attending they were willing to donate their seat back to us. We could then re-sell it or, as a minimum, reclaim the relevant VAT (yes, the scheme was signed off by HMRC). We never fully evaluated this but it was potentially worth up to £20,000 per year.

In later years, the Blue and Yellow Club started and was run by Martin Fielding. Following Martin's very sad early death the group continued and is now run by Iain McNay, one of its founders, and Alex Mitchell. In return for an annual subscription which is donated to the club, they meet three or four times a year for dinner with a representative from the club. In addition from time to time they've clubbed together to help pay a fee for signing a player.

Overall, our approach was that if there was even a hint of a possibility of raising money we had a go.

Looking back now the contribution from volunteers was, and still is, invaluable. A combination of the fact that it was their club – as Dons Trust members the volunteers own it – and a chance to be actively involved meant that in the early days we had almost 300 volunteers.

By my reckoning, in 2008/09 the savings from the work done by our matchday volunteers was worth about £70,000 a season for league games, for matchday hours alone, at a time when our wages budget was £372,000.

Each year we held an annual 'thank you' dinner, drawing once more on the volunteer catering team. In 2009 it was superseded by the volunteer away-day. This was generously sponsored by Iain McNay and we were able to invite all volunteers to a selected away game, with free travel and match entry, plus lunch, drinks and a programme. About 150 people took up the offer every year.

There are many, many other volunteers who have helped over the years, manning the stretcher team, assisting in pitch maintenance, cleaning the stadium, fundraising, hosting visiting officials and much, much more. And away from matchdays we had a host of professionals whose expertise we could call upon. Rachael Wellby was our volunteer in-house legal counsel for a year, while Mike Berry ran the share register for the PLC as well as becoming the club's data protection officer some years later. The club's auditor, Peter Proto, did a thorough, professional job and then donated his fee back to the club. Meanwhile, Dave McKnight, as assistant groundsman, and Paul Raymond, who took on a variety of roles in and around the club, seemed to be there whenever I turned round.

Add to them a range of lawyers, barristers, architects, designers, surveyors, building specialists, marketing specialists, IT consultants, HR consultants and many other people who had nothing to do with our club but liked what we were doing and helped pro bono.

Many of these skills have, of course, been available to the DT and the club through their work on the DT board, all of whom are volunteers and several of whom, such as Matt Breach, Roger Evans, Jane Lonsdale and Sean McLaughlin, served for many years. It is a largely thankless (and unthanked) task to turn up to three- or four-hour meetings and a mass of paperwork every month, plus many ad hoc meetings slipped into the intervening weeks.

There are also old and new fans who have gone beyond the call of duty to help when problems surface. In particular Neil Bolton has frequently been dragged from the terraces when a plumbing problem arose during a game. Similarly, in the early days Adam Hart was regularly fixing our electrical emergencies as we struggled to get the stadium fit for use on a matchday.

While there has naturally been some volunteer fatigue and resultant drop-out, many fans still volunteer on matchdays and many others work in other areas, examples of which pepper the pages of this book. Their commitment is extraordinary and we would be a much lesser club without them. It is very humbling.

18

IT SHOULD HAVE BEEN ME

IN JUST under three months as caretaker manager, Nicky English oversaw a promotion and cup double. Of the 21 league games played under his management we won 18 and drew three, scoring 82 goals and conceding 14. You'd think therefore that he was a shoo-in for a permanent appointment at the end of the season. However, we'd made it clear that his was a caretaker role. We wanted to make sure we got the best person possible. As it turned out, we learned a lot about fault lines in our communications and that trying to treat people well can backfire.

A few things immediately happen whenever a manager's job becomes available. First, the press wheels out the same old names, whether likely contenders or not. Second, would-be candidates who don't think they should have to undergo an interview put their names into focus by contacting the press and denying that they've been approached. And before all that, such is the dog-eat-dog world of football, from the day after Nicky was appointed as caretaker manager we had informal approaches and phone calls on behalf of candidates. ('They don't know I'm calling you.' Of course not.)

For sheer cheek it is hard to better one agent. He called me to say that the next day's papers would contain a denial that his client had been approached and that this story was not of their making. In his eyes he'd put his client's name forward while appearing as innocent parties, subjected to the vagaries of the press. In my eyes a candidate who knowingly employs a sleaze like that is diminished, and if he has an agent who does that without telling him, he's not the greatest judge of people.

It was now two years since we'd started, and Kris was trying to organise the club more professionally. Steve Brindley (who was working with the reserves) had benefitted from Terry Eames's departure and was now advising Kris on football matters. He had drafted a new football management structure which proposed the role of 'football advisors' to the board. Not surprisingly, Steve was one of the nominated advisors along with Lee Dobinson, another of Terry's recruits.

Three weeks after Nicky took up the reins, we advertised for a part-time football manager. For something as important as recruiting a new manager, the DT board was bound to take a close interest but we started recruiting without confirming a laid-down process with them. If we'd done that then, for reasons which will become obvious, I think we'd have started later and we probably wouldn't have ended up being over-ruled by them.

We reached the deadline date for first interviews and, at least as far as I was concerned, Steve's and Lee's roles were unclear. They were pushing for five interviewers at the second stage of the process, presumably so that they could both take part. I felt that this would take the decision away from the FCB and said it wasn't acceptable. Meanwhile, however, they had carried out a first sift of CVs and presented their findings to Kris.

Quite reasonably they divided candidates into three categories, 'must see'; 'maybe see'; and 'no'. Ivor likes to see the detail so he sent a frustrated e-mail to the FCB stating, 'I would like to know who we are not considering and a reason, even if only a one liner like, "no football experience", "He is only ten years old" etc.' I was content to accept the 'must see' recommendations but I wanted to review the marginal candidates. However, without access to the 'must see' CVs I couldn't come to a considered opinion on anyone's pros and cons. In the end, to keep things moving we settled on the recommended eight first interviews and agreed that they should be carried out by Kris and Steve.

But first there was a much thornier issue to deal with. Steve and Lee urged us to consider Nicky English first, separately from the others. Ivor reacted strongly, 'Why would we consider Nick's application separately? How can we consider it first when we don't know what else is on offer? This sounds like a "we don't want Nick so let's rule him out, then choose who suits us best from the rest".' I agreed. It seemed to me that they simply didn't rate Nicky and this was a way of clearing him out of the way.

Steve and Lee argued that if we thought Nicky had done a good job and he could convince us that he would continue to do so, we should give him the job and not continue with the interviews.

For me, that proposal was far too late. If we'd seen this as a possible approach we should have built it in to an agreed process and considered Nicky before we advertised the role. We'd agreed to see who else was out there and had advertised the job. Furthermore, telling the caretaker manager that he wasn't getting the job five weeks before the end of the season struck me as an appalling way to treat him, and we might well end up with him walking away and us having to appoint a second caretaker manager. After due reflection, Kris over-ruled Steve and Lee, added Nicky to the list and started the first interview process.

Clair Richardson, our office administrator, was the note-taker at all the interviews. She recalls, 'Most candidates were interviewed at the Wimbledon Antoinette Hotel in a formal business environment. Kris had a list of set questions, while Steve just sat there silent, eyeing them up. Every now and then Kris would bring him in, but Kris did almost all the talking.'

Two candidates stood out from the first batch. One was Stuart Cash, then the assistant manager to Terry Brown at Aldershot Town, three leagues above us. The other was John Rains, the manager of Sutton United who had just been promoted into the newly formed Conference South, two divisions above us. It augured well that such experienced people were willing to step down two or three levels.

The setting for Dave Anderson's interview was rather less professional. He'd been unable to get away from his job as a delivery driver on the scheduled date so it was agreed that he'd be interviewed just off the M25 at the Hooley Little Chef. Dave arrived early, parked and changed into a suit in the back of his van. He said later, 'I remember thinking, "I'm in a suit in a Little Chef and I'm not comfortable."'

Clair picks up the story as it degenerated into farce, 'We wanted to make sure we got a table so we also arrived very early, just in time to see the waiter delivering a belly-buster breakfast to Dave. So the first part of the interview was conducted while he tucked in to an enormous breakfast! We just had a pot of tea.' Nonetheless, it went well and Dave impressed.

After one more interview, the football club board of Kris, Ivor and I met, along with Trevor Williams and Steve Brindley. We'd been sent

Clair's interview notes in advance, plus a scoring system evaluating the candidates in three areas: managerial and coaching experience, attitude and personality, and overall impression from the interview.

After a long discussion, much of which was around what to do about Nicky, we settled, rather uneasily, on second interviews for Rains, Cash and Anderson. Nicky wasn't included.

Kris wrote to the DTB on the Friday morning, 'informing them' (i.e. trying to avoid a debate) of the second interview candidates and our decision to exclude Nicky. He attempted to head off any resistance by setting out the board's reasons, namely that Nicky's experience and qualifications didn't come close to matching any of the preferred three. Furthermore, we were looking for a long-term manager to take us straight through the league in the next season, be successful in the Ryman Premier and be well placed to take us to the new Conference South within two to three years. Put simply, Nicky wasn't seen as that man.

Kris's attempt to forestall a challenge from the DTB failed. Within a couple of hours the objections started to surface, first that the approach wasn't consistent with our ethos and second wondering if the FCB had sufficient expertise to make such a key decision. Not having agreed a process with the DT board had come back to bite us.

The scheduled DT board meeting the following Monday night was polite but bruising. It was notable because it was the first time (and the last for several years) where the football club board was overruled. After detailed discussions, club board members were asked to leave the room to allow the DTB to conclude privately. On our return we were presented with an instruction, which said, 'There should be an independent football expert involved in the rest of the process in appointing the manager and this person should be approved by the Dons Trust board before the process continues. The football expert will review the interview notes of the eight candidates and consult with the football club board about the suitability or otherwise of the candidates for second interviews.'

A problem for the Dons Trust board was that its elected membership comprised volunteers and it was only scheduled to meet once a month. As a result, there was insufficient time to discuss the consequences of the DTB's decision before moving on to the next topic on a crowded agenda. So what happened next was dysfunctional but, sadly, quite typical of the way we operated then.

It was now nearly two weeks since the first interviews and none of the candidates had been given any feedback. This disturbed Kris and overnight, having had time to think, he concluded that the most pragmatic approach would be to invite Nicky to a second interview and get started on them. This caused an exchange of e-mails where only half the DTB participated. Not everyone on the DTB had the time to respond and one or two members regularly dominated the airwaves through the number and length of their e-mails – another problem with a volunteer-based board.

Meanwhile, someone had suggested that the football insight could be provided by Ian Cooke. Ian had been the captain of WFC's great non-league team in the 1970s. He is strong on his football knowledge but what we really needed was someone to give us insights, for example, about the candidate's reputation within the game. Ian had been retired too long to be able to do that.

The e-mails bounced back and forth for 48 hours and then an exhausted acceptance broke out where members, usually with one reservation or another, agreed that Ian should act as the football expert. He would re-review the notes from the eight interviews but in the meantime the nominated three shortlist candidates, plus Nicky, would be invited to a second interview.

We were on the home straight now but by the time we could meet the candidates we'd lost another week. So all the candidates were interviewed in the first week of May. This time it was Ivor, Kris, Ian and me asking the questions.

We all (including Clair who was asked for a fan's-eye opinion) agreed that Dave Anderson was comfortably the best candidate. John Rains, for all his success at Sutton, was seen as unlikely to sit comfortably in our culture while Stuart Cash was identified as a possible future manager once we got to a higher league. We made a note to keep an eye on his career.

Nicky's interview confirmed the original conclusion. However, we felt that we'd not treated him very well given his willingness to step in and take over at a very difficult time. Ivor has a strong sense of fair play and he was particularly keen to recognise what Nicky had done for us during a crisis. He suggested that we offer Nicky the role of under-18s manager. By then we just wanted to get on and announce Dave's appointment so without a lot of discussion we agreed and thereby created a new problem.

With the decision made, the final game of the season was only three days away. We wanted Nicky to enjoy the acclaim of the fans after our last game of the season, so we agreed to leave an announcement until the following Monday.

Not surprisingly, Nicky reacted strongly to the news. Years later this is how he described what happened, 'I was working in an MP's house [he is a heating engineer by trade] somewhere in the City and Kris phoned me up to tell me what had happened. I said, "That is disgraceful what you've done there, just to phone me up. Why didn't you call me in to the office and explain it to me?" So I said I need a meeting to understand why. I was upset and looking for any reason to be angry.

'When I went into the office Kris said, "We want you to look after the under-18s." I should have said "no". That decision caused a bigger problem and I went on to make a bigger mistake. I should have gone to Dave and said, "What has happened has happened and I will help you any way I can." If it was now I'd have done that.'

Looking back, nearly 17 years later, Nicky is philosophical: 'I wish I'd had the same sort of mind state then as I've got now. I couldn't accept what had happened. Worse than that, with the way I behaved with the under-18s and around the club I made an enemy of Dave and he'd done nothing wrong. I'd done what I thought entitled me to another year, or year and a half. Along with that I was expecting "my" players to be given a chance. It had become my life now, not a part-time job at a football club, but my whole life. My state of mind wasn't adult enough to be involved at that level – I was like a spoilt kid really – and looking back I was so stupid. People said to me "shut your mouth, do what you're told and you've got a job here for life, whether it might be a kit man" but I wouldn't have it.'

The public announcement was made the next day. We had a flurry of protesting e-mails, as is always the case after a potentially controversial decision. But appointing Nicky as the under-18s manager was a good move from a PR point of view because everyone could see that we'd tried to treat him considerately.

19

COME TOGETHER

THE INTERVIEW process looks very different through the eyes of the successful candidate.

Years later, Dave Anderson regaled me with his view of the appointment process. But even before he'd applied he thought he had blown his chances, or possibly lost his job at Hendon.

'John Morris, my reserve team manager at Hendon, had said to me, "You've really got to go and see a game to believe it." Terry Eames had left. It was a Wednesday night game against AFC Wallingford who were second in the league at the time. John and I went in the Tempest End in the back right-hand corner, behind the goal. I had my collar up because I didn't want anyone recognising me. It worked. Nobody noticed me – but about 25 people said "hello" to John!

'We left about 20 minutes before the end.[22] I remember the game was shit and I said to John, "is this real? There's 3,000 people here on a Wednesday night". As soon as we got in the car I said "I've got to apply" and John, who during our long association never asked me for anything, money, nothing, said "would you take me with you?" That's how he became the reserve team manager.

'After that I couldn't think of anything else. I was obsessed by it. If there is anything about you, you want to be in that environment.'

---

22 Anyone who stays until the end is not a 'football person' – they all leave quite ostentatiously at least ten minutes before the end. I think it is partly to avoid the car park crush and partly to show that they have understood the ebbs and flows of the game and don't need to see any more, unlike the crowd they've left behind.

But then he nearly blew it. Shortly after attending the Wallingford game, Dave went for a drink in a mate's pub near Staines. 'He introduced me to a man called Sam, who he said writes some programme or something, and we started chatting. Sam asked me what I thought of a million things but I talked about nothing else but AFC Wimbledon. I was obsessed by them. Then I asked him what he did and he said he worked for the *Non-League Paper*. My heart sank because if this got out it might spoil my chances at Wimbledon for looking too cocky and maybe cost me my job at Hendon. I couldn't let it get into the press so I said, "You can't say anything about this but I'll tell you what I'll do; if I get the job you'll get the first interview."'

The following Sunday, the *NLP* published a short piece under Sam Elliott's byline with the headline 'Hendon Boss in Frame at AFC Dons'. The article quoted Dave as being 'flattered to be talked about in connection with the job' – even though it was Dave who was doing 'the talking about'. Sam had kept his word and he got his exclusive interview eventually.

'My first interview was with Kris and Houllier [the management team's nickname for Steve Brindley] in a Little Chef. They asked me what I knew about the team, who I wanted as a coach, budgets, how many players I wanted to bring in. It was all the usual stuff and I came out thinking "that was all right". Obviously it was only a first meeting.

'The second interview was at the Cobham Hilton [with Kris, Ivor, Ian Cooke and me, and Clair Richardson once more taking notes]. It was the same sort of stuff but with more people and more detail. I was there for two hours and came out with a sore head. I always remember coming out and going through each interviewer thinking, "I've got him," "I've got him," "He's fine, everything's good. I've got them all in my pocket except Erik – I can't read him."'

In the interview I asked Dave how many players he thought we should get from our youth team. I knew he didn't have a reputation for bringing young players through and I wanted to challenge him about it. Dave replied, 'Dale Binns had come through our youth team and if you get one a year you're a genius.' I thought he was flannelling and I was right. I discovered later that Dale Binns did come through from the Hendon youth team, but under Dave's predecessor!

Dave, like most people after an interview, reviewed how he thought he'd done. 'I spoke to my friend, a youth worker who'd done a million interviews. He'd briefed me before I went in. I rang him after I came out and he made me tell him everything I'd been asked, how I'd answered and he said, "I shouldn't say this, but I think you've got it." I felt that if I hadn't got it I could sleep well because I'd given it my best.

'The next thing was Kris phoned me to say that we were going to tell candidates on the Monday. I said, "I'm about to go and play golf in Portugal and I'll be out all day. Can you call me early, please?" The day before the result was to be announced, Peter Rogers, chairman of a previous club of mine, told Martin Murphy, one of my golf colleagues in Portugal, that I'd not got the job. Martin told the others that I'd missed out but he didn't tell me. So when the call was due on the Monday morning, Martin made an excuse to go to the shops and the others went with him – anything to avoid being there to witness my disappointment.

'So I had the house to myself and they all cleared off. Then Kris rang to say I'd got the job but he wanted to speak to the other candidates before making it public, so not to say anything until the evening. I was just thinking "wow", but I couldn't tell anyone. They got back soon afterwards and I was shaking so they thought I'd taken it really badly. It was [Dave's friend] Orchie's birthday so I made sure I was the last one to sign his birthday card, and then put it in the envelope. I signed it "Dave Anderson, AFC Wimbledon manager".

'When we got back from the round Orchie opened the card and said, "Why did you write that?" and that is when they all found out. They'd been treating me with kid gloves all day and I had made the most of it – it was the best three hours of my life! And then we all got very, very drunk. It was the perfect place to be because I had two or three days to let everything sink in.'

And so began the reign of Dave Anderson.

20

MOVIN' ON UP

WE HAD been promoted into the Ryman League Division One. A shorthand way of describing the divisions below the Football League is to count down. So the Conference (since rebranded as the National League) is one promotion away from the Football League and is designated as Step 1. When we started in the Combined Counties League we were at Step 4 so our promotion should have taken us to Step 3. However, at the end of our 2004 promotion season a reorganisation of the football pyramid inserted two new Step 2 divisions, Conference North and Conference South. Below them were the Ryman Premier League (Step 3) and Ryman Division One (Step 4). Although we'd been promoted we were no closer to the Football League than when we started.

Hendon were one of the clubs to decline the opportunity to join the new Step 2 because they didn't want the extra travel costs and the higher wages. As a result, they were now a step lower than before; that demotion in status was a factor in Dave Anderson looking elsewhere for his next challenge.

That challenge turned out to be us and he quickly set about understanding what he'd taken over. His first exposure to our fans was at the family fun day at Kingsmeadow, less than a week after he'd been appointed. It was there that he met Simon Bassey. Dave says, 'I knew him from playing for Aldershot. I knew he'd played at a good level and I just said "talk to me".

'And it was along the lines of "you're going to have to rip it to pieces, all of it". And he was spot on.'

Then Dave also spoke to Joe Sheerin and told him 'you're the captain, you're going to have to trust me and me trust you. Talk to me.' And Joe said 'it's a shambles'.

As Trevor Williams put it, 'Our second season was a party.' Things needed to change and Dave was determined to bring in a much different culture.

My first conversation with Dave convinced me that he was the man to do this. It started with me saying that I knew he was a goalkeeper. He immediately replied, 'No I wasn't.' He let that hang in the air for a moment while I looked puzzled and then he continued, 'I was an *international* goalkeeper.' And we both burst out laughing. He had kept goal for the Northern Ireland schools, youth and B teams. 'Well,' I thought, 'this is going to be different.'

Recently I looked Dave up on Wikipedia and was amused to see him described first as a Northern Irish media personality and second as a former football player and manager. 'Personality' is a very good word for him. He was born and brought up on the Rathcoole Estate in Belfast and this shows both in his accent, which is still strong after nearly 40 years in England, and his down-to-earth manner and language. He's a big man, both in his presence and his physique (he claims to be six feet tall, but isn't, so I started a habit of standing next to every new player to assess their real height, not their 'Dave Anderson height').

Dave fills the room, noisy, talkative and always laughing. And he swears a lot – when I appeared with him on *The Non League Football Show* I was amused to see that he had a big sign saying 'don't swear' propped up in front of him.

What Joe and Simon had told him confirmed what he'd heard on the football grapevine but he wanted to see for himself, so he called the players to a post-season training session at Kingsmeadow. It was held a few days after the family fun day, just before the summer pitch renovations were due to start. And then he started making changes.

First, he brought in Jon Turner, his assistant manager at Hendon. Few clubs at non-league level have a formal recruiting system but they all have someone like Jon who knows all the players at that level and the level above, who's good, who's not, and more important, what their weaknesses are. You need to know more about a player than if he has a cultured left foot. Does he have off-field issues that will affect his game and the dressing room? Dave needed to know the answer to what Brian Clough reportedly said to all his new players on arrival, namely, 'What's your problem; drink, gambling or women?'

The question that was impossible to answer was whether they could play in front of 3,000-plus crowds and not feel intimidated by the occasion. This was no trivial concern. Even experienced players like Steve Butler ('Big Buts' to distinguish him from 'Little Buts', striker Richard Butler), brought in from Hendon to be centre-half and captain, found it daunting. He recalls, 'I'd been at an old-school non-league club like Hendon who get 250–300 spectators and then you come and play your first home game with 3,000. It's something totally different from what you've experienced anywhere else, with people wanting your autograph and things like that which is something I'd never known before – or after – and I personally struggled with that side of it as in, "Why would they want *my* autograph?"'

If, like Steve, you're able to put it out of your mind as soon as the game kicks off, that's fine. But over the early years, quite a few couldn't deal with it.

Dave also brought in Warren Kelly as first team coach and fulfilled his promise to John Morris by appointing him as reserve team manager. A few weeks later, Dave completed his changes when he recruited his physio from Hendon, Mike Rayner, succeeding John Harris. It was a clean sweep of the backroom staff.

He made one other change that would have an effect long after he had moved on. Simon Bassey had suffered several knee injuries but he lived for football. He'd trained hard and wanted to give it one more go. However, as he recalls, 'Training was okay but after every game my knee ballooned up. On a coach to an away game Dave said, "The best thing you can do is retire." I loved Wimbledon and I didn't want to retire – I wanted it to go on forever. But Dave said "no". He told me he liked my opinions on football so he wanted me to help Johnny Morris with the reserves. That was it – I either left Wimbledon then, or retired from playing and stayed as a coach. So I decided to retire.'

Simon went on to become our first team coach for many years. When he eventually left the club he had been with us for 17 years.

While Dave was implementing his changes there were ceremonies to attend. Andrew Judge, then the leader of Merton Council, had announced a civic reception for the team the Sunday after the family fun day. At first I thought it was a bizarre idea to hold a civic reception to celebrate a Step 4 club winning promotion and wondered if it was an indication of a wider agenda from the council.

The club's website duly promoted the event and promised 'that the team … will be processing from the top of Wimbledon Hill to Wimbledon Theatre between 12 noon and 12.30pm' in an open-top bus. Delayed by the usual stragglers, the bus duly set off slightly late with the players, Nicky English and his support staff waving to an estimated crowd of 3,000. Ivor, who is attracted to such events like a wasp to jam, and Kris joined them on the upper deck. I always saw events like this as a duty not a pleasure. So, quoting my insignificance as being merely the finance director (and if I'm honest, anxious to avoid the 'who the hell is he?' question as the bus went by), I declined the offer to ride with them.

The bus made its way down Wimbledon Hill after which it was meant to circle round the town centre's one-way system before spilling the players and management into the New Wimbledon Theatre. However, an over-zealous police officer decided the leisurely pace would cause too many traffic problems so he instructed the bus driver to proceed at full speed. As a result the 30-minute drive took about ten minutes. For many of the fans lined up on the pavement it was like watching a film on fast forward. Whooosh. Blink and you'd missed them.

Back at the club, Dave was getting to grips with the squad. He recalls, 'As stunned as I was outside the dressing room by the size of the club, movie star stuff, I was stunned on the inside, how it was. I looked at players who thought they could hold a gun to my head. They weren't up to the fitness levels we had to perform to. Every time I walked in they were in the treatment room.'

Kevin Cooper had been active in the local press promoting the idea of a new contract, both before the end of the season and, rather unwisely, in a story with the headline 'Talk or I'm off Cooper warns Dons'. He was quoted as saying, 'Without blowing my own trumpet, my phone hasn't stopped ringing with offers… I will be left with little option [other than to leave] if things stay silent.'

Dave was still finding his feet with the board. While he was adamant that there could be no egos in the dressing room he was unsure how the fans, and we the board, would react if he chose to let Wimbledon's all-time record goalscorer leave. So despite his misgivings he opened discussions about the forthcoming season, but not about a contract.

While everyone respected Kevin for the goals he'd scored, they were far from convinced that he would do so at a higher level. Paul Scott says, 'In that league [the CCL] he was perfect. He would never move out of the area. When you've got 60 per cent or 70 per cent of the ball it was fine but my mum would have scored in that Wimbledon team.' Simon Bassey was similarly sceptical.

Dave was very concerned that Kevin's need to be 'the man' would disrupt the team spirit he wanted to engender. Some, like Joe Sheerin, just found his self-focus very amusing, as he recalls, 'The first time I spoke to him he came over to introduce himself when he'd just signed. And then the phone rang and he stopped me, answered the call, went "hello mate" and then covered the phone, said "Lee from Steps" and carried on the conversation – it was a real David Brent sort of moment. I just found him funny because he was so full of himself.' Dave saw this as a problem in terms of team spirit.

The whole saga became an unnecessary diversion, some of it played out in the press. Eventually, Dave brought it to the board and wanted to know our view. We made it very clear that we were willing to take tough decisions and that if he didn't want to offer Kevin a contract then he shouldn't. And so Kevin, scorer of a phenomenal 107 goals and a major part in our promotion the previous season, left amid much acrimony. The press coverage included accusations of reneging on a deal and Dave felt the need to put his side of the story on our website. The relationship was soured for years to come.[23]

New players started to arrive. First was Richard Butler from Ashford Town (Middlesex). Richard was the first player to cost us a fee. The records seem to have been lost but I think we paid £5,000 for the transfer of his registration plus a promise of two pre-season friendly games. Because we'd paid a fee we wanted to make sure we had his services secure so Richard was also the first player with a contract for more than one year. He certainly paid us back spectacularly in that first season. Stocky, with a

—

23 Kevin himself regretted the way it ended. Years later he kindly spoke at a fundraising dinner for our benefit and he said he'd behaved badly and apologised. From my point of view, it was a massive shame that it ended that way because he could have gone on to achieve a never-to-be-beaten goalscoring record for the club.

low centre of gravity, strong and quick he was too much for many defences and scored 30 goals. He also won a lot of penalties, bringing to mind boxer John Conteh's quote after a heavy defeat that he 'went down so easily you'd think he was making a blue movie'.

At the end of July, Dave announced that seven players had agreed terms and many of the players who had feared change when Terry Eames left were released. There is a ritual to be gone through when a player leaves in this way. He says that he accepts the manager's decision and there are no hard feelings but he wants to play first team football elsewhere; the manager thanks him for his contribution and wishes him well. When the statement says anything other than that it's a sign that there were problems between the two and, as always, the manager prevailed and the player moved on.

One arrival who immediately won over the fans was Robert Ursell. He had played as a trialist in a pre-season game and the fans loved him for his outrageous tricks, drag-backs and dribbling, quickly naming him 'The Wizard'. Unlike some players who have a bag of tricks but lack what managers like to call 'an end product', Rob was highly effective. He scored an extraordinary 21 goals from midfield in his first season. With his slight frame he didn't look like a footballer but his skills were such that he was called up for the England Futsal team.

Rob had been offered a trial with Milton Keynes but Dave made it clear to him that if he went there on trial he could never sign for us. The website announcement of him joining said he 'turned down offers from other clubs to sign for Wimbledon, including rejecting the offer of a trial at a League One outfit currently plying its trade in Milton Keynes'. The fans loved this and his instant hero status was enhanced when he scored a brilliant hat-trick in a pre-season friendly against Barnet, three levels higher, including what our website described as 'possibly the finest solo goal scored by a Don in pre-season ever'.

Everyone says you had to see it to believe it. Sadly, I didn't. I was in the bar getting some soft drinks for my family on that scorching-hot day.

Having 'kept all the ones that should have been kept and released the others', Dave set about developing the dressing room culture he wanted. Bringing in Hendon players was a key part of this as he sought, 'To make the dressing room like the Hendon dressing room and ignore the scale of what was going on outside – crowd sizes and all that. And anybody who starts to get carried away with what's out there, they can sod off. They have to buy in to this being a football dressing room. Part of the problem before I came in was people started to believe that they were movie stars or rock and roll stars. But they weren't – they were still Combined Counties players. Things were happening in the dressing room that I wasn't happy with. It was all part of this rock and roll mentality.'

One of the reasons that he let players go was a lesson he learned at Hendon, 'I used to think I could change players – but I learned with experience [that you probably can't]. As Alex Ferguson said, "Don't think you're the guy who can change them." It was the Hendon dressing room that got me the Wimbledon job. If you get it right then they care massively about each other. So when we added to the group we rarely got it wrong. A lot of that came from the players – you'd want a centre-forward and they'd say "go and get him", so the group became stronger.

'I'd heard about the Wimbledon dressing room and I thought it was a disgrace, not just the drinking but it was a behavioural problem.'

Dave wasn't against a few drinks when he was at Hendon, 'You could see the Hendon floodlights from Rob Haworth's house. His wife asked, "How come when you trained at Sutton [over an hour's drive away] you were home at 10.30pm while at Hendon where I can see the floodlights you don't get home until midnight?" He told her we did lots of tactics and video analysis. But we were in the bar and we had that strong social atmosphere. The fine line is managing that.

'The Wimbledon players soon knew where the line was. That's where I thought I was good – no one ever took me on but they knew I was fair.'

The players quickly noticed the difference. Joe Sheerin says, 'You quickly went, "Oh, we can't mess about now." But that change was absolutely necessary.' Simon Bassey adds, 'Dave was more disciplined. Great company, but he had a switch. He was brilliant to have a laugh with but then it was "we're working now".

'He replaced a lot of the players. The ones he brought in were just as crazy as the ones he binned but they knew the rules. Fun and work didn't mix with Dave. He'd have a laugh with the players and some banter but once the dressing room door shut he was the boss and they knew it and they had to do what they were told.'

Kris was responsible for football matters and he'd made it clear to Dave that his brief was to win two promotions in three years. One night, just before the season started, Kris, Dave and I sat in the main stand basking in the evening sun, drinks in hand, just watching the grass grow. Pre-season is one of my favourite times. The pitch looked perfect, the goalposts had just been put back up, the summer clean-up had added a lick of paint everywhere. We were ready. Dave was in a reflective mood so I asked him how he thought the season would pan out. To my surprise, he answered, 'I shouldn't really say this but with this squad we will piss this league.' And we did.

The season started at home to Ashford Town (Kent). The scale of the changes wrought by the new management team meant that only two players from the previous campaign started the game, and it began with a shock as Dave recounts, 'One of the defining moments in my life was when we went 1-0 down in our first home game and Jon Turner said, "Quiet in here all of a sudden, isn't it?" I nearly burst out laughing because while I wouldn't say it was the first time it all hits you, it was funny because you normally think of the crowd and the noise, but we noticed our crowd the other way round. I looked round and the place was packed, over 3,000 people, and you could hear a pin drop. We won comfortably in the end but the thing I always remember is the silence.'

The unbeaten run continued with seven straight wins before carelessly conceding two late goals in a home draw against Leatherhead. Three more victories and two draws meant that we were top of the league when we went to Bromley, only needing a draw to set a new English record of 76 successive league games without defeat. Bromley hasn't been the happiest of grounds for us and our most recent visit had been for the Coney Hall debacle. Bromley took an early lead and for a while it looked as if we were about to see the end of our run until, to quote the report on our website, 'Ursell shrugged off an attempted lunge from Drewett and curled the ball into the top right corner with a quite sublime strike.' The game ran out 1-1 and the record was ours.

Three matches later the run was over. Visiting Bromley's ground once more to play their tenants, Cray Wanderers, we lost 2-0. We had gone 78 league fixtures without defeat, which was just short of a European record. But in some ways getting the 'we mustn't lose' monkey off our backs was a blessing. We lost only twice more in the league that season. One was on New Year's Day and it was our first home league defeat for nearly two years. Steve Butler says, 'Dave brought in breathalysers he'd got from a mate in Northern Ireland before the game and laid them on the table. "If you boys lose today I've going to pick five players at random and test you." We thought he was joking. We lost and I was drawn first out of the hat. I don't know if anyone failed the test.' We also don't even know if the breathalysers worked!

The other defeat was when we went to Walton & Hersham in early April needing only one point to win the league. We were thumped 4-0, and once again Dave wasn't impressed, 'Sky Sports were there to interview us and I went home and saw them interviewing the Walton striker who scored two goals. That was the day I kicked the tray of sandwiches and they landed on [goalkeeper] Paul Smith's head. That was the only time I proper lost the plot.'

Club secretary Trevor Williams was in the room too. He recalls, 'Most of the time with Dave when he was shouty I thought it was an act but he really lost it that day. He decided that they had taken their foot off the gas and he went nuts. I was sitting by the door when Dave threw all the sandwiches up in the air and one with grated cheese landed on Paul Smith's head. He was obviously too scared to remove it. What you don't want to do at a time like that is catch Martin Randall's eye. He said, "Trev, Trev, look at Smudge, he's got a cheese sandwich on his head." I was losing it and when it slowly slid on to the side of his head I had to have one of my coughing fits to cover up my laughing and left the room. I was still laughing five minutes later.'

The title was secured a week later with an otherwise forgettable 1-0 win against Metropolitan Police. In between the battering at Walton & Hersham and sealing the league title, the team had gone to Sutton United for the Surrey Senior Cup semi-final. Missing seven squad members for a game against a team two divisions higher, the odds looked against us, but it was memorable for three reasons. One was Antony 'Frankie' Howard scoring a fine header early in the second half. The second was Dave Anderson being sent to the stand by referee Simon Cook. Dave was dismissed for kicking a water bottle away after first-team coach Warren Kelly had been sent off for abusing the referee. This meant Dave lost a £50 bet with club founder Marc Jones that he'd be sent off at some point in the season.

The third memorable event was Frankie Howard going in goal when Paul Smith dislocated his shoulder in the 90th minute; we didn't have a substitute keeper on the bench. Frankie saw plenty of action in the 11 minutes of injury time during which Sutton bombarded our goal. It quickly became apparent that he wasn't a natural custodian – they usually manage to catch the ball – and after he'd dropped a straightforward catch for the second time the management team were screaming at him, 'Just head it, just head it will you.'

The league season ran out with a draw and two wins, leaving us champions by a clear nine points. That left the final of the Surrey Senior Cup, to be played once more at Woking. To my knowledge, Hans-Petter Bakke wasn't there this time and there was no pre-emptive tattooing being done.

The game was memorable for Steve Butler spending four and a half hours getting from his workplace to Woking, a 50-minute journey normally. He recalls, 'I was stuck on the M25, Dave was ringing me, "Where are you?" and I said, "I'm stuck on the M25 but I left early, no problem." About an hour later "where are you" and I said, "Same place as when you last rang," and he was shouting and swearing down the phone. But the motorway was closed. Dave wasn't happy.'

After getting to Woking and dumping his car on a steward ('mate, I'm supposed to be playing so I'm leaving my car here') Steve arrived at half-time and was immediately brought on as a substitute. He adds, 'Jon Turner took me out on to the pitch. When I saw how many people were there I felt a complete idiot.'

He replaced Steve Gibson, who was unlucky to be substituted after a very good first half. The game was tight and was eventually won in extra time after Rob Ursell's astonishing skill created two chances for Richard Butler within a few seconds of each other. 'Little Buts' scored from the second one. The crowd of nearly 4,000 mainly comprised Dons fans. Of them about 2,000 were once again in the Leslie Gosden Stand, which was a riot of blue and yellow. It was such an impressive sight that when Dave was recruiting players he just showed them the footage of our fans in that stand and said, 'If you want a piece of this, you need to sign here.' It worked.

It was also the first season we were allowed to enter the FA Cup, where the highlight was an Ursell hat-trick at Dunstable, which saw him voted player of the round. During that game, *South London Press* journalist Gordon Law's plea of the previous year was finally satisfied when a male streaker took to the pitch, jumped into the arms of the home keeper and then followed a lap around the centre circle with a ten-yard sliding tackle that comprehensively took out the linesman, much to the delight of the fans.

And so the football cycle started again, with players released, new ones sought, pitch renovations and stadium maintenance, season ticket renewal and an occasional holiday when time permitted.

The season saw the departure of two significant players in our history. Joe Sheerin, our first captain, had injured himself late in the previous campaign. By his own admission he 'came back unfit and a bit overweight and Dave told me I wasn't going to play for him until I got fit. I was taking up a large part of his budget. He said, "I want you to stay but I can't give you what I'm currently paying," and offered me a pay-as-you-play deal, but I told him I couldn't do it.' And then Croydon Athletic offered to match his previous season's wages so he took it but admits, 'I wish I'd stayed and worked to get fit. I could easily have played maybe two levels above where we were at the time and I regret leaving and not trying to make it.'

At the time, and arguably even now, Joe was the most talented player we'd ever had. He says, 'I used to infuriate Dave because he'd say "you're too flicky flicky, full of back-heels and flicks round the corner". One game, just before I came on, he said to me "no flicky flicky, no back-heels" then the ball came to me, first touch, I back-heeled it to Jamie Taylor, he smashed it in the net and Dave looked at me and just laughed.' Joe still comes to the club regularly and says, 'The best time of my career was the time I spent with Wimbledon. People, Ivor, Trev, Kris and Erik, the volunteers, everyone. I miss it, the atmosphere, the matchday. I was really lucky to have those years.' It's a widely held view among players from those times.

Matt Everard, 'The Caveman', retired from football. Years later you can still see fans wearing 'The Evolution of Matt' t-shirts honouring him. He suffered an anterior cruciate ligament injury at Bashley in November 2004 and was still in rehab from the operation the following July. He then had a relapse and more knee operations but that was the end of his career.

In 87 starts and one substitute appearance he scored 37 goals; he was a centre-half! He was admired because he was so down to earth, except when he was apparently hovering a few feet above the ground and scoring signature headed goals. He rejected an approach from Conference side Aldershot to go full time, preferring to stay with us.

After the Withdean 2000 defeat shortly after he joined us, Matt was never again on the losing side in 70 league games (we lost the match immediately following his career-ending injury). He says, 'I wouldn't change a second of it. That 18 months until my career ended, I would do it all again. It was a once in a lifetime opportunity for me. It was magic.'

One issue that hadn't been resolved was the 'Cocaine' song. This was penned by a group of fans and is unique to Wimbledon. In the 'Soapbox' feature in the programme someone had complained about it being sung and the club sought comments from fans. Given that one of its authors was Kris, this was a simple way of first demonstrating that there was a range of views and then saying that since it is neither racist nor homophobic we had no grounds to ban it – and enforcing such a ban wouldn't be feasible. So he'd been open, democratic, and nothing had changed.

Personally, I don't feel strongly about the words but I can't stand 'Sailing', the Rod Stewart dirge to which it is sung.

Finally, the end of the season also marked the appointment of Dickie Guy as president. Unlike WFC we made a point of honouring our players from the non-league days. Dickie was the goalkeeper in 1975 when WFC were one of a very small band of non-league clubs to win away at a top-division side, Burnley in this case. This was followed by a 0-0 draw at Leeds United, the best team in England at the time. In that game Dickie saved a penalty from Peter Lorimer, the man with the hardest shot in football; he remains a club hero to this day. WFC lost the replay to an unlucky deflected goal.

Penalties play a major role in our history. In 1988 Dave Beasant was the first man to save a penalty in an FA Cup Final and they would continue to play a major role in our story as it unfolded. But that's a story for another time.

21

ALMOST THERE

AS USUAL the close-season was busy with social events, ground improvements and recruitment. The summer started with a trip to the Ryman League dinner and awards ceremony. The chairman of the league at the time was Alan Turvey, the dissenting member of the FA Commission in 2002. Although our fans held him in high regard for that stance, we had a fractious relationship with him, mainly because we didn't maintain 'standards'. A lot of this seemed to be about deference to his authority but, bizarrely, it ended up being about dress standards.

Most boardrooms demand that a collar and tie, and often a jacket, be worn by 'gentlemen'.[24] We didn't have such a rule, which irked Alan immensely. Indeed, he couldn't let go of what seemed to me a totally trivial issue.

In my experience the lower down the football pyramid you go the more importance is placed on blazers and ties. It always struck me as incongruous that we were expected to dress so differently from the fans in what was, before canapés and prawn sandwiches became de rigueur, the people's game.

The annual Ryman event was black tie for men and evening wear for ladies. When everyone was seated at their tables, a toastmaster would call for everyone to stand for the entrance of the chairman and his guests, who had to be greeted by hand clapping at a military march rhythm. Alan

---

24 FC United of Manchester dealt with the issue differently. Told by their league that failure to wear ties in the boardroom was a disciplinary offence, they responded by imposing a mandatory tie-wearing policy for their boardroom; they then showed visiting officials to the boardroom door, before saying, 'But we don't go in there.'

would wear a white dinner jacket and he and his wife Margaret would lead the first dance. That was the cue for Eileen and me to leave. Although clubs were mandated to pay for a table of ten, I only went in our first year. Subsequently, we offered the places to club volunteers.

Back at the stadium, we were putting a roof on the south stand, which until now had been known as the Athletics End (it backed on to the adjacent athletics stadium) but was now sponsored by and named after our kit supplier, Tempest. This was the first of a series of stadium improvements aimed at preparing us for eventual promotion to the Football League. A substantial grant from the Football Stadia Improvement Fund helped cover the cost.

The almost immediate consequence of the change was that the 'Kop End' for home fans switched from the north stand, the Kingston Road End, to the newly covered Tempest End which, with steeper banking, had a much better view.

We funded the improvements without any detrimental effect on the playing budget and Dave, named as the Ryman League Division One manager of the year, quickly set about strengthening the squad for 2005/06. It was to be our first in the Ryman Premier League, Step 3 of the pyramid.

In March of the previous season Dave had brought in Shane Smeltz, a New Zealand striker who had played a handful of Football League games for Mansfield Town. During his time with us Shane achieved a number of 'firsts'. He became the first AFC Wimbledon player to win international honours and the first to score an international goal. At the end of 2005/06 he was the first player we sold for a fee. His registration was sold to Halifax Town, a Conference team at the time, for a bargain initial fee of £1,500 with three further increments of £500 depending on appearances, of which only one was paid before he moved on. Shane went on to play in the Australia A-league and for New Zealand in the World Cup – in other words, he was a cut above the usual standard of Step 3 players.

With only three defeats in the previous two seasons the fans were very optimistic about a third promotion in a row. However, there was again only one automatic promotion place. A second spot was available via the play-offs, to be contested between the teams who came second to fifth.

Like most managers, Dave started to manage expectations well before the season started. He commented in the press that two Essex clubs, Billericay and Braintree, were reportedly full-time (we still trained only two nights a week). In addition, Fisher Athletic were reputed to be spending a lot of money on players. We couldn't match that so Dave recruited experienced players who knew the league and what was needed to gain promotion.

He was right to be cautious. After winning the first three games we then won one and drew six of the following nine. By early October we were sixth in the league table. The season then fell into a pattern where we'd ease into a play-off place before slipping down again after a disappointing result. After winning our only two league games in December we entered 2006 in sixth place.

Something significant and hugely beneficial for the club started in December. Usually I sat at the back of the directors' box with my wife Eileen on one side and Iain McNay, a major sponsor and a director of the AFCW PLC board, on the other. Iain is very curious about two things – what is going on and what makes individuals tick – and he would ask me a stream of questions throughout a game. Sitting directly in front of us was Mike Richardson, a lifelong fan of the club who had initially been quite sceptical about our chances of making things work. However, he missed his beloved Dons so in our third season he started coming and paid for a seat in the directors' box. Despite living in the Isle of Man he was able to make most games.

For some reason I missed a particularly depressing 1-0 home defeat to Hendon in the League Cup and Ivor was in my seat, going through the usual interrogation from Iain about what we could afford to spend to improve results. Out of the blue Mike turned round and said he would put some money into the club if we signed 'a big, ugly centre-forward' who would beat up the opposition. Very soon Mike, Kris and Ivor met in The Leather Bottle, a pub in Wimbledon. It was agreed that Mike would pay £25,000 towards players' wages but Kris made it clear that Dave must decide where to invest the money. That was an important principle to establish, but in practice Dave wanted a striker too.

In those days players could be borrowed at any time before 31 March for 28 days,[25] so the temptation to respond to a minor injury or a drop-off

---

25 This system, whereby players could be taken on short-term loans for at least 28 days but no more than 91 in total, was a flagrant breach of UEFA regulations about players only moving clubs within laid-down transfer windows. In 2014/15, UEFA realised that the rules were being circumvented and banned short-term loans. Since then players have only been able to move clubs during a transfer window.

in form was to bring in another player. While it was fairly easy to bring loans in, making them fit quickly into our system was far from guaranteed. Between January and the closure of the transfer window on 31 March, eight players were recruited, including six strikers, but of those strikers only Paul Barnes scored more than a single goal.

One recruit, Dwayne Plummer, inadvertently created one of the season's memorable moments when he was clean through on goal against Braintree in the last minute of a game that was 0-0. The opposition manager was so angry he threw a chair on to the pitch. I'd love to see that feature in 'What Happened Next?' on *A Question of Sport.*

During the season there had been a regular stream of players in and out of the club. In total, 37 players started at least one league game, only six started more than 30 and 20 players started ten or fewer. Undoubtedly Dave was unlucky with injuries to key players. However, as Trevor Williams, the club secretary who had to do all the paperwork, said, 'When it came to new players Dave was like a magpie seeing bright shiny things and wanting them.'

We arrived at the last four games of the season with an injury-plagued team needing to win them all to be sure of a place in the play-offs. Fortunately the other results went our way and our third successive victory, at Hendon, was enough to secure a play-off place. Another in the final game of the season meant we finished fourth with 77 points. The play-offs were one-off matches with the team finishing second being at home to the fifth-placed team, and third at home to fourth. So we were to play away at Fisher Athletic, who we had beaten twice that season.

The timetable was unforgiving. Having played our last league game on the Saturday, the play-off semi-final was on the following Tuesday night. The final would be held at the higher-placed club's ground on the following Saturday. We went into the game with three possible outcomes. If we won and Heybridge, who'd finished second, won the other semi-final we'd be away on the Saturday. If we won and fifth-placed Hampton won then we'd be at home on the Saturday. With so little time I arrived at the game with a couple of thousand explanatory leaflets ready to hand out if we won.

The third possible outcome was what actually happened. We lost.

Managers often complain about injury crises. To his credit, Dave didn't make much of it and said the better team won. However, we'd started with five first-choice players unavailable and during the game both our centre-backs were injured and substituted. Meanwhile, Fisher had recalled Leroy Griffiths who was on loan to Aldershot, two divisions higher. That said a lot about the quality of player they could afford to recruit. He scored, of course. Fisher went on to win the final and were promoted to Conference South. We were pleased about that; we didn't want to compete with that level of spending in the following season.

Our campaign ended with further disappointment. For the second successive year we reached the final of the Surrey Senior Cup, which was again played at Woking FC in front of nearly 4,000 spectators. Our opponents were our tenants, Kingstonian. They scored just before half-time and despite laying siege to their goal throughout the second half we were unable to equalise and they held on to win.

Our season was over. It was time to lick our wounds, learn the lessons of a punishing year and get ready to go again for 2006/07.

22

HINTS AND ALLEGATIONS

ONE OF our fans, known as 'Papers' for the sheaf of documents he always carried about with him, would count the crowds at our games and announce his result on the chat site of choice that evening. Hs figure always differed from ours, mainly because, in line with most clubs' practice, our announced attendances included all the tickets we'd sold, including season ticket holders whether or not they attended.

In practice about 500 season ticket holders wouldn't turn up to games. This meant that we could play a team in a league game one Saturday and report, say, a gate of 3,000 (including non-attending season ticket holders who'd paid for a ticket) when in fact there were only 2,500 fans physically present in the stadium. However, our season tickets don't include entry for cup games so they weren't included in the attendance for cup games. This meant that if we played the same club in a cup game the following Saturday there might be exactly the same number of people in the stadium, but the announced attendance would be 2,500.

The result of this difference was that some teams who visited us were sceptical about the announced attendance. I have a recording of a visiting manager who said in an interview after a cup game at Kingsmeadow, 'There was 2,000-odd here but they've only declared 1,200, it must have only been one side of the ground, I'm sure.' He was fortunate that his interview was intercepted at the editing stage and never broadcast.

This lazy and ignorant slander says more about the speaker than about us, but unfortunately if it's not challenged it becomes the received wisdom. Perhaps it was that sort of arrogant 'I know better' attitude that led one particular club to accuse us publicly of what amounted to either gross incompetence or fraud.

In December 2005 we played St Albans in the FA Trophy at Kingsmeadow. The attendance was 1,953, which was pretty good for a game on a weekend close to Christmas when gates are usually lower than normal. Five days later I sent them copies of the FA forms showing how their profit share was calculated and a cheque for just over £5,400.

A couple of weeks later we received a letter from Sherrards, solicitors, acting on behalf of St Albans. They stated that St Albans FC believed that the gate was close to 3,000 and therefore they were entitled to more than £5,400. Sherrards went on to say that they had viewed the match video which showed 'an unusually substantial' attendance and they were now collecting 'Witness Statements' (do all solicitors think that the arbitrary use of upper case letters is Somehow Threatening?). They demanded copies of the supporting documentation as allowed by the competition rules. The letter was copied to the FA.

Before going on to explain what happened next, it's worth diverting on to the subject of attendances and profit shares. For league games the home club retains all the gate money and profits from match-related activities, such as bar profits, golden goal tickets, programmes, etc.

For cup ties each club gets 50 per cent of the profit, calculated as the gate money, after deducting VAT and the costs of staging the game, such as turnstile operators and stewards (and snow clearance!). The home club keeps the profits from the bar, match sponsorship, programmes, etc. For those of you who are interested in the detail of the calculations I've included a set of completed returns as an appendix.

The overwhelming majority of clubs are very honest but if so minded there's more than one way to skim off some of the profit from a game. The simplest way is to understate the attendance. As a senior Ryman League official said to me, 'Some north London clubs were notorious for gate manipulation,' at that time. There are other ways money might go astray; for example a club might be scrupulously honest but its turnstile operators might not be. At one away game I watched stewards take cash to let fans enter through an exit gate 'to ease the crush' close to kick-off time. There was no way the club could be sure they'd received all the money that was theirs.

The problem was that gate money was almost 100 per cent cash, which is easy to divert. After one particular away cup match our fans' chat site was flooded with comments about dodgy turnstile operators admitting people but not issuing tickets. If they do that it's easy to report low crowd numbers and keep some cash for yourself. After that particular tie I regularly received texts from fans telling me that no tickets were being issued at away games. However, if it was a league match there was no loss to us and it was really an issue for the other club, not us.

Under-stated attendances sometimes had their lighter side. We played away in one of the smaller cups and after the game I drifted into the boardroom. For want of anything else to say, I asked what the attendance had been. The club secretary told me, only to have one of his directors say, 'That can't be right, there were far more people here than that.' After an awkward silence he added, 'Oh, is this a gate share?' I rang their chairman the next day and politely reported the conversation; he added a couple of hundred to the attendance.

The problem with this sort of thing is that if accusations of crowd fixing are made often enough and with the certainty that makes some people type 'FACT' at the end of a chat site post, it becomes the received wisdom that a club is dishonest. So whenever we could we'd stamp on such comments. I recall three clubs where I phoned the chairman to say I'd been told that 'someone in their club' (no names, but he knew I meant him) had been reported as saying we'd cheated them. I was sure this wasn't true but perhaps he could just check to make sure since to do so would, of course, be slanderous.

I should add that assessing the attendance at an unfamiliar stadium is fraught with difficulty. In my files I have a letter from a fan who wanted an FA investigation because he was certain that the crowd for an away game was 'well over 3,000'. The announced figure was 2,200. During the game, but before the attendance was announced, Ivor and I were idly chatting. He thought the crowd was about 2,300 and I thought it was nearer to 2,000.

Sometimes a club's analysis of the attendance would raise eyebrows. For one away cup tie (i.e. a profit share game) the under-16s comprised 20 per cent of the attendance and under five per cent of the takings. Under-16 tickets are very cheap but the percentage of that group at that game was double the average for all the other cup ties we'd ever played.

Is that odd? Yes. Were the numbers manipulated? I don't know. Also, and astonishingly, there was no requirement to issue tickets for the game so there was no way to check the figures back to the records. Still, with such a young crowd that club's future fan base looks secure. That was probably just as well as they also had an unusually high proportion of over-65s, also at a discounted admission fee, so they'd need these younger fans coming through to replace them.

There was one club where we were all absolutely convinced that the attendance and the gate money were under-stated. However, given the club's owners our directors decided that in the interests of our own personal safety it would be best to look the other way.

As for St Albans, they were obviously keen to apply pressure. On the same day that we received the solicitors' letter a journalist from the *St Albans Observer* phoned asking for a comment. The subsequent report quoted 'a source within the club' and specified the amount St Albans had been paid.

I'll quickly skip through what happened next. Kris, quite accurately, assumed that I'd take this personally. I was grateful to him for sending an immediate and very aggressive reply to the lawyers. He also wrote to the FA inviting them to come and inspect our records.

I will let my wife Eileen comment next, 'We were about to go for a brief holiday in the Lake District when that bloody letter arrived. We still went but we were accompanied by all the detailed records which were strewn around the table for the next few days. It was no holiday.'

Having gone through all our records in detail I sent copies of all the documentation to the lawyers and the FA, pointing out that the recent FA compliance visit had reported that our procedures were more rigorous than at many Conference clubs, two divisions higher. Clearly the FA didn't bother looking through it and Sherrards/St Albans must have decided that reading and absorbing it all fell into the category of 'too much hard work'. Three months after the solicitors' letter arrived the FA announced that there was no case to answer.

In fact I did find a few small errors in our records and I calculated that we owed them £13.79. For a while I toyed with the idea of making a huge presentation-style cheque for £13.79 and ambushing their chairman with it in their car park, with the press present. Much as the idea amused me I had better things to do, so I left it.

It's important to learn lessons from such events. We never wanted this to happen again so from that day we invited all visiting teams to come and observe how we account for gate share games. Only one club, Oxhey

Jets, took us up on the offer out of curiosity about 'how bigger clubs do it'. They were lovely people and I still keep an eye on their results well over ten years later.

In one of life's coincidences some years later, Dave Anderson was approached to be the manager at St Albans. The chairman rang me for a reference. I gave Dave a glowing report and then asked if we were ever going to get an apology about the gate-fixing allegations. 'Well you sent us a lot of paper,' was his reply.

23

LET IT BE

AFTER FOUR years we had won two promotions, bought our own stadium and although we'd missed out in the play-offs we felt we were thriving and could confidently look forward to further success. Although attendances were over ten per cent down from that first euphoric year, season ticket sales continued to increase and we were financially very comfortable. And then something happened to challenge our assumptions and, ultimately, make us realise how vulnerable we were.

In early June 2006, commercial director Ivor Heller met Darragh MacAnthony who was interested in putting money into the club. Ivor had already done a little bit of work for MacAnthony, having been introduced by Xavier Wiggins, a lifelong Dons fan and founder member of WISA. MacAnthony had made a substantial amount of money from selling overseas holiday homes and Ivor was excited at the prospect of persuading him to become our stadium sponsor. Ivor was hoping for £100,000 a year which would have transformed our finances.

Ivor takes up the story, 'I went to Olympia where he [MacAnthony] was part of an exhibition promoting holiday homes. He said, "Let's see what we can sort out. We're going to look at this ground of yours."

'We started to walk out and I noticed all these people around us. He said, "This is my main advisor, my PA and my bodyguards." Two cars pulled up and off we went. Then he said he had heard there was a greyhound stadium that would be handy for the football club and decided to go for a look. We drove there and he blagged his way in and started talking about adapting it or knocking it down. This made me very excited.

'We went to the club and showed him around. He spent a lot of money in the shop. Then we went to the Dog and Fox (a favourite pub in Wimbledon). We landed up with a bodyguard sitting in one corner and another in the other corner. I found it very embarrassing.

'We started talking about various options, naming rights, talking around it and got to money and I said £100,000. He said, "You do realise that if we shake hands you're on the hook?" He was saying he wanted to do this and then his right-hand man, his advisor, said, "You want to take the club back into the league?" I replied that if they gave us the money we would do it. We got that close to agreeing a deal.

'Then, just as we were about to shake hands his advisor said, "Darragh, you want to control it, you want it to be your club. Why are you going to spend £100,000 on something when you could spend a couple of million on it and own it all?" I knew that immediately the stadium rights deal was off the table. And then he said, "I'm going to buy the club. I'm not going to sponsor it. Don't worry, you'll have a place in it. Don't worry, I'm going to get the greyhound stadium and go back to Wimbledon and have a right laugh with it over the next 20-plus years." And I thought this was going to be extremely problematic.'

It was agreed that Kris Stewart, then the club's chairman, Ivor, Iain McNay (a member of the DT board who we invited for additional business insights) and I should meet MacAnthony. He was accompanied by his advisor and Xav Wiggins.

My recollection is that although MacAnthony had made his position clear to Ivor, I wasn't properly aware of it before we met. He had flown in especially for the meeting. On the plane he'd watched *Womble Til I Die*, a video about our first season, and was bursting with enthusiasm about his ideas, which included him owning the club. He was very open and didn't try to use clever words to mask his intentions.

He ran through the main points of his ideas. He would acquire AFC Wimbledon and take full control, investing £1m immediately and opening talks with Merton Council about a suitable site for a stadium. His aim was to gain promotion to the Premier League in eight years and he talked about having a new stadium – preferably in Merton – within three years, which would be 'ours' when he moved on. In response to a question he said he felt there was no space for volunteers in the club – we needed to be professional – and that he would make all the big decisions.

I looked back at what Iain and Kris said in Niall Couper's *This Is Our Time*, where the meeting is described in some detail. Kris thought, 'You are kinda missing the point of what this club is about,' while Iain wrote, 'I felt he didn't really understand the principles on which the club was run.' Personally, I thought he did understand but was realistic that they would have to change if he was the decision-maker. I thought his speech about loving what we'd done was sincere, but then he went on to say that he wanted to continue the dream by taking us over; for me that was a serious misuse of the word 'continue'. I said so and we clashed.

A few years later, MacAnthony wrote *From Hobby To Obsession* which devotes a couple of pages to that meeting. He said it was 'one of the worst of my life' and added, 'I've never been in a room with someone who stared at me with such contempt.' It's a shame he thought that because there's a very small number of people I don't like and he isn't one of them. I was amused to read that I spent a lot of time staring at his watch. Presumably he thought I was coveting it.[26]

The meeting broke up and the board members went back to Kingsmeadow where we discussed what we'd heard. Kris was silent for some time and then quietly said he felt a heavy responsibility to the fans because what he said would be influential.

The next step was to take the issue to our parent company, the Dons Trust. Much of what follows is drawn from the minutes of the DT board meeting on 3 July and a subsequent smaller meeting a week later. The minutes record that Kris had sent DTB members 'an e-mail describing the meeting that had taken place with a businessman who wished to acquire the club'. Nine of the 13-strong DT board were present along with Kris, there by virtue of his role as chair of the club. The other people present were Ian Cooke, former captain of WFC and a director of AFCW PLC, and Dave Boyle, then the CEO of Supporters Direct, the body set up to try to increase fans' representation in football clubs.

This felt like a watershed moment. The chair of the DTB, David Cox, asked for initial reactions and for comments 'on whether board members could ever recommend to members that the Dons Trust should relinquish control of AFC Wimbledon'.

—

26 I don't usually wear a watch, although I do have a treasured one which Eileen bought for my 30th birthday. It's a Snoopy watch, which has a tennis bat for the minutes, his paw for the hours and a ball that ticks off the seconds.

The minutes went on to say, 'In general, those present were cautious as to whether the approach from Mr Smith [at the time we weren't disclosing MacAnthony's name] represented the right opportunity for AFC Wimbledon at the current time. IH, MJ and GM were in favour of asking Mr Smith for a more detailed proposal… MJ wanted this so that it could be presented to members. GM thought it would be useful information for the future to know what Mr Smith was proposing and what he thought he could do, even though she was against the idea of selling the club. Others preferred not to seek a proposal at this stage, since it would mean embarking on a process for which the board and members were either not yet prepared or reluctant to countenance.'

The views varied but could be broadly classed into two categories. Six of the DTB members plus Kris said, 'We should not sell the club.' Some of those thought this should never happen while some thought it might happen some day, but 'not now'.

After a long discussion, David Cox summarised. We had three options: first to say 'no' and tell the members that we'd done so; second to ask Mr Smith for more detail which could be reviewed; third to say tell Mr Smith that we planned to engage the membership on our future strategy and if he wished to wait until the end of that process we could talk again.

Nobody preferred option one; Marc, Ivor and Geraldine preferred option two; Tom Adam, David Cox, Nigel Higgs, Sandy Lawrence and I preferred option three. In my view it was the same as option one, since MacAnthony had made it clear that he wanted a quick deal.

A week later the DTB members met again and revisited the options. No one was minded to change their previous conclusions. One board member suggested that supporters didn't care so much about being a fans-owned club but in general it ended with a decision to publish a statement saying what the board had decided. This was released on 17 July.

Subsequently Xav sent an open letter to the football club and DT boards, setting out more details of the sort of ideas which were proposed. An edited version is reproduced in *This Is Our Time* but, in summary, the proposals included a commitment to inject £1m immediately into the club and a similar amount for subsequent years. MacAnthony would leave the ownership of Kingsmeadow with the membership. He also proposed developing an exit strategy that would enable the club to return to the members if he departed.

Xav also said he believed that a worked-up proposal should have been presented to the members. By then it was too late. The DTB had moved on and was starting to plan the terms of reference for a strategic review.

Looking back on it, I think we should have spent more time debating whether or not to take proposals to the members. The whole incident also made me think about a lot of things I'd not previously considered. I concluded that while I believed that we should always do what was best for the club my personal view was, and remains, that if the club was sold to a third party I would stop supporting it.

Very importantly, the debate highlighted a key weakness of the fans-owned model as implemented in the Dons Trust. There was nothing in the constitution that would have prevented the DTB members from committing to sell the club. That couldn't be right; we needed safeguards. By the end of the year initial steps had been taken to introduce 'Restricted Actions' (RAs) into the DT constitution. The aims of the RAs included protecting the club and stadium from being sold in haste by requiring a super majority of members to vote in favour on two separate occasions. Additional RAs with varying voting thresholds were created to cover other matters, such as changing the club's name and increasing borrowings. After extensive debate and consultation the relevant provisions were voted into place in June 2007, almost exactly a year after the first approach.

Later in 2006 Darragh MacAnthony acquired Peterborough United who were at the time in League 2. Since then they have been promoted into the Championship twice and on both occasions been relegated back to League 1 after a brief stay. At the time of writing they are in an automatic promotion place in League 1.

24

FOR ONCE IN MY LIFE

AFTER THE drama of the summer it felt good to see football start again with all the hopes and expectations that each new season brings. And then, five games in, Kris Stewart resigned.

Kris is very bright, principled, a really good strategic thinker and a superb orator. One to one he is very funny and we shared an eye and ear for the absurd and the pretentious. And he was a major driving force in starting the club. But for a long time I had felt that the club was drifting.

Ivor was also very frustrated by the way the board was operating. A few months earlier I had become so worried that the club was drifting that I expressed my concerns to the Dons Trust board, but no action was taken. So I resigned as finance director. The official announcement was fairly anodyne; I saw no benefit in rocking the boat publicly. I was scheduled to stand down once the annual accounts had been finalised. So when Kris rang me one Sunday morning to say he thought it was time for him to go I didn't try to dissuade him. He had been doing the job for just over four years and he no longer looked like he was enjoying it. I thought that so long as it felt like the right thing for him then he should do it.

The day after my call from Kris, he went into the office and broke his news to the staff. By coincidence there was a Dons Trust board meeting scheduled for that night. David Cox was the chair of the DT board and he moved 'what now?' to the top of the agenda.

Members were shocked and surprised. Those who had spoken to Kris commented that he already looked and sounded more relaxed. David Cox reported that he had spoken to Kris who did not feel that he had been pushed out but had made the right decision for himself. Furthermore, he would not be reversing his decision. In fact, he was spending that evening drafting a statement for the club's website.

There followed a couple of hours' discussion, nominally getting to grips with the possible consequences. A lot of it struck me as board members needing time for the issue to sink in. Then Ivor proposed that I be appointed as acting chief executive and I was asked to leave the room while the board discussed it. On my return to the room they confirmed that they'd like me to take over 'for now'.

I was in a dilemma. I hadn't engineered this situation, indeed I hadn't seen it coming, but I welcomed the opportunity. When I resigned I'd talked about needing a break. That was disingenuous but it was the right thing to say at the time; it wouldn't have helped anyone if I'd publicly explained my real reasons. But now I decided that I was going to push very hard for the job and then do it so well that it was impossible for the DTB to consider anyone else for it.

Guessing what was likely to happen at the DTB meeting, I'd talked to Eileen about me taking on the CEO position. She had suffered years of me coming home and kicking the (metaphorical) cat in frustration. But she has always been fantastically supportive of my selfish ambitions. Perhaps she thought that if I was CEO the only person I could now kick was me. Also, when I retired from PwC at the end of 2003 she reminded me of her mantra – 'marriage is for life but not for lunch'. She didn't want me moping around the house.

The next day brought the welcome relief of a game but the good feeling didn't last long because it was a boring draw, making it four draws and two wins in the season so far. After six games we were ninth. The club's up-and-down form continued in the league but, perversely, FA Cup and FA Trophy runs demonstrated the quality in the team. The FA Cup run started against Horsham with one of those dramatic last-minute winning goals that everyone who was there can still picture today.

There followed a home game against Oxhey Jets, who were two leagues below us. Their founder and general manager, John Elliott, was a classic example of the effort, commitment and self-sacrifice that you meet at this level of the game. John created a terrific community club from nothing and when they needed to bring their pitch up to the required standard he put his house up as a guarantee for a £50,000 loan. It's quite humbling to meet people like him. That didn't stop me wanting us to thump them, which we did, 3-0.

One more win took us to a glamour game at Exeter City, also fan-owned and two leagues higher than us. If we beat Exeter we would go into the first round proper of the FA Cup where teams in the bottom two tiers of the Football League enter the competition. It was the first time I'd seen the knicker-wetting excitement by the press about what was in reality the remote possibility[27] of being drawn to play against Milton Keynes.

That was a game we desperately wanted to avoid; we lacked the experience to manage the hype that would have engulfed us. It was only four years since the FA Commission decision, fans' feelings were still very raw and we'd have been very worried about the possibility of trouble erupting at the game. Plus, from a selfish point of view I could never bring myself to shake hands with Winkelman.

In any event, it was academic; the 1,500 fans we took to the Exeter game saw a brave, and slightly unlucky, 2-1 defeat.

Meanwhile, we were making progress in the FA Trophy. After two wins we drew a home tie against Eastleigh, a Conference South club, one league above us. As usual, I was on car park duty for the game – I saw no reason to stop just because I was chief executive – when a member of the Eastleigh football staff approached me. I think everybody, including car park attendants, should be treated with the same respect but that wasn't his style. He told me to fit his mate into the reserved car park 'because he'd come a long way'. I said I was sorry but he wasn't on the list of people I'd been given and if I let him park then someone else would lose their space. Let's just say he didn't agree and after I'd politely refused a couple more times he started swearing.

I asked him if he'd like to speak to the chief executive to complain and he said 'yes'.[28] So I turned around for a moment then turned back, beamed a welcoming smile and said, 'I'm the chief executive here, can I help you?'

He walked away still swearing and promising that we'd struggle to get parking spaces the next time we visited them.

—

27 For that to happen we'd need to have beaten Exeter, after which the odds of drawing the franchise were 78/1.

28 This is what I desperately hoped he would say but actually he said 'no, don't bother'. Everything else is as it happened.

After an experience like that it is even more pleasing to win the game, which we did after a replay at their ground. I didn't have any trouble parking.

In the next round we were drawn away to Conference National club Aldershot Town. This was very welcome but our patchy form in the league was an increasing source of concern to the football club board. A week before the Aldershot tie we were thumped 3-0 at Billericay. We were tenth, seven points short of a play-off place, albeit with a game in hand. Crowds were below the average for the previous season and so was the gate money. We desperately needed to get out of the Ryman League and tenth place wasn't what we'd signed up for.

For several weeks the football club board had been discussing whether we needed a change of manager and the Billericay result crystallised our fears. The issue wasn't so much the league position. We just weren't convinced that Dave could improve results. We thought he needed to change his backroom staff because too much seemed to rest on his shoulders. If you instruct a manager to change his backroom staff you're taking away his authority and you might as well sack him. So, instead, I had a conversation with him about whether he was happy with them; he's a loyal man and he confirmed that he was happy. I reported back to the football club board and we felt we needed a change and we decided to sack Dave.

For such an important decision we needed to get buy-in from the DTB. A DTB meeting couldn't be convened until late in the week so the proposition was that I should sack Dave after the Aldershot Trophy tie. That would leave a full week for the caretaker manager to get to grips with the squad.

To keep these discussions under wraps we needed to meet away from the club. This was how we came to meet in an ill-lit scout hut. Given our reservations about Dave's backroom staff, we weren't going to ask either of them to take on a caretaker role. I had made some discreet enquiries elsewhere and they confirmed our view that Steve Watson, a very experienced member of the squad, would be a good caretaker manager while we recruited a permanent replacement. We couldn't speak to him until after the game but if he refused then our Plan B was Simon Bassey, who was coaching the reserve team and was highly thought of by management and players alike.

And so we went to Aldershot, with me all set to sack Dave after the game. The Recreation Ground is one of my favourite places to watch football. The main seated stand is about 90 years old and the whole place feels old-fashioned, but in a good, solid, attractive way. The stadium has an almost palpable sense of history and it's all the more attractive for it. But that day I was totally unaware of my surroundings – I was mentally rehearsing and re-rehearsing what I'd say to Dave after the game.

If I hadn't been so pre-occupied with what I wanted to say I'd have loved the game. It had drama, possibly the best goal of Chris Gell's life, a stunning, faultless performance in goal by Andy Little and an agonising, tense half-hour – only really enjoyable when it's over and you can look back on it – while we clung on to our lead for dear life.

Aldershot dominated the first half but thanks to Andy's heroics we went in only one down at half-time. Things continued much the same until the hour, with Andy pulling off more last-ditch saves. And then, in a rare attack, midfielder Chris Gell was scythed down, falling as Dave said 'as if he'd been shot by an AK47'. The referee waved play on and as the ball came back towards him, Chris rose, Lazarus-like, to score with a magnificent shot from 30 yards. Possibly the oldest of the many well-worn sayings you'll hear around football is 'goals change games' but it's well-worn because it is true. Suddenly we were on the front foot.

'The immutable law of the ex' is an Italian saying that encapsulates the immensely frustrating experience when players you release come back and play out of their skins against you. That was certainly true for former Aldershot player Roscoe Dsane that day. It was his shot that the Aldershot goalkeeper couldn't hold for Scott Fitzgerald to score our second goal. And then we hung on for the final 25 minutes and easily the best result we'd achieved as AFC Wimbledon.

Ivor says that much as he loved the game, one of the most enjoyable things he's ever experienced in his time at AFC Wimbledon was watching realisation dawn on my face as first we equalised, then took the lead, and then held on to win. What to do? I couldn't sack Dave after that performance. Just to be sure I'd not lost my mind, Ivor grabbed me at the end of the game and said, grinning from ear to ear with a combination of delight at the win and sheer joy at my discomfort, 'Well you can't sack him now.'

Obviously I couldn't sack him that day, but one win, however enjoyable, doesn't save a season. So, on the following Monday I spoke to Dave to congratulate him but to remind him that it was the league he was being judged on. Tenth place wasn't what we were looking for.

The message sank in. He takes up the story, 'Before the game at Heybridge I talked to Jon Turner [the assistant manager] about it and Jon said, "I want you to leave the dressing room." Then he spoke to the guys, telling them, "Dave's under pressure." Despite that the game wasn't going well. With ten minutes to go it was 0-0 and then Chris Gell was sent off. But five minutes from the end of the game, Louis Cook scored a late winner. He ran to the dugout, pursued by the rest of the team, and they all jumped on me. That told me that I had the dressing room with me. The win was important because you [Erik] were going on holiday before the next game so I knew I was safe for at least two weeks.'

We were off on a family holiday to Australia, including the Boxing Day Ashes Test match. Eileen and I returned early on the morning of 13 January and went straight to the next round of the FA Trophy, away to Gravesend and Northfleet, another Conference National team. We watched an outstanding performance and another win. We were through to the last 16 of the Trophy and, including the Heybridge game, we'd taken 11 points from the six league matches between the Trophy ties. Everything was looking much rosier.

And then on the Tuesday morning the sky fell in.

25

HEARING WITHOUT LISTENING

FIRST-TEAM COACH Simon Bassey seems to know everyone in football. He was at Charlton Athletic as an academy player at the same time as Jermaine Darlington, who was two years older. 'Jermaine was well thought of but the reserve team manager gave him pelters,' Simon remembers. So Jermaine left and resurrected his career in non-league football at Aylesbury, where Dave Anderson was the assistant manager. Jermaine was signed by Wimbledon FC in 2001 and played 105 games before brief spells at Watford and then Cardiff, where a knee injury ended his career and he retired from the professional game. Returning to London, he started playing games for Globe Town, a local club playing in the Camden Sunday League.

He registered under his mother's maiden name because he knew that someone with a well-known name like his would be targeted for a kicking. When Dave heard he was playing again he invited him to train with us. We all agreed that if Jermaine could get fit enough for part-time football he would be a fantastic asset.

He made his debut against Harrow Borough on 11 November and received his first booking in the FA Trophy game at Gravesend and Northfleet in January. By that time he'd played for us 11 times in the league, three times in the Trophy and once in the Surrey Senior Cup. The aftermath of that innocuous foul and the resultant booking would engulf us for nearly three months.

On the Tuesday following the Gravesend tie, Trevor came in to the President's Lounge and said, 'I've screwed the club.' Then he sat on the floor with his back against the bar counter and buried his head in his hands. He sat there for quite some time, cursing under his breath. He had received a letter from the Football Association 'seeking our observations' on their concerns that Jermaine had played in the Trophy match without an International Transfer Certificate (ITC).

When a player has been registered with an overseas football association then he can't play for an English club until they've obtained an ITC for him. An ITC confirms that the player is genuinely free to join his new club. The booking had caught the FA's attention; while they see copies of all contracts, they were oblivious to Jermaine because he was only a registered player.

Welsh clubs like Cardiff, Swansea and Newport play in what is now known as the English Football League (EFL). However, they and their players are registered with the Welsh FA which has its own rules and so is 'an overseas FA'. Jermaine's last club before retiring was Cardiff and so any club registering him in England needed to be sure that an ITC had been issued. We hadn't checked.

The scale of the problem quickly became horribly clear. The usual punishment for playing an ineligible player is to be to be thrown out of the FA Trophy. We would also be charged by the Ryman League and if found guilty we would lose all 18 points we'd won in the league games in which Jermaine had played.

We called David Barnard, the former Wimbledon FC chief executive and now a director at Chelsea. In a lifetime in football administration, he has seen it all. David put us back in touch with Jim Sturman QC who had acted for us when we were charged with failing to control our players after the Colne FC game.

We could not have been better represented. Thanks to Jim's sense of outrage at the absence of fair play, we had a barrister working for us who was described in one of the legal directories, with a nod to his football expertise, as 'One of the Galacticos of the Bar'. Free of charge.

The FA Trophy was the most pressing issue because the next round couldn't be played until a decision had been made about our case.

The problem when you're a small club and something like this happens is that there are so many audiences to satisfy and potential ramifications to think through. And initially there was just me to do it; Trev was too upset to deal with it.

We received the letter on the Tuesday after the Gravesend game and by Wednesday night I'd exchanged about 30 e-mails and had several phone calls with Jim (who was conducting a criminal case at the same time); obtained an extension to the FA deadline for our reply; reviewed three drafts of our formal response; written a blow-by-blow brief for the DTB setting out the issues, options and risks; spoken to all the football club board a couple of times and some of the DTB; spoken to Dave Anderson and Trev at length; analysed the options for dealing with ticketing for the next round of the Trophy, a game we were far from sure we'd be playing; consulted David Lloyd, our volunteer PR advisor, about what to say on our website; and taken comments from a range of people on our draft response to the FA. I also spoke to the registrations department at the FA and, no doubt aware of what was going on, they very helpfully accelerated an ITC for Jermaine. It arrived within an hour of us applying. So at least he could continue to play for us.

Everyone wanted to know what was going on. Board members are volunteers and busy with their daytime jobs so you have to catch them when you can. As a result I had to give everyone a grounding, one at a time, in the basic rules. For example, it is each club's responsibility to make sure their players are eligible. So it was our responsibility to ensure an ITC had been issued and we couldn't rely upon, or blame, Globe Town, the first club he played for after Cardiff; they should have applied for an ITC as well.

Even before we'd submitted our reply, the FA e-mailed to tell us where and when the hearing would be held 'if a meeting is required'. I submitted our detailed six-page response late on the Thursday night. At the same time we issued a very brief statement on the club's website saying the FA had asked for clarification of the status of one of our players in the Gravesend game. Our fans aren't daft and they immediately sussed the nature of the problem. The chat site exploded with speculation about which player it was – and the e-mails and calls started coming in.

At 1pm on the Friday the FA confirmed that we were being charged and were required to attend a hearing. We made a further, more detailed, announcement on the club's website.

The hearing was set for 25 January, nine days before the third round of the Trophy was due to be played. Jim and I met at a cafe, just outside the FA headquarters in Soho Square. Jim is immediately impressive. He speaks quickly and as Eileen noticed when he and I spoke on the phone he talks so clearly (and volubly!) that she could make out what he was saying from 30 feet away.

Unlike many very bright people I've met, Jim takes the trouble to explain his thinking and he knows his subject inside out. I was told very firmly to keep schtum in the meeting. He explained that he would argue that ejecting us would be a disproportionate punishment for a simple administrative error by a small club with limited resources. He added that based on the rules we don't have much of a chance but it was worth having a go.

We were seated opposite the three tribunal members; one from the north-east, one from the south-west and the chairman. They took us through the charge. Then there were questions. You know it's hopeless when a 'question' from the northern member is a long diatribe about what we'd done wrong. When he'd finished I asked what his question was but Jim shut me up. He pleaded our case and then ran through a list of precedents where the club in question had not been ejected from the competition. We left the room while they considered the extent of the sanctions – clearly the verdict was never in doubt.

After nearly two hours we were called back in. They'd taken so long because they'd been drafting a four-page summary of the hearing, the judgement and the sanctions. We were told we'd been thrown out of the Trophy and must repay the £7,000 prize money from the two rounds in which Jermaine had played. They added that there would be no additional fine and we could play in the Trophy the following season. It had never occurred to me that they might ban us from that!

Including the prize money from the Gravesend game and the loss of income from the next round, we were out of pocket by about £20,000, or nearly six per cent of our budgeted football income. That hurt. We were told that we could not appeal and that we had half an hour's head start before the decision appeared on the FA site. That was just long enough to get a terse announcement on to our site. I was determined that our fans should find out from us, not second-hand from another body's website.

That outcome was bad but I was far more worried about the Ryman League. We'd now received their letter and were preparing for the hearing. At that stage of the season an 18-point deduction would have put us three points above a relegation spot. I never for a moment thought we might be relegated but such a penalty would kill our promotion chances.

It didn't look good. The rule was common to all leagues and said, 'Any Club found to have played an ineligible player in a match shall have any points gained from that match deducted from its record… The [League] may vary the decision in respect of the deduction of points gained only in a case where a substitute player participates.'

We had to bring the fans up to date so we called an open meeting before the Harrow Borough home game on Saturday, 27 January. We also distributed a statement announcing we'd now been charged by the Ryman League and that we'd written to the FA saying we wished to take their decision to the Court of Arbitration for Sport. Jim had offered to continue to work for us with no fee. Within 48 hours we got a letter from a senior solicitor at the FA saying that the CAS had no jurisdiction over FA competition rules, so we could forget it, although it was said in a more solicitor-y way.

The Ryman League hearing was held at the Gatwick Hilton on Wednesday, 7 February. The panel members were Alan Turvey, the league chairman, Martin Eede from Fisher Athletic, and Dean Fisher from Croydon Athletic. Nick Robinson, at that time the Ryman League company secretary, was there to interpret the rules.

Jim made several arguments. One was that in a criminal case heard by the UK Court of Appeal the Court had directed that the word 'shall' was not mandatory. Therefore, he claimed, 'shall have any points deducted' was not a mandatory directive. He also made the rather less esoteric argument that we'd made a technical error and a points deduction would be a disproportionate penalty.

We thought it went well and we got a sympathetic hearing until Jim said it was quite easy to understand how someone might think playing for Cardiff in the English pyramid would not count as playing abroad. He explains, 'At that point Robinson and Turvey were as one saying, "That was a ridiculous submission, how could anyone who understands football make that submission?" To which my response was, "We're talking about non-league football being administered from a club whose ambition was to go from playing Sunday league back to the professional leagues. You are not talking about a fully-funded, sophisticated club."'

Once again we were turfed out of the meeting and then recalled to be told that they were imposing an 18-point deduction and a £400 fine. We announced it on the website and requested written reasons for the decision.

The next day, we decided to lay into the FA on our website. Looking back I must have been pretty angry when I wrote it and it makes for quite a fun read. In effect it dismissed the FA's responses to our questions as either not answered or 'rules is rules'. It asked why small clubs like us were treated differently from big clubs; for example Liverpool had been given exemption from the rule that a player can only play for two clubs in a season; the Premier League had offered a 14-day amnesty to clubs which may have played an ineligible player in breach of the rules. We even threatened to go to the High Court or the European Court, which was really quite ludicrous when at the same time we were playing the card that 'we're only a small club which has made a technical error'.

We weren't expecting a reply. We were seeking to build on the sense of injustice among our fans so as to energise them into a campaign to get the points deduction reduced or reversed. The principle is quite simple. Fans could say or do things that a club couldn't. So we stood back and let them get on with it. Others pitched in. The Altrincham goalkeeper wrote a long article in the *Non-League Paper*. They had 18 points deducted the previous season for not obtaining an ITC and it very nearly relegated them. He argued we should be treated the same.

Not everyone was unhappy. Publicly, Dave Anderson was saying, 'We did the equivalent of running a red light and got 25 years in prison for it,' in the *London Evening Standard*. However, privately he saw this as his get-out-of-jail-free card. He later confirmed, 'I was thinking 18 points, there's no way they can sack me now. I've got another season.'

Thirteen years later I talked to Nick Robinson, now the Ryman League chairman, about the hearing. He said, 'The panel thought we'd done enough and it would be wrong to deduct 18 points. However, the Ryman League chairman Alan Turvey insisted and was most vociferous that they should apply the rules; if Wimbledon wanted to appeal they could take it to the FA to decide.'

To put this into context, Turvey was very well respected for the job he'd done for the Ryman League but he was very much, as his former roles as a policeman and referee suggested, rules-bound.

Robinson's recollection is very different from how it felt to Jim and I at the time. We felt that the panel was united in their decision. And so to our fans, Turvey went from being a hero, as the dissenting vote at the FA, to an inflexible villain.

A couple of days later we were sent the written reasons and Jim became very angry. He said he wanted to fight it because he, 'Was very committed to winning that case. I hate seeing the underdog being prosecuted so I usually take on the defence – you could say I like tilting at windmills.'

The fans were in uproar and some of them over-reacted. Turvey was the figurehead so he was the target of abusive mail including an anonymous letter put through his letterbox at his home. Lord knows what abuse he'd have suffered nowadays on social media.

It would probably be in breach of data privacy rules nowadays (and perhaps it was then as well) but I persuaded Bruce Badcock, the perennially helpful Ryman League secretary, to send copies of the abusive e-mails to me. I then contacted the senders asking them to back off. Turvey knew his football regulations and, while he had every reason to be upset by the abuse, he clearly knew little about fans because he thought we could control everyone and were choosing not to do so. He was to get even more upset as the campaign went into overdrive.

Russell Smith, a lifelong Dons fan, started an e-petition on the Number 10 website. It quickly gathered pace and signatories. Seeking help and advice, I was introduced to Phil French, the newly-appointed chief executive at Supporters Direct, having recently joined from the Premier League. His help was invaluable in guiding me on how to maximise the effect of our protests, how to manage the media to get them on our side, and how to keep them there. He also reminded me regularly that, while I could express outrage at the injustice of such a disproportionate sanction, I should still speak with restraint if I wanted to influence people. 'Disproportionate' became the key word, to be trotted out at every opportunity.

Behind the scenes Phil was a whirlwind of activity. From his time at the Premier League his contacts were extensive. Breaking his targets down into political, football and media he first spoke to Jonathan Hall, head of compliance at the FA, to understand the process and to push him hard to make the sanction proportionate. We were putting out a consistent message, namely that yet again this little club, formed from an injustice, was battling the giants, trying to survive. Then he went to Brian Barwick, chief executive at the FA, going through the process with him, as well as what could be done and what couldn't be done.

Then came the politicians: James Purnell, later to be the Secretary of State for Culture, Media and Sport; Richard Caborn, Minister for Sport;

and Andy Burnham, Chief Secretary for the Treasury. These men were the key political pressure points because they were the ones who could have conversations with the football authorities. Next, Phil spoke to many members of the All Party Football Group.

If you've got the Chief Secretary to the Treasury who was the founder of Supporters Direct and the future Secretary of State for Culture, Media and Sport, and the Minister for Sport all on your side, they can't say much publicly but it's a powerful combination, all applying pressure. When you add the All Party Football Group with their contacts that is a powerful lobby.

Phil also had 'a difficult conversation' with Alan Turvey. 'He [Turvey] said I should back off and shouldn't interfere in a process and that AFC Wimbledon was a very, very difficult club, always causing problems – and something about not wearing ties in boardrooms.' I didn't hear about this conversation until years later but I was hugely amused to learn that even in the middle of all this strife Turvey was railing about this perceived slight to the fundamental bedrock on which civilised society is based, namely wearing ties to football matches.

At the same time, Siobhain McDonagh, a local MP and force of nature, was working hard on our behalf. She asked me to write a briefing note for Richard Caborn, the Sports Minister. She also presented an Early Day Motion,[29] signed by 84 MPs, which led to the following exchange with Prime Minister Tony Blair in the House of Commons, jam-packed with MPs, because it was immediately before the budget:

'AFC Wimbledon did not know that it needed an international registration for (a former Cardiff City player) to cross the river Severn to play football in south London. Will my right hon. Friend the Prime Minister give his support to the thousands of football supporters up and down the country who believe that there should be justice for everyone's teams, whether in the Ryman or the premier league?'

The Prime Minister

'Actually, I agree with my hon. Friend. She is absolutely right: it sounds like a daft rule, and someone should change it.' (*Hansard*, 21/03/2007)

---

29 An Early Day Motion may be tabled by a Member of Parliament, calling for debate 'on an early day' about a particular topic. In practice, they rarely reach the debate stage in the House of Commons; their principal purpose is to draw wide attention to a subject of particular interest to the proposer.

We were all over the local and national press. Richard Williams of *The Guardian* wrote an opinion piece entitled 'Is AFC Wimbledon's oversight worse than Milan's ref fixing', picking up my point that AC Milan had only eight points deducted for 'four years of trying to unduly influence referees'. Martin Samuel of the *Daily Mail* pitched in too. Meanwhile, we appealed to fans to write to the Sports Minister, the shadow Sports Minister and the FA and exhorted them to 'make your points politely, while making the strength of your feelings clear'.

The whole campaign was sending various football officials apoplectic. Turvey was absolutely livid, especially that Prime Minister Tony Blair had commented in the Houses of Parliament. I suspect that Turvey was no Labour supporter, so this no doubt added to his aggravation. Meanwhile, if I'm honest, I was beginning to enjoy myself.

And so to the appeal hearing itself at noon on 26 March, over ten weeks after the first letter had arrived. We were back at the FA offices in Soho Square in a well-furnished but quite depressing windowless room in the basement. David Henson, the chair of the FA Sanctions and Registration Committee, was in charge of proceedings and Neil Doncaster, then the chief executive of Norwich City, was one of the panel members.

Jim did his stuff again. His argument to the FA was two-fold. First the argument he'd used in the Ryman League hearing about the meaning of the word 'shall' and second the 'proportionality' point. It was, he said, wholly disproportionate to deduct 18 points for what many would view as a technical breach. The argument that the penalty was disproportionate to the offence seemed to get under Turvey's skin because at one point he replied with feeling, 'Well it isn't proportionate that they've got a QC acting for them and we haven't.'

When it was their turn to present they didn't seem to have agreed who would speak. Eventually Turvey made the case that the rules were clear and had left them with no choice. Neil Doncaster asked if the Ryman panel had considered whether the penalty was proportionate. Turvey floundered and I began to think that perhaps the hearing was turning our way.

As before, we were asked to leave the room. Jim chatted amicably with Turvey and Robinson while I made calls and answered some of the barrage of texts asking how it was going.

After what Jim tells me was an unusually short wait for an appeal hearing, we were called back in. David Henson started reading the decision, which was on the lines of, 'The panel confirms that the Ryman League acted correctly and that it did not misinterpret its own League Rule and that the deduction of 18 points was wholly in accordance with the Rules.' My heart sank. But he then added that nonetheless the hearing had concluded that an appropriate sanction would be a three-point deduction. The £400 fine remained unchanged.

I was stunned. Out of the corner of my eye I could see Turvey had gone red in the face. I thought it best not to look at him. We were dismissed and I went up to the lobby where I thanked Jim profusely, and then called Kris who was standing by to put the result on our website. He was so taken aback he couldn't remember the details, which is why the announcement was only two lines long.

Outside Soho Square, a small group of fans had been waiting for the outcome, in a small-scale repeat of the Milton Keynes vigil five years earlier. I went out to tell them the news and then returned to the lobby to make more calls. As Turvey walked past I told him there was a protest group outside but not to worry, given the result they'd leave him alone. That was naughty of me; he exploded.

Later that day we put a longer announcement on our site and asked fans not to be triumphalist; we'd got a good result and that was all that mattered. I thought we'd finally put it behind us and that all that was left was to write thank-you letters to everyone who had helped.

That wasn't the end of it. Turvey took the decision very personally and was clearly unwilling to let it go. A few days later he wrote to all Ryman League clubs asking, 'If they are happy with the action of the FA and, if not, to tell us so that we can decide what, if any, action to take.' This appeared in the *South London Press*. He was later reported in an unidentified publication, a copy of which I have from Ray's scrapbook, volume 21, as saying, 'So far there is only one club that doesn't want to take it any further. The rest are very supportive of the league and very angry with the FA.'

It was true that only one club was supportive of letting sleeping dogs lie but Turvey's statement was highly disingenuous; only 12 of the 66 league clubs replied. In the light of the tepid response he finally let it drop. But he never forgave us.

For Dave Anderson, the outcome wasn't exactly welcome. Years later he told me, 'When it was knocked down to three points everyone was partying and I was crying my eyes out!' The pressure to win promotion was back.

Following the decision the rules were changed and words were added to say that the league concerned could vary the points deduction if the player was ineligible because an ITC had not been obtained. If ever a law was retrospectively amended to fit the decision, this was it.

At the next home game, on Easter Monday, the match sponsors made me the man of the match. I was simply the public face of a lot of activity that fans didn't see and there were far more worthy candidates, but at the time they didn't want public acknowledgement.

* * *

Afterword

You never really know why you've won these things – and I count this result as a clear victory. I'm certain that Phil French's interventions had an effect. And Siobhain McDonagh MP getting Tony Blair onside in PMQs and persuading the Sports Minister to lean on the FA. Was it the press coverage? The e-petition? The barrage of fans' letters? The penetrating logic of a leading QC? Or was it simply that common sense prevailed?

At the time I could see no valid justification within the rules for the appeal panel's decision to reduce the penalty to three points. Indeed, Turvey's argument was that the rules left no scope for any other penalty. But I was later told that as the overall authority on football regulations, the FA hearing *did* have the right to overturn the decision and impose a lighter sanction. So their view was that the penalty was disproportionate and it seems that starting their statement that the Ryman League had followed its rules was probably only a sop.[30]

Quite a few of our fans still believe that the FA has it in for us because 'they've never apologised for their chicken-hearted decision to refer the Wimbledon FC case to a commission'. I think the FA hearing's decision

---

30 Soon after the appeal panel's decision, Phil French was boarding a flight to Jamaica. He was travelling with former WFC stars Robbie Earle and Warren Barton, who were standing just behind him in the check-in queue.

At the check-in desk the attendant said, 'Are you Phil French? The man who helped AFC Wimbledon in their appeal?' 'Yes, I am.' 'Okay, would you like to be bumped up to first-class – and thank you from a Dons fan.' And so Phil travelled first-class while the much more recognisable Wimbledon legends were left in business. As he said, 'I've never been recognised before, or since, and don't expect to be. But that was one of my all-time favourite moments.'

gives the lie to that viewpoint. Personally, I've always found FA staff and executives to be helpful, friendly, highly professional and, my gut tells me, willing to go a little bit further to help because of what happened to us, what we've since done, and how we've gone about it. But there's one area where they continue to get things wrong and this chapter is the right place to raise it.

In September 2019, Grays Athletic were beating Heybridge Swifts 5-1 in an FA Trophy tie when they brought substitute Frankie Hession-Harris on to the pitch for 11 minutes. He had joined them after playing for two other English non-league teams. He played for one of those teams in the previous year's FA Trophy. Those 11 minutes were his only appearance for Grays.

His next club decided to ask the FA about an ITC. It turned out that he had registered but not played for a college team in America over a year before. None of Hession-Harris's other clubs had applied for an ITC but it was Grays who suffered. They were thrown out of the FA Trophy and lost their prize money from that game, plus any proceeds they'd have made from the next round.

Frankie played 11 minutes in a game that was already won. He never *played* abroad. I am sure that most football people would think this is grossly unfair and heavy-handed. I understand that the FA is reviewing its competitions rule after years of draconian punishments of this type. It's about time.

One final point. The Combined Counties League policy is that if we had made our mistake in their league the breach of the rules in the first game would have been seen as our fault. They would regard subsequent breaches as their fault, because they're sent the team sheets and can check. Food for thought for other leagues.

Meanwhile, while all this was going on, the team's form had shown an upturn.

26

REFLECTIONS

THE ANNOUNCEMENT that the FA and the Ryman League were charging us with fielding an ineligible player seemed to galvanise the team and they went on a run of four successive wins. By the time of the Ryman League hearing we were in fourth place, only three points behind the league leaders, Margate.

If the 18-point deduction was applied we would slump to 12th place. So there was no real concern about a possible relegation battle but based on the previous season we would need at least 38 points from our last 15 games to win a place in the play-offs. That sort of run might well have been possible in our Combined Counties days, but it wasn't credible in this league. Our season seemed to be over.

I made one of my very rare forays into the dressing room to tell the players not to worry about the points deduction as we'd sort that out. They should focus on winning points because it would matter when we got the sanction reversed. Either I sounded more confident than I felt or they were very polite because I was taken aback to get a round of applause. Much more significantly, the good run continued as we won three and drew two of the next games. Because the league table wouldn't be adjusted until our appeal had been heard, at the end of that run we were two points clear at the top. However, as the appeal loomed our form fell away and after a mixed bag of results we finished fifth, well short of the league title. Nonetheless, we had secured a play-off place.

Had three points not been deducted we'd have had a sudden-death home tie against Chelmsford City. Instead, we were to play away at

Bromley. We went into the game full of confidence and dominated play until Wes Daly committed two silly fouls in quick succession, the second of them right under the referee's nose. Wes was sent off, leaving us 55 minutes to play with a man short.

We more than held our own until the 57th minute when Bromley took the lead and from that moment onwards the game slipped from our grasp. And so, for the second year running we'd lost a play-off game to a team we'd beaten twice in the league.

The Bromley boardroom has a large window looking out directly on to the pitch. I am a terrible loser but you've got to go into the boardroom and congratulate your opponents. As I stood there, disappointment gnawing away at me, I glanced out of the window. Across the pitch I saw Dave, sitting alone in the dugout, leaning forward, hands on his knees and head down.

Dave knew what was coming. That must have made it all the harder for him to go into the dressing room and thank the team, knowing that they knew it too. He sought me out after the game and we spoke briefly but that wasn't the right time or place. Arguably it would have been braver to have the conversation there and then, face to face, but first I wanted to reconfirm with the board that it was time for a change.

It's impossible not to like Dave. And that made the next day's conversation all the harder. But it was time for a change and his deal couldn't have been clearer; he had to deliver two promotions in three years and he'd not done it.

We published the standard stuff on our website about how grateful we were to Dave for the job he'd done and that we'd reluctantly decided it was time for a change. It's very rare for a club's website to say anything different when a manager leaves. I'd like to have added, 'This time we really mean it.' He had brought more structure and discipline, brought in good players, helped us to move to a better training ground and changed the culture to make us a generally more professional club.

A few days after Dave left we advertised for a new manager. We also spent some time taking stock. Ivor and I had a long conversation where we shared our worries that if we stayed in the Ryman League much longer all our momentum would be lost. At best we'd stagnate. At worst we would start to fall back. So it was critical to get the next appointment right.

I've stayed in touch with Dave over the years and he is an occasional but very welcome visitor to our games. As part of my preparation for writing this book I spent many hours with him. Eileen said all she could hear from the other end of the house was his laugh. I estimate that only about 25 per cent of what we talked about was relevant to this book; the rest was just enjoying his company and exchanging tales about football, managers and Northern Ireland. Some of the stories made their way into this book and some, well I wouldn't dare include them.

After he left us he eased himself back by helping his friend Simon Lane at Windsor before accepting the manager's job at St Albans – 'the worst decision I've ever made and my first ever bad experience with a chairman'. After spells at Northwood (his local club), Slough and Harrow Borough, Dave retired from football management in 2015. He was lured back (or, as he puts it, 'set up by Stuart Cash', one of his successors at Wimbledon) to spend a season and a bit as manager at Chertsey Town. When he took over they were in a relegation position. He kept them up and the next season won the league by 13 points and won the 2019 FA Vase at Wembley, the first time a Combined Counties League club has ever done that. I was in the crowd with Ivor and Terry Brown, his successor at Wimbledon, and when, three minutes before the end of extra time, Quincy Rowe scored the goal of the game to seal the win, we were up out of our seats cheering like everyone else.

It was in the context of this subsequent success that we talked about how he felt looking back at his time at AFC Wimbledon. I asked Dave if he'd ever thought he might not win the league in the first season: 'Yes, every minute of every day – that's how I am as a manager. You have to back your judgement but I worried about it all the time. I remember once when I was at Hendon we were three- or four-nil up at half-time and saying to Jon Turner as we left the pitch, "We can't lose this, can we?"'

I suggested that at previous clubs he'd had limited money and therefore organisation was essential to make up for not having the best players in the league. The first priority was to set up not to lose and it felt to me that was what he did for us, too. As a result, in his first season in the Ryman Premier League we lost six games – fewer than any other team, but we drew 15 and only came fourth. Looking back, was he over-cautious?

'Absolutely, that's what I got out of it. When I'd left Wimbledon, I used to go and spend time with Dean Brennan [the Wealdstone manager] at half-time and after the game. When I saw him on the front foot, Kevin Keegan-ish, I'd think, "Why didn't I do that?" I was scared of getting beat and you have to be different at a club like Wimbledon. You have to be more "go and win it" and get the players to do that.'

When I talked with Matt Everard he suggested I ask Dave if he ever enjoyed his time at AFC Wimbledon. Was he too intense? 'Absolutely. I interviewed Dean Brennan for my podcast, *The Non League Gaffer Tapes*. I'd brought Dean to the club but he was injured and it was a disaster. Dean said, "You changed at Wimbledon. You got too intense for the players." So when I was sacked the first feeling was relief. I remember briefly thinking "if only this or that" but that's not me and it didn't last long. And I also felt that I didn't want to ever get that intense again.

'When I went to Chertsey I decided this is going to be different and it won't take over my life. I retired again after we won the Vase, a decision I'd made some months earlier. Some time later I was leaving a game at Wealdstone and I heard someone say "he won the Vase for Chertsey". That was the first time in ten years I'd overheard someone refer to me as anything other than "the AFC Wimbledon manager". I liked that.'

And so he should. Even then, AFC Wimbledon stayed close to his heart, literally, as we saw at Wembley. After lifting the FA Vase he came to salute the fans behind the goal and, spotting a few Dons fans, he unzipped his tracksuit top to reveal an AFC Wimbledon polo shirt underneath.

With his subsequent experience would he have done things differently? 'You wonder if the job came up at the right time. That was the only time I was ever going to get the job but realistically I'd have loved that moment to have come right now. I'd be much better prepared.'

27

THE HISTORY BOYS

I WASN'T going to write about the franchise,[31] as they are usually referred to by Dons fans. We are proud of what we've done and want to be regarded in the light of what we've achieved, rather than be measured by comparison to any other club. For that reason we've always resisted being defined by our relationship, or lack of a relationship, with them. However, I realise that the subject intrigues many people so I have reluctantly decided to write about the times our paths have crossed, both on and off the pitch.

After we re-formed a lot of people would say, 'I bet you can't wait to play them.' This completely misunderstood us. They aren't our rivals and our games against them aren't derbies. While it is satisfying to beat them, a win doesn't prove anything, nor does a defeat. In short, our issue with them has never been about football. We believe it is more about fairness and what we see as lack of concern for the community from which they uprooted WFC, while themselves espousing the importance of community.

In 2002, the WFC chairman Charles Koppel had not expected the FA Commission to rule in their favour and so there were no detailed plans in place to move to Milton Keynes. Trying to put a brave face on the negative publicity, he talked about '50 per cent of current Wimbledon fans... [continuing]... to support the club at their new home in Milton

—

31 We believe that they've no right to the name 'Dons' and I won't be using it when talking about them. For the purposes of this book I will principally use 'Milton Keynes' or MK.

Keynes'. They would never accept this but we estimate that no more than 50 WFC fans transferred their allegiance and stuck with it.

Unable to move until a temporary home was ready at the National Hockey Stadium, WFC continued to play at Selhurst Park, home of Crystal Palace. Their first game after the FA Commission's decision was in August 2002 at home to Gillingham and was marked by 'The Party at the Park' held by Dons fans to say goodbye to the club that would eventually be renamed Milton Keynes. Simon Wheeler and press officer Kevin Rye, respectively WISA's chair and press officer, spent considerable time making sure the event was well organised and, crucially, peaceful.

About 2,000 Dons fans attended but refused to enter the ground. The event got national coverage thanks to Kevin's assiduous work in corralling the media to attend. It was a huge success, moving the BBC's Garth Crooks to say on live TV, 'The football was an irrelevance. The result today was clear: AFC Wimbledon 1, Wimbledon FC 0.' The official attendance was 2,476 but was actually closer to 600. The announced figure included season ticket applications, the overwhelming majority of which had been withdrawn following the FA Commission's decision; the figure was so ludicrous it moved Crooks to describe it as 'creative accounting'.

The comprehensive disowning of the skeleton of WFC meant that within a couple of months they were playing in front of a crowd of 849, including 211 Rotherham supporters, roughly 200 complimentary tickets given to players' friends and relatives, and the members of Wimbledon's junior teams, who mostly spent the match watching a Champions League game on the TV in the bar. Plus a larger-than-average press contingent, who were there, overwhelmingly, to mock, as indeed did the PA announcer who asked everyone to turn off their mobile phones, as a ring tone echoing around the empty stands might distract the players.

In September 2003, they moved into the National Hockey Stadium. By then they were a very different club. A few months earlier the franchised club had been put into administration and they sold any player who could command a transfer fee. That implied that relegation would follow and it did. Starting the 2003/04 season with one win and one draw from their first 13 games, relegation was confirmed on 6 April 2004, a few days before we won our first promotion at Walton Casuals.

They were relegated to what is now known as League 1, still five levels above us. It was a far cry from Koppel's announcement to the press three days after the FA Commission decision that they were looking at a shortlist of five managers, one of whom 'they hope will lead them back into the Premiership within three years'. They dropped the WFC name at the end of that season and renamed themselves Milton Keynes Dons.

In June 2005, in pursuit of legitimacy, the MKD Supporters Association applied for membership of the Football Supporters' Federation. In advance of their annual conference the FSF committee circulated a resolution to admit them, after first adding a clause that the MKDSA should only achieve membership after the Football League had changed its rules to prevent any further franchising.

WISA had been given early warning about the proposal and submitted an amendment to the resolution, stating that the MKDSA should not be admitted to membership until the WFC history and honours were returned to AFC Wimbledon 'and/or the community of Wimbledon'. Determined to thwart the MKDSA's plans, a hardy band of about a dozen WISA members piled into a minibus and sped down the M4 to the conference venue, just outside Cardiff.

Simon Wheeler, the WISA chair, was one of the organisers of the plan to scupper the MKDSA's ambitions. He recalls, 'We handed out anti-franchising wristbands and I told our committee member Sean Fox that he should speak on WISA's behalf and talk about what it meant to him as a supporter. If I'd done the talking it would have been rather corporate but here was someone who would speak as a football supporter – "Look what they did to us, how would you feel if it was your club?"'

Sean spoke with passion, and thanks to his speech the amended motion was carried by about 90 votes to ten. Simon continues, 'It was all very emotional. The item was first on the agenda and our lot disappeared once the vote was done – they'd only gone for that vote. A couple of the women went and got their nails done and most of the other members went and propped up the bar until it was time to pile into the minibus again. I felt we needed to show support for the FSF so I stayed to the end of the meeting.' And then Simon piloted them back down the M4 to London with 'We Are Wimbledon' being sung on repeat for much of the journey home.

With the MKDSA application stymied, the question for WISA was, 'What next?' By chance an opportunity presented itself almost immediately. In July 2005 Milton Keynes arranged a pre-season friendly at Carshalton Athletic at their War Memorial Sports Ground in south-west London. WISA members had not forgotten their resolution to keep protesting, so they congregated on the narrow road that leads from a leafy suburban street to Carshalton's stadium. Sean Fox was one of the protesters: 'The road to the stadium is a public highway and we stood at the junction where it met the street. The police couldn't be bothered to make us move and our presence perplexed the stewards who had no authority to move people on from a public road.' Everyone approaching the stadium was politely accosted and asked not to attend. Some turned back, some didn't.

And then a Jaguar turned in to the entrance and stopped on seeing people standing in the way. Peter Winkelman, the owner of MK, and his wife were in the car. No one moved. Being smart operators, WISA had taken the precaution of notifying the police of their intention to hold a peaceful protest on the road. They had been quiet and respectful, so the attending police declined to ask them to move saying that, on balance, it would be better if Winkelman didn't proceed. It has become part of WISA folklore that Winkelman protested that he'd taken two hours to drive to the game and Simon told him, 'Well, that's what you and your mates were saying we should do for every home game. Now you know why we didn't want you to steal our club.' He left.

In the greater scheme of things this was a minor victory, giving the protestors almost childish pleasure. But, importantly, it warmed the cockles of the WISA members' hearts and renewed their energy for the campaign to retrieve the club's history.

Simon Wheeler takes up the story, 'We didn't really know where to start trying to get the honours back so we called for a national boycott of any games involving the franchise. Sean Fox and I spent a lot of time travelling around the country talking to supporters of other clubs.'

They were always welcomed but progress was limited. Then came a point where Simon was about to go to New Zealand for a year so he decided to give it one more push. Astonishingly, four Milton Keynes friendlies were called off within a few days of each other. The pressure was telling.

Meanwhile, following the vote at the FSF AGM its chair, Malcolm Clarke, took action, as he explains, 'I decided to see if there was a way of solving this. I ended up going to the Milton Keynes stadium to meet Peter Winkelman to explore whether there was any possibility of dealing with some of the issues.

'I thought I was going to a one-to-one meeting but I was shown into the boardroom and there were seven or eight people there. I thought, "Bloody hell, who are all these people?" I always remember feeling these eyes staring through me; some appeared quite hostile because of the position the FSF had taken over various things. I sat there, like a nervous candidate going in for an interview.

'Then it got worse. At that time the FSF was using Kingsmeadow as our postal address, although we never used it as an office. Someone pointed this out to Peter Winkelman in the meeting. He clearly hadn't known and I thought I was going to be thrown out "because they're even using their address". The tone was that this guy is not in any way neutral, he's just part of them and they're even using AFC's address for their organisation. So it almost didn't get off the ground. Somehow we survived that and the meeting went ahead.'

It was agreed that the FSF would mediate a meeting between Milton Keynes, the MKDSA, the MKD Supporters Trust and WISA representatives. As chair of WISA Simon was an automatic choice to take part, but he recognised that all the MK representatives found him a total pain. If the other WISA representative was another vocal MK dissenter there would be next to no hope of getting a deal. With this in mind WISA decided to send someone who was not on MK's radar, a voice of reason and compromise.

Ross Maclagan was the obvious choice. He didn't post on The Concrete Roundabout (an MK chat site which our fans visit when they fancy winding up their fans) and he had almost no public profile. Most importantly, he would stay calm and be the voice of reason.

The club wasn't involved. We regarded WISA as almost the guerrilla wing of the club. They could do and say things we might agree with but couldn't politically say. And meeting Winkelman would have been an acknowledgement of his club's status; we weren't willing to do that.

Malcolm Clarke recruited Steven Powell to help in the negotiations. Steven was the independent assessor at the Terry Eames hearing (Chapter 14). He is an FSF employee with a background in trade union negotiations and arbitrations. Thanks to a fellow Arsenal supporter who was a partner at London law firm Nabarro, he obtained the use of three meeting rooms. The FSF thought that the professional environment should help to keep tempers cool.

Ross and Simon agreed a good cop, bad cop approach. Simon believed that Winkelman saw him as a rabid Wimbledon fan who wouldn't let things go and that people below him were just going along with him. But Ross managed to convince him that this wasn't the case and that Simon was actually one of the more liberal ones in the organisation because, unlike some, he wanted a solution. Simon was known to be very strongly against MK so if a deal could be struck with him it was highly likely he would carry WISA members with him in a vote.

The mediation started badly. Steven Powell was horrified, 'We started with what, on reflection, was a mistake. We were trying to soften the ground and get people to warm to each other and develop some sort of basic trust. So we kicked off with a plenary session but feelings were running so high that was almost the end of it.' Ross explains, 'Simon was an exceptionally bad cop and Winkelman and the MK negotiating team got into a lather every time he stated that "MK using the Dons name was a beacon of theft".

'Simon wound them all up to the point where they would threaten to walk out. At that point Malcolm and Steven would suggest an adjournment so that everyone could calm down and we split into separate break-out rooms.' Malcom Clarke says, 'It was a classic negotiating situation – the MK group was in one room and WISA was in another. Steven and I oscillated between the two.'

Steven's view was, 'The hero of the negotiations was Ross. He was totally level-headed. Simon was wonderful in his passion but he had a tendency to throw one and we had to adjourn a couple of sessions, otherwise it was going to be a walkout by the MK group.'

At each breakout Ross would speak to Winkelman or Jon Brockwell (the MKDSA chair) and agree with them that Simon had lost it again. He'd then suggest an alternative solution that might be acceptable to both parties. He commented, 'They would discuss it amongst themselves and invariably come back with the idea as their proposal.'

To everyone's surprise, Winkelman wasn't really that bothered about the history. In Malcolm's view, 'Winkelman wanted acceptance and for away fans to come to the stadium. His only interest in all the stuff he held was as a negotiating tool. He wasn't interested in it for its own sake and he wasn't giving up something he really wanted to keep. Instead, he used it as a negotiating tool to gain acceptance. In fact, it was almost the reverse

– the less association there was with Wimbledon the better in terms of the future of the football club.'

They came to a deal within two or three hours. Simon and Ross were delighted that Winkelman was willing to give up the Dons name and all the patrimony, comprising the replicas and memorabilia, was to be passed to Merton Council.

Winkelman wasn't willing to have everything passed directly to AFC Wimbledon as that, in effect, would confirm that we were the authentic club. However, it was agreed that Merton could lend the patrimony, but long-term loans could only be made within the borough. Simon was convinced this condition was Winkelman trying to mock our ambitions and was assuming we would never get into the Football League or return to Merton.

They agreed to meet again to tidy up the finer points. But when they resumed Winkelman had changed his mind about the use of the 'Dons' name and refused to drop it. He claimed that supporters were now invested in it and he had to listen to them. The irony of him listening to fans when he never did so in 2002 wasn't lost on any of the WISA and FSF delegations.

They had reached an impasse. No one moved their position for a couple of hours. Again Ross instigated a compromise. In a scene reminiscent of a gangster movie, while standing next to Pete Winkelman at the urinals, Ross suggested that he release the various trademarks, etc. to AFC Wimbledon's ownership but to do it via Merton Council – again a face-saving formality.

And so the deal was done. WISA agreed to stop campaigning for friendly games to be cancelled and not to oppose MKDSA joining the FSF. They also confirmed that they would not object to Milton Keynes seeking grants from the Football Foundation. This extra clause revealed another reason why Winkelman wanted a deal – the WISA protests were costing him money.

A little while later, Malcom Clarke stood in the middle of the pitch in the empty MK stadium while the mayor handed over the replica FA Cup. A few days later he watched while the patrimony was loaded into a van and driven down the M1 to London, with him following behind. On 27 February 2008 Merton Council held a formal launch of a display of the patrimony in the Civic Centre library. It was attended by WISA, Dons Trust and club representatives, along with Dave Beasant and Lawrie Sanchez, stars of WFC's FA Cup win, and former manager Dave Bassett.

The history had come home. Now we waited for when we would meet them on the pitch, but that is for another chapter.

28

STARTING OVER

IN APRIL 2007 I was promoted from acting chief executive to the permanent role. I persuaded the DT board that they should just appoint me, rather than go through a formal recruitment process. Board members Paul Jeater and Matt Breach were appointed to interview me and satisfy themselves that I met various criteria the DT board had laid down. As Matt Breach told me later, 'We had to do that because of the "we must look at three candidates" rule that we were bypassing. That was as far as we could bend it.'

I was still doing my matchday voluntary duties and this led to a treasured programme headline, not of my making, 'Car park attendant made chief executive'. It was also when David Cox, the Dons Trust chair, told me that I really must have a contract of employment. To be a valid contract there had to be an annual salary. I was a volunteer so he suggested a nominal £1 per annum. I negotiated him up to a guinea; I had a good agent. However, I never got round to signing the contract. Perhaps that is why I was never paid.[32]

From September 2006 when I assumed the role of acting chief executive, life had been hectic. After pursuing a commercial loan for 18 months we had finally agreed a facility with Barclays Bank for £600,000 at base rate plus 2.5 per cent. I felt that this loan was recognition of the work we'd done to establish a reputation for reliability and financial prudence. Even then

—

32 This is not entirely true. At the annual volunteer away-day at the Bristol Rovers game, Iain McNay presented me with a real gold guinea. The guinea is treasured, but the gesture much more so.

I was frankly astonished that a big bank would lend to any football club, let alone one that was only five years old and operating at the seventh level of the football pyramid. The loan enabled us to pay off the last of the debt to Old Man Khosla in November 2006, leaving a substantial sum towards the next phase of our ground development.

Since I'd been appointed we'd also had the Jermaine Darlington affair and in parallel we had to investigate the disappearance of cash from our office safe. We had strong suspicions about the identity of the culprit and decided to install CCTV in the office where the safe was located. This had to be done in secret, so the employee in question was sent on a long-distance errand one evening while the camera was installed.

A few days later I found a discrepancy in the safe cash and went to view the videotape. That was when I discovered that the camera, which was located in the ceiling in the centre of the room, was pointing straight down the cleavage of Clair Richardson, our receptionist. Fortunately, the culprit had knelt beside her desk and we were able to identify him.

I didn't tell Clair about the camera's location until 13 years later when I was preparing for this book. I wasn't sure how she would react but she was very clear, 'I want my boobs in this book.' Anything to oblige, Clair. I still have the tape and view it from time to time.[33]

In the summer, Iain McNay's company, Cherry Red Records, took up the naming rights for the stadium at an increased sponsorship. Iain is a long-term fan and this was the start of a substantial and generous stadium sponsorship that lasted until we moved out in 2020.

Despite this extra sponsorship the budgets for the coming season didn't give us enough money to support a push for promotion. So, a few days after Dave Anderson left I met Mike Richardson to talk about him continuing to put money into the club (he'd topped up our budget in Dave's second and third years). Mike promised to donate £50,000 for the coming season, 'whatever happens', i.e. with no strings attached. He also offered extra money to allow our new manager to be paid on a full-time basis. I use that specific wording because Dave once grumbled to me that it was a full-time job on a part-time wage.

Finally, Mike said he would make substantial sums of money available for spending in future years. In return, he would like 'a say' in the club. He

—

33 This is a joke.

wanted to attend a football management committee meeting (a semi-formal weekly meeting of the board) once a month; a Dons Trust board meeting every other month; to speak to me every week; and to meet the manager every other month. He also wanted 'to be involved in major decisions', defining 'involved' as being allowed to express his opinion, knowing we may not accept it. Mike really loves the club. It's not a pretence and he's always been very generous. Nonetheless, this was a problem because we weren't comfortable allowing anyone, even a long-term supporter and generous friend of the club, to buy influence.

We always seemed to have DT board meetings arranged at fortuitous moments and this week was no different, so I was able to take Mike's proposal to them. At the meeting I suggested a way of making it work. Mike could meet the manager and me for lunch two or three times a season, would get a regular phone call from me on developments at the club, and a guaranteed parking place for matchdays. He wouldn't be able to come to club or DT board meetings but from time to time he would be invited into the boardroom for away games (although he's not really into that sort of thing and I don't recall him ever taking it up). Ivor suggested we create a role of vice-president for Mike and, since he was contributing £50,000 a year, we should make it generally available at that price.

We needed to do something if we wanted to move forward in the league; we simply weren't generating sufficient money to allow us to push for the progress we wanted. Despite that, we were not willing to sell influence but we were willing to allow access in return for the additional funds. There would be fans who hated this idea and wanted us to stay 'pure' but the football club and DT boards were satisfied that this worked and remained within our ethos. And, to be blunt, Mike wasn't really getting a lot for his money.

With this extra money in our back pockets we went out to recruit a new manager. The board now comprised Ivor Heller, Nigel Higgs and me. Ivor was commercial director with a very wide brief, Nigel was primarily responsible for youth development and I was looking after finance and operations.

We were keen to learn from the previous recruitment process. Earlier in the season when we were considering making a mid-season change of manager, the board had come up with a list of 'likelies' and 'possibles'.

Within 48 hours of the play-off defeat and before we'd advertised the role all bar one of them had applied.

I'd drawn up a process, a job description and a list of qualities we were looking for in our new manager and, conscious of the problems we'd had with the DT board last time, I sent them copies. We agreed to appoint John Faulkner as our football expert. John had been a centre-half for Sutton United before being signed by Leeds United. His playing career was cut short by injury but he'd carved out a role as a coach at Luton and Norwich before retraining as a psychologist. He brought sound football knowledge and credibility to our interviews.

We moved quickly. Dave left on 2 May, the advert was placed on 6 May and by 15 May we'd made an appointment. I have the folder of applications. We had 38 candidates, including people who hadn't applied but were of interest to us. That 'people of interest' list was quite prescient; it included the two managers who succeeded Terry!

The press articles fascinated me. The *Non-League Paper* ran an article saying that Terry Brown was favourite to get the job but hedged its bets by naming eight other contenders (four of whom had applied). So when you see an article that says 'as we predicted, X got the job' remember that the first article almost certainly hedged its bets.

We whittled the list down to seven. John Faulkner and I did the first interviews. Three candidates stood out: Terry Brown, Dean Holdsworth and Graham Westley. I've still got the application letters, CVs, our interview notes and psychological profiles for each of them. It wouldn't be right to say too much but it is interesting to compare them.

Dean had played nearly 170 games for Wimbledon FC in the Premier League before being sold to Bolton Wanderers. Sam Allardyce was his manager during his time at Wanderers and Dean talked in glowing terms about how working with Sam taught him how to eke out the very best from players. He volunteered to take no wage, which was clearly attractive to us, but was also a risk because it would make it easier for him to walk away whenever he wanted to. John Faulkner liked him and recommended that we appoint him if he was willing to work with another candidate who hadn't made the final three but who we thought would be a good assistant. There was another problem. He had gone to play for MK after the FA Commission's decision. For that reason alone, some fans wouldn't have accepted him as our manager.

The file on Graham Westley is three or four times thicker than for anyone else. He was the only candidate who actually presented what we asked for, in the format we requested. He circulated a PowerPoint presentation and an equally bulky CV before we met, plus an agenda for what he wanted to tell us.

Graham had all the relevant coaching qualifications and a track record of success in non-league football. He was also a successful businessman, as managing director of his own company, AIMITA. That stands for Attitude Is More Important Than Ability, which was a philosophy he also applied in his approach to coaching.

Terry Brown was the only one to bring his proposed assistant manager, Stuart Cash. Three years earlier we'd decided Stuart wasn't quite ready for a manager's role when we appointed Dave Anderson. However, we'd marked him as someone to keep an eye on.

Terry had the clearest plan to get us promoted. He also had a good understanding of the challenges of managing a club like ours due to parallels between us and his previous club, Aldershot Town (Aldershot had a large fan base and had been forced to start again at the bottom of the football pyramid following the previous club's closure).

Terry also demonstrated detailed knowledge of our squad. This wasn't surprising. Had he stayed, Dave Anderson had planned to bring in Stuart as his assistant and make Simon Bassey his first-team coach. I told Simon that if Terry wanted him we would find the funds to employ him. Simon knew Stuart so he rang him and briefed him at length about the team and where we'd fallen short. Obviously he wanted them to win as that could help him get a coaching role.

Overall Terry was the best fit in terms of football experience and the one who showed a natural understanding of our ethos. Our only concern, and it was a substantial one, was that he'd left Aldershot in the February because his wife, Suzie, was suffering from leukaemia. In the end we decided that he was what we needed and we were willing to take the risk that he might feel he had to step back if her condition degenerated. Even though she was still in intensive care she had insisted that he apply for the job (I am delighted to say that Suzie recovered and 13 years later she still comes to games with Terry). The board offered the job to Terry and Stuart but when we told them the playing budget it was immediately clear that they were taken aback. They asked for time to consider the offer and left.

I called Mike Richardson and explained the problem. He immediately put up a further lump sum to improve the budget – with no strings attached. When I rang Terry to tell him we had found more money it was a relief to both of us. And Simon got the first-team coaching job.

As with Dave Anderson, it was interesting to hear Terry's perspective on the recruitment process when I spoke to him years later. Much of what follows was already known to me, but some of it is new.

'Suzie was still in hospital but I needed to be earning and the job sounded a perfect fit, given what we'd done at Aldershot. She insisted that I go for it. She was lucky because she was at the Royal Berks and John Radcliffe Hospital and she was under some of the best haematologists in the world. You couldn't have got much better treatment than she got under the NHS.

'My next-door neighbour, Russell Smith, is a Dons fan and he was always talking about the club. I'd be asking Russell, "What is Ivor looking for, what is Erik looking for?"

'We'd watched the team, Stuart more than I had. We were both at the play-off game at Bromley. We tried to get a gauge of which players you liked and which ones you didn't. We were careful not to say we wanted to change everything so we tried to pick the pluses we'd like to keep and wheedle out of you who you liked. Stuart had spoken to Simon Bassey and got his views too. I remember getting Mickey Haswell mixed up and saying he's all right-footed and you said he's all left-footed, so I thought I won't go into too much detail here by pretending I know something I don't.

'I couldn't see how there could be anyone with better credentials and experience than Stuart and me. We knew that scene very well and I thought "this is made in heaven for us". Stuart had a number of really good contacts and between us we felt that no one else is going to come to that interview and know more about how to get out of the Ryman.

'After the interview we got back to the pub and we weren't going to take the job. I can't remember the figure but it was nowhere near enough to get us up and nowhere near the Aldershot budget. If you've not got the money to attract players it's a poisoned chalice. Just as I was going to call you [Erik] and turn it down, you phoned up when we were still in the pub and said the budget was better.'

There were three or four turning points during my term as chief executive where something happened that changed everything. This was one of them. Mike's sponsorship, plus Iain McNay's continuing financial support, provided a base on which to build. Without them I am convinced that our progress would have stalled. As I explained earlier in this book, Old Man Khosla was an accidental hero; Iain and Mike were low-profile heroes who made the next steps possible.

So we had our new manager only two weeks after the play-off defeat.

Terry's assistant, Stuart, is possibly unique in that he was signed by two European Cup winners. Martin O'Neill took him to Wycombe Wanderers and Brian Clough signed him for Nottingham Forest when he was at his managerial peak. Almost everyone who knew Brian Clough has a story about him and while it's nothing to do with this book, I am going to crowbar Stuart's story in here, as told to me by Terry.

When Terry and Stuart were managing Aldershot they had an away midweek game at Burton Albion, then managed by Nigel Clough. Stuart spotted Nigel's dad, Brian, sitting in the stand. Stuart isn't normally fazed by very much but he wasn't sure whether to go and say 'hello'.

Terry, 'You should go and say hello. Go on.'

Stuart, 'I'm not sure.'

Terry, 'What have you got to lose?'

Stuart, 'What if he doesn't remember me?'

Terry, 'Well, walk up to him and say, "Hello, Mr Clough, I'm not sure if you remember me, but I'm Stuart Cash and I used to play for you."'

Stuart, 'Okay,' and off he went.

He walked towards Clough and said, 'Hello Mr Clough, I'm …'

Clough, 'The worst f…ing left-back I ever signed.'

Stuart returned to Terry, jubilant. 'He remembered me!'

29

WE GOTTA GET OUT OF THIS PLACE

IN THEIR interview, Terry and Stuart stressed that they thought the team wasn't big enough or strong enough. They set about putting that right.

Terry wanted to bring in strong characters. They started with Marcus Gayle, who had appeared in over 200 Premier League games for Wimbledon FC. Marcus was swiftly followed by three very experienced players in Jason Goodliffe, Rob Quinn and Jake Leberl, who had recently been a member of a Conference-winning side.

Jason Goodliffe was typical of the type of player that Terry was after. He'd played for Terry at Hayes when they came third in the Conference followed by six years at Stevenage where he'd played in an FA Trophy Final and a Conference play-off final. Now aged 32, it was time to drop down a couple of levels and go part-time. He came despite being told that he'd only be backup to the best back four in the division, but when Paul Lorraine unexpectedly left to join a higher-level club Jason stepped up and was made captain, a role he'd had wherever he played.

The risk of signing experienced players is the 'they'll piss it at this level' syndrome where players and managers assume that because they have had a good career they can continue at a lower level; quite often, their legs have gone and they can't do it at any level. So Terry was taking a risk.

He also signed some promising younger players. Tony Finn's manager at Metropolitan Police rang Terry and said, 'I've got this kid and you've got to sign him' (the days when you needed to be a policeman to play for them were long gone). On Jason Goodliffe's recommendation we also signed 19-year-old Samuel Hatton from Stevenage. Both proved to be very important players for us.

Terry insisted that our training pitches were inadequate. I asked Simon to do some research and Terry, Stuart and I piled into Simon's taxi and visited three potential sites. We arrived unannounced at the Kings College training ground, a mile from Kingsmeadow, and less than an hour later we left with the outlines of a deal agreed. Thirteen years later we're still there and have gradually taken over more and more of the space.

And so to the pre-season programme. While at Aldershot, Terry had over-trained his squad and by the time of the first game of the season several were injured. He was obsessed with avoiding a recurrence and his definition of a successful pre-season was that no one was injured.

The change of manager to someone who'd 'been there and done it' generated lots of excitement among the fans, reflected in record season ticket sales. But if the fans were expecting free-flowing football they were going to be disappointed. Simon Bassey says, 'When I was playing, Terry's teams were big and strong and horrible and his team were Herberts but when he came to Wimbledon he'd completely changed. His teams had always been a bit thuggy, strong, aggressive, big drinkers, but he'd gone to Aldershot and changed his philosophy of how he wanted to play. He was a bit older and had gone through personal stuff. He was a completely different person, very calm, quite measured and never really shouted at anyone.'

Terry saw it much the same, but less bluntly: 'At Hayes we were the biggest, strongest most route one team you'd ever seen. We used to play four, five or six centre-halves and it was about not getting beat at all costs, very much defensive-minded coaching.

'I'd built this big ugly side because the Ryman League was not about two-touch football and it still isn't. Coming in to Wimbledon we used the same scenario, big strong and ugly to get out of the Ryman.'

Despite an opening-day victory against Ramsgate the season started inauspiciously. If Terry was in any doubt about the fans' expectations they were made clear at our second home game, a disappointing draw against Staines. He says, 'We were about three games into the season and this man shouted "rubbish Brown" and boshed his season ticket at me. I'm thinking, "We're three games in, behave yourself," but that's the effect of passion.'

Proven goalscorer Richard Butler was still injured and Terry had transfer-listed Richard Jolly who wasn't available to take part in much pre-season training and so wasn't match fit. And then he missed a game for a stag party. Terry was seriously unimpressed, 'Richard Butler would run through a brick wall for you, but Jolly wouldn't run through tracing paper.' We were struggling and after nine games we were 15th.

The FA Cup draw offered a chance of a morale-boosting win at Debenham Leisure Centre FC in Suffolk, a team three levels below us whose previous record attendance was 189. The venue reminded me of Sandhurst, our very first competitive game, because there was just a single crush barrier around the pitch but with a banked-up grass area behind one goal. Such arrangements allow fans to be far closer to management and players than normal and this led to two incidents. The first came at half-time. We were winning 1-0 but the fans were expecting to see us hand out a thrashing, so Terry got some close-up abuse from behind the dugout. 'We'd had them watched – they were big, strong and horrible and we matched them up. Some fans didn't seem to like that,' he says. We went on to win 5-1.

The second incident was when Danny Webb scored our fifth and final goal. He stood, facing the crowd, arms aloft, giving it large. But the fans were close enough for one to call out, 'Danny, Danny, they've disallowed it. You were offside.' Webb's face crumpled for a few seconds until he realised he'd been had. Laughing at what he described as 'great banter', he waded into the crowd to shake the hand of the mischief-maker. That would be John, my younger son. The moment was captured by club photographer Paul Willatts and it is one of my favourite pictures from my time with the club. You don't get that sort of thing at Premier League games.

The signing of midfield player Mark DeBolla was the catalyst for an improvement in form and we rose to third place, albeit nine points behind the league leaders, Chelmsford. They were the big spenders in our division so a resounding 4-0 win against them in the Trophy was seen as a sign that the team was gelling.

And then we signed Jon Main. Everybody knew about Jon. Tonbridge Angels had signed him mid-season a couple of years earlier and after taking a while to settle in he scored 44 goals the following season, including seven hat-tricks. He'd started the current season with a goal a game but

Tonbridge were struggling and they'd sacked their manager, Tony Dolby, the man who'd signed Jon.

We had watched him and Terry had mixed feelings. He decided to get a second opinion. He says, 'I rang Tony Dolby and said, "What's the SP with Mainy? Shall I go and sign him?" and I catalogued the things he couldn't do. "He can't head a ball, he can't trap a ball, he doesn't hold on to it, he can't play with his back to goal." Tony stopped me and said, "Do you want someone to score you 40 goals a season?" I go "well yea, of course I do" and he said, "Well go and sign him then, he'll score you the goals. Things will bounce off him, this ain't right, that ain't right, but he'll score you the goals." And that was it – and he was right.'

I called Nick Sullivan, the Tonbridge chairman. He'd promised Jon that if a decent offer came in he could go. By then Jon had caught wind of our interest and had asked his new manager what was going on. Sullivan told me that his manager was pissed off because he felt we had made an illegal approach to Jon. I said, 'Okay, that's not how we do things. Shall I call it off?' Nick said that wasn't fair on Jon, so after haggling for a while we settled on a fee of £20,000, which was easily a record for us, plus a pre-season friendly and a sell-on clause of 20 per cent.

The only problem was that we didn't have the money! I explained that I just needed to confirm that the funds were in place and we agreed that he would honour the deal so long as we confirmed in writing within 48 hours. I'd taken the precaution of checking the idea in principle with Mike Richardson and Iain McNay and very soon they'd each committed to paying half the fee and the deal was sealed.

There was one other condition. Tonbridge were struggling and they insisted that Jon must play in their game the following Tuesday – which was against us. Terry told Jason Goodliffe, our tough-tackling centre-half, that he mustn't kick Jon because we were going to sign him after the game. This was a first for Jason who was bemused by the idea. He says, 'I played for Terry for eight or nine seasons and he'd only ever told me to whack the centre-forward, so to suddenly be told whatever you do, don't injure the centre-forward was a funny one really. I found Mainy a real nuisance in the first half, chasing lost causes and keeping the ball in. I thought, "This kid is signing for us and he's trying to get one over us." By the second half I didn't care what Terry had said and I left one on him and said a few things to him while he was lying on the floor.'

Jon only found out later that Jason had been told not to kick him, as he recalls, 'But he did in the end. He was getting fed up. He said it was the most unreal experience of his life but he said I was quick and nimble and in the end he said "no, I can't do this anymore" and he larrupped me a few times.'

After the game, Nick Sullivan led us to a small room, just off the main bar. It was just Jon, Terry and me. As Jon saw it, 'Terry was fuming because he'd lost a 2-0 half-time lead [we drew 2-2 and Jon scored]. Obviously, I was desperate to get to the club. I was shocked at Terry's first offer as it was more or less what I was on at Tonbridge. I was thinking £300 a week doesn't make sense. But you were fine and I was thinking if I'd had Erik on my own I'd have got more.'

No he wouldn't. Terry and I had agreed what we were prepared to pay before we went into the room. We played good cop, bad cop and for once I got to be the good cop – and we got away with a bit less than we expected. This was a reversal of my usual role where the manager would talk about me in what we referred to as 'the mad axeman in the attic' approach. 'I'll never get that sort of deal past our chairman. He just won't spend that sort of money.' Or, sensing a good deal, 'I'll try that on the chairman and see what he thinks – I might be able to swing it with him but he can be very difficult.'

We sealed the deal by giving Jon a £100 goal bonus, double what he was on at Tonbridge. Jon travelled to training on the Thursday night, taken aback by the length of the journey, 'I didn't realise how far the ground was from my house!' There was a slightly awkward introduction to Jason Goodliffe, who had so enthusiastically kicked him only two nights earlier, but they quickly became great team-mates. Jason's take on Jon is interesting, 'If you saw him in training you would never play him on Saturday. Technically he's not great and he's not a good trainer but you knew that if you gave him a sniff of goal he would score. He was only interested in scoring goals.'

Jon settled in quickly and had scored seven goals in 11 league games when he broke a metatarsal against, ironically, Tonbridge. It seemed he was out for the season and his injury looked like it had killed our slim title chances; we were now third in the league but 15 points behind Chelmsford, albeit with a couple of games in hand.

Shortly afterwards we were knocked out of the FA Trophy by high-flying Conference team Torquay United, for whom our former player

Roscoe Dsane scored – the immutable law of the ex, once again. The game was most notable for it being the first official engagement of Lord Triesmann, the newly appointed chairman of the FA. I thought it was a nice touch to come to a non-league game first but I was told later it put a few noses out of joint in the organisation.

We were missing Jon's goals so Terry signed Luis Cumbers on loan from Gillingham. He duly delivered with three goals in his first four games. We began to think we had an outside chance of the title and went to Heyridge Swifts on a good run, only for it to come to a juddering halt when Reggie Savage, who'd been on loan with us earlier in the season, scored two goals, in that immutable sort of way.

There was perhaps one last chance. By the time we went to play at Chelmsford we were eight points behind them with only eight games to go. We had to win and with ten minutes left it looked like we would, until two late goals killed us.

Jason Goodliffe was very clear where the fault lay. Luke Garrard had scored a penalty to put us 2-1 up and, over-excitedly, went to taunt the Chelmsford bench. Jason recalls, 'I'd been trying to get him to concentrate and get back into position. They went round him and scored and then did the same thing again, so the two goals came down his side. After the game I got him by the throat up against the wall.'

I never enjoyed going to Chelmsford. If I'm honest that was partly because they were a good team and very likely to beat us. But also, the pitch was surrounded by an athletics track and even though they'd developed a terrace that rolled forward across the track, it just lacked atmosphere. And it struck me as bizarre for a club with a decent following to have all the concession stalls covered in West Ham memorabilia.

The presence of an athletics track meant that there was more than usual space behind the goal. As a result, a mis-hit shot was likely to travel well beyond the pitch. It was the days before multi-ball and so they used several ball boys who seemed to retrieve the ball incredibly quickly if they were losing, while looking busy but somehow taking much longer when they were winning. Nonetheless, there's no denying they were better than us and worthy champions.

This setback seemed to cause a drop-off in form because we then won only three of our last seven games and, thanks to a late run by Staines Town, we yielded second place to them in the final league table.

Furthermore, Gillingham had recalled Luis Cumbers so we'd lost our goalscoring potential.

I'd imagined that as we rose through the leagues we would stop the enormous turnover of players but Terry was determined not to be short of backup. He explained to *Football Hurts*, 'Play-offs are a relatively new phenomenon and I said to Erik, "I need loads and loads of cover. I might not have to call on it, but I need it." We were able to go out and get in three young players, and a couple of scholars. That might have cost us an extra few thousand pounds but that is money well spent. It's a lesson well learned and it's a lesson that I would always use again because play-offs are part and parcel of football now.'[34]

On 31 March, the transfer deadline day, Terry did indeed sign five players on 28-day loans with a clause that we could extend if we reached the play-offs. The incoming players included a welcome return for Luis Cumbers plus Nic McDonnell, scorer of the Bromley goal that defeated us in the previous year's play-offs. Nic was a striking-looking man and knew it, hence his nickname around the club quickly became 'Chocolate' after Archie Gemmill's famous remark about Graeme Souness, 'If he was a chocolate drop he'd eat himself.'

Meanwhile, we'd lost Antony 'Frankie' Howard, one of the best centre-backs in the league and a hugely popular figure with fans and players alike. He'd been offered a life-changing job in America but to accept it he had to leave in April. This sort of thing isn't so unusual at non-league level, where players have full-time jobs and family commitments to meet. In our first season Neil Robson had missed a midweek game because he had a parents' evening to go to. My mantra has always been 'family first' so we hadn't argued with Neil and nor did we try to persuade Frankie to stay longer. But it was a blow.

Before the play-offs there was one more distraction. Some years earlier the FA had tripped up by allowing a suite at Wembley to be named and promoted as 'The Corinthian' without first clearing it with Corinthian-

---

34 Nuts TV didn't last long but they produced the *Football Hurts* series which documented the ups and downs of our season. Terry really didn't want to do it, fearing that they'd only be looking for 'a Peter Reid moment' where, in a half-time rant lasting 40 seconds, Peter managed to swear 23 times. So we negotiated a 'take-it-or-leave-it' deal in which we had editorial rights to remove anything we didn't like. Every week Ivor and I were sent the programme rushes. We never once had to ask them to change anything.

Casuals, the highest-ranked genuinely amateur club in the pyramid. To make amends the FA agreed that Casuals could play a game at Wembley and they had very kindly invited us to be their opponents. As a result, the day after a league game and just over two weeks before the play-offs, we were playing at Wembley. Looking at it coldly, we were foolhardy to accept a game during the run-up to the end of the season, but when it was offered it looked too good an opportunity to miss and it allowed some players to play at Wembley who wouldn't otherwise ever have been able to do so.

We took on all the admin, wrote and produced the programme, promoted the game and sold the tickets. All the proceeds went to Casuals who used it to extend and refurbish their changing rooms. The one exception was that we kept the money we raised from a raffle for one of our fans to take the field for part of the game. Mario 'Mazza' Rajakone got a good 15 minutes on the pitch for an experience he'll never forget. And we had the bizarre sight of a crowd of just over 5,000 watching two non-league teams play a friendly game at the magnificent new stadium.

Wembley didn't cover themselves in glory by indicating that there would be pay-on-the-day facilities and then failing to offer them. Ivor and I managed to smuggle a couple of fans into the game after they had travelled some distance but others were turned away. We won 8-1 and I was delighted for Marcus Gayle to score at Wembley. Simon Bassey also persuaded Terry to let him have a run-out and he duly maintained his record of never scoring for us. The largest cheer of the day was for Casuals' late goal, underlining the stewards' crass insistence that the fans be segregated.

The other good thing to come out of the game was that Jon Main was back and ready to play, if not match fit. Terry underlined his importance to us, 'He's a non-league diamond. His goalscoring record at this level is second to none. I've come to the conclusion with Mainy [that he should] go where he likes. He has an instinct, a knack that you can't coach. He's got a natural ability to be in the right place at the right time so we'd say to the other forwards, "You make your runs off Mainy," because I'd put my house on Mainy being in the right place at the right time.'

After the Casuals game we lost at home to Harlow and with that went our chance of coming second. One of the main frustrations was that we had won only one and drawn two of our eight matches against the bottom four teams. We finished in third place and had a home semi-final with AFC Hornchurch. A disappointing crowd of nearly 3,000 saw us take an early lead through Luis Cumbers and just before half-time Jon Main reminded us what we'd been missing when he doubled our advantage. We had blown enough half-time leads in the season to avoid taking anything for granted and sure enough Hornchurch pulled a goal back in the 75th minute to leave us with 15 nail-biting minutes.

They piled on the pressure and then, right on full time, Luke Garrard cleared the ball off our line. It broke to Steve Ferguson who slipped it to Jon Main about ten yards inside our half. Hornchurch had nearly all gone forward in search of an equaliser but there were still 60 yards and two defenders between Jon and their goal. And he was exhausted, having barely played for two months. But off he set and the player who Terry said 'can't beat a man' went past both of the defenders and, totally ignoring the screams of Tony Finn to pass it to him, hit the ball under the goalkeeper for a decisive third goal. As Terry saw it, 'It's one of them goals where it builds up – he's beaten one man, he's beaten two men and he was knackered by the time he got to shoot past the goalie. He wasn't 100 per cent fit, he'd only just recovered. It was a great, great goal.'

Almost all of the 3,000 crowd can still conjure up the goal and the cathartic release of seeing the ball hit the back of the net. There's little more satisfying in football than a late winner and we all celebrated wildly, including Terry who was captured on *Football Hurts*, racing up and down the touchline when the goal went in, not knowing how or where to release the pent-up tension.

I asked Jon why he didn't pass to Tony Finn who could have simply rolled the ball into the net. He looked at me as if I was stupid and then just said, 'never crossed my mind'. The best strikers are arrogant. Face to face he is self-effacing but on the pitch I've never seen anyone more certain of himself.

Staines came second in the league and won their semi-final so they were entitled to be at home for the final. Their owner and chairman Alan Boon tried to be as accommodating as possible and offered us 1,500 tickets, but even that was less than the number of our season ticket holders. Then he suffered a backlash from local fans and had to reduce the offer to 1,000. Spare tickets were as rare as hens' teeth although reportedly about 60 per cent of the queue for home tickets comprised Dons fans in mufti.

Terry gathered the players at Kingsmeadow for a final training session. His team talk was straightforward, 'It truly is the biggest game of the year – it's not manager speak is it. We're going to be disciplined, we're going to be well organised and we go into the final game of the season without any excuse in the world. We've got a fantastic squad of players. I don't want to offer an excuse. I would never offer an excuse because we're going to win on Saturday.'

The starting team was obvious but with a much-strengthened squad Terry agonised over who should go on the bench. When we signed Jon Main we changed our formation to accommodate him and as a result Mark DeBolla, who had started so well for us back in October, found himself out of the team. He went on loan to Bromley where he was sent off. In those days, bans didn't start immediately and while he waited for his ban to start he was sent off again. In total he was banned for four games and Bromley only had three left to play. So his season seemed to be over.

There was some tension between Terry and Mark but Simon Bassey argued that Mark should be added to the squad, 'I said we've got to put him on the bench. Look at his goals, look at his assists, and so Terry agreed.' I've always left managers alone before big games as they've got more to worry about than chatting to me, so I didn't know Mark was in the squad until I saw the team sheet, an hour before kick-off. Heavily sensitised by the Jermaine Darlington affair, I didn't want to see us win the play-off final and be kicked out for fielding a banned player. I immediately cornered David Charles, who had succeeded Trevor Williams[35] as club secretary, and demanded that he promise me that Mark was okay to play.

David went grey. He disappeared while I paced up and down fretting. After what seemed an age David returned. He had managed to get hold of the Bromley secretary who confirmed that Mark had served three games of his four-game ban. And because he had returned to us at the end of the season the Hornchurch semi-final game counted as the last game of his ban. If he came on as a substitute we were okay.

Lionel Meade, our scout, had told me that Staines looked 'leggy'. They'd had a good run in the FA Cup and as a result they had to catch up on postponed matches and ended up playing nine times in April. Lionel

35 Although Trevor stood down as club secretary he has remained actively involved with the club as a volunteer, acting as joint kit man with Robin Bedford, as well as assisting Terry and all our subsequent managers in a wide range of ways.

was adamant that if we were still in the game after 60 minutes, they'd run out of steam and we'd win. So when I saw it was going to be a very hot day I welcomed it because I thought it would deplete their energy reserves all the more quickly.

In fact, for much of the first half it was us who looked weary. Our normally solid-as-a-rock centre-backs, Jason Goodliffe and Marcus Gayle, looked vulnerable. The game was end-to-end and both sides were grateful to their goalkeepers for keeping them on terms. After about 25 minutes Jon Main pursued a long ball and was bearing down on goal when the Staines captain, Matt Flitter, brought him down outside the penalty area. The Dons fans howled for a red card but the referee, rightly in my view, only showed yellow. Ten minutes later Flitter added insult to injury when he scored from a corner. That wasn't the last impact he had on the game, however.

Terry almost always makes his first substitution after 60 minutes so it was a shock to see Nic McDonnell brought on immediately after half-time. Still we struggled to break through until, as Jason Goodliffe recalls, 'In the last 15 to 20 minutes it was like a switch being turned off and they were running out of energy.' Terry had brought on Mark DeBolla and then Sam Hatton as the last of his substitutes. As he did so he heard former kit man Dennis Lowndes shout from behind the dugout, 'You'll be judged on your substitutions, Brown.'

In the 80th minute I turned to Ivor and said, 'I think it's slipping away,' and started bracing myself to be gracious (I am a terrible loser) in the boardroom. Then we equalised. A long throw from Sam Hatton was fumbled under pressure by the keeper and McDonnell quickly swivelled and crossed the ball for Luis Cumbers to score with a diving header. The Staines players went mad as they claimed that McDonnell had fouled their keeper but I've watched the goal many times and I'm sure he dropped the ball because he was nudged by his own centre-back, Matt Flitter, he of the nearly-red card. Karma?

Two minutes later we won a free kick about 25 yards from goal and up stepped Mark DeBolla. He recalls, 'I was told to take all the set pieces. I remember the free kick very well. I just had a feeling – I felt really confident.

'I think Nick McDonnell was on the end of the wall, where I wanted to put the ball. I told him to move. I sent the ball round the inside of the wall, where he'd been standing, into the corner of the net. I ran to Bassey, as I felt he'd been my champion amid all my troubles, and jumped on him.'

Even though Staines had retained more than half the tickets for their fans, it was obvious from the noise that Dons supporters were everywhere. As Staines regrouped for the kick-off, Iain McNay leaned forward to ask me how long to go and I said '300 seconds'. One by one we counted them down until the final whistle went and the fans invaded the pitch. All three substitutes had had a hand in one or other of the goals. If Terry was indeed to be measured by his substitutions then he'd passed with flying colours.

My first reaction is always to text any member of my family who can't be there. So I immediately texted our elder son who was travelling in Asia and my sister who's always taken an interest in us. When you win a play-off your phone goes off like a machine gun with so many texts you can't keep up. The most treasured one was from my younger son who was at the game. It just said, 'Well done, Dad'.

After the presentations the team climbed on to the bus to return to Kingsmeadow. For the first time in years I travelled with them. Jason Goodliffe remembers the journey well, 'As we came round into the car park the sea of blue and yellow was unbelievable. I felt like I was at a proper club. There were thousands and thousands of blue and yellow. You said to me, "Jason, I want you to be first off the coach." No sooner did I get to the door than I got carried off holding the trophy. It was a brilliant feeling.'

The celebrations went on late into the night. I'm teetotal so I stayed out of the bar. I'm not against drinking, I just don't like the taste, but I've never understood why it's necessary to get drunk to enjoy the success. If I'd had the choice of how to celebrate I'd have asked for a DVD of the game and gone home to watch it again. Instead I sat on one of the concrete bollards in the car park watching everyone being happy and thinking, this is why we do this.

We could breathe easy for a few months. Marc Jones, one of the club's four founders, expressed it very well: 'I said to Mark DeBolla after the game, we're all going to have a brilliant summer now just because he kicked a ball into the net. And that's football for you.'

Terry added, 'Football is a very humbling experience. As a manager at the play-off game on Saturday I'm ten minutes away from being the biggest doughnut in the world after wasting a year of the fans' lives. Or you come back and win and you're a hero.'

On the Monday after the game, Terry Brown released eight players. Mark DeBolla, scorer of the winning play-off final goal and bringer of happiness to fans all summer, was one of them. And, fittingly, Marcus Gayle retired to bring down the curtain on his long and illustrious career with a promotion.

Shortly after this we paid one last visit to the Ryman League awards dinner where we were presented with the play-off winners' trophy and Alan Boon, the Staines owner and generous as ever, delivered a congratulatory bottle of champagne to our table.

I will leave the last word on the season to Terry, 'The title *Football Hurts* summed up the season a lot of the time. I'm now going to enjoy myself for the summer and chill out and get out the Grecian 2000 and come back refreshed for the new year.'

30

THIS LAND IS YOUR LAND

WHILE THE team was battling to get out of the Ryman Premier League we were working to resolve a serious constraint on our ability to gain admission to the Football League.

When Old Man Khosla (OMK) bought the lease from the administrator he didn't bother buying the strip of land that ran behind the north and east stands. The lease on this land had been granted to Kingstonian (Ks) by Kingston Council to enable them to expand if they reached the Football League.

We had cast covetous eyes on that land from the moment we bought Kingsmeadow and now the time was ripe to try to acquire it. Below the Football League the FA specifies ground regulations, arranged by Step – you will recall that Step 1, then the Conference National league, is one promotion away from the Football League.

The regulations cover a host of things, including the length of any lease, the minimum capacity, minimum numbers of places under cover and seats, the size of the pitch, the brightness of the floodlights, requirement for pitch-side barriers, etc.

It was 2008 and we had just been promoted to the Conference South, Step 2, for which Kingsmeadow comfortably exceeded the FA's Ground Category requirements. But we were looking longer term. We already complied with the Football League's requirement for a capacity of 4,000 with at least 1,000 seats in the first season after promotion. But by the start of the second season we would need 5,000 capacity and 2,000 seats. We needed to be sure we could achieve the laid-down requirements for the second year.

We were in the odd situation of having planning permission for the required higher capacity but that permission necessitated building on the perimeter lease – land which Kingston Council, as the freeholders, had reclaimed when OMK didn't buy it. We asked about buying the land and Kingston Council said they were happy to grant us a lease for £100,000, but they wanted Ks (who were still ground-sharing as our tenants) to benefit.

However, there was no one to receive the £100,000. The Kingstonian Supporters' Trust was moribund and the council didn't just want to hand the money to the new Ks owners (when OMK sold the stadium to us he sold the football club separately to some Kingstonian fans). Also, we didn't want to spend £100,000 of cash we'd need for stadium expansion, so we needed to find another way.

We entered into negotiations with Malcolm Winwright, the Ks chairman, to try to find a deal that suited everybody. In the end we settled for a deal whereby Ks got a new 25-year lease, with the first ten years rent-free. The rent-free period was worth about £100,000 which was easier for us to agree than paying out that amount of cash. After ten years they would start paying rent. Crucially, with an eye on our wish to return to Merton one day, the ground-share deal with Ks included a new clause that allowed us to give one year's notice if we wanted to sell Kingsmeadow. In return we agreed a compensation formula if we served notice on Ks. This relatively minor amendment to the wording would prove to be of massive importance nearly ten years later.

Dons fan Dan Norris, who did all the legal work when we bought Kingsmeadow, was asked to prepare the legal documentation to seal the deal. And so we acquired the extra land. We didn't need it yet, but it was reassuring to know that when we won our way into the Football League a major obstacle to meeting the stadium criteria had been removed. Meanwhile, we had another serious matter to deal with regarding the stadium.

When we bought Kingsmeadow it came, as estate agents like to say, with the benefit of planning permission. In fact there were two separate permissions, both of which allowed the stadium to be expanded to the required capacity, but they overlapped. In other words, we could only implement one or the other.

The permission we'd acquired with the stadium in 2003 had been due to expire but in 2006 Hugh Scanlon, our volunteer planning advisor, had navigated us through an extension for a further three years. In the meantime the law had changed and a further extension wasn't allowed. In other words, our planning permissions were due to expire in a year's time.

We faced a choice of re-applying from scratch, an expensive option with a risk that we'd not get what we wanted, or implementing a material operation in connection with the existing permissions. 'Material operation' isn't defined but it can be as trivial as digging a hole (so long as the hole would be needed as part of implementing the permission). After careful thought we opted to improve the stadium as a first step towards qualification for Football League membership.

The demand for seats in the main stand already exceeded availability so we decided to kill two birds with one stone by extending the stand to add over 200 seats. This would easily qualify as a material operation which would implement the permission and protect us forever from it expiring. Furthermore, this particular expansion was included in both our permissions so we didn't yet need to decide which one we preferred.

There was one other important improvement we needed to implement. When Ks increased the number of seats some years earlier they hadn't extended the roof, so the front three rows weren't under cover. We had to put that right.

One of the great things about our club is there's always volunteers with the right skills available to help. The Stadium Working Group temporarily set aside its search for a site for a new stadium in Merton and turned their attention to this project. Tom Adam chaired the group with Mike Dowek, an architect, and Eddie Ridgwell, who had an extensive background in construction, providing input, challenge and support for the project. Mike Presland, a structural engineer, was also on hand to advise on the technical aspects of the design.

We appointed KSS as external consultants and together we looked at how we might expand the main stand. There were now three elements of the project to manage: the project to design, tender and oversee the stand extension; securing the necessary funding; and winning a Football Stadia Improvement Fund (FSIF) grant to pay for part of the project. KSS, Tom and his team looked after the design and build part of the project. The Finance Working Group and I worked on establishing the best way to fund the project, while I wrote and submitted the grant application and liaised with the FSIF.

I learned a lot about C factors (a measure of the quality of the view), safety rules about seating (you mustn't be more than 14 seats away from an aisle), building regulations, planning issues, grant finance and lord knows what else. We eventually appointed Pryer Construction for a tender price of just over £600,000, funded by the unused part of the Barclays loan we'd taken to pay off the debt to OMK, a £250,000 extension to the Barclays facility which, to my continued amazement, they had happily agreed to, and a £140,000 grant from the FSIF.

The tendering, grant applications and clearance from the council all took longer than we had hoped but in mid-September, at our fifth home game of the 2008/09 season, we were able to open the stand. And on budget too! We celebrated with a 3-1 win, but that belongs in the next chapter.

31

BREAKAWAY

FROM DAY one we were very keen to maintain ladies' and girls' football teams.

Following the FA Commission's decision the girls' teams went to Milton Keynes but Wimbledon FC Ladies were cast adrift and operated independently. For a year they continued in the national league. During the 2002/03 season, DT board member Ron Trayhorn got in touch with Carl Sims, the WFC Ladies chairman, and the DTB agreed to fund them. A deal was made, they joined us and started to play under our name. In 2005 Ron was appointed as chairman of the ladies' committee and Bert Dale, also a DTB member at the time, was appointed as secretary. When Ron resigned from the DT board, Bert was elected in his place to ensure the ladies had a representative on the board.

We couldn't afford to fund the ladies to the extent that WFC had done. Nonetheless, in 2005 the team won the Surrey Ladies Cup by beating Chelsea 2-1.[36] However, the reduced funding that the DTB could afford meant that they were soon relegated from the national league.

In 2005 Bert Dale and Maria Bertelli started girls' under-12 and under-14 teams, appointing Toby Crisp and Nick Flinders as the managers. Soon Jackie Saddington joined them to help coordinate their activities and

—

36 Maria Bertelli was captain of the ladies' team and also an international volleyball player who was representing her country in a tournament in Scandinavia immediately before the final. Wanting the best chance for the team, fans using the chat site Weird and Wonderful World clubbed together to fly her home in time for the final. She scored both goals in the 2-0 win.

within a couple of years they had expanded to six teams. And then the whole girls' section ground to a halt; arguably it went into reverse.

The club and the Dons Trust boards were becoming increasingly concerned to ensure that the girls' teams should be integrated into the wider organisation rather than be a stand-alone group. In June 2007, as a means of promoting integration of the ladies and girls, the girls' leadership were invited to join the ladies' board as vice-chair. The offer was not taken up. Over the next 18 months we held meetings, exchanged e-mails and phone calls with Toby and Jackie to explain that they couldn't use the club's name and not be accountable to us in any way. In short, they had to choose between being accountable to the DT, with a large degree of autonomy, or lose their right to use the AFC Wimbledon name.

To cut to the chase, after a combination of e-mails, phone calls, and meetings, the chairman of the girls' committee, Toby Crisp, wrote to me in February 2009 to say, 'Our vision for the continued success of the girls' club is to keep full autonomy at this stage, but with links to AFC Wimbledon.' He went on to say they would have their own club, committee, constitution, and welfare officer. In other words, they would call themselves by our name, play in our kit, hold themselves out to be us, but not be fully accountable to us.

We'd had enough. After consulting the DT board I sent Toby an advance copy of a press release we were publishing later that day. It said we'd withdrawn our permission for them to play in our name and in our kit. We didn't want the girls to suffer so they could finish the season using our name, but after that the teams could separately or collectively join us. However, they could not continue using our name if they chose not to join us.

Of the six teams at the time, three came to us and three played as Wimbledon Town the following season. A couple of years later we had lost sight of Wimbledon Town girls. The saddest part of this whole saga is that, as a result of all this, some girls stopped playing football altogether.

It was now late in the 2008/09 season and, at least so far as the girls' teams were concerned, we were pretty much back at square one. We had already learned with the men's team that committed leadership was necessary to build from a standing start, but the two main leaders had left.

We had little choice but to support the remaining teams as best we could and wait for new leadership to build again.

That is for another chapter and I will return to the development of our ladies' and girls' teams much later in this story.

32

IN THE SUMMERTIME

MANY FOOTBALL fans assume that the close-season is when everything grinds to a halt, except for bringing in new players. That had never been true but stepping up into the Conference South division, we saw a sudden and substantial jump in activity in all areas. We'd never been so busy and there was much more pressure on us. Personally, I welcomed it and I remember saying to Eileen that I felt we were metaphorically and literally in a much bigger league.

Terry Brown had talked about needing to be big and strong to get out of the Ryman League. We had made it – just. Now it was time to rebuild. Terry was very clear, 'We are going younger and we are going more football-orientated than strength and aggression and we're playing the game in a slightly different manner.'

That meant rebuilding the side. Terry's approach to signing the more experienced players was unusual. We set out to recruit Alan Inns, the Hampton & Richmond centre-half. Alan recalls, 'I was on a one-year contract at Hampton. I had no intention to leave, was happy, the money was okay. We had just lost in the play-off final and Dev [Alan Devonshire, the Hampton manager] had pulled me aside, "Are we all right for next year?" I'd said, "Yes, fine."

'Then Brownie called me. As soon as he said Wimbledon, I thought it would be naïve not to go and speak to him. I called Dev straight away and said, "Terry's called me and he'd like to have a chat and out of respect I thought I'd let you know I am going to go and speak to him." Dev was, "Why would you go there? I don't understand, we've just lost in the

[Conference South] play-off final." And I said, "Well they get quadruple our crowds, I think we batted above our average this season, and it's Wimbledon, they're the biggest club in Conference South and [if they ask] you have to go and speak to them."

'Terry and I lived a five-minute walk from each other. He said, "I can take you to the ground and show you round or we can meet down The Rifle Volunteer." We went to the pub and had far too much to drink, maybe five or six pints, just talking football, about the club, where it's been, talking about his time at Aldershot. I thought, "I like this bloke, I love the idea of Wimbledon because I know how big they are, it's going to happen." We didn't really speak about money that much. I called Dev and said, "Look, I am going to do it," and again he didn't really understand. But I signed anyway. Sadly our relationship has never been quite the same since.'

Alan signed and then we recruited Elliott Godfrey, also from Hampton, a couple of weeks later. I'm not sure how many pints that signing cost.

Not surprisingly, players' wage expectations increased as we climbed up through the leagues. One new feature was that some of the players we were talking to (by and large the ones who rejected us) were couching their expectations in terms of 'net' money. In other words, they wanted guaranteed pay, after tax.

We were still part-time and some would-be recruits were saying that taken together with their existing day jobs, our offer would take them into a higher tax bracket. We couldn't do anything to reduce their tax bill, except perhaps to offer to reduce what we paid them! I pointed out the nonsense in their argument by suggesting that they ask their main employers to make up the difference since they paid them more than we did. That went down like a lead balloon. We had no choice other than to watch them go to other clubs who could offer high enough gross pay to absorb the additional tax, or innovative ways round the problem, such as a cash-in-hand signing-on fee.

In early June, David Charles and I represented the club at our first Football Conference AGM. A key item on the agenda was a motion to adopt the constitution, i.e. the list of member clubs for 2008/09. And so, sometime around 11.30am, with no ceremony and very little fuss, AFC Wimbledon became a Conference club. Having already left the Ryman League I wondered if, temporarily, we had been in limbo and not members of any league. Meanwhile, the vagaries of having regional divisions meant that, in the time it takes to snap your fingers, Worcester City went from being a northern club to a southern club in order to keep the two divisions with equal numbers of clubs.

In mid-June David and I were on duty again. Now that the club was over five years old we were entitled to apply for Associate Membership of the Football Association. Our application was considered in a 45-minute interview at Wembley that considered the club's financial strength, our corporate governance and our disciplinary record. We were also asked, 'Why do you want to become Associate Members?' to which I replied, 'To qualify for FA Cup tickets.'[37] We were duly admitted.

While David and I were enjoying ourselves at the Conference AGM in the fleshpots of Blackpool, a team of volunteers was cleaning and improving the stadium as one of the two work weekends. Much of the cleaning was undone when demolition started on the old burger bar at the north end of the main stand. From early June onwards business at the office was conducted in a haze of dust and with the sounds of building works constantly in the background.

The summer seemed to be non-stop meetings with various volunteer groups to discuss what went well and what we could do better in the next season. It was also essential to get feedback from the volunteers who actually ran matchdays, about the problems we might face if we moved away fans to a side terrace so as to reclaim the area behind the goal for our fans at the north end of the stadium.

At the end of June, training re-started and once again there was a sense of anticipation in the air. Every season we tried to make incremental improvements in our training pitches or facilities and this year we had decided to have our first residential training camp. We booked the facilities at Bath University for a weekend – with most of our players in full-time jobs it was the only option.

We believe it is essential for players to understand who we are as a club, where we come from and what we stand for. So straight after dinner on the first night everyone moved to a lecture theatre where there were presentations by the board and by Terry. I started by showing the team the first ten minutes of the final episode of *Football Hurts*, as a good but concise

—

37 Of course I didn't. That would have been the honest answer but it seemed wiser to say something more inspirational which I instantly forgot.

summary of why and how the club was formed. That led to a discussion about how most clubs have an owner, who is usually the chairman. I explained that we had over 3,000 owners who all have a voice through membership of the Dons Trust. It takes players some time to 'get' this (and some never do). It certainly made an impact on some of the players – Alan Inns says, 'You started to realise actually we are part of something here.'

Ivor talked about his expectations of players in areas such as meeting sponsors and the fans; the man of the match award; and attending the Junior Dons Christmas party. He also talked about the pressures of being a Wimbledon player and the importance of treating the fans, who are the owners, with respect. Next, Nigel Higgs explained the club's commitment to youth development, pointing out that two of the participants, Luke Pigden and Steve Gilbert, were products of that system.

Terry was last, talking to the players about the plans for the coming season, the playing formation, the need for the players to be an integrated unit, 'a family' as he put it. He stressed his desire to play attacking football without fear of failing, even if that meant making mistakes from time to time.

On the Saturday there was an intense training session in the morning followed by speed and fitness testing in the afternoon to lay the base data for comparative testing during the season. These were followed by a game of beach football. As Jason Goodliffe explained, 'It was exactly the same at Hayes when I was there. Brownie would run us ragged all day and then suggest a quick game of five-a-side, so that he could win.' And so it was. The management team comfortably won the league of four teams, helped by not having been training all day and having eight players while the other teams had five. Terry 'I was the leading scorer at every club I played for' Brown captained his team to an inspirational win.

The players had a light session on the Sunday morning before dispersing. It needed to be light because, as Terry explained, 'A proper English training weekend wouldn't be complete without the Saturday night bonding session in and around Bath, where I found out that Tony Finn is by far the best dancer in the club.'

By now the fixture list had been published. To give clubs time to load them on the website and get the manager's reaction they arrived about an hour and a half before being made public. One of the perks of being a board member was to be sent an early copy to mull over. Our first fixture was away at Newport County. Suddenly it was real and there was a palpable sense of excitement mixed with trepidation because we were starting our season playing away at one of the title favourites.

When the players are training at most twice a week during the season Terry didn't have much time to show them what he expected of them. So he used pre-season to embed simple but very effective training methods. Ben Judge offered his perspective on training under Terry, 'He was very heavily involved. He showed me the clock, which I'd never heard of before. It means that whenever you're in possession of the ball you should have four, maybe five, options for a pass arranged in a clock position. I don't think many of us had heard of it and it became a joke – "Why weren't you at nine o'clock when I had the ball?" It's not something you ask in a game but it gave us so many options. As soon as the full-backs got the ball the centre-backs knew to drop off to a clock position, with the holding midfielder in another position and it just seemed to really click with us all.'

Terry had also gone for greater pace and a combination of that plus everyone thoroughly understanding their roles meant we were confident of a successful season. We just needed to get that difficult first game out of the way.

33

UP, UP AND AWAY

WE WERE determined to build upon the strong team spirit we'd created during the summer so we decided that we would have our first overnight stay for the opening game of the season. Once again Mike Richardson stepped in, this time to arrange favourable rates at a hotel in which he had an investment.

What followed was transformational in terms of our hopes and expectations for the season. It shouldn't be possible for one game to define a campaign, but this one did, which is why I have lingered on it.

For some players this was their first experience of an overnight stay. Jon Main says, 'I came down and got myself a full English breakfast and ate it all. I didn't think anything of it. I was with Mickey Haswell and I picked up all my food and thought, "Oh, this is lovely." I saw Mickey had scrambled eggs and beans on brown toast and his face just hit the floor when he saw my meal. And I was like "oh, I didn't know" because no one tells you. So I ate it. After that, I didn't do that again.'

Simon Bassey is adamant that at subsequent overnight stays Jon would pinch a couple of sausages and hide behind a pillar while he wolfed them down before having his officially approved breakfast.

Although we'd told the players that fans' enthusiasm was running close to fever pitch, they were completely taken aback by the number of fans who'd travelled for the game. Alan Inns says, 'We had a police escort going into the ground and then "bloody hell, there's quite a few people here and early as well". Then I had a text from my dad and he said "bloody hell, there's loads of fans here". Then walking out, I'm not really a nervous bloke but when I walked out I thought "bloody hell". There were 2,500 fans, most of them Wimbledon, and I thought, "Jesus, this is proper."'

First-team coach Simon Bassey walked out with him, and says, 'I remember it was Innsy's first game. We ran across to the far side, right opposite our fans, to do our warm-up. I went over to give them a clap and I looked round and Innsy was like, "Bloody hell, this is good isn't it?" He was super-excited and it was great to see the child in him.'

Ben Judge had signed on deadline day the previous season on a short-term deal which we extended in the summer. With Jason Goodliffe and Jake Leberl both injured, Ben was the captain. He recalls, 'I remember looking across and seeing what looked like absolutely thousands of away fans. Seeing all of them was frightening and I turned round to Innsy as we did a little warm-up and said, "We'd better perform here because of all these people that are watching."'

And perform we did. In a torrential downpour we were dominant from the beginning. It took 39 minutes to turn that control into goals but when it happened it was special. Mickey Haswell crossed the ball at pace and Jon Main launched himself horizontally and slightly backwards to score with one of the best headers I've ever seen. And remember, this is the man of whom Terry said, 'He can't head a ball.'

Jon went on to score a spectacular second goal and then completed his first hat-trick for the club. Maybe that full English breakfast had a hand in it. Finally, Tony Finn scored another top-class goal. As Simon Bassey said, 'Every finish was like "bang".'

Newport got a late consolation and Ben Judge got the blame. He remembers, 'I got a rollocking from [goalkeeper] Andy Little for not getting out of the way when they scored – the ball deflected off me. He was upset because we lost our clean sheet bonus.'

This unexpectedly good start and the reception the team received from the drenched fans in the uncovered terrace set the tone for the rest of the season. Terry Brown says, 'It was an amazing game. They were well fancied, a big strong side with good backing. We went into the game thinking, "Wow, this is going to be hard," and we played magnificently. Mainy was at his best. It was a completely new side that was playing much more football than we'd played before, even on an awful pitch. The atmosphere after that was "yea, this is all right". Which is ridiculous of course because it is only one game in, and one game into the season doesn't mean anything. But I remember on the coach on the way home thinking "yea, this side is going to do great".'

The day had an even more profound effect on Alan Inns, who admits, 'I've always been a teacher who plays football but when I walked out I thought "bloody hell". I think for those two seasons it made me feel like I was a bit of a footballer. My priorities changed from teaching being my first job and football having to fall in line with that and then suddenly I was not neglecting my teaching ([he's still a teacher so he has to say that!] but certainly the football part of my life was massive and it took over my teaching at times as well. That may not have been a great thing but that was what the club did to me personally. You think, "Bloody hell, I'm part of something here, I need to give it my all."'

We won the next four games, three of them thanks to very late goals which is always a sign of a team brimming over with confidence. The other was arguably our best performance of the season but you wouldn't know it from the result, a 1-0 win at Basingstoke with the winner being an own goal. During this run of games Dean Mason scored his one and only goal for us and was then subject to a dressing room fine by the players for kissing his badge as he ran off to celebrate. The whole bench was groaning, 'You've only been with us a week, son.' I was pleased to find that I wasn't the only one who thought such gestures were naff.

It would be harsh to say that two wins and two draws from the next four games represented a dip in form. But there was a concern that leading the attack with two small men, Jon Main and Tony Finn, didn't leave scope for a Plan B. Furthermore, while only a few clubs employed scouts, all the managers spoke to each other and it felt as if teams were beginning to suss out how to deal with Jon and Tony.

We had known about Danny Kedwell for a while. In fact Dave Anderson had asked to have him watched when he was at Welling, where he had scored a goal every other game. Grays had snapped him up but we had heard he was unhappy there. He wasn't playing well, but we knew he could.

By chance Grays had a Sunday home fixture against Kidderminster Harriers and I ended up joining Terry there. I expect Terry thought that if I went with him it would be easier to persuade me to find the money for the fee. Danny didn't play especially well that day but one thing was very clear – the crowd loved him. Terry's view was simple: we know he can score at our level, you can see he works hard and that's probably why he's so popular, and he offers us something we've not currently got, namely size, presence and a threat in the air. Terry had made his mind up. My philosophy was always to support your manager whenever you possibly can, so we went after Danny.

Coincidentally or not, the next day a coach at Grays told Danny that he could leave. Danny refused because he was on a contract and entitled to be paid. We had heard that Grays were struggling financially so I wasn't particularly generous in my offer. After some haggling we agreed £10,000 which, if press reports are accurate, was less than Grays had paid Welling 18 months earlier.

Danny was full-time at Grays and we were only part-time so he was understandably keen to be paid during the summer. We negotiated a compromise but it was an unbudgeted cost. It was time for another phone call. Once again, thanks to the generosity of Iain McNay, Mike Richardson and Norman Baldock, who each donated £5,000 to the club, we were able to seal the fee and cover the unplanned summer wages.

This wasn't the Combined Counties League and we were never going to be able to maintain this level of performance without a few hiccups. Three defeats in short order, including to title contenders Chelmsford, meant that a third of the way through the season we had dropped to fourth place, eight points behind the leaders. However, we had games in hand thanks to reaching the first round of the FA Cup for the first time. At this stage league clubs joined and Ivor and I were both confident that, given our story, so long as we got a half-decent tie we would be on TV. We did and we were.

We were drawn against Wycombe Wanderers, who were then unbeaten near the top of League 2. Immediately the draw was made Ivor announced that he'd already got a match and a ball sponsor. But the big bonus was that each team was guaranteed a TV fee of £75,000. We also knew that we were almost bound to have a sell-out attendance so we were expecting a very healthy surplus compared to budget, not least because our prudent budgeting always assumed we would lose our first cup game, away from home, so we didn't even budget for any bar income.

With restrictions on how many people we could fit into the ground, the real money-spinner for clubs of our size is the TV fee. To illustrate this, despite the game being a sell-out our profit from everything, but excluding the TV fee, was only £18,983. That must seem odd so, for the curious and the downright nerdy readers, I've shown an example of how these sums are arrived at in an Appendix.

The talk is always about the romance of the FA Cup and it's certainly true that there's a fantastic thrill to be gained from beating a higher-league team. We all know we aren't going to win the cup so we hope for a windfall profit and a bit of fun en route. To get a televised game you need to progress as far as possible to increase the chances of a tasty home draw. That is why in the early rounds most clubs pray to be drawn against 'the lowest left in the competition, at home' so they can win and get into the later rounds when the really big clubs join in and the TV money is even higher.

We had to decide what to do with the surplus funds. That season Mike Richardson had donated £150,000 to top up the wage budget and he had undertaken to do the same the following season. The football club board felt honour-bound to ask if he wanted any of his £150,000 back. After mulling it over he said 'no' but instead he would only put in £75,000 the following season. In effect, that meant the £75,000 needed to go into our back pockets to be spent next season. Nonetheless, the profits from the other cup games, especially the prize money, meant there was still a chunk of cash for Terry if he felt he needed it – and we knew he'd ask eventually.

December brought a dramatic turn for the better for the team, although not for me. We won the return fixture against Newport County 3-0 and that was the last game I saw for a while. I'd been struggling with a cold for some time, while working extra-long hours to get all the paperwork and accounts ready for the PLC's annual general meeting in January. Just before Christmas my younger son came round to visit us and immediately called for a doctor. 'You're grey, Dad,' he said. The doctor arrived and called for an ambulance. And so I was carted away to St George's Hospital with double pneumonia, but only after making the ambulance wait for a few minutes while I put the finishing touches to the paperwork and sent it off for printing. I wasn't going to put in all that work and then have the meeting postponed.

I hadn't realised quite how poorly I was. I found out later how worried my family had been. Frustratingly I missed an upturn in form as the team went on to win three in a row. Soon we were in second place, five points behind Chelmsford with a game in hand.

I'd been able to follow the team's fortunes thanks to Radio WDON, broadcasting an internet commentary on every match. I made a return when we played Maidenhead away in mid-January. We won very comfortably 4-0 against a team which was on the fringes of the play-off places. We were on a roll and by the end of January we were top of the league, albeit on goal difference. This was all building up to the big showdown, at home to Chelmsford.

The kick-off was delayed because of a late rush at the turnstiles. In the end 300 to 400 fans were locked out and had to sit in the bar listening to the crowd noise. From the roars they'd have divined that we scored twice in the first half-hour. We were coasting to victory when Chelmsford scored with 25 minutes to go. But with Jason Goodliffe back in the heart of defence after a stop-start season of injuries, we never looked like conceding an equaliser. And then, in the last minute of normal time with the Chelmsford defence stranded upfield, we broke away and Danny Kedwell crossed the ball for three Dons players to play 'after you, no after you' before Tom Davis pushed the ball into an empty net. Cue total uproar. The fans' post-match celebrations went on long into the night. We had won nine and drawn one of the last ten games and everything looked set for the title.

With the run-in to the end of the season in mind, Terry strengthened the squad with a goalkeeper, two strikers and defender Jay Conroy, for whom it was a return visit after being on loan with us in the previous season. Jay is a very good-looking man and also had a career as a male model. Terry acknowledged this by leading him into the dressing room and saying, 'That's Tom Davis's mirror so you'll have to find one for yourself.'

The astonishing run continued and we had now won 12 of the last 13 games. During that time the Kedwell/Main partnership was lethal. Danny started all 13 games and scored eight goals; Jon started 12 games and scored 17. And to think that none of this would have happened but for my scouting acumen at Grays, back in September!

The extraordinary run couldn't continue – and it didn't. We finally dropped points when we drew each of three successive away games. A subsequent win and a rare home defeat left us on edge as we made our way to Eastleigh.

The match had been even for the first hour when Eastleigh won a corner. Their tall striker Tom Jordan went for the ball, which Alan Inns had covered until Jordan simply reached up above him and slapped it over the line.[38] Everyone waited for the referee to give a free kick but it didn't happen. Despite furious protests, the goal stood and the team lost its composure.

The assistant referee furthest from the goal had seen what happened and Trevor Williams tried to get him to intervene. He says, 'I remember going to the other lino, not the lino who should have been giving the free kick, and I said, "You've seen it. Put your flag up and tell him what you've seen." He said, "The referee's there and the lino's there," and I said, "No, put your flag up and tell him what you think. What have you got to lose? If he ignores you, he ignores you, but tell him what you've seen." But he never did. I don't understand why.'

Shortly afterwards, the referee complained he was feeling unwell and left the pitch. Perhaps he felt sick to the stomach; we definitely did.

With the team unsettled, Eastleigh added a second goal. Despite a late flurry it was too late and we'd lost 2-1. Things got worse, as Alan Inns recalls: 'The referee went off injured and the linesman came on as referee. [As we left the pitch] at the end I was berating the referee/linesman and I said, "Do me a favour. Look at the video and then tell me you're not a cheat." That got me a red card and after the Basingstoke game I was suspended for the last three games of that season.' He would miss the crucial Hampton match.

Ivor is usually very gracious in defeat but in the boardroom afterwards both he and I lost our composure. Trevor wandered in and wasn't impressed by what he saw. He says, 'Our entire board were losing their rag in the boardroom afterwards. I remember walking in and thinking, "Everyone just needs to shut up now." Normally it was the dressing room and the players who were fuming so it was really weird to see people like you losing it as well.'

Eileen dragged me away and we drove home with me grumpier than ever. I promised myself that I would never again let myself or the club down in this way.

---

38 This goal was a strange echo of an incident in October 1977 in a World Cup qualification game between Scotland and Wales. A Scottish player jumped high in the Welsh penalty area and handled the ball. To the amazement of everyone in the stadium, the referee awarded a penalty to Scotland, which they scored. They went on to win the game, ending Wales's hopes of reaching the finals. The player who handled the ball and got away with it was Joe Jordan, Tom Jordan's father.

By now Chelmsford had lost momentum. Following this result, Eastleigh were hot on our heels although our main challengers continued to be Hampton & Richmond, who were three points behind us but with a game in hand. It was fortunate that our next two games were at home. We won them both, but Hampton kept up the pressure by matching our results. And so to Bromley on Easter Monday.

Bromley had never been a very happy ground for us. We lost our 78-game unbeaten run there, the Coney Hall fiasco happened there, and only a year earlier we'd lost a play-off semi-final. But with the game poised at 1-1 our latest loan signing, Rocky Baptiste, had scored what looked like the winner, three minutes from the end of normal time. And then, in extra time, Jay Conroy went down injured just inside our half. Jon Main tapped the ball into touch to allow Jay to be treated and, in line with convention, Bromley were meant to return it to us.

The throw-in went to Bromley's Ryan Hall and he volleyed it long and high. It sailed over goalkeeper James Pullen and into the net. Hall is a very good player and he was quite capable of doing that deliberately, but I suspect it was an accident. We will never know for sure. For the second away game in a row, chaos broke out. What Hall had done wasn't illegal but it was totally against the spirit of the game. Such events are rare but the normal response is to let the opposition walk the ball into the net from the kick-off. Our players and management asked for that but the Bromley players simply lined up for the kick-off.

The referee could do nothing. He asked Del Parnham, the Bromley stand-in manager, to let us score but he refused, so the game ended 2-2. The Bromley manager had recently broken his leg and wasn't in the dugout; he claimed not to have seen what had happened. At the end of the game, Terry was furious but still sufficiently in control to realise that he needed to get to our players before they followed in Alan Inns's footsteps and got sent off. He recalls, 'I can remember being quite proud about how the boys reacted because that could have kicked off into a massive fight. But Dwane Lee, not someone you'd want to be on the wrong side of, was absolutely gonna kill one of their players and I remember saying to Bass, "Stop him, you've got to stop him." [What they did] was a disgrace but you don't do that.'

Parnham was clearly not used to the pressure because, as he left the pitch, he raised a clenched fist towards their fans, as if in celebration of what they'd done. The fury continued in the dressing room. Trevor says,

'It proper went off in the dressing room. Dwane Lee had already had some beef with a couple of Bromley players and he went into their dressing room and started dragging people out. Dwane was normally quite a chilled fellow but he wasn't that day. I was on crutches at the time and I remember trying to hold our players back by holding my crutch across the dressing room door.'

In the stand, Ivor was sitting with club president Dickie Guy. Ivor says, 'There were people behind us in a bar which looked out on to the pitch and they started banging on the glass when they saw how upset we were. Dickie totally lost it and was on his feet banging on the window and shouting at them.'

However, there was some good news. Eastleigh had been hot on our heels but they had a disastrous Easter, losing both of their games; they were effectively out of the hunt. Then we heard that Hampton had been held to a draw at play-off contenders Hayes and Yeading and we retained our three-point lead at the top. So while Ivor was dragging Dickie away I went into the boardroom with the consolation of Hampton's result in my head.

I was determined not to repeat my lapse at Eastleigh. That was immediately put to the test when I was greeted by a Bromley director who said, 'I hear Hampton got a last-minute winner.' He knew it wasn't true and was just trying to wind me up. Tosser. I waited to see the results confirmed on TV and then left. I wasn't in the mood for their hospitality.

The recriminations rumbled on in the press with Bromley chairman Jerry Dolke quoted as saying that they'd refused to give us a walk-in goal because Tom Davis had thrown his water bottle at their dugout. That response was disappointing because Jerry is generally one of the league's good guys and far too bright to believe the 'two wrongs make a right' argument.

Terry used the injustice at the Eastleigh and Bromley games to motivate the team for our penultimate game of the season, at arch-rivals Hampton, a team we'd never beaten. We were three points clear of them with a massively superior goal difference, so a draw would as good as guarantee us the title. A defeat would mean we had to win on the final day at home to St Albans. Everyone wanted to avoid that pressure.

The Hampton game was a sell-out of course. Many of our fans couldn't get tickets from our allocation so they simply visited the Hampton ticket office and bought tickets in the home end, effectively blowing segregation plans out of the water. Ivor Heller recalls, 'The queue went all the way back down Hampton High Street and the stadium itself was jam-packed and largely yellow and blue.'

Once again the game was tight and although we'd had the better chances it was still 0-0 at half-time. In the 53rd minute we switched off and a quick corner followed by a cross-shot was deflected into his own goal by Ben Judge. To counter Hampton's physical presence, Terry had started with the biggest, strongest players available. As a result, Jon Main was sitting on the bench, but not for much longer.

In the 87th minute Chris Hussey was sent racing down the left wing. Two Hampton players went to take him out but instead they collided, knocking the ball into touch and leaving them both prostrate on the ground. Chris quickly took the throw-in to Danny Kedwell who crossed for Jon Main, the man who can't head a ball, to score a fine header. Pandemonium broke out. The Hampton players protested while the team went to celebrate with the Dons fans behind the goal. Jason Goodliffe brought his experience to bear, 'I told the lads to stay up celebrating the goal, don't go back to your positions, stay up. The referee is going to have to come and get us to move and get away from them. If Hampton can't get to him he won't be able to change his mind.'

The view from the stand at Hampton wasn't great and I hadn't seen the collision. I was on my feet celebrating when Ivor turned to me and said, 'Did we just pull a trick there?' I hadn't a clue what he was talking about and after checking that the goal hadn't been disallowed I decided to ask later.

After our moral high horse attitude about the Eastleigh and Bromley incidents, we had benefitted from a dubious goal at Hampton, one that effectively won us the title and promotion. Looking back on it, Eastleigh was blatant cheating, but players cheat in every game whether by stealing forward a few yards for a thrown-in or diving for a penalty. So the real villains were the incompetent referee and linesman – while Jordan shouldn't have done that, he won't be the last to try. Bromley was, I think, a mistake by Hall caused by recklessly hoofing the ball towards our goal. He did nothing illegal but the reaction of the Bromley players and management was disgraceful.

Which leaves us with Hampton. The referee had been letting the game flow and in normal circumstances he'd not have stopped for injuries like that. But usually if there's an injury and the ball goes out of play the referee will stop play. I have to assume that he didn't realise that one of the Hampton players had a serious injury – he had gashed his leg and needed to be carried off. So it was another refereeing error. From an ethical point of view, I think ours was the most marginal of the three incidents, but then I would, wouldn't I?

That is all very interesting but we'd scored, we had drawn, and we were champions all bar the shouting.

In the team coach, en route to the Dog and Fox in Wimbledon, the players took turns to call Del Parnham, the Bromley stand-in manager, and leave messages on his voicemail. Then they disembarked to join the celebrations, which were memorable, at least for those who could remember them.

Sadly that game led to a breach in relations between Alan Inns and the Hampton fans to whom he had been a legend when he played for them. He recalls, 'I was in the stands for Hampton which is my old club. They've still got this thing that after the game there was a lot of mud in the changing rooms, champagne and so on and some of the Hampton fans messaged me and said somebody took a shit and it was smeared across the changing room, which wasn't true. It would have been mud. I went back there once and they thought it was me. I said, "You know me, I was here six years and you know I wouldn't do something like that," but some of them have held a grudge about it since then. That whole relationship at Hampton has gone since the end of that game. We did celebrate and it was very loud, but I didn't think anything untoward.'

There only remained the St Albans match, which was to be Jason Goodliffe's final appearance for the club. He didn't want the day to be a damp squib so when it was 0-0 at half-time, he got busy, 'I was digging a few out and telling them we need to win this game and make it a good day.'

It had an impact. Shortly after half-time Kennedy Adjei scored and immediately donned a swimming cap and slid on his chest towards the fans behind the goal. This was a reference to the fact that he can't swim and the players used to mock him for not getting in the pool. Sam Hatton scored a second and then in a lovely and very fitting end to the game, the season, and his playing career, Jason, our captain, scored our third and last goal in the final minute.

We won the title by three points and arguably it should have been more. The previous season we'd missed out on automatic promotion by taking only five points from our eight games against the bottom four clubs. This season we won seven and drew one, a total of 22 points, in the equivalent matches; we finally had a strike force that would pretty much guarantee goals against the weaker sides and, in the final reckoning, that's what won us promotion.

Interestingly, if Eastleigh had won both their Easter weekend games they would have been champions. My heart bled for them.

There were two more parties. The first one started immediately after Jason had collected the trophy and went on until early the next morning. Jon Main says, 'We were at Oceania [a Kingston nightclub] that night and I had my best mate with me. I lost him and went to some fan's house where people were partying. I came out at about five or six in the morning, totally lost, my phone was dead and I had no cash on me. I didn't know where I was, so I "borrowed" a bike from someone's garden.[39] Luckily I found this shop and said, "Mate, you need to tell me where Kingsmeadow is," and he said, "Oh, you're 15 minutes away." I got myself back to the ground – and my car was there. My pal was asleep in the car. I remember throwing the bike against the fence and having a nap in the car and you [Erik] woke me up [I'd gone to the stadium to catch up on some work]. This would have been nine-ish and Innsy was asleep in the car next to me. We all went round to Fat Boys café and had a big breakfast and then I drove home.'

I was curious, so I wandered round the corner and in another small car park I found several other players, each asleep in his car.

The final party of the season was the traditional end-of-season dinner. The highlight of the evening was a speech by the player of the year, Ben Judge. He was ambushed by the other players on his table who kept ordering Sambucas but while he was drinking the real thing they were drinking water. As a result he was very, very drunk by the time he made his speech, which is still affectionately remembered by everyone present. Also, and incredibly generously, he gave up his promotion winner's medal

—

39 Jon seemed to have a thing about bikes. A couple of seasons later, we played a pre-season friendly at Exeter where, Jon told me rather wistfully, 'We lost 2-1 and I scored my only goal against a Football League team.' What the fans didn't see, which was probably just as well, happened after the team went out on the town on the Saturday night. Arriving back at the hotel at 4am, Jon saw that everyone was still up and sitting in the lobby, 'I thought I'd give them all a laugh and then I spotted a postman's bike. So I stripped off down to my pants and rode the bike into the lobby. They were sitting on a large round sofa so I rode round it a few times then went into the bar. I had the manager chasing me so I hopped off and parked the bike back where I found it.'

for auction. It was bought by a fan for over £2,000 and donated to the club for its trophy cabinet.

But the real reason Ben should be remembered is for his qualities, as described by Alan Inns, 'Judgey didn't look like a footballer in any way but he could read the game better than anyone I've ever played with. Invariably if you were having a bit of a crap time he was the one mopping up behind you. He was fantastic, a really calming influence, never really loses his rag. If he'd been a bit bigger and a bit stronger I think he'd have played at a much higher level.' He had such a good season and was held in great affection by the fans. After all, he was voted player of the year in a season where Jon Main scored 33 goals in 38 league appearances.

A few days later, nine members of the squad were released and the summer cycle started all over again.

I had one last task to perform. Throughout this and the previous season I'd been receiving postcards and letters from an opinionated fan telling me that Terry Brown was clueless and should be sacked. I wrote to the fan and invited him to join me in congratulating Terry on his extraordinary success in gaining promotion at the first attempt in two successive seasons. And I invited him to complete the enclosed season ticket application form.

34

LIFE IN THE FAST LANE

ONLY SEVEN years on from 2002 we'd reached the Blue Square Conference National league (hereafter referred to as the Conference), only one promotion away from the Football League. I looked at the list of clubs and realised this was going to be a huge challenge. Apart from us, the division comprised 11 former league clubs and three clubs which would go on to achieve league status.

The summer had been busier than ever. At the Conference awards dinner at Celtic Manor we'd swept the board for the season just ended. Jon Main collected the Conference South player of the year and the golden boot, Terry Brown was manager of the year and oversaw us winning the fair play league, while he also collected the trophy for winning the league title. We even won the programme of the year award.

Merton Council held a civic reception for us, while Baroness Margaret McDonagh and her sister Siobhan McDonagh MP hosted a House of Lords reception, attended by our board members and a group of our longest-serving volunteers. The FA chairman Lord Triesman and Andy Burnham, the Secretary of State for Culture, Media and Sport, were also present and Andy spoke knowledgeably about us and about supporter ownership. It felt rather surreal to hear our achievements being lauded (pun intended) in such magnificent surroundings. After all, we were still a tiny non-league club.

Back at the club, Kingsmeadow's limitations were becoming increasingly unacceptable as we rose through the leagues. The north and east terraces comprised wide steps with only a small rise between each step; even if you were over six feet tall the view was severely restricted. The only affordable solution was to increase the number and height of the steps. We couldn't add too much height or fans jumping up to celebrate a goal might brain themselves on the roof. So while it was definitely an improvement, I used to say we'd improved the view from crap to piss-poor.

Meanwhile, promotion into the Conference had generated even more interest and we once again broke our record for season ticket sales. However, giving Terry a reasonable budget was a headache, especially when Setanta, who had the rights to televise games, went into administration. We were braced for this and had prepared two budgets; one assumed some TV fees while a back-up budget assumed no such income. Setanta's demise left us facing a budgeted loss but one that the Dons Trust board agreed was acceptable.

At this stage we were one of the handful of teams in the Conference operating on a part-time basis, which meant we only paid the players for the 38 weeks from the start until the end of the playing season. Like other part-time clubs, we didn't pay wages during the summer break or pre-season training. Our playing budget was £420,000 and included wages, any transfer and signing-on fees, goal and clean sheet bonuses, and employers' national insurance. That was probably two or three weeks' wages for a top Premier League player at the time. Our two highest-paid players were on £650 per week.

As usual there was a lot of recruitment activity. Terry went for young, athletic players, aiming to be one of the youngest squads in the league. This was a conscious, strategic choice but it also suited our limited budget.

At that time we signed players on a one-year deal with an option in our favour to extend for another year. This was an idea Terry had stolen from John Still, the Dagenham manager, who also operated on a shoestring budget. While this gave us great flexibility, it was a source of regular anxiety for the players as the season approached its end. Although it helped us to ensure we didn't over-reach ourselves financially, I was never comfortable with the arrangement because it didn't feel like we were treating our players the way a club like ours should.

Terry brought in eight young players to add to those whose contracts were extended or renewed. We stretched the budget to pay fees for two of them, Stephen Gregory and Ricky Wellard. Along with three of the other signings, Luke Moore, Brett Johnson and Seb Brown, they were to play pivotal roles in our drive for promotion to the Football League.

Not all our would-be signings joined us. Terry was very proud of the fact that we had won the league and the fair play trophy. He got quite a bit of flak from fans about that but he was politely dismissive, pointing out that the award was wrongly named and should be 'the good discipline award'. We didn't have the depth of squad to have players banned and missing games. If players were booked for mistimed tackles that was fine; it happens in football. But he made it very clear that bookings for dissent and unprofessional behaviour would be punished.

This approach led to one memorable interview with a potential signing, a player who went on to play at a much higher level. We weren't far into the interview before Terry told him that if he joined us he'd be fined if he continued 'with all that diving around'. He got a much better offer elsewhere so I never found out if Terry could have changed his ways.

The Premier League is always first to announce its fixtures and Football League clubs are next. It has to be done this way to ensure that, for example, a Premier League club isn't playing at home on the same day as a nearby Championship club. In the Conference we were asked to 'pair' with another club so that we didn't both play at home at the same time. We chose Chelsea, not because we saw them as rivals but because we knew that quite a few of their fans came to watch us and it made sense to play on different days. After it dawned on us that Chelsea hardly ever play on Saturdays at 3pm we paired with Brentford, so that we could use some of the same stewards.

Once the PL and FL fixtures had been released, the Conference general manager, Dennis Strudwick, would set about preparing ours, manually. He would lock himself away for a week with some massive sheets of paper and a bundle of pencils. So it was Friday, 3 July before we heard that our first game was to be at home to Luton Town. It could not have been a tougher start because Luton would not have been relegated to the Conference but for a 30-point deduction that had been inflicted upon them by the Football League in the previous season. It was an unnecessarily draconian punishment and, as always seems to be the case, the people who suffer most are the fans who can only stand by and watch helplessly.

Our pre-season games included our first overseas (well, over water) tour to the Isle of Man, once again thanks to the generosity of Mike

Richardson. And now we were lining up to play Luton. One small but very noticeable change was that for the first time we had squad numbers with each player's name embossed on the back of his shirt. It was another sign that we were sailing in deeper waters.

Jon Main, winner of the golden boot after scoring 33 goals in the previous season, was on the bench. While most fans were taken aback by this, it didn't surprise him, as he remembers: 'The gaffer wanted to go 4-3-3 instead of the diamond formation we'd used in Conference South. To play in a 4-3-3 formation you have to be able to run with the ball and I'm no good at that, so I knew I was going to struggle. I wasn't a confident all-round footballer but put me in front of goal and I'll fancy my chances of scoring. But I couldn't do a job in a 4-3-3 formation.'

Terry agreed, 'Jon Main knew what he was good at and didn't try stupid things he knew he couldn't do. We tried to evolve into more of a footballing side. He needed an early ball that he could get on to and get behind them. We were playing more tippy tappy, playing to Dan [Kedwell], getting it back, playing it wide. Jon suffered a bit from the way we changed our style. He was ideal in a diamond but not for 4-3-3.' Despite this, Jon made 20 league starts and eight substitute appearances, scoring 12 goals, before a medial cruciate ligament injury ended his season in March.

Having been left out of the team for the Luton game, there was a certain irony that Jon was brought on as a substitute and won and then scored a penalty. That slightly fortunate point ensured we maintained our record of never losing an opening match of the season.

In some ways the day was more memorable for other things. First, the Luton fans were feistier than any we'd seen before at Kingsmeadow, as Haydon, our Womble mascot found when he went too near them and had his head ripped off. He never went near opposition fans again.

The Luton directors were an open and friendly group with whom we developed a long and very good relationship. However, they were still coming to terms with three successive relegations and the shock of finding themselves outside the Football League. We were very amused to overhear one of their boardroom party say, 'We've got to get out of this league. We can't keep coming to places like this.'

The season was packed with incident, on and off the pitch. In October we sold Chris Hussey to Coventry, at the time a Championship club. Chris had been released first from Brentford and then Woking but John

Morris, our reserve team manager, took him on. Chris arrived with a bit of a reputation for a bad attitude but Simon Bassey, who was then the reserve team coach, took him under his wing.

There's an awful lot of players in non-league football who have talent that belongs at a much higher level but who simply lack the commitment or attitude. So a lot of effort went into getting Chris to understand what he needed to do to succeed. As Simon said in the *Non-League Paper* at the time, 'A lot of the pride that we take from Chris's achievement now comes from the change in him as a person, rather than just his ability as a footballer.' What Simon didn't say was that his mentoring didn't stop when Chris left; he stayed in active touch with Chris to encourage and support him throughout the ups and downs of his career.

We'd been aware of interest from several Championship clubs but it was Coventry who made a move. Chris Coleman, the Coventry manager, came to watch him personally as a last check before making an offer. We spoke to Chris and made very clear what size of fee he'd need to offer. As a result, we were offered £100,000 plus additional payments including for appearances and promotion, plus a 20 per cent sell-on clause. Out of mischief I asked that the clause be raised to 50 per cent if Chris should be sold to Milton Keynes; this seemed to amuse Ray Ranson, the Coventry chairman, who agreed without hesitation.

It was a season of strange events. Terry was sent off at Rushden & Diamonds for 'sarcastic clapping' in response to a referee's decision going our way for the first time during the game. The Conference rules were that a manager who'd been dismissed must leave the stand and go somewhere he couldn't observe the rest of the game (you may recall that when our manager and physio were sent off at Chessington they simply stood behind the dugout). However, Terry sweet-talked a steward into letting him into an empty sponsors' box, from which he watched the rest of a hard-fought 1-0 win in comfort, with his feet up and a drink in his hand. All he needed was an old-fashioned voicepipe direct to the dugout and he'd have been set for life.

Rushden were to suffer financial meltdown some years later but nowhere near as dramatically as Chester City, who were issued with an HMRC winding-up order in January 2010. The Conference suspended the club – which had been put up for sale – for breaching its financial rules and for cancelling matches. A month after the winding-up order was served

Chester City were dismissed from the league with all results annulled and future fixtures cancelled. A year later the club was wound up.

I was on the Conference board by this time but, if I remember correctly, I didn't vote for their expulsion because of a conflict of interest. This was because all the results from their fixtures were to be cancelled and while all the clubs above us had taken points from them, we had lost the game we'd played against them. So we benefitted from their dismissal. Because the game was totally expunged from the records, Jon Main 'lost' a goal from his record – I jokingly asked him to repay the goal bonus but he just grinned. Another anomaly of that match was that it was the only one in which Nathan Ashton, sitting in for the departed Chris Hussey, played for us. But because it was expunged from the records he never officially existed.

In December 2009, Allen Batsford, our revered former manager, died suddenly. He led WFC to three successive Southern League titles and the extraordinary FA Cup run I referred to in Chapter 20. Those glory days formed the foundation on which WFC's Football League membership was achieved in 1977. Allen's achievements merit a book in their own right and his loss was keenly felt by fans.

The league season started well and by the halfway mark we were sixth, one place and two points short of a play-off position. But once again we were plagued by serious injuries and Alan Inns, Lewis Taylor and Ross Montague all suffered anterior cruciate ligament injuries that put them out for the season and, in effect, ended their careers with us.

In the FA Cup we fell out with Crawley, an easy club not to love for various reasons, over ticket prices for the tie at their ground. We felt the prices were excessive given the nature of the game and took it up, as was our right, with the FA. This was a fruitless exercise because, as we later realised, the FA will side with the home club in all but the most extreme circumstances.

After drawing 1-1 at their ground we won the replay 3-1, despite playing half the game with only ten men. We set off to play Millwall at the New Den with Crawley manager Steve Evans's typically graceless comments ringing in our ears, 'There has been one team in this cup tie over two games, one team that has played all the football – and it is that team that has gone out.'

Millwall treated us royally except on the pitch where we lost 4-1 after being in the game until four minutes from the end. The crowd of just under 9,500 was disappointing, depressed by the police demanding that it not be played on a Saturday or Sunday because of other pressures on their resources. Millwall fans have always been well-inclined towards us and, as expected, the game passed without incident.

Unfortunately, the season didn't end as well as it had started and we witnessed a late collapse in which we lost five of our last six matches without scoring. This included a Wednesday night 5-0 thrashing at York where we were unable to deal with their pacy, strong, tall forwards. The travelling fans, many of whom had already made a fruitless trip to the first, postponed, match, started to shower abuse on goalkeeper James Pullen, who was certainly not the main reason we were losing. Pullen reacted strongly. Trevor Williams said, 'Pully has no amber. He was green to red, bless him.' He made the mistake of arguing with his own fans and the consequent supporter disaffection probably contributed to his departure at the end of the season.

This proved to be a golden opportunity for Seb Brown, who had been signed at the beginning of the season as a stop-gap while our other principal keeper, Andy Little, recovered from injury. Seb had been released from Brentford who told us, informally, that 'he has a mistake in him'. So it was no great surprise when he spilled the ball and gave Fulham a goal when playing on trial in a pre-season friendly. At the time I assumed that had killed his prospects of a deal but Terry signed him. Terry was vindicated when Seb shone after injuries to James Pullen gave him his opportunity, including two penalty saves in the drama-laden last five minutes of a 1-0 away win at Mansfield. James, dropped to the bench after the York game three days earlier, was the first on to the pitch to congratulate Seb with a huge hug.

It's hardly a spoiler to say that Seb was central to our promotion the following season but if Terry had decided that his mistake versus Fulham wasn't acceptable, or if James hadn't fallen out with the entire contingent of travelling Dons fans, then Seb's career and our play-off final result the following season might have been very different. It's these little things that sometimes add up to something momentous.

And so the season ended with us 14 points short of a play-off place and 35 behind the league champions, Stevenage. Nonetheless, we were eighth and comfortably the highest-placed part-time club. The foundations had been laid. Now for a promotion push.

35

UP WHERE WE BELONG

TOWARDS THE end of the 2009/10 season, in what turned out to be a pivotal moment for the club, Terry put the case for us to go full-time. His argument was simple but very persuasive, 'If we want to progress we need to go full-time. And we won't be any better placed to do that one year or two years from now. So why wait? If we are going to do it, let's do it now.'

I advocated the proposal to the football club board who were also persuaded. We were ready to present the idea to the DT board when, following a particularly awful end-of-season home defeat against already relegated Grays Athletic, Terry told the post-match press conference, 'It will be better when we're full-time next season.' That's not how you'd want your parent board to find out about such a radical and arguably risky proposal. I was very upset and he was very apologetic, but the cat was out of the bag.

That was all very well, but could we afford it? By going full-time we would move from paying players for a 38-week season to 44 weeks – we still wouldn't be paying for their summer breaks. That change alone would add nearly 16 per cent on to the wage bill for exactly the same players.

Every year we compiled a detailed budget starting from scratch. We re-examined every area of the business and calculated the likely profits and costs. We left the players' wages out of the process so that the profit that resulted from this approach was what we could afford to spend on them. The early drafts showed a total of £243,000, which was nowhere near enough and, indeed, a long way behind the previous year's total. The budget commentary, which I will spare you, went into great detail about why we had so much less than the previous year; the single biggest factor was a drop in income of £98,000 due to the loss of TV fees following the demise of Setanta. It was a relegation budget.

Once again, Iain McNay and Mike Richardson came to the rescue. As vice-presidents they committed £50,000 each to the budget. Once they'd heard the figures, they undertook to pay a further £100,000 between them if we didn't earn it elsewhere, for example, from an unexpectedly good FA Cup run. As Iain said at the time, 'At least we shouldn't get relegated.'

All of this had been done without Terry's knowledge and before the conversation about going full-time had arisen. There was one more twist to the story. The benefits for being a VP were trivial – a smile, a 'thank you', and lunch with Terry and me three or four times a year. At one of these lunches, and unaware of what Iain and Mike had already committed, Terry explained how he needed two more players. Mike immediately chipped in to fill the shortfall, saying that he'd had some good news that morning.[40] Terry said, rashly in my opinion, that we now had a chance of making the play-offs.

At this stage we had a budget of £440,000, which was £20,000 more than the previous year but it had to stretch across 44 weeks, not 38 as in the previous season. By my calculations it put us about 14th in the wages league table. By coincidence, journalist Stuart Hammonds had done some research and come to the same conclusion in an article published in the *Non-League Paper*.

By the end of the 2009/10 season Terry was clear that if we were to go full-time he couldn't afford to retain some of the more senior and expensive members of the squad. As a result he had released 11 players. He'd now had a core group of young players who had been blooded in the Conference, plus the experience of senior men like striker Danny Kedwell, now our captain.

He set about recruiting more young players, almost all of them from lower leagues, and by the time we played our first league game we had our youngest starting squad yet, with an average age of under 22. It was coming together nicely. And then, on the eve of the season, we received a bid for Danny Kedwell.

—

40 I am pretty sure that Mike was saying he'd had some good fortune because he wanted Terry to believe this was a one-off. He used to say he'd funded the Vegas trips from a bet when in fact he was dipping into his own pocket; for some reason he seemed uncomfortable about being seen to be so generous.

Five days before our first game of the season, I was watching our reserves play at Walton Casuals when my phone rang. It was Steve Evans, the Crawley Town manager. He asked, politely, how much we wanted for Danny.

We couldn't sell him. He was our top striker, captain and our best chance of the goals we needed to make the play-offs, so I thanked Steve for his interest, said Danny wasn't for sale and rather naively hoped that was an end to the matter.

I hadn't really registered that Crawley were the new moneybags club in the Conference until I looked them up. In the past they had always looked as if they were on the verge of financial difficulties but, suddenly, they were awash with money.[41] In July they'd paid £70,000 to sign Matt Tubbs, who went on to win the golden boot that season, and then Sergio Torres for £100,000. So I shouldn't have been surprised when a fax arrived the next morning offering us £40,000 for Danny.

We had a protocol for signings. When we signed each player we told them that we were aiming to get into the Football League *with* them. We also said we wouldn't stand in their way if a good offer came in for them but that 'a good offer' did not mean a club in our league or, indeed, from many of the clubs in the two leagues directly above us. Selling to a club in the same division as us would probably undermine any promotion hopes while telling the squad that we have no ambition.

I quickly checked with the board and then responded that none of our players was for sale. Now that I was aware of their riches, out of a sense of mischief and to wind them up I added 'at any price'. By 1pm we had a second and final offer of £60,000; minutes later Crawley had a second rejection in exactly the same words. Steve Evans phoned Terry the next day and told him, 'Your chairman is an idiot because all players eventually have a price you'll sell at.' And of course he's right – about the price, anyway. You can make your own minds up about the rest of it.

---

41 Crawley's newly found wealth led to a further major spending spree. After failing to sign Danny they paid £165,000 for Richard Brodie from York City. By the end of January 2011 they'd reportedly spent over £600,000 on transfer fees alone (*Non-League Paper*, 23/06/20). That was 33 per cent more than our wages budget (including transfer fees) for the entire season. Meanwhile, Evans was boasting to Terry that they'd be flying to long-distance away games and telling the *Non-League Paper* that he had a war chest of £1m to spend in the January window.

Later that day we announced that we'd rejected Crawley's bid for Danny. We thought that news would be a major boost to our fans' morale and so it proved. Evans went into the press saying that we'd 'broken a verbal agreement' to let him go if we received an offer for £60,000, which was an invention. This was all knockabout nonsense but it set our fans into action.

As fate would have it, the fixture list had us playing Crawley at home a few weeks later. If we won we would go top. Evans was already despised by our fans for his touchline histrionics and non-stop hectoring of referees and his latest rant added petrol to the fire. So, unknown to the club, a group of fans produced T-shirts bearing the legend 'Some things money can't buy' above a picture of Danny. Wearing the T-shirts, the fans were there in force to welcome the Crawley team coach and loudly mock Evans.

The portents for the game weren't good. Due to injuries we had two players making their debuts in a back four which now had an average age of 19. Behind them was first-choice goalkeeper Seb Brown, aged all of 20. They would face this expensively recruited team, including Matt Tubbs who would go on to score 37 goals that season. I braced myself for defeat.

If we could have written a script for the game it couldn't have bettered the events of that evening. Losing 1-0 with 13 minutes to go, Sam Hatton equalised and then, two minutes later, who else but Danny Kedwell scored the winner with a fine looping header. The fans were almost delirious with joy.

After the final whistle, Danny went to soak up the adulation from the crowd. He was handed one of 'his' T-shirts which he put on as part of the celebrations. Thinking that we'd produced the T-shirts can only have added to Evans's black mood. As he left the pitch he was loudly abusing me and the stewards who, as they do with all controversial figures, were escorting him to the dressing room.

Despite this result, we knew we weren't going to win the league, given the enormous amounts of cash now being spent by Crawley. Nonetheless, we retained top position at the halfway stage of the season although they had two games in hand and were only two points behind. One point behind them lurked Luton, with one game in hand over us. Nonetheless, Terry had got the players performing brilliantly and the extra fitness following the decision to go full-time was underpinning our success.

In the January transfer window we had money to spend, thanks to fees from our televised games, so we authorised Terry to recruit. We needed to strengthen our attacking options as Jon Main wasn't the force he had been before his cruciate ligament injury and Terry felt we needed more experience in defence. In came centre-back Jamie Stuart from Rushden & Diamonds and Gareth Gwillim, a left-back on loan from Dagenham & Redbridge after our previous loan left-back, Chris Bush, was recalled by Brentford. James Mulley and Kirk Hudson came in to add pace and penetration to the attack.

In March, our form faltered with a draw and two successive defeats. And the next game was away at Crawley. Effectively it was our last chance to re-open the title race.

It was race week at Cheltenham and in previous years Mike Richardson had taken the first team and football management there for the day. With such a massive game looming, Terry told the squad that they were not permitted to go, especially as the fixture had been brought forward to the Friday night. So he was stunned when he heard that Mike had taken five of them anyway, only a couple of days before such a crucial match.[42]

This illustrated perfectly the problems with accepting money from wealthy fans, however well-intentioned. Terry was furious and laid into the players. As he recalls, 'I remember having a face-to-face bust-up with Jamie Stuart about it and saying, "Jamie, you either go along with me on this or you're out of the door." He was arguing that they didn't have a drink, they weren't doing this and they weren't doing that and they shouldn't be fined.'

Terry knew that if he didn't fine them he would lose face and possibly lose the dressing room. But if he did fine them we might alienate a major benefactor. The issue was clear to me. First we had players who'd breached club discipline and second, you back your manager. This was a matter of principle and so we fined them. It was important that the squad could see

---

42 The outings to Cheltenham were well known for their excesses. In 2014 Mike invited Jon Main and his partner Stephanie to join some of the team at the races. Jon says, 'I was just coming back from the toilet and Mike had obviously been chatting to Stephanie. We'd not been going out long but Mike said if I proposed on the spot he'd pay for the wedding. Stephanie started nudging me so I called Mike's bluff, saying "throw your car in and I'll do it". Mike threw the car keys on the table. It was a brand new Aston Martin. By now Stephanie was nudging me really hard and I chickened out. Every year I get a tweet from team-mate Luke Moore. It has a photo of the car and one word – idiot.' Jon and Stephanie are still together.

that we wouldn't tolerate this sort of selfish behaviour and no one, however wealthy, could protect them if they broke the rules.

We lost 3-1. Crawley were worthy winners despite being reduced to ten men for the second half. Terry was down, 'I felt really let down at the Crawley game. Danny said he was unwell and didn't play and as a team we didn't turn up. If ever I was going to walk away I'd have walked away then.' Talking about it years later, he added, 'But you backed me and said, "What do you want to do and we'll support you."'

Trevor Williams always regarded that incident as the turning point when the team really came together. Terry hadn't registered that at the time, 'I'd never looked upon it as a turning point but some of the other boys were having a go at them for what they'd done. They [the players who went to Cheltenham] were some of the strongest characters in the dressing room but some of the others stood up and said, "You were well out of order there, you were totally out of order." That's not something you manufacture and without it we could have gone under.'

Instead, Terry brought them all together to analyse the game, review where we were in our challenge and what we needed to do from now on, given that the league title was now beyond us. Crucially, at the end of March we signed the final piece of the jigsaw, Kaid Mohamed, and went on a run. As Simon Bassey put it, 'Crawley was a bump in the road that maybe we needed. From then on we didn't lose. Maybe they felt they'd let Brownie down but they went on a run and we just blew teams away.'

Four successive wins followed, including what everyone said was our best performance of the season, possibly best performance ever, at Cambridge United. We sealed a play-off place three games before the end of the season. One more win effectively secured second place and home advantage in the second leg of the semi-final, so Terry's thoughts had already turned to preparing for the next few weeks. He recalled Jon Main from loan and, in a lovely gesture, brought him on to the pitch in the final game of the season for everyone to show their thanks for a much-admired player. Despite straining every sinew, Jon couldn't score in the half hour he played but he was applauded all the time he was on the pitch and was still named man of the match!

We ended the season in second place with 90 points, trailing some way behind Crawley but very comfortably ahead of third-placed Luton. In our promotion campaign in the Ryman League, Terry had bemoaned how many points we dropped to the bottom four teams. This time we got it right. One reason for the team's success was the ruthless demolition of the bottom four teams; we won all eight games with a goal difference of 24-3.

Our semi-final was to be against Fleetwood Town, who had come fifth. I thought this suited us. Fleetwood would play passing football and we believed we were the best team in the league at that. Fleetwood were another team that was bankrolled to an extent well beyond their fan base. However, unlike almost all other clubs who are funded in this way Andy Pilley, their owner, was putting infrastructure in place and building for the long term to try to make the club genuinely sustainable. So despite being in the bottom quarter of the attendance league table, they were third in the spending table according to Stuart Hammonds's article.

After the Cambridge game the whole squad knew we could beat anybody on our day and we went into the play-offs full of confidence. We won the away leg 2-0. Terry was delighted, and nervous. He recalls, 'I thought we played really, really well, a disciplined performance. We won 2-0 and then the nerves came in unbelievably after that because it's yours to mess up. However you dress it up, if you come back to Kingsmeadow and blow it you might as well walk out of the door.'

Terry had been very worried about the inroads the Fleetwood left-back, Junior Brown, had made into our defence in the first leg, so he called an old friend, the Kidderminster Harriers manager Steve Burr. Steve's advice was simple, 'Don't worry about him. Just play the ball into the gaps that he leaves behind and you'll kill them.' As Trevor Williams said, 'You could sneak a double-decker bus into the space Brown left behind him.' Against two centre-backs who weren't very mobile and lacked pace, we were able to pull their defence all over the place.

For the second leg, all the pre-match publicity was that the first goal would be crucial; if they made it 2-1 on aggregate it was game on. If we scored the tie was effectively over.

We scored after 37 seconds. Brett Johnson hoofed the ball towards the corner flag, centre-back Sean Gregan chased out to get it, but Kaid Mohamed bundled him off the ball, held off Junior Brown and slid the ball under the keeper.

By half-time we were 3-0 up after following the tactics to the letter. This scoreline was a little unfair to Fleetwood because they'd had two one-on-ones with Seb Brown, both superbly saved, and had a lob cleared off the line by Sam Hatton. But it was 5-0 on aggregate. The only worried person in the ground was Terry Brown, 'Scoring after 30 seconds took an enormous weight off my shoulders but when they got their goal early in the second I was half thinking "oh no". We were 5-1 up on aggregate but that sums up how ridiculous the thought process was.'

We ran out 6-1 winners and 8-1 on aggregate, a Conference record. Kaid Mohamed scored a hat-trick and James Mulley scored the goal of the game against a demoralised Fleetwood. Terry had told the team before the game to hit the ball wide and drag their centre-backs out of position, because 'they can't run'. After the game, we found Sean Gregan's boots on the peg in the away dressing room.

We were about to play a one-off game a week before the ninth anniversary of the FA Commission's decision and the reward for the winners was a place in the Football League.

36

SHOOT IT IN THE RIGHT DIRECTION

NO ONE understood the importance of practising penalties better than Terry Brown. As Aldershot manager he was twice thwarted by shoot-outs, losing a play-off final to Shrewsbury in 2004 and a semi-final against Carlisle a year later, despite being 3-1 ahead at one point. So it was hardly surprising that the team started practising them six weeks before the play-off final.

This was all new to Lee Minshull, who had signed from Tonbridge and given up his job as a quantity surveyor to grab a chance of reaching the Football League. He says, 'Everything was done very professionally. Every penalty taker had to start with a walk from the halfway line to make it as realistic as possible.' The approach obviously made an impact as he has since successfully used it twice in his current role as assistant manager at Concord Rangers.

First-team coach Simon Bassey kept score from behind the goal, and recalls, 'If you missed you had to do a lap of the training pitch in a given time. The only one who never missed was Kaid Mohamed.' They settled on their first five penalty takers long before the semi-finals, let alone the final. A few days before the final the TV cameras visited the training ground and that day our penalties were awful; perhaps it worked out well because it's best to get these glitches out of the system before the big day.

The last training session before setting off for the final wasn't a great success, as Simon explains, 'In all the big games we've played the last training sessions are shit. No one wants to train, you're frightened that you're going to get injured, that you're going to roll your ankle. As soon as it's finished and everyone's fit it's been a great session, even if it's been a shit session. You've got your team, they know what they're doing, what you've been telling them all year, we know we're good and fit and mentally we're in a good place. So you don't get negative about the session not being as great as you wanted it to be because that's only going to affect the players. You just say "it's been a brilliant session" and they have to walk off believing that.'

The final was to be played at Manchester City's Eastlands stadium, now the Etihad, because the Champions League Final was being played at Wembley a week later and UEFA demanded that the pitch remained unused in the run-up to their final. Excellent as Eastlands is, the change of venue was a disappointment for both teams' players and fans alike with the extra travel time and cost knocking at least 10,000 off the attendance.

Nothing was left to chance. Watching everything close-up, Trevor Williams was in no doubt, 'Our build-up to the final was perfection. Terry did not put a foot wrong in terms of the way we trained, the time we trained, the penalty practice. We gave ourselves the best chance to win that game. If we'd lost you could still say we couldn't have prepared any better.' Throughout the preparation, Terry had reinforced his message at every opportunity with comments like 'when we get to the final', and, 'We came higher than Luton by six points. We're better than them. We deserve to be there.'

The team travelled up to the Village Hotel in Ashton-under-Lyne to stay overnight before a key part of the preparation, a training session on the pitch on the Friday morning, the day before the game. Rather than keep the players cooped up in the hotel on the Thursday night, Terry sent them off across the road to the bowling alley and arcades.

Every club has a joker who lifts the mood and releases tensions whatever the situation. Reece Jones was ours. He wasn't going to make the squad but his presence lifted everyone. As Trevor put it, 'He's an absolute fruit-loop and dressing room gold. He was silly arseholes, he was brilliant, the boys loved having him around. If he was signed to do that it was a genius move. If the players were nervous he'd say or do something silly. It was incredibly juvenile stuff but it was what was absolutely needed at the time.' On the Thursday night he excelled himself, performing a range of exotic moves to the dance machine to howls of laughter from the squad.

The next day came the serious stuff. A lot of it was about getting familiar with the surroundings and taking the souvenir snapshots. As Simon said, 'We wanted to get the tourist bit done and out of the way so that on Saturday the team could focus.'

We were given the away changing room but that soon changed. We got on very well with the ground staff. One of them told Trevor Williams, 'You lot, you came up, you were respectful, agreed a time, worked with us about what you wanted to do, went on the pitch when we wanted you to and looked after it. Luton went to Spain, didn't want to do a session on the pitch and then decided they did.' Another of the ground staff told Simon, 'They relegated us, with David Pleat running across the pitch.[43] They're in the Conference and they are trying to tell us when they'll train. I've never liked Luton so you can go here.' And that is how we got the home dressing room.

The Manchester City dressing room was decorated with motivational statements and photos of their players above their allocated spaces. After the players left training, Robin Bedford, universally referred to as 'Rocket', and Trevor put up photos of our goal celebrations, great saves and tackles, all photos they'd prepared especially for the day. Trevor says, 'We put squad photos and individual photos, so that when they walked back in on the day of the final the boys felt a little bit more at home.' Furthermore, Terry had insisted that the entire 'family' travelled to the game, including all the expanded first team squad, even if they weren't in the named 16 players on the day. That is why when Jon Main arrived the next day he found his full kit hanging up and his photo on his place, replacing Argentine international player Carlos Tevez's photo for that one day.

Rocket also carefully placed a lion and a dog in pride of place. Earlier in the season Mark Francis, a psychologist, had worked with the team and introduced them to the idea, as goalkeeper Seb Brown explains, 'He was saying you can't just be a lion strutting around thinking you're the best. You have to have a bit of the dog in you, do the dirty stuff, do the hard

—

43 Twenty-eight years earlier, in 1983, Luton won the last game of the season 1-0 at Manchester City's Maine Road ground, saving themselves from relegation at the expense of City. As the final whistle blew, Luton manager David Pleat famously celebrated on the pitch by performing what looked like a barefooted walk on hot coals, while wearing a beige suit and brown slip-ons. Football fans don't forget or forgive – and neither do fashion gurus.

work and all of that as well.' Seb adopted the idea, bought two soft toys and started taking them everywhere with the team.

Seb continues, 'Rocket took care of them when we went anywhere overnight. He had pictures of them in the gym, on the weights bench, they just became a bit of a running joke, getting them in different positions. I'm sure that indirectly it helped the group to bond. Initially the boys went away saying "what was that all about?" but it ended up bonding everyone together.'

The night before the final saw the usual ritual where players and management staff on their first away trips have to perform a song of their choosing. Some struggle through to the amusement of their peers; others are more confident, like Sammy Moore (injured and missing this game) who had asked if he could have ten minutes when it was his turn a couple of years earlier. The next morning the team had an early breakfast and a light lunch at 11.30am, three and a half hours before kick-off.

We'd played Luton twice that season, getting thumped 3-0 at their place and earning a slightly fortunate point at home. We didn't score in either game so we needed to put that behind us. So, in between the two meals the football management put the likely Luton team up on the notice board and went through them all. It was, 'Him – loser, him – lost this game, him – he doesn't want to be there and the other players don't like him, him – lost a play-off before, him – he's a shithouse. When the chips are down they are losers and they will lose.' It was very disrespectful but it did its job, reinforcing the team's self-belief.

Later, Terry gave a more conventional speech. 'I wanted them to go away thinking, "Wow, we are here now, let's deliver," not, "Oh my God, this is it."' He didn't try to be Al Pacino in *Any Given Sunday* (which was just as well, as Pacino wasn't interrupted by one of his players forgetting to switch his phone off). He kept it short.

'This is our day, this is our moment, our time.[44] We've actually planned this for a year, or two years, but within the last six weeks we've really focused on the City of Manchester Stadium, we've really focused on getting to Eastlands. "When we get to Eastlands," we've been saying, "it will be

—

44 As Danny Kedwell gathered himself to take the deciding penalty in the shoot-out later that day he turned to his team-mates and, drawing on Terry's speech, said 'this is our time', which became the title of Niall Couper's excellent record of our first ten years.

our day. When we get to Eastlands we will play our football." You played on it yesterday. It's made for us. It's big, it's beautiful. Everybody down here loves us, everybody hates Luton, it's absolutely made for us.

'We planned better for this game than for any day I can ever remember. We're fitter, we're sharper, we're hungrier, we're unbeaten in the last ten games. We've got one game to go. We sat down after Crawley and went, "This ain't good enough for us, we've got to improve, we've got to win, or not get beat, in ten games." You've done the shitty stuff, you've done the hard part, this is your glory day, this is where you get to show how good you are, this is where everyone, on the telly, your friends, every bugger that's there in the 30,000, or whatever it is, people [see] how good we are, to set a marker for the second division and the managers there going "shit me, they play some stuff".

'Eastlands, we've got our dressing room – we've got the home dressing room – it's our pitch, our tempo. The most important thing I'll say to you, our tempo. Good luck gentlemen.'

At 12.30pm the coach set off for Eastlands. Everyone was relaxed. Terry had done a magnificent job getting everyone into the right frame of mind. We were massive underdogs. Their wages budget was nearly triple ours at £1.3m compared to our £440,000. We were inexperienced; Luton had two players who had both made more league appearances than our team put together. But it didn't matter, it just didn't matter; we were going to win.

At Eastlands the players wandered out on to the pitch. Luton players were checking out the pitch for the first time, taking photos and absorbing the feel of the stadium. Terry was bemused that they'd not visited Eastlands before the game, 'We trained on the pitch on the Friday. I think that was a real mistake they made [not doing the same] because it got you out there. We felt it was one we'd got over Luton and I couldn't believe they didn't train on it – it beggars belief. It was a totally different surface from anything we'd played on all year.' Whether or not this made a difference to Luton's performance, it added to the belief in our dressing room; we'd already got one over them.

Off the pitch the fans were arriving, filling 26 coaches, each named after a member of the playing squad. It was much easier for fans to remember that they were travelling in the Kedwell coach as opposed to coach 22. I went outside and wandered around a sea of yellow and blue, chatting to friends, old and new, before joining a large group in the FanZone that had been set aside for us outside the stadium. I'd said from the very first time we put together a five-year business plan that I thought the major challenge would be getting out of the Conference; staying in League 2 would be much easier. And here we were, in what was probably the defining game of our short existence. To my surprise I was totally chilled, even though I feared that, given our meagre financial resources, if we didn't win today it might be years before we could challenge again.

Back inside the stadium I joined the other board members and invited guests. We'd invited the player of the year from each of our previous seasons to join us for lunch and in the directors' box, but most politely declined and chose instead to sit with the fans. I liked that; it said a lot about the relationship between fans and players.

Eileen and I travelled up separately from the team to stay with my sister and her husband. On the morning of the game they were amused to see a van with a large satellite dish on its roof draw up outside their house for the first of many, many interviews. Press interest had started immediately after the play-off semi-final and continued until close to kick-off on the day of the final. There was a relentless edge to many interviewers' questions, asking how I felt about the possibility of being only one division below the franchise, while I reminded myself not to call them that publicly. As usual the response was, 'We are immensely proud of what we've achieved and refuse to be measured by comparison to anyone else. And anyway, they're not playing here, so let's talk about today's game.'

Only four members of the Wimbledon team and five members of the Luton team appeared in both the 3-0 hammering earlier in the season and the final, but the reasons for the changes were very different. After a spectacular falling-out with their fans, Luton's manager Richard Money had been sacked 13 games before the end of the season. His assistant, Gary Brabin, had been appointed as caretaker. Brabin had, like Terry, lost a play-off final and a semi-final, the latter on penalties. He had set about making the team younger and by the time of the final the average age of their starting line-up was 26, down from 27.5 in the game earlier in the season. Meanwhile, Terry had quietly added experience to the squad although we were still younger than Luton, with an average age of 25. It represented a major addition of experience compared to the average of a touch under 23 in the earlier game.

Luton also arrived full of confidence. Brabin felt their build-up had been near-perfect, 'We'd got a good formula for the semis, we were in real good form. We won 3-0 away at Wrexham – we were fantastic, we could have won 7-0. I remember coming away with 3-0 thinking it's a nice comfortable lead but we should have put this thing to bed tonight with four, five or even 6-0, we were that good on the night.'

Terry and assistant manager Stuart Cash went to that game to assess the possible opposition in the final and saw it through different eyes. Terry told me, 'I came away thinking we're going to win this. Wrexham were unlucky, a decent side, but everything Luton tried came off. I remember thinking we'll have more legs than Luton.'

One person who was unusually nervous before kick-off was first-team coach Simon Bassey. He recalls, 'Every time we'd played Luton they were much better than us, even when we beat them 2-1 at Kenilworth Road in the previous season. It's the only time I've ever done this – I went in the toilet at Manchester before the game and I was puffing with nerves. I knew this was our one chance. We had a mid-table budget and we'd put a really good team together but it would break up after the season. If we went up we might be able to keep hold of a few. If we didn't go up they'd leave and then we'd be starting from scratch with a poor budget. And that's a hell of a job.'

He was absolutely right. We knew that several of our players were being watched by league teams and that we could never match the offers they were likely to receive; in fact we couldn't even match the wages that other Conference clubs could offer them. This was it. Make or break. And still I was completely chilled. After all, we had our own club, in our own stadium and nine years earlier we had nothing.

The players went through their pre-match rituals while in the background they could hear Jamie Stuart throwing up. Jamie had joined in January to add experience to the defence – he accounted for nearly 200 of the 240 league starts in the team. While not as tall as most centre-backs he had, as footballers say, 'a good leap on him'. He had a real physical presence and a stare that felt like he blinked only every 60 seconds.

Jamie's warm-up routine must be unique, as Seb Brown describes, 'He would neck down a few bottles of a sports nutrition powder, probably laced with caffeine. He'd be in the showers doing sets of different press-ups to get pumped up and he'd be sick every so often. One minute you'd hear "aaaarrggh" in the toilet being sick and the next he'd be belting out press-ups in the showers. And the smelling salts, he used to love the smelling salts.'

Eventually, after the pre-match ceremonials the match got under way. The game was very open, high on quality and entertaining. There were several key incidents. First, Danny Kedwell had the ball in the net after seven minutes but he was offside. I interviewed Danny nine years later and, as you'd expect from a striker, he is still adamant that the goal should have stood; the DVD shows he was at least a yard and a half offside!

From then on the final was finely balanced until the last five minutes when Luton's Jason Walker collected a pass in the penalty area. He overran the ball as he tried to round Seb Brown. But as Walker ran on, Seb clipped his leg. I was convinced it was a penalty but the referee played on, possibly distracted by the frantic activity as first Sam Hatton and then Jamie Stuart made desperate last-ditch blocks.

Only two minutes later, Luton broke free again and Walker, rising unchallenged to a cross, headed the ball firmly into the net. Or at least that's what it looked like to everyone in the stadium, including me as I sat directly in line with it. But the ball hit the inside of the post and rebounded straight into Seb's grateful clutches. Luton boss Gary Brabin was on his feet celebrating and even now can't understand why the ball didn't go in, 'You look at Jason's header and think with the law of gravity, how has that not gone over the line?' That's not how physics works but I know what he meant. Meanwhile, Terry Brown was also thinking it was going in and he'd lost another play-off final.

At 90 minutes it was 0-0. In extra time we were comfortably the better team. James Mulley had a clear chance, Kaid Mohamed hit the post and, in injury time, Ismail Yakubu missed an unchallenged header from a few yards out. Years later, Danny Kedwell still hasn't forgiven him. Sam Hatton crossed the ball perfectly from the right. It was heading straight for Danny, who remembers, 'It was a free header, my eyes lit up and then Yaks came from nowhere. "What are you doing?" but he hit the side-netting.'

And so in our 49th game of the league season, it all came down to penalties. I was very calm but Eileen can't bear to watch penalties and went off to hide in the ladies'. I was thinking about Terry. How must he be feeling, having lost a semi-final and a final in penalty shoot-outs?

The penalties were to be taken at the end where the Dons fans were stationed. The format is well-worn. Five penalties each and if it's still level then continue until one team scores and the other misses. Terry called everyone together. Lee Minshull had come on as a substitute and was keen to take one. He says, 'Kaid Mohamed had cramp in extra time and I said to Terry, "I think I should have his penalty." Mine had been really good in practice. But Kaid said, "I want one, I want one," so we said okay.'

We had eight offers to take a penalty and three just didn't want to know.

Some people, like Eileen, can't look. Others, like Simon, have their lucky routine, 'I always cross my fingers and squat down, just like that and we've never missed one.' Ivor was a total fidget, unable to sit still. For reasons I've never understood, I sat totally still; the more critical the situation the calmer I became.

Luton's Alex Lawless went first and Seb, diving to his right, saved it. Sam Hatton was first for us. As he walked towards the penalty spot all I could think of was an awful penalty he'd taken years earlier in an FA Cup match at Horsham where we'd lost on penalties. But this was a different time and place, a more experienced and more confident Sam Hatton, and a different result. He thwacked it into the top corner of the net.

George Pilkington converted for Luton and Luke Moore, who'd had a fantastic game and was my man of the match, took his. This was another high-quality penalty, lashed into the angle of the post and crossbar; as the Brazilians say, 'where the owl sleeps'. After the game I asked Luke about his perfect penalty and he said, 'I didn't mean to hit it that high.' And we fans think these things are all planned; sometimes it's better not to ask. Nonetheless it was unstoppable and 2-1 to us.

Then Adam Newton scored for Luton and Kaid Mohamed limped forward. He'd had cramp for the last 20 minutes of the game and I thought, 'He's going to miss.' He did, with a weak shot that Luton's Mark Tyler saved easily, and it was 2-2.

I was watching Terry. What must he be thinking? He'd been here before and lost from a winning position. And here it was happening again. I've watched the DVD several times and the strain is etched on his face. He's a good man and a fine manager and I was desperate for him to succeed.

And then came the turning point. After first congratulating Mark Tyler, the Luton keeper, 'because that's what you do, however gutted you are for your team-mate', Seb settled down to face Jason Walker's penalty. Before the shoot-out started Seb had been seen studying a scruffy piece of paper, which looked like it had been torn out of a spiral-bound pocket book – as indeed it had. It listed the names of four Luton players who'd taken penalties and where they'd placed them. In the days before widely available match videos that was all Seb could find on YouTube. Only he knew that of the four names on his list only Jason Walker was on the pitch. Seb had found six penalties that Walker had taken; four were hit down the middle of the goal and two to the keeper's right.

Seb takes up the story, 'When Walker was walking up I half-knew in my head that I had to hold on a little bit. If you watch the penalties, in a lot of them I went quite early to try and cover the ground. With Walker I thought I've got to hold on as long as I can. I was going to dive right but I knew that I had to delay it and ultimately that was what transpired. If he had blasted it down the middle it would have been hit or miss whether I got a foot to it or a toe to it and if that would be enough to keep it out. Luckily he went slightly to the right with not a lot of pace and obviously the rest is the rest.'

Seb saved it. So much of football is narrow margins and this was a classic example. Walker had tried a Panenka penalty,[45] striking it not very hard down the middle of the goal. If he'd hit it harder Seb probably wouldn't have been able to stop it. Ironically, if he had done a 'classic Panenka' and hit a slow, lazy chip down the middle, Seb would probably have completed his dive and been lying on the ground as the ball drifted past. When they go in you look cool and the goalkeeper looks foolish. When they don't, however, it's a different story.

Gary Brabin couldn't believe his eyes, 'I remember Jason Walker doing that penalty in practice and the lads had a go at him over it and said he should do it properly. I was going to say something to him but I never did because I'd seen the players having a go at him. I thought "well that's him told" and I didn't want to put something in his head. But I don't think anyone in the stadium could believe what he'd done.'

—

45 This type of penalty is named after the Czech player Antonin Panenka, who scored with this technique in a shoot-out in the 1976 UEFA European Championship Final, consigning Germany to defeat by doing so. If it isn't done well, or if the goalkeeper simply stands still, the taker can look foolish. In 1992 Gary Lineker attempted it in an England international match against Brazil; if he'd scored he would have equalled the England goalscoring record. He didn't. He never scored again for England.

For a moment no one registered what they'd seen. The TV commentator said it was a goal, until he realised that Seb had stuck up 'a strong hand', as the goalkeeping coaches say, and saved it, even as he dived to his right.

Up stepped Ismail Yakubu to take his penalty. Terry wasn't confident, 'Yaks was the one I wouldn't have fancied. He had been practising them before. People said he used to wait until the keeper moved before hitting it, but I don't know how you do that. I took penalties and only missed one and there's no way in a million years I would have the nerve to do that. But he took a beautiful penalty, didn't he?' Indeed he did; he took two steps and coolly side-footed the ball, not very hard, one way as Mark Tyler dived the other. I have watched the DVD many times and I always enjoy Steve Bower, the commentator, going almost full Partridge with, 'Oh and Yakubu.'

We were nearly there at 3-2 to us and set point. Midfielder Steven Gregory, who had been due to take a penalty until he was injured and substituted, turned to the TV cameras, raised a finger and almost screamed 'one more'.

Back to Terry. He was now animatedly, and yet distractedly, chatting to a policeman who had wandered on to the pitch and ended up beside him. Later I asked him what he was talking about. 'No idea. No idea at all,' was the answer.

Each team had one penalty left. If Luton missed, or if we scored, we were in the Football League. Jake Howells, at 20 the youngest player on the pitch, stepped forward and scored a perfect penalty to make it 3-3.

Next was our club captain and top scorer Danny Kedwell. In moments of great tension some behaviour is completely irrational and so, as Danny set off, Simon Bassey shouted at him, 'Pull your socks up, you look a tramp. It looks tired, it looks messy.' Immediately Terry shouted in response, 'Just leave him alone.' Simon continued to grumble, 'It's not a good look, socks round your ankles, it don't look good.' Danny ignored him.

I asked Danny if he'd wanted Howells to miss, in which case we'd have won 3-2 and be in the Football League without needing him to take our fifth penalty. Or did he want Howells to score so that the decider lay with him? He's a striker so the answer was obvious, 'I wanted Jake Howells to score so I could get the winner.

'My previous penalty was at home versus Rushden. I'd missed the one before that and Bass had said, "In future, just smash it. When you smash a ball no one's going to save it because you hit it so hard." I took one in training and smashed it into the roof of the net and he said, "There you go, that's how you do it," and that's how I did it after that. Bass was great like that.

'At Manchester I thought, "I'm absolutely leathering this." Don't aim for the corner, just leather it. I wasn't nervous – it was really weird. As I walked up I was thinking, "How am I going to celebrate? Do I jump into the crowd, do I run to the players?" The referee had the ball in his hand and he went to pass it to me and I said "drop it on the floor". I don't like taking it off the referee. I don't know why.'

I wouldn't be going into such detail if Danny had missed, and if we'd not been promoted to the Football League you probably wouldn't be reading this book, so it can't be a surprise to read that he scored. It was 4-3 and, as Radio WDON co-commentator Rob Cornell shouted in an over-excited voice that ratcheted up to castrato levels, 'We're in League 2.' Lee Minshull, who was next in line to take a penalty if Danny missed, felt a huge wave of relief sweep over him.

Danny ran to the corner flag. Jon Main was so sure that Danny would score that he'd already set off, which is why, despite his injured knee, he was the first to reach him. I looked for Terry but I had lost sight of him in the pandemonium on the pitch so I set off to offer condolences to Luton. Their directors, Gary Sweet and David Wilkinson, said, with a great deal more dignity and good grace than I suspect I'd have been able to muster if they'd won, 'If we had to lose I'm glad it was to you,' a sentiment later echoed to me by Gary Brabin.

I returned to my seat just in time to see a shirt-sleeved Terry on the pitch, discovering the child within him, smashing an imaginary penalty into the roof of the net and running, arms aloft, towards the fans to celebrate. Eileen surfaced from the ladies' and discovered that club president Dickie Guy's wife, Josie, had locked herself in the next cubicle while the penalties were taken. Eileen had heard the roars and they were so loud she assumed we'd lost until, as she emerged, someone in a blue top raced past the ladies' door, screaming with delight. A steward confirmed the result.

Trevor Williams, one of the club's founders, broke down in tears in the dugout: 'I just sat there and started crying and one of the stadium staff came up to me and said, "Don't worry, mate, Luton are a massive club, you'll be back next year."' Fellow founder Ivor Heller, who isn't one for being able to hide his emotions, looked like he was going to burst with joy as he fist-pumped and jumped up and down in the directors' box. It made for great TV.

From somewhere in the crowd an anthem struck up to the tune of 'Blue Moon', very appropriately since it's the Manchester City fans' song. 'Nine years, it only took nine years,' came the chant. I love it when a club has a song that is theirs alone, whether it is 'I'm Forever Blowing Bubbles' at West Ham or 'You'll Never Walk Alone' at Liverpool. Now we had another one to add to the 'Cocaine' song. I love it when our fans start singing it, because it takes me back to that day. I've often wondered who came up with it.

I have no recollection of the trophy presentation. Afterwards, Ivor and I went down to the dressing room where there were handshakes all round and suddenly I found myself being hugged by a naked man. I was grateful there were no cameras there; nowadays that would have been all over social media.

After waiting for the best part of an hour for Danny, who had been randomly selected for a drug test but was so dehydrated he couldn't manage to pee, we all went back to the hotel where there was a buffet laid on for us. The players were soon out on the town where they met up with Mike Richardson, whose support had made much of this possible and who, appallingly, I'd forgotten to invite back to the hotel. I don't really want to know what happened that night but I've been assured by more than one player that they landed up in a club where by the end of the evening absolutely everyone was singing 'we're going up'.

The next day the team, with many of the players looking very green around the gills, returned to Kingsmeadow on the coach. They were greeted by a couple of thousand Dons fans and after many handshakes and pats on the back, off they went into town to continue celebrating.

I missed all this. On the Saturday night Eileen and I travelled up to the Lake District for a short break, much of which was spent completing a grant application for a safety control room, a mandatory Football League condition for membership. You don't get long in football before the 'what's next?' question needs addressing.

The aftermath of promotion was very different for different people. For Luton, Gary Brabin had to pick up the players, which left him little time to pick himself up. He recalls, 'The players were devastated. I remember Jason Walker's family were at the ground waiting for him and he never even went in – he just went home. Once I'd done the things I had to do, the interviews and all that, I just remember that the big part was that I wanted to get away from everyone, to be on my own.'

For Luton players it wasn't just losing a final. A while later, Dons midfielder Lee Minshull met some ex-Luton players who told him that they would have received five-figure bonuses if they'd won. Our bonuses to be spread across the entire squad of 20-odd players came to about £50,000.

Lee, who had given up a good job to try to make it as a professional footballer, found the effect transformational, 'Being promoted changed our lives. We got Football League contracts, we were Football League players and we got PFA pensions, things like that. And when you get up to League 2, it's almost like if it doesn't work out you've got the Conference to go to. So you've got another chance at full-time. But if you're with a Conference club and it doesn't work, then you're probably going to have to go back to part-time.'

For Jon Main, hero of Conference South and golden boot winner two years earlier, it was a success tinged with sadness because he knew this was the end of the road for him. He would never play in the Football League. Years later I asked him whether, not having played in the play-off final, he had felt able to take part fully in the celebrations. He said, 'I absolutely got the club. It was a farewell and I knew what it meant to everyone, and what the fans wanted and as much as it hurt me leaving I was just so happy. I love the club and it was a lovely farewell really. My dream was to play league football but it was the perfect goodbye.' And they say there is no such thing as a club man nowadays.

Jon's departure was formally announced three days after the final. Among the other released players was Ismail Yakubu, scorer of that oh-so-cool penalty in the final. Even the lion and the dog disappeared, never to be seen again. Football doesn't stand still for long and there is little room for sentimentality.

Promotion affected lots of people in different ways but I think my favourite memory of the post-match celebrations was when I overheard Traci Sleet, widely known as Traci Turnstile for her matchday volunteering, say 'I'm a Football League turnstile operator now.' How lovely.

37

NEW KID IN TOWN

WHEN WE bought Kingsmeadow in 2003 we knew we were buying a non-league stadium. However, we were confident that we could make it comply with the Football League's requirements. Now we had to prove it.

To help clubs to prepare for promotion the FL circulates a 102-question self-assessment checklist covering areas including the size of changing rooms, quality of floodlights, pitch dimensions, the overall capacity, and the number of seats. One mandatory requirement was that before the start of our first FL season we had to erect a control room to monitor crowd safety; that is why I spent the first two days after our promotion-winning game completing a grant application for such a room. So much for a holiday.

FL entry is in two stages – 'admission' and 'membership'. The admission standards set out what is acceptable for the first year in the FL. For example, we only needed a capacity of 4,000 to be admitted but for full membership we had to have 5,000 by the start of the second season. Failure to comply could mean expulsion. In effect, the FL was saying, 'We'll let you in, but if you don't improve your ground to the required standard within a year we can throw you out again.' This sounds very threatening, and it is wise to respond accordingly, but in practice the FL staff go out of their way to help.

Reaching 5,000 capacity was a major problem. The planning permission showed a potential capacity of over 6,000 but that required a comprehensive rebuilding of the stadium and that wasn't affordable. Our existing capacity of just over 4,700 qualified us for admission but I couldn't see how we could possibly increase it to 5,000 at an affordable cost. Furthermore, one of the FL's requirements meant we needed to install more seats. These would have to be created in place of existing standing areas and, since seats take up more space than standing, the capacity was likely to go down, not up.

Help was at hand. Although the FL lays down criteria for membership, it is the local authority which issues the licence to operate the stadium, including the specified capacity. So we turned to the council's safety advisor for help. He recommended that we bring in a terrace specialist to advise us on possible options.

The basic calculation is simple; you can stand 47 people in each ten square metres of terrace. So multiply the area of the terrace by 47 and divide by ten and you get your theoretical standing capacity. But the resultant capacity must be reduced by factors which take into account the quality of the view and the adequacy of safety arrangements such as emergency exits and stewarding. To get the required capacity above 5,000 we had to be inventive; we ended up including every square metre of the stadium that could be occupied, including places no one would ever stand, for example around the floodlights. It was a complex and time-consuming process which ended up with a theoretical capacity of about 5,300. We then had an honest conversation with the council's expert about how many fans we could safely accommodate. As a result, we agreed to restrict the operating capacity to 4,850. It was then simple arithmetic to 'reverse engineer' the adjustment factors to scale the capacity down to 4,850.

The FL was happy because the capacity was certified as being over 5,000 and Kingston Council was happy because we were limiting the crowd to a number we all agreed was safe. And we were satisfied that the resultant capacity wouldn't put fans at risk. The risk of ejection from the FL had gone away.

While I was preoccupied with making sure we weren't going to be thrown out of the FL, Mike Richardson had taken the players to Las Vegas immediately after the play-off final, fulfilling a promise he'd made if they won promotion. Three days after the final, and with the squad in Vegas, I received a call from the Gillingham chairman, Paul Scally, making a transfer bid for our captain and leading striker Danny Kedwell. I wasn't surprised because Paul had enquired about Danny's availability the previous October.

We tell all our players when they sign for us that we will not sell them to a club in the same division. But I immediately knew this approach was going to be a problem because Gillingham was Danny's local club, which he'd supported since he was a child. The following morning, having as usual consulted Terry and the board, I formally rejected the bid; Paul asked to be kept informed if things changed – and of course they did.

Very soon Danny's agent was on the case. After long discussions with Terry we agreed that we had little choice other than to let Danny go but to help with how this was presented to fans, we would insist that he ask for a transfer. The request duly arrived and we decided to announce that Danny had asked to be put on the transfer list. This was to make sure that our fans knew that we weren't selling him willingly. Another reason was to advertise his availability. Gillingham would argue that he would move to them and no other club, so we didn't have much of a hand to play, but we were hoping to attract other bids to make it competitive.

We dug our heels in and in late June we received another, much improved, offer which we again rejected. We were approaching the start of training for the coming season and Terry didn't want an unsettled player around as it wouldn't be good for team morale. But we guessed that Gillingham would want Danny ready for their start of training so we held our nerve. Sure enough, an acceptable bid arrived. At £75,000, and given the circumstances, we felt we'd done well – the basic fee was triple the original offer. We had agreed to forego some add-ons to achieve that fee but we didn't think Danny would be sold for a substantial profit and we wanted to maximise the guaranteed fee.

While this had been going on we had also received a formal approach for our star midfielder Steven Gregory. We had heard on the grapevine that several clubs were interested in him, but it was a surprise when League 1 club Bournemouth made an offer in late June. In line with our undertaking to players when they sign, we told Steven of Bournemouth's interest and he was clearly very attracted by the idea of testing himself at that level.

Again we resisted but they were persistent. Four separate offers were made and each was refused on the basis that we didn't want to sell any of our players. For a while it seemed that the deal was dead but when the add-ons were improved we reluctantly agreed to the deal. This all happened so quickly that Steven's transfer ended up being announced a couple of days before Danny's. To add to our problems, Kaid Mohamed, who had been on loan at the end of the promotion season, had chosen to move to Cheltenham in preference to us. We could never have matched the offer they made him. So six weeks after the season ended, and before we'd even kicked a ball in League 2, we had lost both our first-choice strikers and our key midfielder.

Despite this, Terry was determined to give the squad a chance to prove themselves in League 2 and so recruitment that summer was limited. He had already recruited Jack Midson to bolster our attacking options; now Jack was our principal striker. With only a couple of other newcomers much of the summer was spent re-signing existing players, because they now had to have standard 52-week Football League contracts.

While all this was going on, club secretary David Charles and I flew to Cyprus for our first Football League AGM. A substantial part of the meeting was discussions about club finances; my meeting notes say, 'Clubs in all three divisions voted in favour of developing rigorous new measures aimed at delivering a "break-even" financial model.' Given the financial disasters of various clubs over the ten years since that meeting it's hard to believe that everyone was fully committed to what they voted for.

Being promoted to the FL meant an introduction to the Salary Cost Management Protocol. The SCMP, better known as the wages cap, imposed a limit of 55 per cent of turnover to be spent on players' wages. The terminology used about the cap is confusing so, for those who are interested, Appendix 1 shows how the process worked. For the purposes of this chapter I'll just say that we complied quite easily; indeed I was left wondering how on earth clubs managed to spend up to the allowed level.

On the first night of the AGM I was sitting on the hotel patio when I was approached by a vaguely familiar figure. He introduced himself as Brian Mawhinney (a former Home Secretary and, more relevantly, a former chairman of the FL). He suggested that he and I should sit down with Peter Winkelman, the Milton Keynes chairman, to discuss how we might normalise relations between the clubs. Taken aback by this out-of-the-blue approach, I replied that I didn't think our owners, the fans, would want me to do that. He paused and then said, 'Did you know I'm a Lord?' before going on to suggest that the fans wouldn't know if we dined at Westminster, away from prying eyes. I explained that I'd need at least the support of our parent board to do that and I was certain it would be refused. From that day when any family discussions aren't going my way I draw myself up to my full height and say, 'Did you know I'm a Lord?'

David and I went straight from Cyprus to the Conference awards dinner at Celtic Manor where Terry Brown received the warmest reception of the night when he went forward to collect the award for winning the play-off final. The Conference AGM was the next day and after many farewells it was back to Kingsmeadow to await the release of the fixture list.[46]

The most enjoyable event of the summer was an invitation from the Combined Counties League who presented us with an award to recognise that we were the first CCL club to go on and be promoted to the FL. It was a lovely gesture and very much appreciated. I thought it was right to invite Kris Stewart, a founder and chairman during our time in the CCL, to accept the award on behalf of the club.

The fixtures landed us with a plum first game against Bristol Rovers, newly relegated from League 1 and expected to be promotion contenders. Ivor always has an eye on the historical significance of games and so we obtained FL permission to play in a kit that was based on the one WFC wore for their first FL game against Halifax Town in 1977.

The media coverage was non-stop, including interviews with half a dozen overseas publications. I bounced from one interview to another and eventually they all seemed to merge into one. It was a great day for us. Unfortunately, the result wasn't. Terry kept his word to the promotion squad and nine of them started the game. Two others were on the bench and only James Mulley was missing, injured, from the players who remained from the play-off final.

The game started at a frenetic pace. For most of the first half we were thoroughly outplayed and were quickly 2-0 down. I began to fear for us in League 2. The team gradually settled down and mounted a comeback, only losing to a late penalty. It was the first time we'd lost an opening league game of the season.

—

46 Before the league season started we were required to play a preliminary round of the League Cup. We were drawn away and lost. In our first six years in the FL, we were drawn away every year in the first round of the League Cup and lost every game. Finally, in our seventh season we were drawn at home in the first round; we lost. At the time of writing (September 2020) we've just played this season's first round. We were drawn away and we lost, making a total of nine first-round exits in our ten years in the FL.

Centre-back Jamie Stuart had two reasons to remember the game. First, after only four minutes he earned the doubtful accolade of being the first of our players to be booked in the FL. No one was very surprised. The second reason was that he scored our first FL goal with a fine glancing header. Everyone was surprised.

Many of my fears were put to rest when we won our next game, away to Dagenham, and then again at Plymouth. We were settling in well. Our 12th match was at Morecambe, where we won 2-1. Terry Brown remembers, 'We were brilliant. Their crowd were shouting about typical Wimbledon hoofing the ball and the Morecambe skipper came over and said, "Are they watching this game, you've outplayed us."' After that game Terry said to me, 'Well we're not going to get relegated, are we?'

And then we started losing. It's not always obvious why results suddenly turn for the better or worse, but perhaps part of it was that clubs had now seen us. As Terry put it, 'By then most people had sussed that we wanted to play out from the back and they pressed us.'

Simon Bassey thought Morecambe was a turning point, 'Celebrating on the bus back was probably our downfall. All those young, hungry boys who were striving, thought they'd cracked it and [when things went a bit wrong they] couldn't get it back.'

We lost the next three games badly, conceding 12 goals. Just before the third, Terry had to rush home to deal with a personal matter. Stuart and Simon took over, decided we needed to stop conceding goals so easily and ground out a very negative, but oddly satisfying, 0-0 draw at Shrewsbury, who were then in a promotion spot. Simon observed, 'There comes a point where you've just got to stop losing. We bored the life out of everyone at Shrewsbury but we got a terrific point by just shutting the game up. Then Terry came back and did what he wants again and as a coach your job is to try to keep the players believing.'

The poor run continued and home defeat to Swindon in January 2012 was our sixth loss in a row and with only three draws in the previous 12 games we had slumped to 17th in the league. While our excellent start meant that we were still eight points clear of a relegation spot, it was clear that we needed to change things. In most clubs, three points from 12 games would have led to calls for the manager's head and protests on the terrace. I was very surprised how few fans were demanding a change of manager. It reflected the affection in which Terry was, and still is, held and the fact that we hadn't dropped into a relegation spot – but we feared we would unless something was done.

We weren't playing badly. We were creating chances but missing them. In such circumstance the gossip soon starts that the manager has lost the dressing room, but not in this case. Trevor explains, 'The management use me and Rocket [Robin Bedford, the kit man] as a lightning rod. When things are going badly they are very interested in what the fans think because they understand that once the fans turn then a manager's position becomes very difficult. But I don't remember there being a fear of Brownie losing his job other than "it's a football manager, anything could happen" and I don't remember [the players] being particularly fearful of relegation.'

As soon as the transfer window opened in January we were able to sign new players. Following the Swindon defeat we had nearly two weeks free because our game against Macclesfield Town had been postponed thanks to their involvement in the FA Cup. Terry used that breathing space to focus on scouting recommended players. After travelling the length and breadth of the country, he told me that he wanted to bring in George Moncur and Billy Knott, aged 18 and 19 respectively. I was taken aback. I always tried to be positive and support our manager's football judgement but I found myself saying, 'Are you telling me that two kids are going to save us?' It was my Alan Hansen moment.[47]

A few days after they signed we turned the corner with a win at Port Vale. The match report said, 'The midfield duo of Billy Knott and George Moncur particularly impressed, adding quality and tenacity.' So much for my opinions on football. Jason Euell, a hero of the WFC days, had been brought on loan from Charlton but to everyone's disappointment he was injured and didn't complete the game.

The next 21 matches yielded 25 points and we finished in a just-about respectable 16th place with 54 points, ten above the relegation places. The cause of our problems was clear. We were in the top half of the table for goals scored, but third-bottom for goals conceded. The precarious nature of FL membership was illustrated by Macclesfield Town who mimicked our awful run but couldn't wriggle free of it, taking only seven points

---

47 In August 1995, Alan Hansen said on *Match of the Day* that 'you'll never win anything with kids' after a young Manchester United side had lost the first game of the season. The team, including those 'kids' (Beckham, Scholes, the Neville brothers and Butt), went on to complete a league and cup double that season.

from their last 23 games to finish bottom and be relegated. I couldn't help thinking back to our early-season 4-0 thrashing at their Moss Rose stadium when a smug Macclesfield chairman had told me we were doomed.

We ended the season on a positive note with a win against already-promoted Shrewsbury, but Terry knew we needed to make changes and released the majority of the remaining players from the promotion squad. But that summer it quickly became apparent that he had got his recruitment disastrously wrong. A pre-season 7-0 thumping by Premier League Reading was an early warning of problems and four defeats from the final five pre-season games reinforced the alarms.

Our first League 2 match of the season was at home to Chesterfield. We won 1-0 but it was one of those days where you wonder how on earth we managed to take one point, let alone three. In the next two, away at Burton and then Bradford, we conceded 11 goals and looked horribly adrift.

We'd had a bad run the previous season but this felt different. It wasn't long before board meetings were devoted to discussing what we should do. We took only one point from the next three games and, significantly, this time we no longer believed that Terry could turn things round. I spoke to Terry regularly and it was clear to me that he was similarly unsure. Years later he told me, 'During the Reading game I thought we are in trouble here, then we got thumped by Bradford and Burton.'

We had a midweek home game against Torquay and Terry asked to come and see me beforehand. He went straight to the point, 'How long have I got?' I said that we needed a positive result that night. That would reduce the pressure and give us some breathing space. He said 'fine' and that, whatever happened in the game, he and Stuart would come to the scheduled board meeting the next morning.

In fact, we played well that night but lost to an absurd goal, the type that teams concede when things are generally going against them; Seb Brown hit an attempted clearance against Rene Howe's ample-sized arse and the ball rebounded into the net. We gave a better performance but still lost 1-0.

Simon Bassey, heartened by the performance, was surprised by Terry's reaction, '[Terry] came in and shook my hand. I said "we done all right tonight" and he said "no, that's it" and walked into the changing room and shook everyone's hands. Then we had a good party in his office. In all honesty I think it might have been a relief to him in the end.'

The next morning Terry and Stuart came to meet the board. We were very down because, first and foremost, we all respected Terry as a man and as a manager, and we were uncomfortable sacking the man who'd delivered our dream of returning to the FL. Before they arrived I reminded the board that however painful we might find this meeting we mustn't feel sorry for ourselves; it was Terry and Stuart who were being sacked.

Terry was friendly and smiling; he's a decent man and he'd clearly decided to make it easy for us. He was obviously anxious to secure his financial position since this was his only job, so he raised the subject of termination pay, as he recalled when talking to me about it recently: 'I remember saying how does that leave me financially and Ivor saying, "Would you take a cut in the money [if you get another job soon]?" and I went, "No, I won you three promotions and the payment should reflect that," and you interrupted and said, "No, no, no, we signed a contract and that's what we will honour."'

While writing this book, I asked Terry how he felt about how we treated him. He replied, 'I didn't have a problem with it at all. I always thought from pre-season the recruitment's wrong here. There are so many facets to being a manager and you need to get them all right. You might get away with a couple but recruitment isn't something you can get wrong. You can't win games without centre-halves and without any legs.

'To this day Stuart thinks we were sacked far too early [but you were proved] to be right. Neal [Ardley] had enough time, so he had the opportunity to change things and bring different players in.'

Simon remembers, 'We played Bognor in pre-season away and got murdered even though we won. It was a tough time and we didn't get it right. It was hard, with a small budget.

'It was important to stay in League 2 so we needed to do whatever was necessary to win games but Terry had gone away from that. We talked about it a lot and I was saying, "Let's go pragmatic and get a couple of draws, get some confidence back in the team," but he said, "I ain't doing that again. I am not watching that sort of shit every week."

'Terry succeeded at Hayes, with a very low budget and got them high in the Conference. It wasn't pretty. They did what had to be done with what limited resources they actually had. Now he'd insist that he wanted Seb Brown to throw the ball out – but that will kill you because Seb's confidence was shot to pieces and so he didn't want to throw it out. So he held it longer than he should and that gave the defender who got it less time to make a decision. Maybe Terry thought the work he'd done to [win us promotion] would buy him the time.

'Terry never lost the dressing room. Even towards the end, he came in every day, he never once made an excuse. Despite everything that was going on Terry came in and always conducted himself with class and dignity.'

Terry had been with us for five seasons. In that time he won three promotions and established us in the Football League. It was an extraordinary achievement and, not surprisingly, he is held in high esteem and much loved by our fans and, tellingly, also by the supporters of his former clubs, Hayes and Aldershot. Given his track record, I still struggle to understand why no other league or Conference club sought him out to make him their manager.

All the board were desperately unhappy at his leaving, but we all felt that we had no choice. It was time to start the search for a new manager.

38

TEENAGE KICKS

WIMBLEDON FC was renowned for producing Premier League-quality players from its youth scheme. WFC owner Sam Hammam liked to refer to the Academy as his manufacturing unit – 'We manufacture top players.'

When the move to Milton Keynes was sanctioned the Academy went with them and with it a route for local boys to the top levels of football. The WFC community football scheme, basically fun football for children of all ages, survived another year before WFC culled it.

From the start it was clear that to retain the things we loved about WFC we would need to recreate a thriving academy. Commercial director and club founder Ivor Heller realised the need and approached a Dons Trust board member, Nigel Higgs, to ask him to take it on. They weren't the only ones to spot the need. Very soon Paul Bentley, who with others ran a couple of boys' teams, approached the DT through first team manager Terry Eames and suggested that AFC Wimbledon adopt his teams as a means of starting a youth programme.

Nigel agreed that the following season we would re-enter those teams in their existing leagues but under AFC Wimbledon's name and in our kit. At this stage we paid for everything, including the kit, league fees, and much more.

Paul was very astute at recruiting the best teams and the section was hugely successful in the premier league of local-area football. Teams were coached by parents and the parent stayed with the team, and his son, as they moved through the age groups. Some parents displayed extraordinary levels of personal commitment, but despite all their dedication that approach meant that each team had its own ethos. We wanted to focus on developing skills, not winning at all costs, but not everyone got the message and some coaches were over-competitive. As a result, we started to get a name for being an unpleasant club to have as opposition. Nigel set about changing the ethos; it was clear we needed to be professional in everything we did. It wasn't always easy, but that was the aspiration.

The first real push was to get players to pay their way because we couldn't afford to subsidise the growing number of teams. The next stage was to insist on using professional coaches instead of parents. This idea went down like a lead balloon with many of the parent coaches. However, the football club board was clear; the youth scheme was about excellence and we needed to make it more professional.

Because of the fairly unstructured way the youth scheme had initially developed, we had two teams in most of the age groups. This wasn't practical or affordable and we had to drop one of the teams in each year. We endured some very uncomfortable meetings with parents, with Nigel taking the brunt of the complaints. Football is a sport that stirs strong emotions. Add the parent-child relationship to that and it is probably an understatement when Nigel says that pushing these changes through 'wasn't pleasant'.

Some teams wouldn't accept the changes and walked away, so at least three age groups had to start from scratch. However, by 2010 the process was pretty much complete. As it turned out, that was just in time because that was the start of the season we were promoted into the Football League and we needed to acquire Centre of Excellence status. That would have been impossible if we'd still been using parent coaches.

At that time we recruited Jeremy Sauer, who very quickly established himself in overall charge of the 'minis', the seven-to-11-year-olds. Although we were now moving to paid coaches it wasn't all plain sailing. Jeremy recalled, 'Some of our coaches were 17- or 18-year-old boys, trying to manage a team where the opposition manager was often a middle-aged man walking up and down the touchline shouting and looming over them. Some opponents' managers took it upon themselves to tell the parents that our managers didn't know what they were doing. There was some truth in this because most of our coaches had learned their trade by coaching in schools not by running games, which was a completely different skill set.' But they quickly learned.

We also had to deal with parents coaching their children from the sidelines, sometimes getting so close to the pitch that the assistant referee couldn't run the line unhindered. Jeremy recalls, 'I was really irked that parents thought it was okay to coach so I bought stakes and ropes and put them out before every game a few feet back from the touchline. The other coaches thought I was mad and wanted to use cones but I insisted.'

An even bigger decision was to tell parents that we would leave their child out of the team if they persisted in coaching during games. These changes weren't popular but we had to be more professional and the board supported them without reservation.

While we were building the youth development schemes we also needed to defend our corner in regard to community football. We faced a massive challenge when, in 2003, WFC stopped offering community football and Fulham wanted to step in to the gap. But we were adamant that we were the natural community club in Merton so Nigel, supported by the then-football club chair Kris Stewart, teamed up with Tooting & Mitcham FC and persuaded Merton Council not to let Fulham use their parks.

That gave us a base from which to build our own community scheme. We explained to parents that we were going to continue the WFC scheme at Wimbledon Park and that other clubs weren't allowed to use those facilities. Some years later the community football scheme transferred to the club's charitable arm, the AFC Wimbledon Foundation, but we'd have been swept aside long before then if Nigel, supported by Kris, had not stood his ground.

For the last eight years[48] I've chaired the foundation as we have expanded our work across Merton and the adjacent boroughs of Wandsworth and Kingston. With a mission statement, 'To help our community pursue their dreams by improving their skills, resilience, well-being and confidence,' and led by our director, Philip Rudling, we've grown and expanded our work into health, social inclusion, education and sports development.

In the last year, initially as a response to the Covid pandemic, a massive volunteer force of well over 1,000 people spread across the three boroughs has been providing a concerted, well-organised response to need, including

---

48 I am retiring from this role round about the time this book will be published. That brings to an end my active involvement in the wider club, other than as a fan.

food poverty, IT equipment for children and household furniture for low-income families.

This initiative, known as The Dons Local Action Group, is now integrated with the foundation to provide a powerful, hugely positive force for effective intervention in areas of most need. DLAG's work has had national recognition in the media while the club and Foundation were invited to 10 Downing Street some years ago to honour our community work.

Meanwhile, as part of our long-term planning to anticipate Football League status, we formed an under-18 team in 2006/07 and it really got going under Mark Robinson's tutelage. He also took on our star year. That group, introduced to us by Tony Wilson, went on to win 104 successive games. Some years later, as an under-14 team they entered a national competition for youth teams from non-league clubs, winning the final at Derby County's stadium. I was among a few hundred Dons fans that day cheering them on. The undoubted star of that team was Patrick Roberts, who was signed by Fulham shortly afterwards.

Patrick wasn't the only one who was sought after but we fought hard to keep the others. We were very good about selling the dream and the pathway and we emphasised the family aspect, the 'you're not a number' feeling. Very importantly, players and parents got a real sense that we were supportive and that we cared. As a result, we were in the extraordinary situation where we had lads turning down professional clubs to play Sunday league grassroots football – and paying £300 a year to do so.

But did we sell them a false dream? We can't be sure, but of that team, Ryan Sweeney played a handful of first team games before being transferred to Stoke City for £200,000 and Dan Agyei was sold to Burnley for £100,000. Team-mates Egli Kaja and Ben Harrison played nearly 30 first-team games between them and the other members of that squad now play at various semi-professional levels. Would they have done better if they'd accepted offers from those other clubs? I doubt it, but we can never know.

From then onwards we were plagued by requests from Football League clubs to take our boys on trial. Scouts and agents would sell the dream to the boys but we thought it was cynical; terrified of missing a real talent and with no constraint on how many recruits they brought in for trial, they took boys who we knew wouldn't make it with them. And when they didn't meet their club's needs they simply sent them back.

We hated this. If a boy went on trial and the club liked him, we'd lost him for no compensation. If, and this was usually the case, they rejected him we'd have to try to re-assimilate a miserable and very demotivated boy back into our squad. This was lose-lose for us, so we decided that if anyone went on trial to another club we would not take them back. This was also very unpopular with some parents but we weren't prepared to exist simply as a pool for bigger clubs to fish in and throw back the ones they didn't fancy. As Jeremy says, 'The message it sent to others was really powerful.'

A problem that all clubs face is finding suitable places to play and train. When Mark first started coaching we were playing in Sunday leagues and coaching in public parks. Mark says, 'I would turn up with a bag of balls and little more than jumpers for goals. Once you got to know which other teams were training there and what time they arrived, I'd make sure to turn up an hour earlier to bag the best spot.'

At one venue Jeremy Sauer used for under-seven to under-11 games, the brick building, which would be flattered to be called a pavilion, was a popular location for drug users. On a Saturday morning he would get there early and make the place presentable. He set up pop-up goals and AFC Wimbledon banners and made it look more professional. Mark Robinson also used the facility and he recalls, 'Homeless people sometimes used to sleep in the pavilion overnight. I used to get there an hour before the lads turned up to clear it all out because there'd be cans of beer and sometimes needles. There was one guy who was always a bit reluctant to move on so I bought him a Happy Meal a couple of times to ask him to let us take over for a few hours.' It's not exactly the glamour that some people associate with football.

All of this was very hard work and challenging, especially as Jeremy and Mark weren't full-time. Mark recalls, 'The early days were difficult, but it was exciting. It was seven days a week and it was just constant. But it was also very stimulating and exciting because it was just constant challenges.'

A lot of our problems were resolved when Terry Brown joined us as first team manager. He wasn't happy with the first team training facilities and, as explained in Chapter 29, we started using pitches at Kings College. Overnight we had a home and somewhere to play youth team matches, with proper changing facilities.

Our objective was to develop lads who could play for the first team. But with three promotions in four years the youth team went from trying to develop boys who would be good enough to play in the Ryman Premier League, the seventh tier of the football pyramid, to trying to prepare them for the Football League.

We needed to demonstrate to parents and boys alike that there was a path through for them. We had seen Chris Hussey work his way from the under-18 and reserve teams into the first-team squad where he went on to play 70 league games before we sold him to Coventry for £100,000. But he had joined at age 17 from Woking and we desperately wanted to see authentic graduates, who'd been with us several years, make it to the first team.

Everything came to a head when we reached Conference National, just one promotion away from the Football League. As Jeremy Sauer put it, 'In the first year [of the Conference] we started thinking, "Shit, what happens if we go up?"' Then in 2011, at the end of our second season in the Conference, we won promotion. So Jeremy, Mark and Nigel found themselves travelling back from the play-off final in Manchester and asking, "Shall we go for it?"' In this case 'it' was being recognised as a Centre of Excellence.

Mark recalls, 'Until then we had muddled through in terms of facilities and whatever and used that to our advantage [when talking to parents] as in the fact we haven't got the best facilities doesn't matter because we're Wimbledon, the perpetual underdogs, this is what we do. Now, all of a sudden, we had to apply for Centre of Excellence status and of course the quality of the facilities did matter because you got inspected.'

The timeframe was really tough; we had six weeks to get signed off as a Centre of Excellence. To everyone's delight they achieved it and it was only then that Mark and Jeremy were employed full-time. In a very short space of time we'd gone from little more than jumpers for goalposts in public parks to a formally recognised Centre of Excellence in the Football League. Almost immediately another daunting challenge came along; the Elite Performance Player Plan (EPPP – said as 'E-triple P') was launched. We had a year to qualify to become an academy if we wanted its funding.

EPPP was a Premier League-inspired idea to improve the quality of youth development. Clubs which achieved academy status were awarded (in our case) £210,000 per season on condition that we complied with the EPPP policies and procedures and we spent £1 for every £2 the PL gave us (that wasn't difficult since we needed to spend far more than that to comply with the EPPP requirements).

There are four categories of academy. Category 1 is the highest while Category 4 only runs teams from under-17 upwards. The higher the category the better the facilities, the more staff who must be employed and the higher the qualifications they must have. We applied to be Category 3.

Mark says, 'That was a completely different ball game and a stressful period. I was academy manager then. But I was still doing the youth team and Jeremy was doing the younger age groups up to under-12. The EPPP brought in new criteria and the academy manager wasn't allowed to coach the youth team.' There was no way that Mark would have given up coaching so when we went through our first audit Nigel put himself down as academy manager.

Jeremy was designated as operations manager, another of the roles we had to be seen to be filling. In practice he did most of the head of academy role but without the title, so much of the credit for the successes of the academy should rightly accrue to him. The idea was to do and say what was necessary to achieve academy status and sort out the detail later. Mark says, 'When they audited us it was quite clear that we didn't have the right people doing the right roles. Nigel quite obviously wasn't the academy manager and they could see that.' Not surprisingly we failed the audit but it was marginal so we were given a chance to try again. This time Jeremy was made academy manager, Mark was head of coaching and Nigel was the board member to whom they reported. Various other improvements to practices and policies were made and at the second attempt we were proclaimed a Category 3 academy.

A major benefit of academy status was that EPPP put in place a matrix for calculating compensation if another club took one of our players. The compensation was, at least nominally, designed to recognise the amount of our investment in developing a young player. For a Category 3 academy player in the under-nines to under-11s we would get £3,000 for each year they'd been with us. Above that age it was £12,500 per year. So if a boy joined us at age eight and went to another club from our under-12s team we would get three lots of £3,000 plus £12,500, equalling £21,500. On top of that we would get a five per cent share of any profit if he was subsequently loaned out for a fee or sold. We would also get £15,000 per match if he played a PL game for his club (reduced to £2,500 for a Championship game and further for Leagues 1 and 2).

In practice the matrix was rarely applied and we negotiated a fee but at least we had a baseline and, more importantly, protection from the poaching that plagued us until we reached the Football League. Compare this to what happened to us when we were a non-league team. You may recall that one of our teams won 104 games in a row, including a national tournament. The star player, Patrick Roberts, was then signed, perfectly legitimately, by Fulham for no fee. Five years later they sold him to Manchester City for £11m. Had the matrix been in place we'd have got £21,500 immediately, as calculated on the page opposite. The five per cent share of the profit on the subsequent transfer would give us another £550,000, plus a payment, dependent upon the division, for each senior game he played. In fact, we got nothing.[49]

We're delighted for Patrick and proud that one of our young players has done so well. And Fulham would no doubt argue that the majority of the £11m transfer fee was earned thanks to their development of Patrick. The key point is that while we remain a FL club with an academy, that can't happen to us again.

There is one final, but absolutely critical, twist to the compensation calculations. Once a boy signs to become a scholar at age 16, the matrix no longer applies and we can negotiate a fee. If, on reaching 17 he is offered a professional contract but refuses it, he is free to move but we can claim compensation. If compensation can't be agreed between the clubs then we can go to a tribunal. For how this worked in the case of one of our players see Chapter 44.

Our philosophy was that we weren't just about football and everything we did needed to reflect our values. We were determined to make sure that the boys had these values instilled in them and that they clearly understood what our club was about and what we stood for. These standards are implemented in a host of small but practical ways, from ensuring the boys sweep the dressing room, home and away, after a game, to getting some of the more senior ones to turn up for the volunteers' work weekend to help

—

49 It is not quite true that we got nothing. Patrick was loaned to Glasgow Celtic by Manchester City and thanks to an arcane UEFA rule about international loan transfers, Celtic contacted us to say we were entitled to training compensation. So in the end we got £3,300 for an £11m player. That is 0.03 per cent of the fee. Ah well.

out. This sort of spirit creates a bond between club and players although, as we've moved up the leagues, it has proved harder to instil.

The adjustments to roles that we made to pass the EPPP audit highlighted an issue within the newly fledged academy. The academy manager isn't allowed to be a team coach and Mark's forte and love is coaching so we created a head of coaching role for him. But EPPP envisages that the football philosophy will be set by the academy manager. And Mark and Jeremy didn't agree about some quite fundamental, albeit technical, aspects of how best to develop the boys.

In theory the academy manager's view should prevail but Mark had Nigel's ear. While this seems a trivial and technical matter it was far from it. Their differences were only fully resolved several years later by which time Nigel had stepped down and Mark had been promoted to the first team management group, leaving Jeremy a freer hand to determine the academy's football philosophy.

In most clubs there is a natural tension between the academy and the first team and we were no different. There comes a point where academy coaches believe some of their boys are ready for first-team action, while the manager has to assess whether he shares that view and to choose the right moment to bring a young player in. They are bound to disagree from time to time. Of itself this is not a bad thing.

When we reached the Conference these differences started to emerge. Mark and Nigel would champion one or two players as being ready for the first team while our managers, first Terry Brown and then Neal Ardley, weren't always convinced. My stance was simple; we appointed a first-team manager and we made it plain to him that we were keen to bring through our own players. The manager had targets of his own, whether it be to win promotion or avoid relegation or simply consolidate. He would make the final decision and be judged on his results. All our managers have shown a willingness to play academy graduates but they will never select a player unless they think he is better that the incumbent.

Things changed when Jeremy took over as academy manager. He told me, 'I sensed that there was some concern within the board that academy players had been pushed too quickly. So I focused on building a relationship with you. It was important to demonstrate that I understood that the first team was about getting ready for the next game and winning. I thought that there were things the club could do better for young players but the starting point for that conversation had to be a good relationship between the two of us.'

This worked. Jeremy went out of his way to demonstrate that the academy was justifying the investment. He invited us to hold him accountable for the money that we were investing and wanted to have the pressure of comparing what the academy does with what else the money could be spent on.

We were now getting many of the same messages but with much clearer explanations. Instead of a view that we didn't need to recruit boys to bolster the various teams, this was now presented as a vision. In the meantime, with limited resources the academy focused on putting greater emphasis into recruitment at pre-academy level, so as to get boys in and train them in our ways. We became very effective at this and a real nuisance to other London clubs as we were taking one, two or three of the best under-seven and under-eight boys into our academy from those clubs.

This might make you think that we rarely introduced academy boys to the first team. To date the academy has provided 14 players who have made more than ten first team league starts (mainly, but not all, for us). Of the boys who've played their games with us, the most enduring is Will Nightingale, who joined when he was nine years old and is now club captain, and Anthony Hartigan, who joined at the age of 14. They have, at the time of writing, both played nearly 100 league games for the club. More recently Jack Rudoni has graduated to the first team and is now a regular, playing 30 games to date. Meanwhile, Ryan Sweeney, a graduate who went to Stoke aged 19, has played nearly 150 league games for a range of clubs.

These figures are important in a less obvious way, because every three years we were audited to make sure we continued to comply with EPPP policies and procedures; if we didn't comply we could lose our academy status. A key criterion in the assessment was our productivity over a ten-year period. This is a measure of how many games our graduates have played, whether with us or other league clubs. The greatest credit is given for Premier League appearances, then Championship, and so on down the divisions.

In the early years when we were a new academy it was impossible for us to have an established track record. We were marked down for that, completely unfairly in our view because if you've only been a league club for a few years you can't have a ten-year track record. Now that the academy is nearly nine years old we should be getting a higher productivity score.

While, to the best of my knowledge, we've yet to produce a player who has appeared in the Premier League, it was good to see that academy graduates Joe Bursik and Toby Sibbick have played 15 and 30 games respectively in the Championship.

Nowadays the academy audit no longer puts such a heavy emphasis on productivity. In some ways (now that we've got a track record) that is a shame. A very useful management tool would be for the Premier League, which oversees the audits, to publish an anonymised chart of appearances, by club, much like the turnover and club spending chart that the Football League publishes (see Appendix 1). Then each club could assess its actual and relative success in the most important result for an academy – how many of its boys end up playing league football.

Apart from meeting the criteria set by the EPPP, one of the biggest challenges for any academy is to prove that it is value for money within a club. I looked at this from time to time. Ignoring the spending for our first four years in the Football League by treating it as set-up costs, there was still a hefty deficit on income from transfers compared to spending. But there are other, less immediately obvious financial benefits. To measure them, Jeremy and I developed a simple model to calculate the hidden savings from academy players. While many clubs won't admit it, academy players who graduate into the first team are generally paid less than externally recruited peers for the first year or maybe two while they establish themselves. So we calculated the notional saving in annual wages of having an academy graduate as a first-team squad member compared to the cost of the nearest equivalent external recruit. This made a healthy dent in the deficit.

Finally, there is contingent income. Several boys have left for substantial sums over the last few years and one or more of them may well yield a significant sell-on bonus to us. It only needs one major sell-on to cover our costs for several years. The important thing is that it is measured and reported upon.

To end and to be clear, I am a strong supporter of an AFC Wimbledon academy but I think it is important to understand what it costs and what we're getting from it. And of course it isn't only about the money; there are substantial intangible benefits from being a local, community club which brings young talent through. And there is always the great thrill of seeing 'one of our own' come through to the first team and then succeed. Long may it continue.

39

SISTERS ARE DOIN' IT

AFTER THE problems during during 2008/09 (see Chapter 31) we had only three teams playing under the name of AFC Wimbledon girls. We were, in effect, starting from scratch, with no training facilities.

Around that time Dennis Lowndes started to get involved and ultimately he assumed the chair of both the ladies' and girls' operations. Over the next few years we gradually increased the number of teams, as Dennis explained, 'At first we brought in the under-11s. The next year they became the under-12s and we brought in a new under-11s team.' As the teams which had stayed with us at the time of the split got older they migrated up to the first team or the reserves, but by then we had grown organically.

Within a few years this growth meant that we had all age groups from under-11 through to under-18. And by going out talking to schools, local authorities, the playing field associations and other groups Dennis somehow managed to find pitches for them to play on, despite a desperate shortage of suitable facilities. Eventually, thanks to him we reached agreement for all our girls' teams to play their games at Archbishop Tenison's School.

When we started our boys' teams they paid subscriptions to play and this continued until the men's team were promoted into the Football League. Shortly after that we became an academy, partly paid for by a substantial financial contribution from the Premier League and we were no longer allowed to require subscriptions. The problem for the girls is that at present there is no similar infrastructure to provide funding, so they continue to pay to play.

The ladies' teams have never been asked to pay subscriptions and they are funded by the Dons Trust, a couple of sponsorships and underwriting of losses. Step forward again Mike Richardson, who has generously made up shortfalls in spending for the last few years.

Meanwhile the structure is gradually being changed. For many years the girls' teams were primarily social, which is an important community initiative, but there was no clear pathway through to the first teams. As a result, there was a real risk that after playing for us for up to ten years we could lose our best young players. In 2015 David Growns was asked by the DT board to help to deal with these issues. With Dennis wishing to step down after his long stint, David took over the chair of the ladies' group and soon afterwards Debbie Francis took the equivalent role for the girls. Working together and supported by other volunteers the girls' teams are gradually establishing a clear route for players to graduate to the first team while, crucially, still maintaining our community-based football for girls' teams from ages ten to 18. It is a delicate balance but they are getting there.

In 2016 the ladies' team won promotion into the National League South East Division One, and has remained in that league since then. By 2021 we have a first team, reserves and an under-23 team plus two teams each at under-16 and each year down to under-11s, making 15 teams in all.

Looking forward it is difficult to see an easy path through to the stage where the ladies' team joins the ranks of the professional clubs. At present the top tier in the Women's Super League is occupied by clubs with equivalent male Premier League or Championship teams and almost all are heavily subsidised. The next step down is the WSL Championship where some apparent outsiders, such as Lewes and London Bees, play, so perhaps we can aspire to that.

At the time of writing we are two steps down from the WSL Championship. The medium-term aim is to gain a promotion into the level below the Championship, which is still an amateur level. The plan is that once there we can reappraise and set new targets. To gain that promotion we will need to see the fruits of the youth development element of the girls' teams and more funding, whether by sponsorship or gate money. Pressure is growing for the ladies to play at our new stadium and if we are truly a community club then that must eventually come, along with the extra gate money and sponsorship that will allow the team to develop further.

40

RESCUE ME

THIS WAS the third time we'd recruited a manager and we were keen to waste no time. Terry's departure was announced on 19 September 2012, the day after the Torquay defeat, and we advertised the vacancy the next day, with an application deadline of 25 September. Even before the advert was posted we'd had approaches.

For the previous two appointments we'd had a football specialist to advise us. Ivor had always stayed close to Dave 'Harry' Bassett, a club legend for his playing and managerial career at WFC. Harry went on to manage several other league clubs, most notably Sheffield United where he also achieved significant success. I was sure that Ivor harboured hopes of persuading Harry to take on the caretaker manager's role, but he was having none of that. However, he did agree to help us.

We ran through the applications to date. In many ways this was the most useful part of Harry's involvement. We'd name an applicant and he'd say, 'Do you want a manager who doesn't go down to the training ground very often?' Those were things we couldn't easily know and it helped us to thin down the list. We had 40 applicants of whom Harry thought only three or four should be interviewed, but we added some late applicants to give us a total of seven.

We agreed that Harry and I would carry out first interviews and that all four members of the football club board, namely Ivor Heller, David Charles, Nigel Higgs and I, would conduct the second interviews.

While the preparation for interviews was going ahead, we still had matches to play. We asked first-team coach Simon Bassey to take on the caretaker manager role. I was very relaxed about putting Simon in charge. He was recognised as an excellent coach by both his previous two managers. His first step was simply to remind players how good they were and rebuild their confidence. Seb Brown was one who showed an immediate improvement once Simon encouraged him how to simplify his game. Then he took striker Byron Harrison aside and worked with him in training to get him back focusing on what he's best at, namely getting on the end of crosses. It worked; Byron scored in four successive games.

Trevor Williams observed Simon's management style close up, 'The Wycombe game [Simon's first in charge] is one of my favourite, favourite AFC Wimbledon games. Bass was in charge and it had been his ambition forever to be a football manager and to be the manager of us even more so. Bass's stuff in the build-up was brilliant, the way he spoke to the players, he was calm and clear. He was brilliant.'

Even at that time there was still something of a non-league club about us. At half-time Simon had brought on Frankie Merrifield, one of our academy graduates. After about five minutes Frankie was bent double and, as footballers put it, blowing through his arse. In a break in the play Simon asked him what was wrong. He replied, 'Sorry Bass, I had three plates at pre-match.' He'd never joined the squad for a pre-match meal before so he had helped himself to three plates of pasta: he could barely run. Nonetheless, even though we only had ten and a half men we played well and deservedly won 1-0.

Terry and Stuart, sacked only three days earlier, were at the game in a box, next to the away fans. Trevor says, 'Brownie got the adulation he deserved from the fans who were there. After the game all the team went up to see him in the box. It was the wrong side of the stadium but Bass made them all go up into the box and say goodbye to Brownie.'

By the time of our next game, Harry and I had conducted our first interviews and narrowed the field down to four. I wanted a sports psychologist to help with the second interviews and Harry introduced me to Steven Sylvester. He was immediately impressive, so we added him to the interview team as an observer, to feed back his thoughts after the interviews.

The shortlist comprised four people: Simon Bassey, who was caretaker manager during the process; Lee Bradbury, who was the only candidate with league management experience; Rob Page, the first-team coach at

Port Vale who had been recommend by his manager, Micky Adams; and Neal Ardley, a much-loved former WFC player who had come through the academy ranks at WFC and had been the academy manager at Cardiff City for the last six years. We told them to bring their proposed assistant with them; we wanted to assess the proposed management team, not just the manager.

Neal's involvement was a real *Sliding Doors* moment. Only dimly aware that Terry had left, Neal was in London scouting a couple of youngsters for the Cardiff academy. Visiting a local pub with his dad one night, he bumped into a fan who assumed he was in London for the job and mentioned it to Ivor. The next day Ivor rang Neal to say, 'I hear you're in town. You know our job is available? If you're interested I'm making no promises, but I am sure you'll get an interview.'

We planned the interviews carefully, trying to introduce some features that would test various aspects of the candidates' skills. Steven was keen to see how they performed under stress by introducing a bit of theatre to see how a manager would deal with it.

The candidates' discussions with Dave were a great opportunity. Steven asked Dave to react strongly when they presented their weekly training schedule. Dave took him literally, banging the table before going to the flipchart to reveal one of his favourite statistics. It said 55 per cent of goals conceded the previous weekend in the Premier League were from set plays – 'And you're only going to spend part of Friday morning on them.'

Their reactions were very different. Simon said later, 'Dave Bassett was on about set pieces and I should have argued back instead of trying to be nice.' Of the candidates only Neal went to the flipchart, took the pen from Dave and set out his own thinking, politely but clearly saying where they differed. Personally, I didn't care whether or not there was a right answer. I wanted to see someone who was unafraid to speak their mind rather than try to play the politics of the interview.

I also had a question that was designed to elicit a reaction and test the ethos of the individuals. John Terry, the Chelsea captain, had just been banned for racially abusing another player. So I asked, 'It's the night before the biggest game of the season and your star striker racially and obscenely abuses a young apprentice. What would you do?'

Neal's answer was easily the most considered. Eight years later I found out why. He and his assistant manager, Neil Cox, turned up at the hotel half an hour early. Neal went to the toilets and went in a cubicle. Immediately, in came the two previous interviewees who were talking about that question. As they left the hotel they saw Neil Cox and asked who he was with, to which he replied, 'Neal Ardley – he's in the gents' at the moment!'

After we'd done all four interviews the evaluations started. Dave was quite circumspect but it was clear that he favoured Rob Page. I thought that was because Rob was more direct and more combative. Even though he didn't have a vote in the selection process, we asked Steven for his views. He also put Rob first because, 'He clearly had this force from being a captain and an assistant manager at Port Vale … [he] was very clear in his thinking and quite abrasive and I thought that was just what the club needed at the time.' Both had Neal as a close second.

The board took a different view. No doubt we each had different reasons (for example, I assumed that Neal's academy background weighed heavily in Nigel's thinking) but three of the four of us were in favour of Neal and one was undecided between Neal and Rob. Looking back on it, Neal's view was, 'I thought Dave Bassett would favour Rob Page because Dave was very close to Micky Adams and Rob was Micky's assistant at Port Vale. So I thought I was going to be up against it when I knew Rob was one of the other candidates.'

Travelling back on the train from the interview, a friend told Neal that Rob Page had gone from 6/1 to 7/4 favourite and that Neal was now 9/1. 'Then I got home and obviously you rang that night and I was expecting you to maybe say, you know, "Thanks for the interview but unfortunately …" But you just said, "You've got the job. It's yours if you want it," and then you the next thing you said was, "But you won't get rich being our manager!"'[50]

When we appointed Neal there were accusations that we were being romantic by appointing a former club hero. Eileen will tell you that 'romantic' isn't a word she associates with me. We chose Neal because he was clearly the best candidate. Also, Neil Cox came across very well as a proposed assistant, personable, and relaxed but quite willing to put his own views across; we thought he would be a good foil for Neal. Nonetheless, we were taking a risk because neither of them had been first-team managers

50 I really don't recall saying that. But it was probably what I was thinking!

before and nor did they have experience of leagues at our level. Neal was taking a risk too, as he explained later: 'It wasn't as if I was out of work, desperate for a job. I was in a really cushy number and was enjoying my time and the family were enjoying living in Cardiff. I wasn't thinking I was going to blow you all away and get the job, I was thinking I was going to go to the interview because it's good experience and see how I go. But it felt right because it was back where I and my family originate from and it was going to be potentially working for fans that know me and would hopefully give me the chance. I knew that the board was full of fans who would 100 per cent want it to work if I did get the job because I was one of theirs. And I thought, being a romantic, it was the ideal first job.'

It might have been very different. One of the applications was from Chris Wilder who we held in very high regard. We'd heard that he wasn't happy at his current club and there was intense speculation about whether or not he'd be offered a contract extension. True or not, if he had gone through with his application he would have been hot favourite. However, he withdrew. I suspect he could see that we were unlikely to be able to give him the budget he'd want.

Neal's appointment was announced on 10 October, three weeks after Terry left. In the intervening period, Simon had taken charge of four games, including the win at Wycombe. He oversaw two victories and two defeats and, with a little better luck, it would have been three wins. At Oxford we were 2-1 up and missed several very good chances before eventually losing 3-2. That was of particular interest because, at the time, the Oxford manager was under pressure from the board. Had they lost he might well have been dismissed and things might have turned out very differently. Why? Because the Oxford manager was Chris Wilder.

An early decision was what to do about Simon, who had been with us from day one. We quickly agreed that Simon's knowledge of the players at this level made him invaluable to the new management team. And, let's be blunt about it, paying him off would cost as much as retaining him for the rest of the season; drawing on his experience and network of players was far more likely to help us survive the relegation battle ahead.

Once again, Trevor Williams was able to observe from close up, 'Straight away you could tell we had stepped up a gear, as in how everything was planned and what was expected from the players, what was expected from everybody. Ards was smart enough to know that you just can't come in and be a force, you have to carry people with you. He did that brilliantly; everyone knew what their jobs were. When Bass took over there was more training, stuff was better organised and everything was timed. And then Ards came in and did similar but to an even greater degree. Every minute was planned and it still is as impressive as any manager we've had.'

On the day Neal was appointed we had played 11 games and were 21st in League 2 (only two of the 24 clubs would be relegated) with ten points, six of which Simon had won in his four matches as caretaker manager. Neal's first game was at home to Cheltenham, who were in a play-off place. With a strong sense of theatre he waited until all the players, substitutes and staff were on the pitch before making his way to the dugout to a resounding welcome.

A problem for any new manager is that people expect an instant impact. In fact Neal had only met the players for the first time on the Thursday and had asked Simon to take the Friday training. Many newly appointed managers sit in the stand, partly to see the game better but, in my view, as much as anything to make it clear that this isn't yet their team. We lost.

By the end of December we had taken nine points from Neal's first 12 games and were bottom of the league, three points adrift of safety. We were in a parlous situation as Neal recounts, 'We were away at Torquay on New Year's Day and on New Year's Eve at the hotel Ivor was his usual bubbly self. He said, "You all right gaffer?" and I said, "Nah, not really." He was shocked when I said, "From now to the end of the season we need play-off form to stay up," and he was like, "Oh blimey, I didn't know that." I'd done the calculations and I was thinking we have to get to 53 points, which is as high as anyone has ever had to get to avoid relegation.'[51]

Relegation was an awful prospect. We'd won our league place on a low budget and I was far from sure that we could repeat the feat if we went down. Financially it wouldn't be calamitous but it would be very painful. From the beginning Neal's focus was to get us to the January transfer window and now it was here, with us needing play-off form to stay up.

Two days later the transfer window opened. The recruitment in January would make or break our season.

---

51 In the previous five seasons, starting with 2007/08, the points needed to stay up were 43, 38, 45, 48 and 45. This season was different because there were so many teams who were much of a muchness. Neal was right: it transpired that 52 points were needed.

41

THE SCRIPT

WE NEVER talked about it publicly, but it was only good sense to produce a relegation budget, in case the worst happened. Relegated teams immediately lost the Premier League solidarity money and, at that time, only received a parachute payment of half a season's FL distribution.[52] Taken together, we would be £410,700 worse off in the first year, as well as suffering a fall in gate money and sponsorship income. At the time our players' wages budget was £904,000. We would have survived but it would have been very bloody.

All our players were on contracts which reduced their wages by 30 per cent if we were relegated. Some of the highest paid players also had a 'right to walk' clause, allowing them to end their contract and leave for a nominal, or no, fee. We might not want to lose them but we would be unable to afford them in the Conference so we would have had to let them go.

Players' contracts expire on 30 June but we have to pay them for any part of July where they haven't found another club. If they sign for someone else for a lower wage we are obliged to make up the player's new wage to what we were paying them until the end of July. As a result of this rule, some clubs invited players to train with them in July and gave them a

---

52 Having faced the effect of this calamitous drop in income if we were relegated I instigated an initiative at the Football League to increase the parachute money to the full amount in the year after relegation to the Conference and 50 per cent in year two. Relegated teams would still lose the solidarity money but at least the FL money would soften the blow a little in year one.

contract starting in August, so we had to pay them while they trained with their new club. I felt that was taking the piss, so for players with the right to walk if we were relegated we stipulated that if they didn't have a new club by the second week of July the walk-away clause ceased and we could ask for a fee. We never had any intention of retaining these highly paid players but setting a deadline date would have the effect of concentrating the minds of their agents as well as the clubs who wanted to sign them. We wanted to get them off our books at the earliest possible moment but we weren't going to be screwed around.

Despite a good run of two wins and two draws in January we ended the month bottom of the league and two points from safety. Neal was desperate to add players with strength of character to help the club through what was going to be a very difficult and stressful last 19 games. Signing players is never easy and it's several times harder when you're struggling. As Neal explained, 'We were trying so hard, but no one wanted to come. We were bottom of the league and we were the worst team in the league. We needed captains, with a bit of know-how.'

He had targeted a striker, Gary Alexander of Crawley Town, and Alan Bennett of Cheltenham Town, a centre-back. We could afford them because of the FA Cup prize money and fees from two televised games we'd had earlier in the season. Gary and Alan weren't being selected for their clubs so we had something valuable to offer – game time and a chance to do something memorable by keeping us up. And in the case of Alan Bennett, something else too.

Simon Bassey made the first approach to Alan a couple of weeks before the deadline. He says, 'I'd been speaking to a few people and they told me that when Benno was at Brentford and they won the league they went to Vegas and he loved it. So I rang him up and said, "Is that Alan Bennett?" and he said "yes" and I said, "Do you want to come to Vegas?!" and he went, "Who is this?" So I explained who I was and he was still laughing. I told him that I'd heard he'd enjoyed himself in Vegas and he said he loved it so I said, "We're going if we stay up, all paid for, blah, blah, blah!" because Mike Richardson had promised that we'd go at his expense.'

Alan didn't want to leave Cheltenham even though his manager had signed a young centre-back and told him that he couldn't guarantee him his place in the future (that phrase is football manager-ese for 'I'm going to drop you'). So despite Simon's entreaties and the lure of another trip to Vegas, he wasn't moving.

Our other main target, Gary Alexander, had fallen out badly with Crawley. They had a new manager who didn't, as footballers say, fancy him and he was out of the team. He also felt they were messing him about so he told them he was going to sit in the stand and make them pay him for the rest of the season. Neal didn't argue with him, he just listened and tried to keep him engaged. They had played alongside each other at Millwall and the mutual respect kept Gary talking longer than he might otherwise have done. But he was quite stubborn and wasn't to be persuaded.

Meanwhile, Cheltenham were keen to sign our striker Byron Harrison. Neal was willing to let him leave but only if Gary came in as a replacement. And Gary wasn't moving. So on the last day of the transfer window Alan had turned us down, Gary was staying put and as a result Byron was staying with us.

In the sort of mild hysteria that comes when everything seems to be conspiring against you, Simon, Neal and Neil lay on the floor of our sponsors' lounge singing songs about Gary Alexander and transfers to the tune of 'American Pie'. By 5.30pm, with no hope of any deals, everyone went home. And that was it. To all intents and purposes the window had closed without us being able to bring in either of our key targets. The future looked bleak.

Gary may be stubborn, but Neal is persistent. As soon as he got home he started texting him and continued throughout dinner. After a little bit of toing and froing Neal started to smell an opportunity so he rang Gary and said, 'Look mate, let's do it.' Suddenly Gary was onside and agreed to come.

Gary had weighed up the options and made up his mind, 'Northampton had come in for me as well. They were sitting in third or fourth place that evening. And I had a choice. It was like, do I go and challenge for promotion? But I was coming towards the end of my career and I just felt, you know, it's a different challenge. If we can stay up it's going to be an unbelievable feeling. It'd be like winning the league. So I chose Wimbledon.'

Although he didn't say so, perhaps there was also an element of 'I'll show them they were wrong' about his decision; Gary was released by Wimbledon FC at the age of 12. Neal then had to ring Byron Harrison, me, club secretary David Charles and everyone else to get back to the stadium so that we could receive Byron's contract, faxed from Cheltenham for him to sign, while I finalised the transfer fee negotiations.[53]

It was now urgent, in fact desperate. Time was fast running out. But it was exciting too. Everyone milled around trying to dissipate their nervous energy when actually there was nothing to do but wait. Wait for Byron to arrive, get him to sign the contract and then send him off to join Cheltenham. They'd been so keen to sign him they did so without a medical.

As Byron left via one door in came Gary through another. Club secretary David Charles was desperately trying to finalise one deal while drafting a loan agreement with Crawley to take Gary until the end of the season.

As we were relaxing with the negotiations agreed and the formalities under way, Alan Bennett rang. He'd changed his mind. I've often thought we are a lucky club and we certainly fell on our feet that night because the Cheltenham officials were still at their stadium finalising all the paperwork for Byron. If they'd not been there the deal with Alan wouldn't have been possible in the very limited time that was left. We sat around checking our watches every 30 seconds or so, praying that he could get to their stadium in time.

It was too late to get all the paperwork done for Alan to transfer to us. The only solution was for him to cancel his contract with Cheltenham before the 11pm deadline and then sign for us the next day; a player without a club can sign for another club at any time in or out of the window, so long as his contract was cancelled inside the transfer window. This meant Alan was being asked to trust us to complete his deal the next day; if we didn't keep our promise he'd have no club and no income. Fortunately, his agents at the time vouched for our integrity. Alan signed the next day. We had got both of our targets.

---

53 This was when I first discovered what the prize money was for promotion from League 2 – not a subject that had ever previously concerned us. I asked for a bonus payment if Cheltenham won promotion and was told, 'Only if we go up via the play-offs.' This was because the prize money for the first, second and third automatic promotion spots was £25,000, £10,000 and £5,000 respectively, whereas a Wembley appearance would be worth anywhere between £100,000 and £250,000 depending on the attendance. There's something wrong with a system when the team that loses the play-off final makes up to 50 times more money than the teams which are automatically promoted.

Later I asked Alan what caused him to change his mind and he said, 'It just kind of snowballed. There was humming and hawing and back and forth. I drove to Cheltenham stadium [and] it was nearly 11pm by the time I got to the ground. There was a risk [of cancelling his contract with no new one until the next day] but there'll always be a risk I suppose and [Alan's agent] Bobby Bowery spoke highly of Bass and the club, so I was happy to go ahead.'

Things started to come together in mid-February when we beat Bradford 2-1. Bradford were having an astonishing season and were the first League 2 club to have reached the final of the League Cup. We played them a week before that final and I was hoping they'd take it easy, not wanting to get injured. But with seven minutes to go we were 1-0 down. Then Jack Midson scored and Gary Alexander did what we'd recruited him for, scoring a winner in the last minute of stoppage time.

All football fans love a last-minute winner, especially when it takes you from the depths of despair to ecstasy in a millisecond. Anyone who was there (and many who weren't there have heard the tale so often they now believe they were there) can recall that goal in great detail.

This started a good run and by late March we'd taken 20 points from the last ten games, which is automatic promotion form. We were now 16th and seven points clear of a relegation spot. We had six games to get the three or four points we needed for certain safety. At the following week's board meeting spirits were high and everyone agreed when I suggested that I should tear up the relegation budget. Ah, hubris.

I am not superstitious. I never worry about tempting fate but if ever anything was going to sow doubt in my mind about that attitude it was the following few weeks. We lost three successive games 1-0, each to a late goal. One of those was against Barnet who were also relegation-threatened. We battered them for the whole match, made one mistake and they scored. Football, eh?

We were in trouble. Neal was concerned about the dip in morale and wanted to raise it. I'd put him in touch with a sports psychologist and after that meeting he recalls, 'One thing that stuck in my mind was how the players react to adversity, going behind, conceding a goal. They beat themselves up, they haven't got the belief and every time the opposition score it's, "We can't keep clean sheets, the opposition are going to score." When you think like that it's going to happen.'

He wanted to give them a theme, a belief to fall back on in the face of adversity. So he told the players, 'I believe it's written in the stars that we're gonna stay up. You need to understand that every time an opposition score a goal, or every time we fall behind, it's just part of the process of us staying up. It was going to happen and we should just say to each other "it's in the script". So don't worry, get on with it, don't let it affect us and we'll be okay.'

And so 'it's in the script' became the simple but effective mantra. Unless motivational slogans on the dressing room walls are part of a coherent vision of the team's beliefs, they are simply words written on a wall, no more than that. This was a very simple message: if we encounter adversity we will overcome it, because it's in the script that we are going to be fine. It had an effect on midfielder Harry Pell who was painting the house he had just bought. He stencilled motivational phrases all over his wall and sent photos of his handiwork to the rest of the team.

Our next game was at home to Exeter and we saw the players reacting well to adversity, coming back to get a hard-earned draw after twice falling behind. But we were still three points from safety with only two games left and our next game was away at Gillingham, who were about to be crowned champions. Their top scorer was Danny Kedwell.

But, importantly, we'd stopped the rot. At first it didn't look that way as the team left the pitch at half-time, 2-0 down. Usually the management team of Neal Ardley, Neil Cox and Simon Bassey would spend a few minutes agreeing the key messages for the players before entering the changing room but today they just thought 'let's go straight in' and told the team to go for it.

Neal says, 'We changed our shape and made a couple of other changes to give us an opportunity to put them under pressure. I just said to the team, "It's in the script. You go out there and act like you're the champions, smother them. They think that they're getting the title today. You make this second half the most uncomfortable second half they've had all season. Smother them with energy, tempo and play with a belief that it's in the script."'

The transformation was astonishing. Simon adds, 'They probably went in at half-time thinking they'd won the league and this lot are shit. We came out and really upped our game and when we started playing they struggled to bring their performance back up.'

After non-stop pressure from the Dons, Jack Midson scored after 65 minutes. Then with only seven minutes to go, Jon Meades scored his only, but vitally important, goal of the season to make it 2-2. We might even have won; Gary Alexander hit the post soon afterwards.

The players and management left the pitch to find that all the other teams in the bottom five of the table had won and our one point wasn't enough to stop us dropping into a relegation spot. But then realisation dawned; two of our rivals had to play each other in the final game of the season. If we won, both of them couldn't get enough points to stay above us. However, our goal difference was far inferior so we would be relegated if we could only draw. At least it was clear-cut; win and we stay up, don't win and we go down.

Although tension had mounted towards the end of the season, anyone turning up at the training ground would never have believed we were fighting to stay in the league. The place was full of smiles, Bass had brought in a dartboard and the players would stay behind to play darts. They were having fun, even in training. Our best chance of staying up was if the players didn't feel the pressure, so the aim was to keep it away from them.

The tactics were simple. Neal says, 'We knew we weren't good enough to get the ball down and pass it so we talked about the percentages, we'd get in behind them, we'd deliver crosses. We weren't gonna focus on anything other than producing stats that give us a chance of winning the game. And so we did it all in training and we kept going on about how we are going to win the game.'

What isn't visible to everyone is the pressure on families who can only stand by and watch. On the day of the game, Neal's wife Sarah was in the bar with their elder daughter Libby. Neal says, 'I got someone to go and get them and brought them down to my office and Sarah just burst out crying. It was my first job as a manager and she knew the importance of getting it right for your own career, let alone the hard work you've put in to succeed in the first place. She was crying her eyes out and I just said not to worry as it's all under control, I'm calm, the team are ready, just go out there and watch the game, enjoy it. She walked out feeling a bit more positive and I took a deep breath because I was literally shaking. I just went "come on". I knew that I had to go and deliver the team talk in a minute and I needed to get myself in the right place. I needed to get the emotion that I was feeling out of my body so I just took five minutes on my own to be able to go in.'

We played well against Fleetwood but it was one of those games where you wonder if failing to take our chances would cost us dear. Finally, in the 61st minute, Gary Alexander powered in a header from a free kick to give us the lead and hope of salvation. But three minutes later a Fleetwood corner skimmed off the head of their striker, hit Gary on the thigh and rebounded into the net. Gary was distraught, 'One minute I thought I'd saved us, the next minute I thought I'd relegated us.'

Neal adds, 'You could have heard a pin drop at that point. But that was a moment when I realised the power of "it's in the script" because that could have been the moment when it was over but I saw a group of players all saying that same thing together, clapping their hands saying, "Don't worry, it's in the script. Don't worry, keep going." And I thought I didn't even need to try and lift them, they're doing it themselves.'

And then, with seven minutes to go we were awarded what I thought (and was very grateful for) was a soft penalty for a foul on full-back Curtis Osano. Jack Midson picked up the ball to take it. This one kick would probably determine the club's future for the next few years. I'd gone to stand behind the goal at the other end of the pitch; it seemed the only place to be for a game of this importance. Meanwhile my wife Eileen, who'd hidden in the toilets to avoid watching the penalty shoot-out at the play-off final, was unable to get away from her seat in the directors' box in time to hide, so our friends covered her head with coats.

Every one of the players and management I've spoken to was very confident that Jack would score, even if, as in the case of Simon Bassey, it was solely because he was doing his lucky crouch with his fingers crossed!

And score he did. Now we needed to survive seven minutes plus injury time to be safe. Alan Bennett tried hard to explain the situation to the Fleetwood players, saying, 'You're safe you know, you're mid-table, you're on holiday, you should have your flip-flops on. What are you doing running around here?' He told me, 'We were desperate, we needed these three points, so you push whatever buttons you can.'

The message didn't get through as Fleetwood threw another striker on to the pitch and then pushed a centre-back up front. Trevor Williams was sitting by the dugout. He recalls, 'Graham Alexander [no relation to Gary] was the Fleetwood manager. He's a big mate of Neil Cox and I remember Coxy looking at him saying, "What are you doing putting strikers on off the bench?" and they were really giving it a go.'

After eight never-ending minutes of injury time the final whistle went and we were safe. The crowd invaded the pitch and I made my way back to the boardroom to discover that Barnet had lost and been relegated. I remember commenting to the Fleetwood chairman that their performance showed the integrity of our league, because they did everything they could to take a point from that game. After doing his press commitments a visibly emotional Neal bumped into me outside the boardroom and, well aware that I'm not keen on physical contact (is that a northern thing?), he said, 'I know you won't like this, but,' and gave me a big hug.

We were safe for another season and it was time to start rebuilding. In the meantime, Mike Richardson kept his word and a couple of days later the team flew out to Las Vegas where he treated them royally, as Alan Bennett recalls, 'I remember one night we were in a bar and like everything in Vegas it's all set up for money – you get what you pay for. We'd got the top table, right at the side of the dancefloor. And the Rotherham squad was there too, but they were at the back, sat near the toilets. They kept coming up to us saying, "What's going on here? You're the third worst team in the Football League and you're like Premier League players there partying. We won automatic promotion and we're pretty much sat outside."'

Some years later I asked Alan how important it had been to him to keep us up. I was surprised by his answer, 'You meet people in the car park when you're walking to your car, they're all saying the same thing about their club but in different ways. And you don't really get that at many clubs where everybody in the group, the whole tribe, is thinking the same thing and regaling the same message, about where they came from and how they came up and "oh, we've got this far and we can't go backwards", etc. So that was a higher meaning, that's what I felt anyway.

'At the start it [learning about the club] was from Google and then it was just chatting to Bass on the phone. And then most of the interactions were heading from the car towards the ground on matchday and bumping into fans at away games. So it was constantly in your psyche that you're seeing it and people are talking about it and they're tagging you and stuff. And that's it, that's osmosis there for you, it just seeps into your psyche. And you just kind of believe that you're playing for something bigger than what you are.'

42

A POCKETFUL OF MUMBLES

WHEN WE reached the Football League we found that agents[54] were playing an increasing part in our recruitment so I thought that this would be a good place to write about how they operate and how we sought to interact effectively with them.

Do you fancy being a football agent? It's quite easy really. All you need to do is pay £500, tick a few boxes and confirm to the FA that you're a decent person and you're all set. It's that easy. Seriously.

Until 2015, football agents had to pass an exam that covered subjects such as contract law, immigration laws and registration rules. They also had to pay an insurance bond. Then world football's governing body, FIFA, changed the rules and a qualification is no longer required. As Mel Stein, the chairman of the Association of Football Agents, said, 'It is wrong that "a bloke in the pub" could now offer to represent players.'

Why did this happen? The reason was that transactions were getting more and more complicated. As one example, some players signed with multiple agencies even though the contracts are meant to be exclusive. As a result, a player would move to a club and all the agents would turn up and demand payment because he was contracted to them. FIFA were finding it impossible to enforce the rules in a number of recalcitrant or downright incompetent national associations and its dispute resolution service was overwhelmed by cases. So they took the simplest way out and scrapped pretty much all of the qualification requirements.

—

54 All of this chapter is pitched at dealings with agents at our level in the football pyramid and not the multi-million-pound deals that you read about in the papers.

One change that arose at the same time was that agents were renamed intermediaries because they often work both for clubs and players. However, I will continue to refer to them as 'agents' because that's still the term that is most frequently used – and it's quicker to type.

There are still some FA rules that regulate how agents can operate. Contracts with players must be renewed every two years and players can move on at no cost if they wish. There are pluses and minuses with this arrangement; players can't be tied down for unreasonable lengths of time but on the other hand for some agents the time limit is motivation to do a deal and take their cut sooner rather than later, in case the player moves on and they get nothing. The earliest stage at which an agent may sign a player is in the calendar year in which they become 16, so many boys sign aged '15 and a bit'. If an under-18 player signs an agency agreement it must be counter-signed by a parent or guardian. Agents are also not allowed to pay players to join them or offer any other inducements. In practice, some do.

There is no set fee for an agent's services. Both FIFA's and the FA's regulations suggest a three per cent fee but the most common level is five per cent of a player's gross annual wages plus VAT. The fee is usually paid in advance at the beginning of each season. Strictly speaking the player pays the agent and so the fee is his responsibility but this is tax inefficient for them. So, instead, the norm is for the club to pay the fee and the player only pays the tax on the fee as a benefit in kind.[55]

—

55 Non-accountants may wish to switch off at this point. Say a player is on £80,000 a year. If the agent's fee is five per cent then he gets £4,000. Add VAT = £4,800. If the player paid this out of his post-PAYE income, taxed at 40 per cent, he would, in effect, need to earn gross wages of £8,000 to pay the fee. However, if the club pays the fee, the player is only taxed on the £4,800. From the club's point of view it's cheaper to pay the agent's fee directly rather than pay the player a large enough sum to be able to have PAYE deducted and still cover the cost of the fee.

The club can't reclaim the VAT on the agent's fee because the contract is between the player and the agent; you can't reclaim VAT on someone else's transaction. This has led to widespread use of 'dual agency' agreements, where the agent is argued to be working for both the player and the club. If the assumption is a split of 50/50 then the agent invoices the club for 2.5 per cent and the club can reclaim the VAT on that. The dual agency split is variable but most clubs go for 50/50 to avoid arguments with HMRC. Where the agency fee is in millions it's in the club's interests to argue that all the work done by the agent is for their benefit. The player also benefits from a dual agency agreement because now the club is only paying the balance of the fee, i.e. 2.5 per cent, on his behalf, so his personal tax liability is lower. Everybody benefits – except the tax payer.

For the pedantic accountant – and there's a tautology for you – for ease of explanation, the above example ignores National Insurance.

For many years we refused to pay agents' fees. We couldn't see any reason to do so, especially when younger players were getting the benefit of being in the shop window for bigger clubs. This continued until we reached the Conference National, at which point the pressure to make payments increased sharply. We were no longer the big fish in our league. In our second season there we went full-time. We were now competing for players who were making their living from the game but, by and large, we continued to be successful in resisting agents' demands for fees. Our stance was that we were willing for the agent to get a fee but we only had (say) £800 a week to spend; if the agent was paid a fee then it would have to come out of the £800 and the player would get less. At that level most agents didn't press for a fee.

By the time we reached the Football League it was getting much more difficult. In the previous chapter, Neal talked about the difficulty of attracting players. We were a small club, we had a low budget, we were playing in what was really a non-league stadium and our training facilities compared poorly with those of other clubs. And we didn't pay agents. The last of these was far from being the most important factor, but it didn't encourage agents to point their players in our direction.

So, gradually, we started paying them, although not for every deal. For players at the beginning of their careers where we were, in effect, giving them exposure and who were on £350, £400 per week, it would have been foolish for agents to claim a fee. They held fire in the hope that the player would move to a bigger club and a better wage. Conversely, we were less likely to pay an agent for players towards the ends of their careers; to be realistic, we just didn't need to.

There are lots of stories about bad agents and I'm sure most of them are true. We certainly came across a few but by and large they were fine to deal with. My problem with them was that a lot of them did nothing visible to earn their money, especially when they were simply discussing a contract renewal. They'd come in to discuss their player's new terms and we knew they needed to be able to demonstrate they'd improved the contract, so we'd concede an extra £50 on the goal bonus and honour was satisfied. Some were more of a problem. I remember Tony Finn's agent saying to Terry Brown and me that not offering more money to his client was a form of abuse. Terry had him out of the room almost before I realised; he knew I'd explode on hearing that so he ended the meeting.

The area of our greatest concern about agents was young players. With increasing money in the game there are more and more agents, many of them ill-qualified other than having paid their £500. And the competition for players is such that they are targeting younger and younger boys, often with a direct approach to the boy after a youth team game, mumbling vague and undeliverable promises.

We tried to protect our boys but initially we were slow off the mark in trying to keep agents under control. One agent told me that in the early days he could just walk in to watch our youth team games. No one would challenge him and he'd simply walk round to watch the player he was interested in. To control this we introduced security but even then it was far from watertight because chancers blag their way in by saying they are a player's cousin or whatever, and the steward finds it hard to object.

We got a real wake-up call when a man got in to our training ground one Saturday morning where our youth teams were playing their matches. He stood out because he clearly had no experience at all. He was targeting, among others, some under-12s. It was then that we realised just how young they were aiming their sights and how great a risk we were facing. We kicked him out but other, similar ones appeared. We tried to manage this by making anyone seeking entry tell us which boy or team they were watching and then escorting them to a carved-out area by the relevant pitch, from where they could watch. That had some success in restricting their pervasiveness.

But physical security isn't enough. Some of the bigger agents employ 'runners', young lads who basically worm their way into academies and get phone numbers to feed back into their employers' network; they are Artful Dodgers for these latter-day Fagins.

Then there are the insiders. We are aware of instances where some clubs' academy coaching staff were also on the payroll for an agency. It started to dawn on us when agents got a boy's phone number and his parents' contact details. Also, nowadays some agencies are tied in with club employees, or ex-professionals who have been in a particular club and earn a little bit on the side from passing on information. Like water seeping through the smallest cracks, they get everywhere. For example, we know of a young player who is doing private training sessions, away from his academy, with a friend of a friend of an agent – who turned out to be a coach at the boy's academy. And of course if a senior academy coach leaves to join an agency then you can soon expect to see your best players targeted by that agency.

Approaches don't just take place at the training ground. With social media being such a big part of young people's lives it's hardly surprising they are tapped up by that route. One of our young players had an agent contact him directly on his Instagram account when he was only 14. We rang the company, of course, and the boss said, 'Oh yes, that's one of our new lads, we'll have to give him some education as we don't approve of that sort of stuff.' As if. It's just spivvery. There are serious child protection and safeguarding issues around such behaviour and, I fear, a disaster looming in the wings. And tapping up players via social media isn't far away from being a form of grooming, but it's an easy way for an agent to get in with a family so it's very attractive to them.

There were quite a few parents at our academy who appointed an agent simply because they were getting endless calls, e-mails, and direct approaches to their son, which eventually felt intrusive to the point of aggression. Our response to this was to brief parents of 13- or 14-year-old academy boys. We talked to them about agents, how they operate, pitfalls, the rules; everything they needed to be aware of.

We also built relationships with half a dozen agents who we felt were open and honest and tried to keep the boys' interests foremost. If we could see that a player had some interest around him our academy staff would normally try to link that player to the pool of agents we'd created. We'd encourage some of those agents to come and watch a boy 'because there's interest in him'. We would suggest that the family speak to at least three agents so that they could make their own decision. When this worked we had a chance of developing a good working relationship that would give the boy a development focus and not an agent-driven financial focus.

The problem then was that some agents tried to set the parents against the club with messages like 'they're only doing it to keep control of your boy' and 'they'll treat your son like a piece of property' and 'the agents they're recommending are in the club's pockets – don't trust them'. All of this is very hard for parents to deal with.

Some parents have appointed themselves as their sons' agents and they can bring different but equally difficult issues to the table. At the mild end of the scale we noticed that whenever one of our first-team midfielders, who was represented by his father, was coming to contract renewal time,

Ivor Heller, left, with Glenn 'Trigger' Mulcaire

Kris Stewart

Trevor Williams

Marc Jones, standing, with Glenn Mulcaire and Lee Sidwell

Terry Eames, left and assistant manager Lee Harwood, at the Wimbledon Common trials, June 2002

Triallists warm up on Wimbledon Common, June 2002

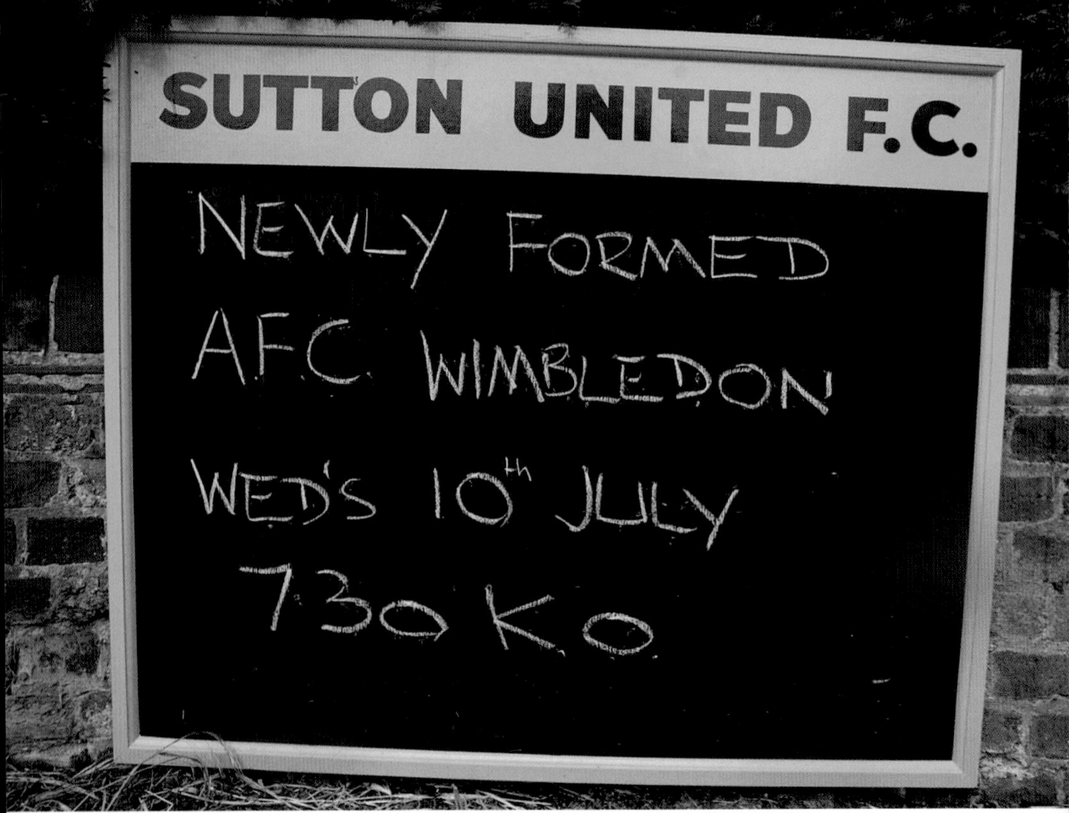

Marketing campaign for our first ever game, July 2002

Press conference at Sutton. l to r: Miles Jacobson, Sports Interactive; Ivor Heller; Kris Stewart; Terry Eames; Joe Sheerin (captain); Julian King (player/coach), July 2002

Joe Sheerin, right, leads out the teams at Sutton

A cameraman perched on the dugout roof films the goal celebration at Sandhurst Town.

'Table for 1,000 please.' Dons fans queue for curry at Southall

Dons fans under the Feltham FC roof. Three seasons earlier the same fans watched us at Old Trafford and Anfield

Kevin Cooper at Chessington & Hook. Andy Sullivan (left) and Lee Passmore look on. The white kit never recovered

Nicky English is chaired by fans after sealing the Combined Counties League title at Walton Casuals

Fans arriving for a night match at Kingsmeadow

Kingsmeadow, our home for 18 years, seen from the Paul Strank main stand

Steve Butler (left) and Chris Gell lift the Surrey Senior Cup, May 2005

Simon Bassey moved into coaching with Dave Anderson

Dons fans take the ferry to the Hampton & Richmond game

Richard Butler's last-minute goal at Walton & Hersham put the Dons in play-off contention. Manager Dave Anderson (left) and assistant manager Jon Turner couldn't wait to join Luke Garrard and Paul Barnes in the celebration, April 2006

Jason Goodliffe holds the trophy aloft after winning the play-off and promotion to Conference South, May 2008

Jon Main celebrates the equalising goal at Hampton, effectively sealing promotion to the Conference National, April 2009

Danny Kedwell dons the fans' t-shirt after scoring the winner v Crawley Town, who had earlier tried to sign him, September 2010

Manager Terry Brown looks happy after beating Crawley Town

Christian Jolley jumps for joy after scoring our fifth goal v Fleetwood Town in the play-off semi-final, May 2011

Left to right Rashid Yussuf, Kaid Mohamed, Danny Kedwell, Ricky Wellard and Stephen Gregory celebrate Mohamed's hat-trick goal v Fleetwood Town. Referee Andy Madley looks on, May 2011

Seb Brown dives to save the first penalty, play-off final v Luton, May 2011

Sam Hatton scores. Wimbledon 1 Luton 0

Luke Moore scores. Wimbledon 2 Luton 1

Left to right, goalkeeping coach Paul Priddy and manager Terry Brown hardly dare to look. Assistant manager Stuart Cash watches

Seb Brown reaches up to save Jason Walker's penalty

'Oh and Yakubu'. 3-2

the press would start reporting that he was being watched by Charlton, or Brentford, or whoever.

Meanwhile, some parents were simply greedy for more money irrespective of the effect on their son's career. For example, one player's agent got him £4,000 a week as an 18-year-old but the parents were continually pushing for much more. Eventually the agent didn't renew their contract because morally and ethically they no longer wished to represent him.

By the time I left the club every 18-year-old player had a professional agent, apart from one or two where the parents took on the role. Of those professional agents, about 50 per cent were agents we thought were not just in it for a quick buck. At age 15 and 16 about 50 per cent had representation. For academies at higher-level clubs that percentage is much greater.

Occasionally we came across Billy Big Bollocks agents, which was an education for us all. One such self-aggrandising nitwit called to arrange to talk about his client. It was quickly apparent that he'd never seen him play or even spoken to him. We made the case that a move might not be the best thing for the boy as he could soon be getting first-team football with us which would stand him in good stead for a later move. In response he simply said, 'Ah okay, that's good to know, good to learn a little bit more, but he's too big for a club like this.' And so we lost him. It did amuse me, however, that we clearly didn't have a clue who this terribly important man was; that would have upset his fragile ego.

This isn't a one-way street. Clubs can be as bad as agents. There's a well-known story about a young player who was called in to see his manager and told he was being released. 'But you can't do that,' he said. 'I'm on a contract.' The manager replied, 'What, this one?' Then he took the contract out of his top drawer, tore it up and dropped it in the bin. That player would have benefited from having an agent!

Having said all this there are, of course, many very good, decent agents. The better ones work with the clubs to develop young players and put a lot of effort into building relationships with the player and the parents. When everyone is working to a common and agreed objective it is so much better for the boy in question.

To take an example, one agency built a relationship with our academy manager. Over the next few years they worked with us, reinforcing the same messages to one specific boy. We agreed that the player in question should ignore the interest from around him and aim to get 50 games in the first team. If he got 50 or so games in League 1 then he would be likely to attract interest from clubs at a higher level. And if it turned out that League 1 or 2 was his true level, then he'd be a well-established player with a career for life laid out in front of him that would give him good rewards if not making him a millionaire.

Nowadays, the better agencies recruit young players much the same way as clubs by having potential clients watched on at least three separate occasions by different scouts. Each scout collects and submits extensive data on the player, the situation (for example, the strength of the opposition, the pitch conditions, and the quality and experience of the players around him). Once a potential recruit is identified good agents approach the parents first, so that a trusting relationship can be built up. And rather than harvest lots of players, for each age group they only recruit one and never more than two players for each position.

Controversially, some agencies employ coaches to offer supplementary training to their clients. This isn't wildly popular with the clubs because they fear that it will run counter to their training regimes; the agencies argue that a player can benefit substantially from tailored one-on-one training. This is a practice I frowned upon when I was CEO but I can see that there are times when a player may feel he needs to confide a lack of confidence about a specific skill but be worried that he might jeopardise his position at his club if he said so to them. For example, I'm aware of a couple of boys who've made it to our first-team squad but still needed to learn to head a ball properly.

Some agencies also employ psychologists. Again the argument is that, rightly or wrongly, some boys worry about any admission of doubt or weakness to someone who is employed by their club. And let's be clear-eyed about this. The agencies do these things because they want their clients to develop as successfully as possible because by taking the longer view they are aiming to maximise their returns. Like any business relationship, it's best if it can be win-win.

Most of this chapter has focused on the role of agents with young players. That is because it's the area where we see most day-to-day interaction and where we need to take proactive steps to protect our younger players. It is also the area where it is possible for clubs to work with agents to help young men build a career for life.

Finally, I will end with an example of how one particular agent was extremely helpful to us, simply by doing their job conscientiously. When we signed Mitch Pinnock from Dover he was under 24 so we knew we would need to pay compensation. Although we weren't a long way apart, we couldn't agree a fee with Dover and it became a point of principle not to yield any further. So we went to a tribunal.

Both parties submit written evidence to support their case and then attend to present their arguments and answer questions. Dover's presentation set out that Mitch had played 102 games for them, 60 as a substitute, across three seasons and had been loaned out to another club as part of his development. It was persuasive, as it should be.

However, the agent was able to give me a match-by-match analysis of how many games Mitch had started and how many minutes he'd actually been on the pitch (for example, a substitute appearance sounds good but if he only came on to the pitch in the 85th minute that puts a rather different emphasis on its significance). As a result of this analysis the panel's decision was much closer to our wishes than Dover's. Some months later I bumped into one of the members of the panel and asked him what he thought of it. 'Well, you did all our work for us,' he said, 'and that made the decision clear and very easy to make.'

On reflection, I would rather agents didn't need to exist but I recognise that many players need independent advice and support, especially the young men who have known little other than football from an early age. The trick is to find an agent who takes a long-term view that is aimed at development and giving the player a career, not merely a one-off deal that gives short-term rewards. An agent should also be there for setbacks, not just the good times, and to support a player and help him find a new club if he doesn't achieve his ambitions at the current club.

Overall then, if a parent asked my advice about whether to appoint an agent for their son in an academy I would say 'yes'. But it shouldn't be them!

43
LITTLE BY LITTLE

IN THE struggle to escape relegation a total of 43 players appeared in league games in 2012/13. Fifteen of them were loan players who returned to their clubs; a further 19 were released during or after the season.

Now that we were safe we were looking for stability and a much more comfortable league position. And we wanted any excitement to be a cup run rather than a relegation threat.

It was easy to see where we needed to strengthen; our goals conceded and our goal difference had been easily the worst in League 2. Of the previous season's back five defenders, only Alan Bennett survived both Vegas and the post-season cull. Play-off final hero Seb Brown was relegated to the substitutes' bench.

It proved to be a season with a new drama that we could well have done without. We started very well. After six games we were third and playing lovely, attacking football.

Then, despite no discernible difference in training, tactics or player commitment, we took only five points from the next eight games and found ourselves 15th in the table. The problem with a flying start is that it can, as it did here, flatter to deceive. Then when the downturn comes many fans' expectations have been unrealistically raised. If we'd got to 15th place with a more even set of results then I think the majority of our fans would have been quite content. Instead some started looking for someone to blame for 'the collapse in form'. Our season continued in stop/start fashion and by the end of 2013 we were still 15th and looking comfortable.

One of the problems with taking loan players is that if we work on developing and improving them and they are a success then the vultures, in the form of other clubs who would love a big goalscoring striker, start to hover. And so we lost Michael Smith, who had been a great success, leading the line well and scoring ten goals. We had taken him on loan from Charlton until 1 January but we wanted to keep him until the end of the season. However, he was in the final year of his contract. Facing the prospect of him leaving at the end of the season for nothing, Charlton understandably cashed in. So, off he went to Swindon for a £150,000 fee. Bummer. But I couldn't blame Charlton – it made good business sense for them.

Fearing this outcome, Neal had already targeted two loan replacements, Danny Hylton from Rotherham and Charlie Wyke from Middlesbrough. Both players went on to do very well elsewhere but neither was a success for us, scoring only five goals between them. Danny was coming back from an injury and never really got match fitness back. Charlie was a young lad who was obviously talented but was too young and raw.

Struggling to score goals, we went on a long run of poor form and although in mid-March we were still in 15th position, six points clear of a relegation spot, we were starting to look over our shoulders. Getting a win in our home game against Cheltenham had become critical.

The match was an extraordinary one of changing fortunes. With just over 20 minutes to play we were losing 2-0 and then in the space of two minutes and seven seconds[56] we scored three goals; the first and third were two of the three Danny Hylton scored in his stay with us, while the middle goal was scored by a former Spurs youngster called Jake Nicholson. The drama continued with Cheltenham pulling the score back to 3-3 before we scored a winner in the 97th minute.

That win effectively put us within five points of safety with seven games to go. While we weren't going to forget that we'd prematurely relaxed the previous season, we felt we could look forward to a comfortable run-in to the end of a season of satisfactory consolidation.

Eileen and I almost invariably go out for dinner – nothing posh – after a home game. As we sat down to eat that night my phone rang. It was club

---

56 The timing is taken from a YouTube video called 'How quickly can AFC Wimbledon score three goals?'

secretary David Charles to tell me that we had a problem. Jake Nicholson shouldn't have been playing.

Historically, player contracts run to 30 June but relatively recently a new 'multiplicity' contract had been created. These could extend for one or more whole months but didn't have to run to the end of June. We had taken Jake on trial and liked him, so a convenient way of making him available to play for us while extending the trial was to give him a one-month multiplicity deal. However, it had expired the day before the Cheltenham game; we hadn't noticed and we hadn't extended it.

We were stuffed. We would lose the three points we'd gained only a couple of hours earlier and that would mean we were now only four points clear of a relegation spot.

I decided not to ruin Neal's evening by calling him straight away; instead I ruined his Sunday, as he told me years later, 'There was a rollercoaster of emotions that we went through in that game because we hadn't won for a while and things weren't great. So that win was a massive relief. Then I just remember the Sunday morning when you phoned me. You know straight away from somebody's voice that something is not right – and then you said, "Are you sitting down? I need to tell you something." I just remember vividly that I thought you were going to tell me that you were seriously ill. Then you obviously told me the news and I remember actually kind of feeling quite relieved because of what I thought you might have been about to say. Then I realised where it put us in the league and went back to feeling worried again.'

We were, once again, in crisis management mode. I'd briefed the board before speaking to Neal and we agreed that we should keep the news from the players because we didn't want to put pressure on them. Neal agreed but then, very unfairly, I told him he couldn't tell his staff either.

That didn't work, as he explained to me years later, 'Coxy [Neil Cox, the assistant manager] knows me well and straight away he turned round and said "there's something up". You'd told me I wasn't allowed to tell the staff because it mustn't get out, but Coxy was like, "What's the matter?" No one quite knew what was up with me and they didn't know whether it was a problem at home or whatever. On the second day I couldn't keep it in any more. I couldn't keep it secret because we all needed to know and we needed to come up with a plan of how we were gonna get over it. So I ended up having to tell them all, but I told you I hadn't because you told me not to!'

First thing on the Monday morning we set about damage limitation. David contacted the player administration department at the Football League and explained what had happened. Their initial response was that perhaps we need not be charged. We were asked to send our comments in time for an FL executive meeting on the Wednesday. Jim Sturman QC, who had acted for us in the Jermaine Darlington case, offered to represent us at any hearing. However, we were advised to look at the composition of any panel before asking Jim to act: the rule of thumb was that our representatives should be commensurate in status with the people on the panel.

Then I had to tell the Dons Trust board. At that time Matthew Breach was the chair so I called him to explain the background. And finally I consulted David Lloyd, a fan and retired PR guru to whom I went for advice about how to deal with the public relations surrounding major issues. Given that this was the second time we were facing a points deduction for using an ineligible player, I knew there was bound to be a shit-storm when it got out.

David wrote a comprehensive plan for us but we could only implement some of it. I've always taken the view that there will be some mistakes in any walk of life and the measure of the person or the club is how, and how quickly, they respond. So his advice included, 'The most sensible approach, no matter how taxing, is to take the initiative and own up and deal with the situation head on.' But we'd already agreed with Neal that we shouldn't tell the players so we couldn't do that; instead we prepared a statement for release if the news leaked out and guidance for club staff, football management and the board on what to say. In a perfect world that wouldn't be needed until we were absolutely clear we were safe from the threat of relegation.

I never believed that the FL would treat the issue as an admin error and sure enough we were charged. They assured us that nothing would be made public but I struggled to believe it wouldn't get out.

We took two points from the next three games and although on the face of it we were six clear of a relegation place we knew that a deduction meant that would only be three. Our next game was away at Southend, who were in a play-off place and on a good run of form. Neal was worried that the team was too relaxed, thinking we were safe, so he laid it on thick in his pre-match talk. 'I went to town on the team talk saying, "If I find any player not running, if anyone pulls out of a tackle, I will drag you off, I will nail you." I went into one, really went for them. I said I wanted them to go through the game like it was a final, like their lives depended on it. Everyone was looking at me as if to go, "All right gaffer, we're 16th here, what are you worried about?" Bayzo [Ashley Bayes, the goalkeeping coach] loved listening to the team talks and afterwards he said, "The hairs on the back of my neck were standing up." But we went out there and were outstanding and we beat Southend.'

After that game the football club board was celebrating wildly, to the bemusement of the Southend directors who couldn't understand, and couldn't be told, why we were so delighted. We were now 14th with 52 points. However, the bottom teams had won, so after the expected penalty points were deducted we would still only be three points from safety. In fact, if we'd lost to Southend we would have been equal on points with Northampton, who filled the second relegation place. No wonder we celebrated.

The stress was enormous, not least on David who was facing the possibility that his oversight might cause us to be relegated. I've never lost sleep over anything at the club, but some of my waking moments weren't pleasant during that period.

It didn't get any easier. In the next game we were 2-0 down to Newport County and anxiously watching the other results. For the second match running Kwesi Appiah, on loan from Crystal Palace, was outstanding and scored as we came back to draw 2-2. However, the other results had gone against us and we knew we were still only three points clear of a relegation spot.

It was Easter weekend so three days later we made the long trip to Plymouth. Once again Appiah was outstanding, setting up Jack Midson for our first goal and scoring the second as we came back from conceding an early goal to win 2-1. Even after deducting three points we would still have 53 and we were safe. The celebrations were even louder than at Southend and Neal felt able to tell the team on the coach journey home. He says, 'I got back on the coach and I said, "Lads can you get to the back," and I told them what happened. I said, "This is the story, you can't tweet it, you can't say I said it, but I have been hard on you and this is the reason why." I told them what the win had done [for our league safety] and they were all like "oh my God" after the event.'

In fact, the story had started leaking out during that game and it was all over the chat site that evening. But we were safe and making the announcement became a much easier proposition than if we'd still been struggling to avoid the drop.

Quite rightly the DT board felt it should act and appointed the vice-chair, David Growns, to carry out a review to establish what happened. In the week when Jake Nicholson's contract should have been renewed I was away on holiday and David Charles had turned up for work unwell. He and I spoke on the phone regularly and being on holiday didn't change that but when I realised he was struggling I sent him home. That explains what happened but it doesn't excuse it. An error that could easily have cost us our Football League place is potentially a sackable offence, so I think David Growns's report and recommendations for improvement were very restrained. Ultimately I was responsible for everything in the club and so I seriously considered resigning because there had now been two incidents while I was CEO. I was persuaded not to do so after informal conversations with Matthew Breach and David Growns but we all knew that another mistake like that would cost both David and me our jobs.

We went to a hearing and duly had three points deducted, despite tabling examples of where other clubs had lesser penalties for similar sins. In Chapter 21 I had a rant about the disproportionate nature of the punishment for an admin mistake so I won't repeat it here.

Were we right to keep it from the players? Later I asked Neal and veteran centre-back Alan Bennett if they thought it was the correct decision to keep the matter secret. Alan's view was, 'Yeah, I think so. Coxy and Bass, they're experienced guys and they just knew that it would work. Then you could tell the players at the point we were safe whereas if you did it earlier it would have been a risk.' Neal was more direct, expressing a view that you should never give a group of players an excuse for failure because some of them will use it. My logic was simple; it would become the only topic of conversation with the press and the fans and I didn't want that extra burden on the players.

But for the points deduction, 2013/14 had been a season of steady progress and now we needed to build on it. We had stopped leaking so many goals but we still weren't scoring enough, as illustrated by the fact that Michael Smith was our top scorer, despite having left halfway through.

Still searching for the right combination, we released Jack Midson, scorer of the penalty which had kept us in the league two seasons earlier, and Seb Brown, whose penalty saves got us into the league in the first place but whose confidence seemed to have deserted him. The summer became a story of two strikers. The more visible one, in every sense, was Adebayo Akinfenwa, who is a shade under 6ft tall but 16st, or 102kg. Rated the world's strongest footballer by one of the well-known computer football games, he had branded himself 'The Beast'.

We'd tried to sign him the season before but Gillingham had offered him a deal to play in League 1 and he wanted to give it a go. Neal told Bayo he'd be disappointed if he didn't want to try his hand at the higher level, wished him success and said we'd be keeping an eye on him. So when he became available again a year later the relationship was already established and the signing was fairly straightforward.

This wasn't the case with our second target, Matt Tubbs. Only two years earlier he'd been bought by Bournemouth for £800,000 but after losing half a season to injury he'd slipped down the pecking order and had been out on loan a couple of times.

Matt was based near Bournemouth and had got an inkling that Portsmouth were interested in him. They had the advantage of being nearer and a bigger club so his agent kept stalling us. We knew that if Portsmouth came in for him that would have blown us away. But Neal finally got him over the line after persisting and persisting. Pursuing a player can become all-consuming and can take over your life. It became so bad that it took over a large part of his family's holiday in Greece. Neal says, 'I kept saying to my missus, "I've got to take this call, it's about Tubbsy." In the end I think they just kept hearing the word "Tubbsy". After one long call out on the balcony I came back in and my daughter Bella, who was quite young then, just said, "Well Dad, have we got Tubbsy or not?" and I thought, blimey, that sums up where I am.'

Eventually he signed and Neal's efforts quickly bore fruit when he scored six goals in his first six games. Throughout the season we never looked like being relegated and fleetingly flirted with a play-off place. But by the end of March we were safe with 53 points and seven games left to play. Neal decided to experiment and played a more adventurous formation for several games which, while hugely entertaining, gained us only five points. We finished a respectable 15th place in the league; we would have needed to win six of those last seven matches to get a play-off place.

Yet again we found ourselves with our top scorer having been with us only half a season; in the January transfer window Matt Tubbs was lured away to Portsmouth, who had previously shown no interest in him. If we hadn't been aware that Portsmouth were interested in him it would have been apparent when we played them at Fratton Park in mid-December. Matt scored and we won 2-0. He was substituted near the end at which point we were subjected to the cringe-making sight of the then Portsmouth chairman giving him a one-man standing ovation as he left the pitch. Sigh.

Bayo ended the season equal top scorer including a goal in the FA Cup against Liverpool, the team he supports. We'd reached the third round after a replay against York City and then a win at Wycombe Wanderers. Earlier in the season we'd lost to Wycombe in the league. It seemed that every time Bayo went for the ball the opposition defender went down. Dons fans were convinced they were faking it and that the referee was being conned. As a result, when the cup game came round the Wycombe manager, Gareth Ainsworth, a much-loved former Dons player and one of the very few who showed solidarity with fans during the protests, ended up being booed. I was mortified; Gareth is one of the good guys.

We prepared well for the Wycombe game, with training being at 100mph to simulate what we would be facing. But possibly the most important preparation took place on the day. Neal found the referee on the pitch and asked him to judge whether Bayo was a big strong lad or whether he'd committed a foul.

Neal always picked his battles carefully and refrained from publicly criticising referees. So referees knew that if he made a point it was worth listening to. He didn't ask for favours, he just politely asked the official to watch out for something. Sure enough, early in the game Bayo went up for a header and the Wycombe player went down holding his head. The ref waved play on.

And so to Liverpool. The FA Cup draw was made while we were playing a reserve game at Merstham, home of the cheese rolls. Within two minutes I had a call from a Liverpool radio station asking about the tie. We were clearly going to be under a strain for the next few weeks.

We could only offer Liverpool 100 seats and 750 terrace tickets, which was hopelessly inadequate. For the one and only time I found dealing with the police difficult. They were adamant that Liverpool fans would try to get in by any means necessary; climb walls, forge tickets, sneak into the ground a day or more before the game and hide. We put extensive controls in place and no one was allowed in the car park without first presenting a valid ticket for the home stands at a temporary barrier at the main road. We were certain we had it under control. About an hour before kick-off I went into the car park and the first man I saw asked me, in an unmistakable Scouse accent, if I had a spare ticket!

Before the game Neal was asked if he hoped Steven Gerrard would play and replied that we should want him to play because our players should want to play against the best, not play against the kids. We lost: AFC Wimbledon 1 Steven Gerrard 2. He scored two goals and headed a goal-bound shot off the line. Maybe Neal should have stayed schtum.

The TV fee was very welcome and so was the press exposure. We decided that it would be wrong to increase prices and saw a national daily paper announce '£4 to watch Liverpool'. They were right; the under-18 ticket for a terrace place was £4 and the PR of not increasing prices was worth far more than the extra £7,000 I calculated we'd have earned if we'd put prices up 25 per cent.

At the end of the 2014/15 season we were firmly established as a League 2 club. Now it was time to look upwards. The squad contained seven players who would feature prominently the following season but once again we needed to bring in a goalscorer. Get the right one and we were ready for a push for promotion.

44

YOU CAN'T ALWAYS GET WHAT YOU WANT

TRIBUNALS ARE a feature of football where many fans see the results without having the process explained. This chapter takes you through why they arise and how they work, illustrated by a specific example in which we were involved.

First, a very brief history. In the bad old days players were attached to clubs under what was known as the 'retain and transfer' system. It meant that players were not entitled to leave a club at the end of their contract; the 'retain' part of retain and transfer. Furthermore, if an out-of-contract player asked for a transfer the club could refuse to pay their wages, while still being able to prevent them from leaving. This arrangement was known by players as the 'slavery contract'.

Following a legal case brought by George Eastham in 1964, astonishingly only two years before England won the World Cup, the 'retain' element was amended in several ways. Importantly, it was the start of a tribunal system to resolve disputes over the fee to be paid by the club to which an out-of-contract player moved.

Fast forward 31 years to 1995 when Jean-Marc Bosman won a case at the European Court of Justice. The decision allowed players in the EU to move to another club at the end of a contract without a transfer fee being paid.

An exception was for those under the age of 24 where a player could leave his club and join another but 'compensation' had to be paid for the investment in his development. There is no fixed formula for determining the amount; instead there are laid-down criteria from which it should be determined.

Compensation is usually settled amicably when an out-of-contract player moves from one club to another. But when the amount payable can't be agreed then the dispute may be taken to tribunal. These cases are generally known as Bosman transfers.[57]

The tribunal in question involves Will Mannion, a goalkeeper. Our academy takes boys from age eight upwards but we are always on the lookout for talented recruits at all ages. Will was one of those later arrivals. He had been at Watford, Reading and then Dagenham & Redbridge where he was released after less than a year. That is a soul-destroying situation for a 16-year-old boy to be in; sadly, it is very common But then Ashley Bayes, our first-team goalkeeping coach, saw his potential and we offered Will a scholarship in May 2014, at the age of 16.

For the next two years he trained alongside our first-team goalkeepers, under Ashley's direct tuition. After taking a while to build up his confidence, Will's quality began to show during his second season; his outstanding performances played a large part in our FA Youth Cup success when we beat Newcastle United and then Watford. Both of those clubs' academies are much better funded than ours.

Will was spotted by the FA's talent scouts and he was called up to an England under-18 training camp in January 2016. This was attended by only eight other goalkeepers from around the country. Thanks to Ashley's tutelage and the developmental environment of our academy, Will had gone from reject to the fringes of the England team in 18 months.

What happened next was not Will's fault in any way; it happened simply because he was a talented young goalkeeper.

In December 2015 we told Will we'd be offering him a contract and followed it up with a formal offer in January. From our point of view, the problem with England camps is that players at lower level clubs attract interest from higher up the pyramid.

—

57 The massive transfer fees you see in the press are to acquire a player's registration while he is still contracted to another club. In these cases there is no obligation on a club to release a player but they may choose to do so, either as an economic judgement or because they think they won't be able to get the best out of an unsettled player if they make him stay and see out his contract.

We'd been hearing rumours about approaches from other clubs and we'd rejected a couple of requests for Will to go on trial. This was our policy for all boys because for us it was lose-lose. If the other club liked a boy he'd arrive back desperate to join them, making it easier for that club to pressure us into accepting a low fee. If they rejected him he would arrive back desperately disappointed and we'd be left to pick up the pieces of his shaken confidence. So we always said 'no' to such requests.

Then in January we received a bid from Hull City, who were a Premier League team at the time. They offered £20,000 and a sell-on clause of ten per cent of the profit Hull made. We rejected the offer out of hand and made an improved contract offer to Will.

If he rejected our contract offer Will would be free to leave when his scholarship expired at the end of June, although we would be entitled to compensation. We decided we should try to negotiate a sale now rather than wait until the summer when there was a chance, albeit a small one, that he might not find a club and we'd get no compensation. Or, more likely, he'd find a smaller club which couldn't afford a decent fee. We decided to listen to offers while quietly trying to drum up interest from the other clubs who'd watched him; we wanted to create a bidding war.

It was May before we received a further written offer from Hull – £30,000 plus an improved sell-on clause at 20 per cent. By then it was becoming clear to us that no other clubs were interested in bidding. So we rejected Hull's offer and took the initiative by phoning them and asking for £75,000. That figure was fairly arbitrary but had been arrived at after substantial input from our academy manager, Jeremy Sauer, and a look at our cash flow needs at the time.

In June, Hull sent a final offer of £40,000 but with the sell-on clause reduced back to ten per cent. We refused the offer the same day. A few days later Hull wrote to say they planned to sign Will on 1 July, the day after his scholarship ended. In accordance with the rules they would then lodge half their offer, i.e. £20,000, with the Premier League.

On the same day that they signed Will, Hull referred the dispute to the Professional Football Compensation Committee. The PFCC is an FA committee which determines the amount of compensation to be paid in circumstances such as these.

Most people in football recommend avoiding a tribunal like the plague 'because you have no idea what they will decide'. However, we concluded that any tribunal would be unlikely to reduce the compensation below Hull's offer of £40,000. Furthermore, when Hull made their final offer they would have factored in the likelihood that a tribunal would only increase it.

In the meantime we'd had some good news. Will had made his debut for the England under-19 team and, however good their coaching, Hull could hardly claim the credit for this. We felt this would support our valuation.

On the deadline date for submitting their case, Hull's club secretary phoned me to ask if we really wanted to go through the hassle of preparing papers and would I like to talk to their vice-chairman. After discussing it with the board we decided to go back and ask for a lot more than our earlier request for £75,000 on the grounds that sum had constituted an offer 'to get the deal done' at a time when we needed the cash. That situation no longer applied. Furthermore, Will had now made his debut for the England under-19 team which justified a higher valuation.

We had also become aware that the England under-19 first-choice goalkeeper had just been transferred from Sheffield United to Bournemouth for a reported fee of £800,000.[58] Special circumstances relating to that transfer massively increased the fee but, nonetheless, we wanted to reference it in our submission.

We decided to ask for £300,000. This was nonsense, really, because Will was out of contract and therefore the compensation would be based on the laid-down criteria; fees paid for players like Ramsdale who were under contract were not comparable. But our thinking was to get a higher figure into the tribunal members' heads. And anyway, what harm could it do to shoot for the stars?

I rang Hull, who had been hoping to pitch the agreement somewhere between £40,000 and £75,000, so this was a huge shock to them. With such a disparity in expectations we agreed that we might as well go to a tribunal.

It was now mid-September. Expecting that the negotiations would be unfruitful, we'd been gathering comparison data from other clubs to try to get evidence to support our valuation. There is no central database of

—

58 The goalkeeper was Aaron Ramsdale, who later joined us on loan. His performances helped us to avoid relegation in the 2018/19 season.

previous decisions to call upon, so we used search engines and called one or two particularly helpful clubs to try to identify precedents. We quickly identified several examples that might help our case and I called the CEOs of the relevant clubs. Most clubs at our level have had experience of losing highly valued players to bigger clubs, so without exception everyone I approached was very willing to help.

Everything proceeded at a snail's pace and it was February 2017 before we were able to send our submission. On 3 March Hull responded and we exchanged responses, then responses to responses. On 16 May, ten and a half months after Will signed for Hull, we attended the tribunal at the Park Plaza Sherlock Holmes Hotel in London. A bit above our normal pay grade!

Hull brought their club secretary and a sports lawyer to the meeting. We'd decided not to bring legal representation but instead to discreetly play the 'small club versus Premier League club' card. Rather than saying 'we can't afford a lawyer' I'd say, 'Well, I'm not a qualified lawyer, but ...'

We'd been advised that for youth team players it looked good if the first-team manager attended, so as to demonstrate his interest in youth development, so we added Neal Ardley to our presentation team. It now comprised Neal, Jeremy Sauer, our academy manager, Ashley Bayes, our first-team goalkeeping coach, and me.

The hearing had a QC to act as an independent chair, plus a rather daunting list of panel members, with one each from the Premier League, the Football League, the League Managers' Association and the Professional Footballers' Association. Before we started the panel interviewed Will with neither club present. From our point of view the problem with this was that the player's loyalties are naturally with his current employer (it was, therefore, pleasing to read in the 'reasons' document we were sent after the decision was announced that Will had been very complimentary about our club, about our insistence on him completing the educational component of his scholarship, and especially about the coaching and guidance he received from goalkeeping coach Ashley Bayes).

Hull's lawyer went first and focused on the eight criteria on which compensation should be based. These are:

- The status of the transferor and transferee club – our lower-league status would tend to depress the fee but, conversely, Hull's Premier League status would increase the fee

- The age of the player – an older player is more likely to attract increased compensation
- Any fee we paid to sign Will – this was zero and therefore not helpful to us
- How long Will spent with us – it didn't help our case that he was with us for only two years
- The contract offer we made to Will – a higher wage offer would increase the compensation, but we didn't pay a lot to first-year professionals
- How often Will had played and any international recognition – he hadn't featured for our first team, which didn't help our case, but he had received international recognition, which was very helpful
- Substantiated interest from other clubs – if we'd had any other offers that would have helped to justify an increased fee; the requests for trials from other clubs wasn't considered relevant
- The costs of running our academy – the compensation is designed to cover the development investment in the player but, being a Category 3 academy these costs were not massive when spread across the number of boys in our system
- Previous tribunal decisions – each club presented the most helpful examples to its case and we added fees paid or offered for young players at our club and elsewhere.

When it came to our turn, I led our presentation. We had rehearsed our points more than once. Ashley hadn't been in such an environment before so he worked from a script, but his natural passion and enthusiasm soon surfaced as he talked in detail about Will's talents and what he'd done to develop him. Neal and Jeremy added their points and I focused on the fees for comparable transfers.

I came away thinking that we'd done as well as we could but that we'd struggle to get a six-figure sum because the compensation was driven by the criteria. So I was pleasantly surprised when we were awarded £100,000 plus up to a further £100,000 based on first-team appearances for Hull. There might be further payments, contingent upon England recognition at under-21 and full levels, plus a 20 per cent sell-on clause.

A couple of days later we received the tribunal's detailed reasons for the decision. There was no definitive calculation, nor could there be, but it seemed to me that the decision was based largely on the value we'd added during the time he was with us, the fact that Will had been signed by a Premier League club, and the international call-up. They had, by and large, discarded most of the comparative figures both we and Hull presented.

Looking back on it, both sides had reason to be frustrated. Hull had to pay more than they could have settled for several months earlier, while we missed out on a higher fee if we'd offered Will a contract at an earlier stage. So we concluded that we needed to revisit our policy on when we should offer contracts to promising youth players. If Will had been on a contract we'd have been able to seek a much higher fee. On the other hand, no other club had come in for him and perhaps Hull wouldn't have offered the sort of sum we'd have wanted if he'd been on contract, so it might have been self-defeating.

There's a couple of tailpieces to this story. First, a few months later Hull asked if we'd be interested in them buying out the 20 per cent sell-on clause. Their offer wasn't very generous so we declined. We were following advice I'd been given years before, namely that it's always worth giving up a few thousand pounds in a transfer deal in return for a higher sell-on percentage. You only need one of the players to be sold for a large sum to more than compensate for the relatively small sums you forego.

And finally, at the time of writing Will is 22. He played one game for Hull's first team, in the League Cup, and most of his experience was on loan at Aldershot and Kidderminster, both National League clubs. His contract expired at the end of the 2019/20 season and he joined Pafos, a Cypriot First Division side, on a free transfer.

45

WHO ARE YOU?

ONCE IN a while a player emerges as if from nowhere, sparkles and dazzles like a shooting star and imprints himself on your mind forever. And then he's gone, as suddenly as he appeared. Bobby Shillinde was such a player.

Observant fans will first have noticed him after the play-off final in Manchester in 2011, when he tweeted as he left the hotel with the team. Over the next couple of seasons his personal stats show that he made 19 appearances as a right-sided midfield player for our under-21 team and eight for the first team.

Born in Botswana, Bobby came to England when he was 13. He was desperate to play for the national team, The Zebras, rated 97th in the 2013 FIFA rankings. Never shy about promoting himself, he pressed the Botswana FA to call him up for their next training camp.

Step forward, Comfort 'Big Fish' Ramatebele, Botswana's first FIFA-registered agent (at the time you had to pass exams to achieve agent status). Ramatebele was under a cloud for introducing Nigerian striker John Abimola to Botswana Premier League rookies BR Highlanders. Unfortunately Abimola didn't live up to the hype and nor was there any evidence that he was actually in the records of the Nigerian FA, even though he claimed he had played for Nigerian junior sides. The Highlanders' coach Teenage Mpote very quickly kicked him out.

Bobby Shillinde was manna from heaven for Ramatebele, who desperately needed to redeem himself. Although Bobby was a relative newcomer to the Dons team, and we were struggling in League 2, he was highly rated. The *Botswana Sunday Standard* quoted Dons manager Neal Ardley as saying, 'I can confirm that he is registered with our under-21 reserves but has plenty of first-team experience. He is a very well-disciplined, hard-working youngster with [an] abundance of pace and skill. Bobby has been with us from the 2010/2011 season and one thing I admire about the youngster is his persistence. He has always proven his worth in the team.'

And indeed he had. He featured in the League 2 Team of the Week and was delighted to tweet a photo of himself with the match ball, 'signed by The Lads', after being voted man of the match. It was all going so well. 'There is no doubt that he would be promoted [to the first team] next season,' added Neal in the *Sunday Standard.*

Arrangements were made through the Botswana Football Association to bring the 'genius', as Big Fish had proclaimed him, to Botswana for close assessment. Mmegi Online (Mmegi is Setswana for 'The Reporter') pictured Bobby arriving at the Sir Seretse Khama Airport on 13 March, saying, 'All eyes will be on the 21-year-old Shillinde, who plies his trade at AFC Wimbledon in League 2.' Bobby headed straight to the Zebras' camp.

And then. Days down the line, Botswana fans were told that Shillinde could not make his international debut because he did not have a local passport. Although it was an understandable oversight, many Botswana fans were disappointed. But, as reported in the *Sunday Standard*, word coming from the camp was that Shillinde was not what manager Stanley Tshosane had expected.

And then. Marina Hyde of *The Guardian* had picked up reports that Bobby might not be exactly what he said. In an article on 20 March she reported our press officer saying, 'I've checked with a few people. This player has never played for AFC Wimbledon as far as we are aware. Just to point out also that AFC Wimbledon does not have an under-21 squad at the current time, nor a reserves squad, though do we have a development squad.' It seemed that he'd Photoshopped himself into the team of the week in place of Joel Grant of Wycombe Wanderers. And as for that photo of the signed match ball!

Shortly after Ms Hyde's article the club received a 'cease and desist' letter on headed paper from a firm of solicitors based in the north-west of England telling us, in solicitor-ese, to lay off Bobby.

It was already too late. A group of fans had adopted him. A Botswana flag flew proudly at the away game at Aldershot on 16 March. Following a 1-0 win, first-team coach Simon Bassey tweeted, 'Great result and all without our star player Bobby Shillende.'

Big Fish wasn't too downhearted, as reported once again in the *Sunday Standard*, 'Bobby's issue has opened my eyes about this business of being a FIFA agent. It's a demanding business which needs someone to be a perfectionist. But I'm not going to put my head down because of this scandal… Ramatebele is a person who takes chances and the fact that the whole country is talking about me right now is because of the player who I brought here in good faith but it turned otherwise. Some of the chances I take are going to be disappointing but I'm ready to take the bullet.'

And so Bobby Shillinde joins Adrian Shankar at Worcestershire County Cricket Club and Ali Dia at Southampton FC in a pantheon of players who weren't quite what they advertised. No doubt there are others over whom a veil has been drawn by the clubs which were involved.

Bobby, if you're reading this, please be assured we're not mocking you. Your persistence and perseverance bordered on the heroic and is much admired by Dons fans.

And once in a while, when a striker misses an open goal from three yards out, you'll hear some of our fans mutter, 'I bet Bobby would have put that away.'

46

HIGHER GROUND

THE 2015/16 season dawned. The previous two campaigns had been about establishing ourselves as a League 2 club and building for the next stage. We now had the core of a very good squad and just before the previous season ended came a turning point.

Our experience of being within 17 minutes of relegation two years earlier had made me very nervous about the consequences of going back down to the Conference. While we would survive such a drop I saw it as a serious threat to the likelihood of us getting our new stadium. So, after talking it through with the football club and Dons Trust boards we decided to try to create a cushion by going for promotion to League 1. If we were then relegated back to League 2 we would be able to manage that relatively easily; but going back to the Conference would be a problem on a much larger scale.

Every year we produced a 'bottom up' budget. All that means is that we start at a very detailed level and then bring it all together to produce a club budget. So, for example, commercial director Ivor Heller would be asked to estimate sponsorship income which he would do by listing the existing sponsors who were likely to renew, then add in new deals he thought he could make. Then he'd do the same for all the other areas of income and expenditure. I'd review it, challenge him to earn more income and we'd agree a departmental budget.

This was done for the entire club with the exception that we didn't calculate the players' wage bill. We didn't need to; the idea was that we would spend the total profit from all our other business areas. Of course, it was never as much as we would like it to be and it usually led me to go back to Ivor and see if he could generate more profit.

When I had the figure we felt we could afford I would deduct National Insurance and an estimate of the agents' fees and items such as clean sheet and goal bonuses. That would leave me with a figure that I could tell Neal was his weekly wages budget. If he wanted to buy a player then I'd convert the fee back into a weekly wage and that came out of his budget. He would take the budget and produce a marked-up team lay-out, with two players for every position. Where we already had a contracted player he'd write in the name and wages. Otherwise next to each position he'd write, 'new player £XXX per week'. And the total had to add up to the budget. Simple really.

Neal treated the money as if it was his. If he could bring in a player for £100 per week less than he'd allocated for that position he could spend more on another position. And, unusually among managers, he would hold some money back, in case of injury or if a bargain signing appeared.

This year I met Neal at the training ground and talked about the budget. I had persuaded the Football League to produce a table showing league position compared to wages budget over a four-year period.

I talked it through with Neal. The chart shows unequivocally that on average over the four years, the top three or four places in the league were occupied by teams who, as a minimum, were in the top half of the spending league table. But what is also showed was that the fifth, sixth and seventh places were frequently occupied by teams much further down the spending table. So this was his challenge. If we could get him up to 14th or thereabouts in the wages table could he have a real go at promotion?

Neal came at it a different way. We'd agreed a minimum target for each year was to be four places above our position in the wages league table. That way, if we were the lowest spenders in the league we'd still expect him to over-perform and avoid relegation. So he said, 'Well, by your reckoning then, if you got me to 12th in the budget table I'd have to over-achieve by four or five places. You're challenging me to do that.' I agreed we would try to find the money and we had a deal.

Shortly after that meeting, Neal and his staff held a two-day meeting entitled 'What does promotion look like?' We had retained a core of players who would be the mainstays of the team and now they turned their attention to what we needed to complete the jigsaw.

Recruitment was never easy, especially for a team with what amounted to a non-league ground, which didn't pay top whack and which had yet to finish in the top half of League 2. But the planning and analysis paid off and by mid-July we had signed four of our main targets, including Lyle Taylor.

Lyle hadn't been a success in England, scoring goals at a reasonable rate only when he was on loan in Scotland. Nonetheless, Scunthorpe United had seen something that made them pay £150,000 for him, but then he fell out of favour and was fifth in line for a place in their team. But we knew all about his qualities and had watched him several times over a couple of years. Our approach to recruitment was usually that Neal and I would agree the parameters and he would negotiate the deal. My role was to be 'the madman in the attic', so that Neal could tell the agent, 'I'll never get that past my CEO,' or, knowing he'd got a good deal, 'Let me see if my CEO will agree – I think I can persuade him.'

We rarely paid fees but Scunthorpe wanted one and at that stage he asked me to step in to negotiate the fee. He recalls, 'I'd met the player, the agent, and agreed the terms, etc, etc. And it got down to the fee, which wasn't a king's ransom, but they wanted something for him. It was just where we would be willing to go on that. I was going to my mum and dad's and I remember pulling over in my car to ask you to jump in and get the deal done and find whatever it needed to be a solution.'

I rang Scunthorpe and after some haggling we agreed a fee of £10,000. They agreed, even though I'd heard on the grapevine that they still owed an instalment of the fee to Sheffield United. But when you're letting an unhappy player go, the decision criteria include getting his wages off the payroll as well as any fee. We only ever agreed to pay add-on fees out of extra income so I was quite relaxed about agreeing an additional fee for reaching the play-off semi-finals and another for reaching the final. Surprisingly there was no added fee for winning the play-off final; maybe nobody believed that would happen.

Lyle signed and the same day he made his debut in a friendly at Basingstoke. He scored a hat-trick and I watched, certain we'd done a great deal. A few years later he ran down his contract and left for Charlton. While he was there, Brentford offered £3m for him. Not bad for a £10,000 player.

Our other new striker, Tom Elliott, had been released by Cambridge but we also knew him very well and were delighted to get him. We now had four strikers; Ade Azeez with sizzling pace, Bayo with phenomenal strength, Tom Elliott with height and power and Lyle Taylor, the most natural goalscorer of the four.

Recruitment was pretty much complete when we re-signed Jon Meades (a midfielder or full-back who had been on loan with us two years earlier), Andy Barcham (a skilful and hard-working wide midfielder), and Paul Robinson (a massively experienced centre-back with over 350 games behind him, most of them at a higher level).

There was a different feeling around the place that summer. Neal, his assistant Neil Cox, and Simon Bassey were all highly energised. I recall thinking it was like one of those action films where the first half is about creating the team. And, just like in those films, some of the main characters took some persuading to join us.

Neal says, 'You mustn't cut your nose off to spite your face when deals aren't going your way. You have to understand the player's motivations. I agreed a deal with Tom Elliott and then got told he was going to Port Vale. I just said, "Well is there anything I can do?" The answer was, "No, he's going to Port Vale," who were in League 1 at the time. So it was okay, wish him good luck and then I left it. I was waiting for him to be announced as their player, but nothing, nothing, nothing. On the off chance I rang the agent and said, "What's happening? Why has he not signed?" He told me they were messing Tom around and I said, "Well look, I'm still here. I really want him. Surely the lad wants to be loved and I will do that. I'm not messing around." Soon afterwards, he rang me back and said, "Let's do it."

'It was the same with Paul Robinson. The deal was agreed and everything was done and I remember taking a call and the agent saying to me, "I'm really, really sorry." I was gutted because I thought he'd be a big piece of the jigsaw. Then, I rang him [Robinson] up a couple of days later and said, "Look, no hard feelings, I wish you all the best." He just went, "To be fair I think I have made a bit of a mistake. He's not going to play me." I said, "Listen, I'll take you, come. I'd love to have you." So he signed.'

It is in the nature of some fans to carp about everything and be grudging in their praise. It clearly got to Trevor Williams, who had a close-up view of the recruitment and development of the players, and recalls, 'I would kill for some of that squad still. This is what winds me up and what still winds me up, "Oh we got lucky we got Lyle, we got lucky we got Tom." We didn't get lucky. Lyle didn't turn up at the training ground on spec and go, "Can I come and train with you?" Bass was talking to me about Lyle for three years because we all knew he was a good player but we knew he had never really settled down anywhere. Tom Elliott had had a quiet year [at Cambridge] before that but we knew all about him and took him as soon as he was released and Bass worked hard with him.'

By the end of October we were tenth, one point away from the play-offs. New recruit Paul Robinson was encouraged, 'There was a really good feel about the place from day one. I felt in the first half of the season we had the potential but we should have done better, we'd have a good result and then we wouldn't really back it up the following week. But I always felt we had a good team. We had four decent strikers, especially once we got them all fit and firing, and then it just felt like a matter of time before something was just going to click.'

However, a poor November saw us slip back to 12th. Then on 12 December we played Stevenage at Kingsmeadow in a game that was to be a turning point in our season. We played poorly and conceded the sort of goal that no one can quite believe. Our regular keeper, James Shea, was very good but he had lost a bit of confidence and we'd taken a young player on loan from Cardiff. Stevenage hit a long, aimless free kick from their own half and he called to let it come through to him. But he'd come too far from his line and the ball bounced over his head into the net. We lost 2-1.

The team had arranged to go to Manchester for their Christmas party and wanted to get away promptly. George Francomb, who'd been voted man of the match, was desperate to avoid missing the train but Ivor wasn't ready – eventually, after hanging around for some time, George went. It was a perfect storm of an awful performance, a joke goal, the team buggering off, a missing man of the match and making things worse by posting photos of what a good time they were having on Instagram.

It got worse: one of the fans who was baying for blood got involved in a Twitter spat with the loan keeper who reacted with, 'You're still paying to watch every week and helping towards my wage. I'm laughing and you're losing out.' Ooof. We sent him back the next day.

It became folklore among the cognoscenti that this all led to a revolution. Some fans even claimed that Neal had lost the dressing room, a story that gets trotted out every time we had a poor run – 'FACT' as some of the keyboard warriors like to proclaim. This is fantasyland writ large as Trevor explains, 'I have heard that the players rebelled and took over. That is just utter nonsense. It is a narrative among certain of our fans that the players took over. We had a strong dressing room but the idea that this wasn't Ards's promotion is just bollocks, utter bollocks. I don't care if you like Ards or not, I have no issue with that, but if you are telling me the players took over in the dressing room I will tell you as someone who is at training and who is in the dressing room, that is blatantly just shit.'[59]

In fact, we knew we weren't playing badly. It was a time before expected goals became widely used but they showed that we were second in the expected goals league, behind Portsmouth. We just had to stick with it.

Despite the vitriol from some fans, so far as the players and management were concerned the much-derided Christmas party was a major success. Paul Robinson recalls, 'In a way it was a turning point for us as a group. You could think that when you've lost the game you have to go home, shut your door and mope for a few days but throughout my career I found a team night out or some kind of bonding exercise is more effective. The session really brought us together as a group. It was pretty much every member of the squad so everyone was there and I think it created that bond between us. Sometimes a good Christmas do can, ironically, make your season. It's a long, hard, tough season in League 2. Travelling around the country, going up to Carlisle and then down to Plymouth, you've got to dig in and fight for each other and get results. That bond, that friendship, that kind of togetherness, that's when it all came into focus, really.'

There were some significant changes on the pitch. For all his strength, Bayo wasn't our most mobile player. Simon Bassey had been working with Tom Elliott since he arrived and he judged the time was right to promote Tom's case because, 'If we played Tom Elliott we could press. I remember Ards coming to my room in the hotel [before an away game at Exeter, just after Christmas], something he never normally did, and saying, "You think Tom Elliott?" and me saying, "I'm telling you now, Tom Elliott." He scored that day and it was the start of a really good run with Tom starting and Bayo as a sub. We really kicked on.'

---

59 'The manager has lost the dressing room' is a regular cry from fans when a team is on a poor run. It is almost always nonsense. This was one of the few issues where Ivor and I clashed. He likes to get close to the players and would pick up all their grumbles. I refused to listen to him because players love to grumble. As Terry Brown once put it to me, 'Of course they're unhappy that we've lost a few games. So they should be. I want them to care.'

Indeed we did. On 1 February goalkeeper Kelle Roos joined on loan from Derby County and kept nine clean sheets by the end of the season. With seven wins from the next eight games we were fifth by late February. But not everyone was happy. Like most players, Bayo was desperate to start but Tom was now preferred to him in the starting line-up. Our good run ended when we lost 2-1 at home to Oxford. Neal brought Bayo off the bench, 'For something different, but he didn't try a leg. It was one of the first times I ever did it but I rang him that night when I got home. I was that angry and he was like, "All right gaffer?" and I said, "No, not at all, I want to see you on Monday. You've killed me today." On the Monday he didn't come up and see me and I went down and hauled him up to the office. I said, "I can't have you being a non-trier and that's what you were on Saturday." It cleared the air and he was immense for the rest of the season. We wouldn't have won promotion without him.'

A dip in form meant we took only two points from the next five games and dropped out of the play-off places. And then we put the final piece in the jigsaw. Late in 2015, Simon Bassey had travelled to watch Darius Charles, who was recovering from a serious injury. 'But he could hardly run, so we let it drop,' said Simon. In March we watched him and he was fit again. He couldn't get in the team at Burton Albion so we took him on loan. Six wins from the next seven games and then a draw at Stevenage in the penultimate match of the season saw us firmly fixed in the last play-off place.

We had taken 45 points from the second half of the season, which was automatic promotion form. We had strong characters in the dressing room, such as Barry Fuller, Darius Charles and Paul Robinson, who were all natural leaders. Not everyone is a leader. It takes all types and they need to be managed. Trevor says, 'Lyle was massively important. He was brilliant for us but he wasn't a strong leader in the dressing room. Danny Bulman used to play '80s music just to annoy him and once they got him to have a complete hissy fit by playing Justin Bieber over and over again just to wind him up.'

Confidence was sky high and we didn't care who we got in the play-offs but, nonetheless, we were interested to see who it would be. Accrington were second in the league and in fantastic form, with eight wins and three draws in their last 11 games. They were massive favourites to gain automatic promotion, needing only to beat lowly Stevenage on the last day of the season. But they could only draw and were pipped to one of the three automatic promotion spots when Bristol Rovers scored a winning goal in the 92nd minute of their game. So Accrington came fourth and would play us, the seventh-placed team.

It was ironic that Accrington would be playing us because earlier in the season at Kingsmeadow they'd been deprived of a win by what is probably the worst refereeing decision I've ever seen. At the end of the first half they shot from about 12 yards out and after the striker had hit it and as the ball was in the air on its way to our net, the referee blew for half-time. We drew 0-0. If that goal had counted they'd have had two extra points and won automatic promotion.

In general, the majority of teams that miss promotion on the last game of the season find it hard to re-motivate themselves for the play-offs and don't succeed. Furthermore, having assumed they would win, 'Everyone was devastated and there was no Plan B,' said Mark Turner, the Accrington club secretary. It also threw manager John Coleman's plans out of the window; an avid Liverpool fan, he had tickets to see them in the Europa League Final in Basel on the day of the second leg of our semi-final.

We hadn't realised quite how off-balance Accrington were. They travelled down to the first leg at Kingsmeadow on the morning of the game but, unable to arrange anywhere to train because most clubs were carrying out close-season maintenance, they had to train in a local park.

The first leg was a typically tight game. We won 1-0 in the 93rd minute when academy graduate Tom Beere, on the substitutes' bench because of a late injury elsewhere in the squad, scored. It was the only goal of his first-team career with us.

And so to the second leg. By now the players had declared themselves to be 'the wolf pack' with Darius Charles, Barry Fuller, Callum Kennedy and George Francomb leading extended howling sessions before the games. The noise reverberated round the Accrington dressing room which, as Trevor said 'is tiny, very cramped. But I'd never complain about Accrington because they were always so good to us – even after the semi-final when we broke their physio couch thanks to eight players sitting on it!'

Neal prepared the team by telling them that for the last ten weeks of the season Accrington had played every Saturday and Tuesday to catch up on a fixtures backlog. He says, 'Part of my team talk was you've got one team who have rested their players, who are delighted to be there, everything is geared around being there, and another team which is devastated to be there and hasn't had any rest.'

In fact, from the beginning of April until the end of the season, only one of their seven games was in midweek. But that didn't matter; what mattered was that our players believed that we had a fitness advantage and played accordingly.

The game started badly for us and by the hour-mark we were 2-0 down, losing 2-1 on aggregate. Centre-back Paul Robinson wasn't worried, however, 'Even when they scored that second goal I still felt really calm, it just didn't feel like we were out of it. I still felt confident that we would come back and get goals and, like Neal made out with his team talk, we'd finish the stronger.'

Nine minutes later Bayo, who'd come on as a substitute, scored a thumping header to bring the aggregate score level, taking the semi-final to extra time. The team talk before extra time is crucial and Neal showed his qualities by saying nothing. He recalls, 'We got everyone around and then Darius just went off. He's a big character and he just started saying, "We're stronger to a man. I've started telling their players they've gone, we've got you now." He was going round every one of our players saying, "To a man, we're stronger than them, we're fitter than them and we will not lose this game, mark my words." I'd gone in ready to say my bit but I just stood back and let Darius talk because he was in the zone, the players were listening to him and they believed him. I didn't need to say a word.'

In the first period of extra time, Jake Reeves, all non-stop energy, skipped past a couple of opponents and homed in on the goal. An Accrington player came to tackle him as he got his shot away and they both fell to the ground. The keeper saved it and the ball spun up to a lurking Lyle Taylor who scored. I've watched that goal many times but the bit that always catches my attention is that as the defender tries to get up off the floor to block Lyle's shot, Jake (inadvertently, naturally!) slings an arm across him and holds him down. It was 3-2 on aggregate and we were going to Wembley.

Or were we? Accrington have six floodlight towers, three down each side of the pitch, and with eight minutes to go all five lights on one of them failed. The referee played on. A minute later all the lights on another tower failed. The referee stopped play. Immediately Neal was on the pitch to tell him that he mustn't abandon the game.

Mark Turner, Accrington's secretary, had just had a radio message that there was smoke coming out of the control box on the floodlight. It seemed that the choke, a key component part, had overheated and tripped the light. To prevent anyone tampering with them, the control boxes were high up the towers. 'We were lucky,' said Mark. 'The man who rewired the lights a few years ago was in the crowd. If you watch the match video you can see somebody climbing a ladder to the box – that's him. He quickly worked out that only one bulb had failed and, after isolating it, he got the other bulbs back on.' The second tower came back on and the conspiracy theorists in the crowd settled down. Speaking to him later, Paul Robinson said, 'To be fair to the Accrington players, they all wanted to get on with the game. Nobody mentioned abandoning the game.'

Did the thought cross Turner's mind? 'Yes. If I'd been a cheat I would have turned everything off and said "sorry". But that wouldn't have been the right thing to do. If we don't play, that isn't fair.'

A few minutes later the final whistle went and we were going to Wembley. As everyone leapt to their feet to celebrate, I noticed Neal shrugging aside the hugs from his management team, as he explained later, 'My staff were jumping on me and all I could think about was, "Get off me, I'm gonna see them. I'll celebrate after doing the right thing first," so I went on to the pitch and picked up a couple of their players. I was one of the last to get to our fans because I wanted to go around and pick up some of their players.'

Ever since I saw the iconic photo of Freddie Flintoff with Brett Lee after one of the most exciting Test match finishes of all time, back in 2005, I've thought *that's* the way to behave. First respect your opponents, then celebrate.

As we drove home that night I'm afraid the accountant in me kicked in as I realised that we would be able to reward the players properly for their performance. We aren't high payers, so we give the players a share of our extra profits when we succeed. The players were on 20 per cent of our share of the gate money if we won and ten per cent if we lost. The profits from the four semi-final legs are pooled; the FL takes 50 per cent and the clubs get an equal share of the rest. In effect we got an eighth of a pool that was disappointingly small because we and Accrington had low attendances. If we'd lost the bonus would have been so little I'd have been embarrassed to offer it to the team. I'd calculated that if we won, our share of the Wembley gate would be £250,000 – and ten per cent or 20 per cent split between the players was worth having, given our basic wages.

The final was to be played at the end of May. We had a fantastic volunteer work weekend before the final. More fans than usual turned up, as they put it, to prepare the stadium for League 1 and, I suspected, to work off some of their nervous energy. It was certainly a very welcome distraction to be so busy for those two days.

The end-of-season dinner was scheduled for the weekend before the final. When Ivor planned it we didn't know how the season would end but with a final in prospect we had no problem selling out. The highlight of the evening was Paul Robinson's rabble-rousing speech. To roars of approval he ended with a Conor McGregor quote, 'We're not going there to take part, we're going there to take over.' That became a shout around the dressing room, followed by wolf cries, naturally.

Trevor Williams had déjà vu over the preparations for the final, 'I think we got everything right in the same way that Brownie did at the City of Manchester Stadium. We all went to Wembley then ate together at the nearby TGI Friday's. We did the Wembley experience and went in the dressing rooms, exactly the same way we did with Cashy and Brownie. On the day of the game me and Rocket did our usual thing of putting loads of pictures up for the players, like we did at Manchester, to try and make it look and feel a bit more like home.'

Neal's focus was on getting the players mentally prepared, 'In those 12 days we only really trained for four. We did hard sessions on a Tuesday and then Thursday and took them to Wembley on the Wednesday to get all that out of the way. The only time we really focused on the game was the two days prior to the Sunday.'

Once again the opposition fitness was a focus. Neal adds, 'We'd been told by several people that Plymouth were doing double sessions and training too much, the season had caught up with them and their legs had gone.

'On the day of the game we decided to keep everything real and stay in our tracksuits. When we got there Plymouth were on the pitch in their new suits. I remember Darius coming back into the dressing room saying, "Lads, we've got this, we've won. Look at them all in their suits taking selfies. They're here for a day out. We're here to get promoted."

And that was the theme. It wasn't arrogance, just this incredible belief within that squad.'

Paul Robinson put it into context, 'I played at Wembley a couple of times for Millwall. It's important that you take away the mystique and know your routines coming up to the day, otherwise you can get carried away and before you know it, the game is starting and you're not ready. So it was really good that we went. Everyone knew what they had to do on the day, where their family was going to be sitting, and that really made a difference. If you look at Plymouth on the day, they all turned up in their suits and were taking photos. They were enjoying the occasion but I'd said to a few of the lads along the way, it wasn't about getting in the play-offs, it was about *winning* the play-offs. I'd learned from Millwall when I went to Wembley the first time. We lost but I felt a little bit like maybe the achievement was getting to Wembley and getting to play there. But no, it should be, "We're going to Wembley to win the play-offs." That was what I learned, to get everyone used to it and ready for the occasion.'

We had help from other quarters. Neal says, 'Paul Cook [the Portsmouth manager] rang me. They'd played Plymouth in the semis and he said, "Graham Carey is their best player. Stop him and you've got too much for them." So I changed the formation slightly to allow Danny Bulman to do a man-for-man marking job. Carey never got a kick.'

Another key feature of the preparation was assigning our sports psychologist, Steven Sylvester, to talk to Tom Elliott on the morning of the final. Neal had asked me if we could recruit a psychologist to work with him on how the team reacted to and recovered from setbacks so I suggested Steven, who had been an advisor to the panel when we appointed Neal.

Tom had been substituted in both semi-final legs and Bayo had done well after coming on. Neal was keen to bolster Tom's confidence so Steven was briefed to reassure him about his value to the team and remind him how well he'd played that season. It paid off; Tom had a fantastic game, hassling and harassing the Plymouth centre-backs and then, in a defender's nightmare, after enduring that for an hour Bayo came on in his place to bully them with his extraordinary strength.

And so, to the game itself. First-team physio Stuart Douglas remembers coming out into the stadium, 'We were in the tunnel. Darius was shouting and although I never was involved in the old Crazy Gang from what I've been told it was probably the closest to that. It was "we are going to intimidate you and we are going to beat you". Everyone was really pumped. Darius was shouting "we are the wolf pack, we're the wolves, we're going to win" and everyone would shout and howl. It was relentless. Plymouth were just standing, not saying a word, like rabbits in headlights. It was almost like *Gladiator* when they're about to come out and you've got Russell Crowe, who's ready for it, and you've got the other gladiators a bit scared before the door opens. Plymouth were like the small gladiators who knew their time was up.'

With the game poised at 0-0, wide midfielder Andy Barcham went down injured. Stuart says, 'Me and Barch got on really well and before the game I'd said, "Listen Barch, it's Wembley, whatever you do, cramp, dead leg, just get me on so I can say that I've been on the pitch." And he said, "All right, all right, I'll do it." Then he goes down and I ran the whole width of the pitch to get to him. I got there and I was like, "Barch, top man, you got me on the pitch. I'm buzzing, I'm gonna be on Sky." And he was like, "No, no Douggie, I'm struggling, I'm really struggling." And I was like, "What?! I thought you went down just to get me on."

'He went, "How long's left?" and I went, "We've got five minutes, you'll be fine. Just work your nuts off for five minutes and that's it, game done." He said, "All right, I can do that." They've got massive screens at each end of the pitch and we're standing on the line waiting for him to go back on and he looked up at the clock and he was like, "We've got 15 minutes!" I said, "Oh, yeah, yeah, 15 … I got it wrong." I knew that if I'd said 15 he'd have said he couldn't do it, so I just pushed him on to the pitch. After the game he was like, "Douggie, I would never have lasted if you'd told me it was 15 minutes. My knee was killing me. By the time I realised it was 15 it was too late and I was back on."'

Three minutes later Lyle Taylor scored and from then on we were in total command. We went on to win, comfortably, 2-0, in front of a crowd of nearly 60,000. Neal says, 'There was one point in the second half when we were 1-0 up and Coxy came up to me and said, "We've got to be careful, we need to tell the players to slow down, not get so far forward." But the players were in the zone so I said, "Nah, I'm not stopping this, let them carry on." They didn't need me to tell them to just sit there, so I just said, "No, no, no, no. They're all right, leave them."'

As Trevor said, 'Ards was the most chilled man in the world. His only real worry was that if the game went to extra time he might miss his flight that evening to go on holiday.'

In the final minute of injury time, Ade Azeez broke away and won a penalty. We had the unsavoury sight of Bayo and Callum Kennedy tussling over the ball to take the penalty. Not surprisingly, Bayo won and then put his kick away to make it 2-0. I was convinced he only wanted to take it so that he could tear off his shirt and reveal a t-shirt promoting his 'Beast' brand on national TV.

As usual, Eileen started to make her way out to avoid watching the penalty but I persuaded her to stay on the grounds that if Bayo scored it was 2-0 and the game was over. If he missed, the referee would immediately blow his whistle for full time. Instead of leaving the Royal Box she covered her eyes with a scarf. He scored and she started helicoptering her scarf above her head in celebration. Very soon Ivor joined in and then, in a moment that was caught on Sky TV and went viral, he spotted a friend lower down in the crowd and started to flick Vs at them. Not exactly the sort of decorum you'd expect in the Royal Box.[60]

The celebrations went on long into the night but Eileen and I, as always, sloped off to the Lake District for a break. We were in League 1. Neal caught his plane – just – and went on holiday. All our plans had come together. And we were 13th in the wages league table. See Appendix 1 for an explanation of how it is calculated.

---

60 A few days after the final, a football club board meeting was interrupted by a member of staff bringing in a letter from the FA. In the standard wording of such letters it asked for our observations about 'a club official … making inappropriate gestures towards fans in the lower stands' and mentioning possible disciplinary action. I was taken aback while Ivor played it cool, although later he was seen pacing up and down in the club's office cursing the FA. Ivor sought advice from former Wimbledon FC CEO David Barnard, who told Ivor that it was pretty serious and that while he might be fined there was little chance of a ban. It was round about then that the office staff decided they really ought to tell Ivor they'd faked the letter. David was in on the prank. One of the reasons I think it worked was that I was unaware it was a joke and thought it was genuine until I saw David's reply to Ivor.

47

THE PRETENDERS

SOMETIMES, EVEN when you've been expecting something for years, it is still a shock when it finally happens. And so it was when we were drawn to play Milton Keynes in the second round of the FA Cup.

The draw was televised late on Sunday afternoon in early November 2010. I walked in to our living room just as it was announced 'number 13, Ebbsfleet or AFC Wimbledon', a pause, and then 'number five', another pause, 'Stevenage or Milton Keynes'.

It was the worst of all worlds. We'd always known that we'd have to play them one day but we had hoped that the first game would be away from home. We thought that it would release years of pent-up anger and that when we subsequently played them at home some of that anger might have dissipated.

It didn't help that both teams had drawn their first-round fixtures and so by the time we knew the results of the replays there would be only 11 days until the tie itself. We were very worried that outsiders would come to the game to cause trouble and at that time our systems weren't good enough to ensure that our fans, and only our fans, could get tickets to the home areas of the ground.

In 2010 we were still in the Conference National league. Teams at that level join the FA Cup in the fourth qualifying round which, thanks to the expansion of the competition over the years, is actually the sixth set of games to be played. Teams which win in the fourth qualifying round go to the very posh-sounding 'first round proper' (formal attire to be worn?), at which stage the 48 League 1 and League 2 teams join.[61] We all know we aren't going to win the cup, so the rule of thumb is to hope to draw the lowest-ranked team left in the competition, at home. For us, three such ties might allow us to reach the third round, at which stage the Premier League and Championship teams join. That's where the money is to be made, either playing away at one of the giants or at home to a higher-league team, where the TV people sniff a possible giant-killing and the game is televised with a large facility fee. If we didn't get one of those ties we'd hope for a game against a team we'd never played as AFC Wimbledon, to give everyone a taste of something different and perhaps a new ground to visit.

We'd beaten Maidstone in our qualifying round match and to our disappointment, and no doubt theirs too, in the first round proper we drew Ebbsfleet, a team from our league. So no television fee and no higher league team to try to giant-kill, just a really tough game with a so-so attendance which wouldn't earn either club much money. The match was as dour as I feared, with no goals and enlivened only by a sending-off from each team. While the result was disappointing, 'at least we were still in the hat' as the mandatory cliché goes.

Milton Keynes were two divisions above us in League 1 and had drawn their away fixture at Stevenage, a League 2 team. Both of us needed to win our replay for the dreaded tie to go ahead.

While the draw was very unwelcome, we'd prepared for it. Going through my old files I found a plan I'd developed with Kevin Rye, then a communications executive at Supporters Direct. The plan split the actions we should take into: what to do if there was any possibility of getting them in the draw; what to say if we did get them; and, finally, comms and PR in the build-up to the game. I've been so good at erasing them from my consciousness that I didn't recall that document at all.

At the training session the day before the Ebbsfleet match I talked to the players about the possibility of getting Milton Keynes in the next

—

61 A total of 759 teams participated in the FA Cup that year. There's an extra preliminary round, a preliminary round and four qualifying rounds before the first round proper, and seven rounds, including the semi-finals, to whittle the numbers down to the two finalists. Only a handful of clubs have a realistic chance of winning but for smaller clubs like us the prize money is very useful and a TV facility fee can transform the finances for that season. But the big prize was an away game at, say, Arsenal which at that time was reported to be worth about £750,000, nearly double our annual wages budget.

round. If that happened they were simply to respond to press questions by saying we'd be aiming to win the game; any other questions should be directed to me.

As soon as the draw had been made I was on the phone to Ivor, who was equally mortified at the prospect of playing 'that lot'. We agreed who we would each phone to make sure the PR message was consistent.

Whoever summarised the draw on TV completely missed the significance of the tie but the schedule arrangers didn't. Before we knew it our first-round replay with Ebbsfleet was to be televised on a Thursday night, two days after MK were due to play their replay against Stevenage. The second-round tie itself had been made the televised Saturday early kick-off game. The rearranged replays meant that we would now have only nine days to sell the tickets. Nightmare.

The strength of feeling towards MK was illustrated by a members' resolution put forward at a Dons Trust meeting in June 2005 which required us to refuse to play them if we were drawn against them in any competition. This was opposed by the board and voted down on the simple basis that if we enter a competition then we agree to abide by its rules; if we don't want to do so, we shouldn't enter.

Hardly anyone wanted to play them, but we still wanted to win the tie against Ebbsfleet. The franchise would just need to lose their game. I 'watched' the closing minutes of their replay on Teletext. They led Stevenage until the 95th minute when Darius Charles, who was to join us some years later, equalised. Extra time didn't resolve the deadlock and it went to penalties. I endured the slow, step-by-step agony of watching the outcome of each penalty being flashed up on the screen. MK wasted a golden chance to win it during the first five penalties and eventually lost 7-6. My relief was palpable – we just weren't ready to play them yet.

We had fallen on our feet. In anticipation of us playing Milton Keynes the replay with Ebbsfleet was televised (fee £36,000 – replays are awarded half the full fee) and so was a dreadfully unappetising game against Stevenage (fee £72,000). We scraped past Ebbsfleet with a goal in the last minute of extra time. The only memorable thing about the Stevenage match was the severe overnight frost that placed it in doubt. The TV fee was critical to us so when we found that the goalmouth at the athletics end of the stadium was frozen solid I got Trevor Williams to persuade the referee to inspect the other end. Meanwhile, we parked the tractor in the goalmouth with its exhaust pointing down on to the worst-affected areas. The ploy was a success but we weren't and we lost 2-0.

The money from these two televised matches effectively formed part of the kitty we spent to strengthen the team and go on to win promotion to the Football League that season. It's nicely ironic that Milton Keynes inadvertently played a substantial part in our promotion that year.

The evil day had been put off, but not for long. Now that we were in the Football League we would go into the FA Cup and the League Cup draws in the same round as them. We were also in the Johnstone's Paint Trophy (commonly known as the Paint Pot and contested by League 1 and 2 clubs only) which was drawn on a regional basis, increasing the chances that we would be drawn against them sooner rather than later.

It happened in 2012 and again the tie depended on the outcome of two FA Cup first-round replays. This time we had been drawn away, which was a small consolation. Once bitten twice shy, the TV companies committed to broadcasting the game only if we both won our replays. We might have lost our away match at York City if striker Charlie Strutton had missed the train. With the boarding time fast approaching he was nowhere to be seen. Simon Bassey eventually located him by the entrance to the Northern line of the London Underground where he said he was waiting because, 'You said we were going north.'[62]

Charlie scored a late equaliser at York and in the televised replay he scored two goals and laid on another. We won 4-3 in extra time and Charlie's three goals across those two ties were the only ones he ever scored for us. The following night Milton Keynes comfortably beat Cambridge City, from four leagues below them, to ensure the dreaded tie would go ahead.

As soon as the replays were over and the game was definitely on we were deluged with requests for access, interviews and information from all round the world. As a small club we found it incredibly difficult to manage the circus that came with the game. I dug out the action plan.

The main issues were about making sure our fans were safe and so we insisted that we should control ticket sales for the away part of the ground.

—

62 When I interviewed him several years later, Simon said, 'I'm not sure that he actually said that. I might even have made it up for the banter with the players!' Nonetheless, this tale is now an established part of the club's folklore and there's no reason to let the truth spoil it.

We were also determined to say nothing inflammatory; if there was trouble at the game we didn't want anyone to be able to say we stoked up the emotions. So only accredited spokespeople should speak to the media. By and large, Milton Keynes took the same approach although their manager, Karl Robinson, infuriated many of our fans with some inane comments.

We also agreed that we would make no recommendation to fans about whether or not to go. Our directors would not accept hospitality but would instead sit with our supporters and refuse media requests for comment on the night. In response to innumerable questions about meeting their officials and shaking Peter Winkelman's hand, I was persuaded to issue a statement explaining that I'd sought guidance from the Dons Trust board and after a long discussion, they decided they would not accept hospitality on the day of the game. They instructed the football club board to do the same. The statement ended, 'The fans (who own the club) … don't want us to go in to the boardroom. Therefore, there will be no hand to shake.'

Neal Ardley had been in his post for just over three weeks when the draw was announced. This was an enormous amount of pressure to put on someone new to the role of a first-team manager. As he said later, 'I'd have to be in the Premier League to get the same exposure as a manager as I got in the build-up to that game. Just think about the minefield that I was potentially walking into with the media.'

To minimise the interruptions and distractions we held a press day at the training ground and refused other requests for interviews. The interest was extraordinary. Neal says, 'When we did the press day there was press there from as far away as Australia, New Zealand, all over the world and they were all talking about how it's the most emotional of games that has been played in football. And when you hear people start a sentence like that, you're going, "Jesus, I know what this is about but blimey, I haven't really thought of it like this." And you start thinking one wrong move, you know, you've upset our fans, you could upset their fans which wasn't as much of an issue, you could say the wrong thing about the FA. So it was a real political nightmare for me to get through that whole thing and say the rights things with the right passion for our fans but not say anything that really landed me in it or upset people.'

Although he was still settling in to his new role, I was totally confident that Neal would be pitch-perfect in everything he said. In fact, it was me who screwed up when, in what was probably the first interview I did, I called for them to drop the name 'Dons'. What was that about saying nothing inflammatory?

The question-and-answer session with all the press was quite fun in the end. I spent a fair bit of time trying to explain to journalists who were new to the story that this game wasn't a derby, nor were we rivals, let alone 'arch-rivals'. Instead, as our PA announcer Chris Philips succinctly put it, 'This is not a rivalry but an unwanted obligation.' Sometimes these interviews offer an unexpected opportunity, as when the Sky reporter asked, 'Who are the real Dons?' to which the answer was 'AFC Wimble*don*' – the clue is in the name.'

There were several journalists who knew us and our story extremely well. I particularly remember Jim White, who'd written several positive articles about us, getting straight to the heart of our real concern by asking, with a mischievous grin on his face, 'What about a replay?' All you can do at times like that is resort to the standard politician's answer of, 'Sorry, but I don't answer hypothetical questions.'

The extent to which we were being watched was reinforced when both clubs got a letter from the FA asking us to remind people carrying out interviews not to inflame 'what we appreciate is a potentially difficult game for all concerned'. We were also asked to instruct our players, 'If a goal is scored not to antagonise opposing fans or otherwise gesticulate to the crowd.' We didn't really need any reminding – the FA was just protecting its position so that if anything happened they could say publicly that they'd warned the clubs. And, since we'd been warned, any sanctions would be harsh.

The game was moved to a Sunday to accommodate the TV schedules and was sufficiently high-profile that the day before, Winkelman and I were interviewed (but not together) on the *Today* programme on Radio 4, normally a politics and current affairs show.

I didn't go to the game. I felt very strongly that for years we had implicitly supported WISA's campaign for fans to boycott their teams' games against the franchised club and here we were queueing up to attend the very first time we played them. I understood that people wanted to support their team but going would have felt hypocritical to me and I was very disappointed when our other directors chose to attend (some years later Ivor Heller, our commercial director, told me that he was so emotional about the whole event that when he got off the coach at their stadium he burst into tears).

Trevor Williams and Robin Bedford took the kit to the ground the night before the game. Trevor recalled, 'It was an early kick-off so me and Robin went down there the night before to set all the kit up and they basically man-marked us. They had two guys who followed us around everywhere until eventually we told them to get out of the dressing room.

'Me and Robin weren't usually with the team when they arrived, but on this occasion we travelled with them because we'd been there the night before. We got off the coach and to one side of us was our fans and to the right was their fans. Our fans started cheering and their fans started singing "you're not the real Wimbledon". Our fans went nuts and started pushing the barriers back and you could see that's when their fans twigged that this wasn't a friendly footballing rivalry, our fans absolutely detested them. That was the moment where the frannies [franchise] realised that our lot actually hated them and hated everything about their club.'

As for the game itself, we were playing a team with much greater resources. As their erstwhile manager Paul Ince once said, 'What can you do with only three million pounds?' Well, one answer is 'pay our budget more than twice over'. Neal was very aware of the disparity in the two teams' quality and says, 'We spent probably more time preparing for that game than for any game. Given the gulf between the teams at the time, we needed to get a lot of things right and drill it so that the team knew their roles. How we lost the game I'll never know.'

Everyone said we played superbly and were unlucky to lose; in the third minute of injury time a wayward shot from a Milton Keynes striker hit one of their players' heels and was deflected in. He was looking in a completely different direction. That was the difference between the teams.

I like it when fans use humour to make a point. So, to ram home the 'club thieves' point the Dons fans sang, to the tune of 'Bread of Heaven', 'Where were you when you were us?' throughout the game, while a plane flew low over the stadium towing a banner that said 'We are Wimbledon'.

I didn't watch it on TV. Instead I took my granddaughter to the local playground and looked up the result when I got home. I was disappointed we'd lost but was massively relieved that we didn't have to host a replay at Kingsmeadow. We received TV facility fees worth £72,000 and spent the money in the January transfer window, recruiting players who helped to ensure a successful survival bid (see Chapter 41). Once again they'd inadvertently played a substantial part in our success, this time in avoiding relegation.

Having played them once it would be wrong to say that the boil had been lanced. However, having that first game behind us did make subsequent meetings easier, not least because the next two against them, in the 2014/15 season, were also at their stadium. We lost a League Cup tie 3-1 and then a couple of months later in the Johnstone's Paint Pot we beat them for the first time, 3-2.

While it was good to win it proved nothing, no more than losing did. Winning didn't make us better than them; we already held the moral high ground and results on the pitch will never change the shameful way they came into being. Nonetheless, it mattered more to the players than I realised, as Neal told me years later, 'The players knew the significance of it, regardless of whatever competition it was. I remember as soon as they came in the dressing room, I think it was Matt Tubbs dived on to the kit wheelie bin and went flying across the room with him on top of it like Superman. They were all going nuts and shouting and hollering in there because they knew what they had done and how the fans felt.'

Our promotion to League 1 meant that we could not avoid playing them at Kingsmeadow in the 2016/17 season because we were now in the same division. To allow our fans time to get used to the idea we asked that the game at Kingsmeadow be in midweek in the second half of the season; the Football League obliged.

I asked Neal how the first home match compared to that first meeting in the FA Cup. He says, 'It wasn't as bad, because the first time was ridiculous, but it was the first time they'd come to us and there was immense pressure. I didn't enjoy playing them because it went beyond me losing a game of football. If I didn't get a result it got quite personal and quite nasty and aggressive because of the emotion and the feeling there. So the pressure on me when we played them was pretty immense. I didn't enjoy having to deal with it and I didn't enjoy the games because I knew whatever happened, you know, being a hero is great for five minutes, but if it doesn't go well it ends up quite nasty.'

Centre-back Paul Robinson gave a player's perspective, 'Just as soon as we came out for the warm-up it was one of those nights where it's almost like they've turned on full power, you know, like the electricity in the stadium. Everything about it just felt, yeah, this is gonna be a proper night.

'What was really notable was there was media from all over the world taking a real interest in it, which took me aback. It was worldwide and Neal did well to control that. On the Thursday before the following Tuesday's game he made sure it was all done and out the way and then it was just preparation for the game really. I think obviously, Neal being a Wimbledon person, he felt it more than most and knew what that game was going to entail too.'

Did the players get it? Robinson continues, 'Yeah, they did. They definitely did. Especially that night. We all knew as well being the first game at home that it was one that we wanted to make a mark in and get a result in and it worked out that way.'

We won, deservedly, 2-0 and the crowd loved it, every second of it. One man who didn't was Peter Winkelman. Much as we disliked the idea of having their officials in the stadium we had no right to ban them, so we invited their safety officer to visit. We showed him the facilities, which were the same for all visiting clubs – the away directors' seats are surrounded by our fans and to leave our tiny boardroom to go to the toilet they'd need to walk through our sponsors' lounge. It wouldn't be pleasant. They decided to copy what our directors had done and stand with their fans on the away fans' terrace.

To avoid any confrontations, the MK fans were required to come in official coaches and were escorted into and out of the ground by the police. There was speculation that Winkelman wouldn't come but I was sure that his ego wouldn't let him stay away. And sure enough, quite close to kick-off, he appeared in the crowd. I don't suppose he enjoyed the taunting from our fans or losing the game. He tried to slip away early but the police wouldn't let his car down the access road and he had to wait until the end, along with their supporters.

I am very aware that this sounds awful and in many people's eyes doesn't reflect well upon us. So be it. I think any passionate football fan would be totally unforgiving if his or her team was pirated some 60 miles away up the motorway to facilitate the building of a hypermarket. I always think that MK supporters should be relieved that our protests were very civilised compared to how some other clubs' followers would have reacted.

We played them twice more the following season. Although they won at Kingsmeadow they ended up being relegated, despite having one of the largest budgets in the division. But that wasn't the end of it.

After our second home game against the franchised club we received a letter from the Football League explaining that they were 'formally investigating an allegation relating to a potential breach by AFC Wimbledon (the Club) of Regulation 3.4 in relation to the approach of the Club to arrangements in the build up to and during the above Match [the home game played on 2 September]'. The letter went on to state that the FL's regulations require, 'In all matters and transactions relating to The League each Club shall behave towards each other Club and the League with the utmost good faith.' And furthermore, 'No Club, either by itself, its servants or agents, shall by any means whatsoever unfairly criticise, disparage, belittle or discredit any other Club or The League or in either case any of its directors, officers, employees or agents.'

In the precise language which lawyers use to ensure they can't be accused of pre-judging the issue, we were told that we were being 'investigated' to see if we had failed to comply with these regulations because: we had not put their name on the front of the programme; we had not referred to them as Milton Keynes Dons on the tickets or on the team sheet issued to guests on the day; the scoreboard had referred to them as 'MK'; and the PA did not announce their goals. We were given 11 days, subsequently extended by a week, to provide copies of all and any documents, texts, e-mails, voicemails, in effect anything, whether internal or external, relating to the game.

We were deeply suspicious of Rule 3.4 when it was introduced into the Football League's rule book the previous summer. We believed that it was being introduced so that we could be charged. Matthew Breach, the Dons Trust chair at the time, specifically challenged the FL about this at the annual AGM in Portugal and was assured by the FL that this wasn't the case. And here we were being charged under this new rule.

Our response was sent on 17 October and in it we argued that we hadn't breached the rules because we hadn't criticised or disparaged them in connection with that game or, indeed, at any time. We argued that the complaint should not be brought unless Milton Keynes had themselves complained and, if they had, we were entitled to see the complaint so that we might respond to it. We set out a long list of rejoinders but the real, unstated issue was that we simply refused to use the name 'Dons' to refer to an entity we regard as club-stealers.

We knew our reply would make no difference. Sure enough, in December a letter arrived from the FL, charging us with the misdemeanours set out opposite plus some new ones. These included that we '[did] not use the full name of Milton Keynes Dons FC or use the name Dons in respect of that club in its [i.e. our] internal documentation'; we had 'adopted a policy of "avoiding fraternisation with or accepting hospitality from officials of the club"' along with 'a policy of minimising contact over and above the necessary for the safe and proper conduct of matches'.

So we were, among other things, being charged for not referring to Milton Keynes by their full name in our internal documents. And, because we don't respect the way they acquired their club, for setting a policy not to accept their hospitality. I've worked with enough lawyers to know that their opening shot is to start with an extreme stance, so as to be able to concede something as part of the debate. But, really, threatening to charge us for how we refer to another club in our own private internal documentation?

Following some wise counsel from a well-respected third party, in April 2018 Shaun Harvey wrote to me saying that the FL would drop the charges if we agreed to mediation with a view to finding a solution in respect of the clubs' relationship. We had advance warning of this letter and so I was able to write back the following day accepting the offer. The FL issued a statement announcing the mediation a few days later.

Prior to agreeing to enter into the mediation, the Dons Trust board had extensive discussions about the approach to take and what to say to members. This illustrated the dilemma of a fans-owned club very well. On the one hand we should communicate with members and fans and it was argued that we should explore what they felt would be acceptable. The converse argument was that deciding our policy in public would undermine our negotiating position and we should instead come to the best deal we could and then take it to the members for approval.

The DT board agreed that the nominated representatives would work within guidelines agreed by the board with various red lines which they could not cross in any circumstances. In other areas they were given flexibility but in the knowledge that any deal would have to be approved by members.

And so it lies. On behalf of the club I signed a non-disclosure agreement about the mediation and I am honouring that because I don't want to put the club in a difficult place. However, I don't think it is a breach of any great secret that the talks are in limbo; after all, any agreement, or a breakdown, would have been announced. It is also fair to say that the departure of chief executive Shaun Harvey from the FL meant that most of the momentum was lost.

When, at the end of that season Milton Keynes were relegated to League 2, the issue of our next meeting was postponed for a while. But they were swiftly promoted back into League 1 and so the problem has resurfaced. At the time of writing we had just played them at Plough Lane, but with no fans and only one visiting director present. The issue has in effect been postponed for another year.

Finally, from time to time people make remarks on the lines of 'it's time you moved on'. I understand this point of view, but we *have* moved on. We're no longer encamped and protesting outside the FA, WISA negotiated the return of the patrimony and agreed to stop lobbying fans to boycott their games, we've set up our own club, won back a place in the Football League, built a new stadium back home in Plough Lane, a couple of hundred yards away from our old ground, and stayed rooted in our community. We have moved on, in trumps.

But for our fans their continuing use of the name 'Dons' is first a nonsense – they abrogated all rights to the history years ago – and second an offensive reminder of what they did, and many of us don't want a reminder of that broadcast in our stadium. If they quietly dropped the 'Dons' name I suspect that relationships could be normalised, although never be cordial. So, it's time people urged them to move on; we already have.

48

THE LONG AND WINDING ROAD

IN 1990 Sam Hammam, the owner of Wimbledon FC, persuaded Geoff Smith, then the leader of Merton Council, that the old Plough Lane stadium could not realistically be upgraded as required by the Taylor Report. Hammam argued that to build a new stadium elsewhere in the borough he needed to sell the existing ground and use the money on the new project.

In return for a payment to Merton reported to be anywhere between £300,000 and £2m, Smith agreed to lift the restrictive covenant which required the site to be used for leisure/sports use only, effectively preventing its sale. In 1998 Hammam sold the site for supermarket use for a reported £8m having already moved WFC to ground-share at Selhurst Park. There followed years of wrangling in which Hammam, who was much more media-savvy, very effectively dumped the blame on to Merton for not finding a new site in the borough.

Andrew Judge, by then the leader of Merton Council, says, 'I felt this was grossly unfair and that Merton had gone to great lengths to accommodate alternative sites.[63] So in October 2001 we published *Wimbledon Football Club. A Home in Merton*. The document listed all the steps we had taken to help in the search for a new site. It also assessed 13 possible sites, looking at two in particular. One of these was the Wimbledon Greyhound Stadium site, about 200 metres up Plough Lane from the old football stadium.'

—

63 Andrew Judge was leader of Merton Council from 2001–2006 and leader of the opposition from 2006–2008. He then took on a cabinet post in the council's leadership team, and his actions played a major part in our return to Plough Lane.

Seven months later the FA Commission allowed WFC to relocate to Milton Keynes, which directly led to the formation of AFC Wimbledon and our renewed search for a stadium back home.

A documentary film of our first season, entitled *Womble Til I Die*, includes a scene where club founders Kris Stewart and Ivor Heller peer through a fence to see the now-derelict and overgrown Plough Lane stadium. They talk about buying the land for a new stadium but permission had been granted to build housing on the site and the likely price had escalated well beyond the £13m they talked about. We didn't have access to those sorts of funds. In fact we had access to no funds at all at that stage.

Meanwhile, the Stadium Working Group, chaired by Tom Adam, had been looking for a site back in Merton. In 2003, less than a year after we were formed, the SWG produced a 'Site Options' report which looked at 13 sites, most of which were also on Andrew Judge's list. However, the report didn't consider how we might pay for a new stadium and we had no money.

It seemed to me that we had to take a long-term view. At the time we had next to nothing to offer. We were a brand new club operating at level eight of the football pyramid, with only a very small amount of cash, few assets and no business track record. We needed to build a reputation for reliability, financial prudence and community involvement. I hoped that my background as a former partner in PwC would add a degree of credibility when we got to the point where we sought partners to work with and finance for our plans.

A key element of this strategy was that we needed, as soon as we reasonably could, to work our way up through the leagues so that with all the other factors in place we were a credible organisation to Merton Council, lenders and stadium development partners. Most importantly, even if we knew we were pissing into the wind for the first few years, it was essential we were seen to be actively searching for a new stadium. In particular, we had to keep ourselves within the thoughts of Merton Council.

Over the next few years we focused on Merton for our community work, even though Kingsmeadow is in a different borough, Kingston. This had the twin benefit of reminding everyone that Merton was our home and keeping our ambitions clearly in the minds of the local politicians.

In 2008 we asked Roger Hobkinson of Colliers International, an expert in property development and planning (we have an expert for every occasion in our fan base!), to lead a team to produce a new report on potential stadium sites. Working with one of their town planning specialists, they searched Merton for potential locations. Our principal aim in commissioning the report was to influence Merton Council's core planning strategy which was under review. This was a very dry but crucially important document which would set the council's development strategy for the foreseeable future. We needed to get ourselves embedded in the strategy to give us any chance of progress.

Roger's report achieved its overall purpose, not least because its messages were reinforced by our fans, as Tara Butler of the council's Future Merton team explains, 'Out of the blue in 2009 we got hundreds, maybe even thousands, of responses from AFC Wimbledon fans from all over the world saying "bring AFC home, bring us back". These messages didn't directly connect with the broad, dry strategic planning document but we got all these e-mails, postcards and letters saying "we want to come home".

'I was thinking at the time "this is a bit odd" but we reported it to the councillors and a change was made to say we'd got loads of responses from AFC fans and of course we'd support them coming back to the borough. The statement is quite benign and neutral but in hindsight that change was very helpful when, in 2009–2010, things started to roll forward. Somebody – it wasn't Merton – had urged the fans to write.'[64]

Change was afoot elsewhere. In 2005, Risk Capital Partners (RCP), a private equity investment firm, bought Greyhound Racing Association Limited (GRA) which owned six greyhound tracks. Wimbledon Stadium was one of those tracks. We quickly concluded that RCP didn't plan to operate them as greyhound stadiums and speculated about whether they might be open to a buyer. To help to keep our ambitions visible to Merton in June 2008 I wrote to Luke Johnson, co-founder of RCP, asking to talk through our ideas for the site. We got nowhere.

In 2009 we had won another promotion and were now in the national division of the Conference; that felt like a game-changer. Following that promotion the Mayor of Merton held a civic reception for the club. This turned out to be a pivotal moment and also one of the few times when I nearly fell out with Ivor. After the event Ivor told me that Merton

64 These responses were almost certainly triggered by a request from Tom Adam, then the chair of the SWG, urging fans to write to Merton supporting the return of the club to the borough.

councillors were desperate to get the club back to the borough. I thought it was wishful thinking and pooh-poohed the idea but then had to apologise when Tom Adam, the SWG chair, fed back an identical message. For the last few years when we had talked to Merton about coming home they would say, 'Bring us your ideas and we will look at them.' Suddenly we were being asked, 'How can we help?'

Things were gaining pace, although 'pace' is a relative word given that it took 11 years from that visible change in the council's attitude to opening the new stadium. Determined to get cross-party support, Ivor and I met Stephen Alambritis, by then the leader of the Labour opposition (from 2006 there had been a minority Conservative administration), to talk about our plans. Alambritis swears that as we ended a very encouraging meeting I said, 'We will keep in touch with you because you might be leader soon.' Tactless perhaps, prophetic yes.[65]

In the background, Andrew Judge continued to think about how to get AFC Wimbledon back to Merton. There was little he could do unless Labour was in power. In 2010 the local elections took place on the same day as the general election. He decided to stand as the Labour parliamentary candidate for the Wimbledon constituency and at the same time he stood as a councillor in the Abbey ward of the borough; the loss of the three Abbey seats to the Conservative Party in 2006 had been a major cause of Labour losing control of the borough. He says, 'I thought that if I focused my constituency and council campaigns on Abbey ward, I might win a seat and help to swing the balance of power back to Labour.'

He was right. He was elected a councillor by 98 votes. With the Liberal Democrats winning two seats from the Conservatives, Labour now had the most seats on the council and formed a minority administration.

Judge had stood down from the Labour leadership in 2008. Thanks to winning the Abbey seat, his successor as leader of the opposition, Stephen Alambritis, became leader of Merton Council in 2010. As a senior councillor, Judge asked for and got a cabinet portfolio of planning, regeneration, property and street management. He could now directly influence policy on a range of issues, including a new stadium.

—

65 Stephen Alambritis was leader of the opposition from 2008–2010 and then leader of the council from 2010–2020. He actively promoted the idea of our return to Merton to local MPs and two Mayors of London. I think I made a good call.

The next step was a new initiative. Tara Butler says, 'In 2011 Andrew Judge and Stephen Alambritis launched the Call for Sites initiative. Instead of waiting passively for people to come forward with ideas for development we did a media programme and they were interviewed by property press and other media saying, "Let us know who wants to build what in Merton. We are open for business, we are pro-active." We got lots of coverage and as a result we got lots of sites and one of them was the greyhound stadium, by the then owners, GRA Holdings. James McGinlay [who had been appointed as Merton's head of sustainable communities earlier in 2011] was also instrumental in being pro-development and going out to the property press. The initiative came from the leadership but James was instrumental in percolating it down within the council.'

McGinlay had previously been at Islington where he was a contractor advising on the Emirates Stadium. That experience of having been 'on the other side' was to prove invaluable later in the negotiations.

Alambritis cleared another hurdle out of the way when, in June 2011, he apologised publicly for the council lifting the covenant on the Plough Lane stadium back in 1990. He explains, 'When you're the council leader and the fans think you're partly or wholly to blame, it is important to move on and an apology does that.'

Alambritis also approached Luke Johnson, co-founder of RCP, who were still the owners of Wimbledon Greyhound Stadium. Alambritis says, 'I'd heard that Luke Johnson wanted housing so I thought I would go and discuss the issues. He was very polite but he said, "I'm sorry to disappoint you but it's got to be housing and housing only." I said there was also this football club that wanted to come back to the borough. He wasn't empathetic and he didn't think you were going to come back into the Football League. We agreed to disagree and I left that meeting fully aware of where they stood. But I knew there was another player in the middle and that was NAMA.'

NAMA is the Irish National Asset Management Agency. Its role was to maximise the recovery of property development loans it had taken over from various Irish banks following the financial crisis of 2008. Among those loans was about £50m that was used to finance the acquisition of the greyhound stadiums.

GRA Limited (which was still owned by RCP) now owed the £50m to NAMA who could call for the loan to be repaid at almost any time.

In short, nothing could happen on the Plough Lane site without their approval.

Judge and Alambritis were both intent on relocating the club to the borough. With the Call for Sites there was now a real possibility of developing the greyhound stadium.

Judge says, 'One of my priorities was to find a stadium site. It was a personal objective after all the work we'd put into campaigning for the retention of Wimbledon FC. I felt that AFC Wimbledon was a successor to that tradition and we ought to do everything possible to get a stadium in Merton for the club to return to.

'The only way that could be afforded was to allow some ancillary development that would produce a profit that could be used to build the stadium. The only likely development which could achieve that was housing, which is so valuable that it could well do the trick.'

Alambritis, a Fulham fan, had come to the same conclusion, 'I grew up by Craven Cottage and for me the idea of a brand new football stadium was fascinating. Council officers talked me through enabling planning legislation where we can dangle housing in front of a developer but they could only build it if they accommodated a football stadium. For me that opened doors – why wouldn't you do that if you were the leader of a council?'

We had also spotted the opportunity, as Roger Hobkinson explains, 'For years we'd been saying there's this stadium, it's 12 acres of under-used, vacant land and property in high-value south-west London. At some stage somebody was going to be all over it to build housing. We knew that it had sporting use as a greyhound stadium and we needed to preserve that sporting status to give us some leverage when it was developed. So with the SWG chair, Tom Adam, we drafted a letter to send to Merton saying it was essential that the sporting designation be retained.'

Andrew Judge says, 'The planning designation for the Wimbledon Greyhound Stadium prevented housing development, so I worked with Tara Butler to create a new planning designation for it.'

Tara Butler recalls, 'It was a team effort. We spent ages trying to work out what we could do. However much the councillors and the fans might want us to pick AFC Wimbledon we, as planning officers, couldn't pick one organisation over another.'

The solution they settled upon was to designate the stadium site as 'a suitable location for an intensification of sporting activity with supporting enabling development'. That rather abstruse phrase was a major breakthrough for us. There could be housing but there also had to be a stadium.

Having formed the policy, it was embedded in a much longer document entitled the 'Sites and Policies Development Plan' which was subjected to public consultation, followed by an independent inspector's hearing. That hearing wouldn't take place for several months so we had time to prepare.

Suddenly there were other bodies interested in developing the greyhound stadium. In April 2012 we were approached by Newridge, a development company owned by Stephen Sexton. Sexton's plan was to acquire the greyhound stadium by going straight to NAMA. Here was someone who was proposing to build housing while also making a payment to help build a stadium for us as part of the deal.

In June 2012 we entered into a Memorandum of Understanding[66] with Newridge. The MoU specified that we would be given land on which to build our stadium and a substantial lump sum towards the building costs. The agreement was exclusive to Newridge for nine months; in other words we couldn't talk to anyone else.

In July 2012 we submitted our response to the Call for Sites, setting out our objectives for a football stadium on the site but, by agreement, we didn't name Newridge. Importantly, Newridge's architects had demonstrated that a stadium could be fitted on to the site as well as sufficient development to make the plan viable.

Shortly afterwards, Newridge approached NAMA to open negotiations. We wrote a letter of support for the approach. This triggered a very surprising response when I took an irate phone call from NAMA asking what on earth we thought we were doing. Later that day I received a more conciliatory e-mail to agree a date to meet Galliard[67] and NAMA together

—

66 A Memorandum of Understanding describes the broad outlines of an agreement between two or more parties. It sets out the mutually accepted expectations of all of the parties involved in a negotiation. While not legally binding, the MoU signals that a binding contract is imminent.

67 Risk Capital Partners acquired GRA Limited which owned Wimbledon Greyhound Stadium, among others. They subsequently entered into an agreement with Galliard, a London-based property developer, to seek to build housing on the stadium site. Although Galliard did not own the stadium they were clearly authorised to commit to a deal with Merton and AFC Wimbledon. For simplicity, from now on I've referred to them throughout the document as the owners of the land.

to discuss our proposition. I think the best way to describe the attitude towards us in that meeting would be dismissive.

Meanwhile, Alambritis had received two other approaches. One was from Paschal Taggart, an Irish businessman and former chair of Bord na gCon, the Irish Greyhound Board. He wanted to build a new stadium on the site to help revitalise greyhound racing.

Over the following three years Taggart was an active campaigner for the retention of greyhound racing at the site. He met Alambritis to promote his plans and was encouraged to submit a planning application. However, despite lots of noise he never did submit one. I concluded he was happy to wait in the wings, believing that other bids would fail. If that happened he would be in a much stronger negotiating position to take over the site from Galliard.

The second approach was when Stephen Conway, the Galliard chairman, arranged a meeting with Alambritis. Galliard wanted to build housing on the site and were aware that it didn't have a planning designation that allowed housing.

Alambritis says, 'I explained that the council were proposing to change the site designation to allow housing but also to include sporting intensification. If Galliard wanted to develop the site, they would have to create a substantial sporting use; I made it clear that meant enabling us to build a stadium.' This was a message that was repeated consistently throughout the planning process.

Both Merton and the Greater London Authority had policies which required that up to 40 per cent of the development be affordable housing, which is much less profitable for the developer. In return for Galliard providing some of the stadium funding, Merton offered to accept a reduced level of affordable housing. In other words, Merton were saying instead of sinking some of your profit into affordable housing you should divert it into helping to build a stadium. This type of arrangement is known as enabling development.

Alambritis ended the meeting by writing my name and phone number on a piece of paper and saying, 'That's the person you need to speak to.' But by then we'd signed the MoU with Newridge and its terms meant we couldn't talk to Galliard. Furthermore, at that stage Stephen Sexton was very confident that he could do a deal directly with NAMA and cut out Galliard.

Sexton's confidence increased when he secured a chunk of land on the site. This extra land would allow a more integrated development across an enlarged site, with more housing and therefore greater profitability. He wrote to NAMA to tell them this. Their reply ended, 'I cannot stop you wasting time and money but emphasise that you are given no encouragement to do so whatsoever and indeed, you are probably simply causing difficulties for the very party you profess to be supporting namely Wimbledon AFC [sic].' It struck me as very odd that a body whose role was to maximise the recovery of the loans was so unwilling to discuss an alternative offer.

Frustrated with our insistence on honouring our agreement, Galliard director Mike Watson rang to say that since we wouldn't talk to them they were now talking to a rugby club. I asked him to hold off for a few days because Newridge were due to meet NAMA and after that our position would be clearer.

Newridge made one further bid to NAMA but again it was rebuffed. Sexton then agreed that even though we were bound by the MoU we could speak to Galliard. This cleared the path for us.

By mid-2013 we were working actively with Galliard to develop a planning application for the site. They had allocated a chunk of the 5.1 hectares[68] to us and, working with Derek Wilson of architects Wilson Owens Owens, we started to develop a stadium which would be capable of holding about 20,000 fans but which would start with about half that number.

Overseen and co-ordinated by Andrew Williams, our project manager, the design team worked with us and with Galliard's specialists to overcome the many complex issues around the site. Until you're close up to this sort of project it's hard to understand how much work goes into designing a site that included 602 housing units and our stadium. The consultations between us, Merton and Galliard were long and frequent.

We were all proceeding on the basis that Merton's 'sporting intensification' policy would be adopted, but it had still to be approved by an independent inspector. In January 2014, nearly two and a half years after the Call for Sites was launched, the hearing started. It lasted for over

—

68 5.1 hectares is 12.5 acres, an area about the same size as eight football pitches. We were allocated about 40 per cent of the site to build our stadium although Galliard director Mike Watson regularly claimed we had over half and, occasionally, nearly 60 per cent of the land area.

a week, with almost two days considering the stadium site. By this time we were working with Galliard and had been allowed to make a relatively late joint submission to the hearing.

The case for a greyhound stadium was submitted by Paschal Taggart. Clearly upset by us teaming up with Galliard, his submission was preceded by a bad-tempered grumble about the lateness of our submission and Galliard's 'clear intention of running into the ground the tracks with development potential'. In the hearing itself, Taggart shouted across the room to demand that I publish our business plan for the site.

All the signals from the hearing were positive and so we proceeded to work with Galliard and by June 2014, when the inspector's final report approved the site designation, we were ready to consult local residents and businesses about our joint plans.

We had PR advice throughout the consultation and planning committee process. Our main day-to-day advisor was Daniel Francis, who recalls, 'After the planning hearings in January 2014 we started to ramp up our activities. We went to see Ravi Govindia, the leader of Wandsworth Council, Stephen Hammond, the MP for Wimbledon, Sadiq Khan, at that stage the MP for Tooting next door to the site, and Richard Tracey, the GLA assembly member for Merton and Wandsworth. It was all about warming people up before the May 2014 elections.

'At that stage Merton was a minority-controlled Labour council. Stephen Alambritis was concerned that the Conservative councillors were more susceptible to influence from opponents to the scheme so, with everything pointing to Labour winning overall control in the May 2014 election, we delayed the consultations until June.' He was right. Labour won a sweeping victory in the council elections.

The site is on the boundary between Wandsworth and Merton so we decided to hold two consultation events in each borough. We knew some of the loudest opposition would come from the Wimbledon Park Residents' Association (WPRA), so it was ironic that we needed to hire their hall for the two Merton consultations. They didn't make it easy, allocating us the minimum amount of time for the two events. When we sought a third event or longer slots there was no budging them.

On the night of the first event WPRA opened up the hall and then went along to a Paschal Taggart presentation for a greyhound stadium; we'd known nothing about that alternative event, which was held nearby.

We concluded that so far as the WPRA were concerned it was 'anything but football'.

The consultations were intense. Daniel Francis says, 'Normally, at a busy consultation I'd expect 60 people through the door in six hours but we were getting 300 people in four hours. We had a team of 20 to 30 people, with experts to answer questions on all possible topics and a dozen volunteers and officials representing the club because many of the visitors were fans.'

Everyone was urged to comment, whether or not they had attended a consultation meeting. To enable us to show councillors that the opposition was coming from a minority, we had the responses analysed to get a more precise understanding of where the opposition to our plans was centred.

We presented councillors with the analysis which showed there was majority support across both boroughs. We also provided councillors with a map showing the location of supportive households in their borough. It was a very unsubtle way of reminding them how much support we'd received from people who could vote in future council elections.

Finally, after taking feedback into account, we submitted the application in December 2014. Aided by David Wood, a planning expert colleague of Dons fan and real estate lawyer Dan Norris, the detailed negotiations between us, Galliard and Merton about what would go into the s106[69] agreement took a year to get to the set piece of a planning committee meeting, on 10 December 2015.

The planning committee comprised six Labour and three Conservative councillors, plus one from Merton Park Residents' Association. The chair was Linda Kirby who first had to confirm she was eligible to carry out

—

69 A section 106 (s106) agreement is a legal agreement between a local authority, in this case Merton, and developers, in this case Galliard and us. Such agreements are required when, as in this case, a development will have a significant impact on the local area. The s106 agreement required Galliard to make contributions towards, among other things, local traffic calming, pavements and education. For us it stipulated the number of games we could play each week, closing time on matchdays, etc. Most significantly for us, the agreement specified the level of affordable housing which Galliard were committed to build and their £14m contribution towards our stadium costs.

The reason it took so long to agree was that the application needed 'substantiation' in a number of areas. These included liaison with the Environment Agency, Transport for London, and the GLA. It also involved agreement to the overall scheme viability calculations, which was really a discussion between Galliard and LBM although we were party to those discussions.

the role for this application, as she explains, 'I went to Legal and said to them, "I'm chairing the planning committee with this major application, am I legally okay to do it? I was a season ticket holder at Wimbledon FC but I haven't been to any AFC games." My sympathy for Wimbledon was probably the same as for any other councillor in the borough in that we'd like to see progress. But first and foremost, planning is quasi-judicial and you have to make a decision on what you see, not what you'd like to happen.

'Committee members have to remain impartial, so if you voice an opinion on an application you should declare yourself incapable of chairing the meeting. I knew I had an open mind.

'Before the application comes to committee the officers report whether it complies with the planning regulations. The committee then has to decide on planning grounds which are all listed: how big is the building, where is it located, is it on a flood plain, the room sizes, the amenity space, etc.'

The meeting started with the officers presenting their report. Next the objectors and proponents spoke, then councillors from the ward where the proposed development was sited had an opportunity to speak. Once they had finished, nobody else was allowed to speak except the committee.

Seven people wished to object at the meeting. Each speaker was allowed a maximum of three minutes. To keep it balanced, the proposers are allowed as many speakers as there are objectors. So we had seven speakers and 21 minutes in total.

Our speakers were carefully chosen to respond to specific concerns. They included Jackie Valin, the head of Southfields Academy, just down the road from Plough Lane, to talk about the community benefit the stadium would bring; Tim Hillyer, a local resident (and fan) who had lived in the area when WFC played at Plough Lane and could rebut many of the allegations about the poor fan behaviour, and Kay Skelton, then the director of our charity, to talk about the community work we were doing in Merton.

Daniel Francis was there to help us through, 'I remember there were seven of you. We'd rehearsed you to make sure you didn't over-run. I had a stopwatch and throughout your sessions I was literally sitting on the floor behind you. No one could see me but I was kicking the chairs to tell you your time was up.'

After about three hours of presentations, questions and answers, Linda Kirby asked the committee members to vote. She says, 'I had no idea what was going to happen when it went to the vote. It was really scary. As the chair I don't express a view; my role was to make sure everybody else expressed a view.'

Having finished scuttling along behind us and kicking our chairs, Daniel Francis had returned to his seat immediately behind the Conservative members of the committee. Here he overheard their deliberations, 'They were talking while Linda was summing up. One councillor said to the other, "What are we going to do?" My recollection is that their hands went up last. They looked around and one of them said, "Shit, we've got to put our hands up here."' They clearly didn't want to be seen to be the only dissenters to a hugely popular decision.

The moment I saw six hands had been raised in favour I stopped looking and started texting Eileen to let her know. It was only when I left the chamber 15 minutes later that I realised that, with the slightly belated votes from the Conservative members, the application had been approved unanimously.

Throughout the process Stephen Alambritis had been very positive that we would win the vote but I was nonetheless taken aback that it was unanimous. I wasn't the only one to be surprised. Planning committee chair Linda Kirby says, 'I remember being absolutely freaked when it got to the vote when I said, "Can we move to the recommendation? Can I see those in favour?" And when I looked around and saw everybody's hand up I was, well, shocked. Absolutely shocked. I wanted to pump the air!'

She couldn't join the celebrations because she had to chair the rest of the committee, 'Some people had to wait for their planning application to come on after yours and I was apologising to them for the delay. They were all going "don't apologise" and cheering. It was an amazing evening.'

We now had a 'resolution to approve' our application. However, to get final planning permission we still had several hurdles to clear.

Any substantial planning application has to be signed off by the Greater London Authority (GLA), in effect by the Mayor of London. At that time the incumbent was Alexander Boris de Pfeffel Johnson. On 22 March 2016, just over three months after the Merton planning committee vote, came a bombshell when Johnson 'called in' the application. This meant that he was taking over from Merton the role of granting – or refusing – final permission. He was throwing everything up in the air.

Everyone at Merton was bemused. The GLA officers had recommended that Johnson should leave the decision with Merton. So when Merton officers called their counterparts to ask what it was all about, they were told, 'We've got absolutely no idea.'

The decision was doubly frustrating because Johnson had already announced that he was not planning to stand again in the London mayoral elections which were taking place two months later. Theoretically he had time to review the application before standing down but in practice we knew it wasn't going to happen. We would have to wait for a new mayor to settle in before we could start lobbying for a reversal of the decision. On reflection I concluded that it was no bad thing that the final decision wouldn't be taken by Johnson, who is so susceptible to influence by lobbyists and notoriously uninterested in detail.

The good news was that Sadiq Khan was elected mayor in May. He had been the MP for Tooting, the constituency which adjoins the stadium, so he knew the issues well. I'd briefed him some months earlier and found him open, approachable, funny and, best of all, a football lover. He'd expressed his support for the move so we were optimistic; we just had to give him time to settle in.

Sure enough, Khan launched a 14-day further consultation (which I am certain was to make sure his decision was legally unchallengeable) and received over 8,000 responses, almost all from Dons fans of course. This level of response gave a powerful message but the GLA had to read them all so it also slowed things down a little. Nonetheless, on 22 August, five months to the day after Johnson's announcement, Khan returned the power to make the decision to Merton.

We will never know for sure why Johnson called it in. My suspicion is that it was a combination of lobbying on behalf of Wandsworth residents by Richard Tracey, the GLA member for Merton and Wandsworth, and by Wandsworth Council who saw many of the benefits going to Merton while they would suffer the cost of providing education to the child yield (the ugly expression for the number of children who would live in the new flats). Wandsworth had good access to Johnson because his deputy mayor and chief of staff Eddie Lister, the former leader of Wandsworth Council, was very close to his successor, Ravi Govindia. Maybe I am being too cynical when I say that it struck me that they felt it would do no harm for a Tory council to be seen to be supporting objectors in a Labour-held parliamentary constituency in their borough; then again, maybe I'm not.

It was clear that Alambritis held Wandsworth responsible, at least in part, for Johnson's decision because he greeted the news that the decision had been returned to Merton with a tweet that said, 'Great result. Merton 6 Wandsworth 1 (Johnson og).'

A few months later I was told that Johnson had confided to a close aide that he called in the application because he was being pestered to death by a GLA restaurant waitress who was a greyhound fan. Sometimes I found myself lost for words.

In the end all major planning decisions are inherently political. We would not have had a stadium but for the political will of Stephen Alambritis and Andrew Judge. Johnson's intervention was almost certainly also triggered by politics. His decision cost us eight months, from December to August, but in the greater scheme of things it was a temporary setback. We had won the overall battle and we moved on.

Or so we thought. It wasn't over yet. Citing concerns that the stadium would put undue pressure on the transport infrastructure and services, Wandsworth Council wrote to the Secretary of State, Sajid Javid, to ask him to assert his right to call in the application. Once again the politicians had over-ruled their own officers' recommendation to let the application proceed. Javid mulled it over for six weeks before announcing he wasn't going to intervene.

And yet, it still wasn't over. The Save Wimbledon Stadium Action Group submitted a 44-page dossier to Historic England (HE) asking that the stadium be listed. HE had taken a very brief look at the site early in the application process and reported that there was nothing of any great interest, but they were now required to look again. Their report, which came to the original conclusion, wasn't published until June 2017, 18 months after the resolution to approve our planning application.

With limited cash resources we couldn't afford to continue the design work during all these delays so we had suspended it while we awaited decisions by the mayor and then the Secretary of State. Towards the end of 2016, nearly a year after the planning committee's resolution to approve our application, we felt sufficiently confident to resume. We will never be sure how much the delay cost but I estimate that the combined effect of another year's inflation in the construction industry and the cost of stopping our work and then starting again came to over £1m.

The next task was to negotiate the Development Agreement, a contract between us and Galliard setting out our respective responsibilities and commitments. Once again we were represented by Dan Norris of Hogan Lovells.

There followed a year of protracted negotiations and seemingly interminable meetings hammering out points of principle and arguing over the detailed wording. Getting the agreement right required the ability to think through the commercial issues as well as the fine detail of the legal wording. We were very fortunate to have Dan to lead us through this phase.

I found many of the meetings deeply frustrating and I thought I'd give readers a flavour of the downsides of being part of such protracted negotiations. For example, during the planning process the GLA demanded that we introduce some 'animation' into the stadium, to enhance the pedestrian thoroughfare that runs along the length of the site. The GLA was concerned that the imaginatively named north/south street would be narrow and dark.

We responded by agreeing to introduce a crèche to cater for the 'child yield' from the housing and a café, built into the side of the east wall of the stadium. The crèche would be built into the east stand of the stadium but paid for and let by Galliard.

We needed to negotiate with Galliard to establish how this would be achieved. Galliard's lawyers started the discussion by demanding a 999-year lease on the relevant part of the stadium. I'm well used to people starting negotiations from a fairly extreme position and then moving towards the point at which they would be willing to agree, but this was simply ludicrous.

If we agreed, then for a thousand years we wouldn't be able to change that part of the stadium or be able to demolish or rebuild it without Galliard's or their successors' agreement. In such situations it is impossible to know whether the lawyers are acting on their client's instructions or whether they are just dick-swinging to impress them. Either way they are just wasting everyone's time.

Dan patiently negotiated a more realistic agreement but it took time and energy, plus quite a lot of good will, to get there.[70]

The same 'start at one extreme' approach was mirrored in the first draft document, presented to us by Galliard's lawyers as the starting point for negotiations. It set out obligations on us to do a whole load of things. Subject to negotiation we were okay with that. But there needed to be reciprocity and I got used to Dan's mantra, persistently demanding that what we were being asked to do had to be mirrored by Galliard. A lot of that deal was harder to agree because they started from such an extreme position, which I don't think was very clever. Again, I don't know where that stance came from – Galliard or their lawyers, but it was a waste of either their lawyers' time or Galliard's money.

One major success for which Dan should be given all the credit was securing the freehold of the stadium land. The deal was that Galliard had to give the land to Merton, who would then transfer it to us. Initially the council proposed to grant us a lease and they appointed a consultant to try to come up with a suitable structure to do so. Dan argued, over a prolonged period of time, that to minimise the risk to the council of any repercussions if the club was ever to go under, we should be granted the freehold rather than a lease.

There had been talk of an annual rental of £100,000, ratcheted up as we rose through the leagues. If we had been granted a lease it would have been for either 250 or 125 years – that's what councils usually grant. A 250-year lease at £100,000 per year would have cost £25m, so persuading Merton we should own the freehold was quite a saving.

Finally, on 13 December 2017, two years and three days after Merton's unanimous resolution to approve our application, Stephen Alambritis, Mike Watson and I signed the s106 and Development Agreements, huddled

---

70 We always thought the crèche and café were impracticable but the GLA officers saw these as key to livening up the area just outside the stadium. Merton's Tara Butler sorted it out, 'The location wasn't suitable for that sort of environment, without any outside space and embedded in the stadium walls. We ended up with a crèche, a café, and the entrance to the club's shop to try to liven things up. We went to the Merton Education team who said unless you have an outside space no one is going to be interested in operating a crèche. So we kept going back to the GLA and saying it will never get used in this location and then we would have a white elephant. So they took it out.'

The requirement for animation was deleted from the planning permission by means of a subsequent s73 'variation application' which also dealt with anomalies that had gone through in the original document. So all Dan's patient negotiation re the crèche was wasted.

together under a small AFC Wimbledon marquee, erected on the pavement outside the Plough Lane site. Dan was there to see the end result of his labours and make sure we signed in the right places. Stephen then handed me the official decision notice and we were finally there.

Actually, we weren't. There was one more obstacle we might need to overcome, if a protestor were to apply for a Judicial Review of the decision. The only acceptable grounds for doing so, however, are if the process that was used to arrive at the decision was not followed properly, or if the decision defied logic.

We were very confident that a JR would not succeed. However, anyone can apply to a judge for a JR and, for a relatively small outlay, they could cost us a further substantial delay while the judge assessed whether to accept that there was a prima facie case to answer.

I was confident that Wandsworth wouldn't be seeking a JR; in July I'd bumped into Ravi Govindia, the leader of Wandsworth Council, in the gents' toilets at Wimbledon during the tennis championships. He told me that they wouldn't be seeking a JR. Nonetheless, for the six weeks after Merton issued the decision notice we held our collective breath until the time period for an appeal had expired.

Of all the things we've done as a club, this planning application was probably the best example of everyone working together effectively. Stephen Alambritis says, 'I got so many nonsenses when I was leader. Someone from an organisation would turn up and then the next day someone else from that organisation would turn up and say something different. What I found was that it was just you and Ivor, consistency and continuity. It made all the difference.'

From the council, Alambritis led the way, smoothed out all the political obstacles, and was always available to resolve any problems. Andrew Judge had the vision and worked assiduously over several years to make it happen, supported by James McGinlay, who was excellent in both public and private meetings, Paul McGarry, Future Merton manager, who made sure that the stadium was a consistently high priority of the team, and Tara Butler who, with her comprehensive knowledge of the planning issues and calm manner, steered the key planning designations past the independent inspector.

On our side, Tom Adam, Roger Hobkinson, Andrew Williams and Dan Norris contributed hugely to our success. And, of course, Ivor was always there, tirelessly banging the drum for AFC Wimbledon and Plough Lane.

The team done good.

49
OPPORTUNITIES

ALL THE time we were calculating the cost of the stadium we were looking for different and innovative ways of raising the necessary funds. This chapter deals with three of the initiatives we took, leading to two successes and one abject failure. I start with the failure.

In the eyes of many of our fans Sam Hammam is the devil incarnate, because he sold Wimbledon FC to the Norwegian businessmen (see Chapter 2 for more detail). Much worse, in 1998 he sold the Plough Lane stadium to a supermarket chain without having a permanent home for us to move to. He did well out of it – it's widely believed that he pocketed £20m for the club and £8m for the stadium.

In August 2001, the day after the proposed move to Milton Keynes was announced, Sam appeared at a WFC pre-season friendly at Brentford and was bemused to be harangued by a very angry group of Dons fans. He never understood this. In his eyes he was the innocent party and he felt bitter that he had been 'very cruelly' abused by the supporters. Ever the victim, in his view he had been cast into the wilderness, 'I was thrown out by the old Wimbledon and that night I was thrown out by the new Wimbledon.'

So, you can imagine my surprise when he turned up at Kingsmeadow on a Monday night late in 2014.

Kingstonian were playing that night. I left early because my office was next door to the changing room and I struggled to concentrate when the team's music was pounding away through the wall. As I got into my car I noticed a small, grey-haired man hanging around, looking lost. He looked a bit like Sam but I thought it couldn't possibly be him and set off to drive home.

But maybe it was him? I decided to check. I pulled the car off the road and rang Peter Miller. Peter had been a director at WFC and the only boardroom voice against the move to Milton Keynes. Rather than resign, he decided to continue so that he could secretly brief the fans' association, WISA, about their plans. After being seen at our first game at Sutton United, he was told by Charles Koppel, the WFC chairman, to stop going to our games or be sacked. So he resigned.

Sam is an inveterate networker and, as such, he stayed in touch with Peter. So when I said, 'Do you know where Sam is?' Peter was able to say, with confidence, that he was in the UK. 'Well,' I said, 'not just the UK. He's at Kingsmeadow.'

I was curious about what he was up to so I turned the car round and went back. Surely he wasn't thinking of trying to get a voice in the club? When I pulled in he was still wandering around looking lost, so I invited him into my office. After chatting idly for a while I decided, on the spur of the moment, to show him our plans for Plough Lane. He was charming and very interested but before long his ego took over and he was telling me how to do it better.

From time to time the football club board had discussed approaching Sam to suggest that he should donate a chunk of the proceeds of Plough Lane towards our new stadium. We could try to sell the idea by telling him it was a way by which he might get the credit he deserved for the many good years he brought WFC. And here he was in my office.

A substantial contribution from Sam would obviate the need for a bank loan and we could enter the new stadium almost debt-free. Perhaps this was the opportunity the board had discussed. If so, I didn't want to rush it and wanted to consult Peter. I was due to be home so I introduced Sam to the Ks board members and left him watching the game with them in the directors' box.

The next day I called Peter. We agreed that while it was a long shot, we should have a go. Sam had given me his mobile number so after a couple of weeks I called him and suggested that we meet the next time he was in the country.

We met four or five times over the next couple of years. We got on very well, unless and until I gently suggested that I understood why fans might be so disappointed that he'd sold Plough Lane. At that point he'd go off on a rant, about how he'd been shafted by Merton Council, how the fans were ungrateful, no one gave him credit for what he had done for the club and, astonishingly, that WFC and AFC Wimbledon were both 'his babies'. I got so used to hearing it that I think I could have repeated it verbatim.

Eventually Peter and I decided we should take the plunge. Peter knew him better than I, so he offered to raise the subject. A great opportunity to do so presented itself in September 2016. The Secretary of State had just declined a request to call in our planning application and we could now say that the new stadium was definitely going to happen.

Peter wrote a carefully crafted letter to Sam. In it he said that no one begrudged Sam selling the club. However, selling the stadium had lost him the respect of many people, including former players, officials and directors. Now he had a chance to rectify this. A substantial donation was a one-off opportunity to cement his special place in the club's history and for him to be properly recognised. We didn't offer Sam anything in return, other than a chance to do the right thing and open the door to his possible rehabilitation with the club. And, of course, the idea would need to go to the Dons Trust membership for ratification because it would be likely to cause controversy. Then the members could decide; we'd only be offering them an idea.

Sam wasn't having it. He and Peter met in a London hotel and Sam told him that he had gone too far. He again brought up the abuse he was subjected to at the Brentford game and how the supporters had cruelly betrayed him. It got quite loud and a tense peace was only restored after an intervention by a waiter. We could clearly forget about any money.

Peter hasn't seen Sam since and I've not heard from him either. Some fans will no doubt berate us for supping with the devil but we thought it was a chance to make a massive difference to the club and worth trying. If we'd persuaded him to accept our suggestion he'd no doubt have been a nightmare to manage, but I was sure we'd get by.

So that was how Sam missed out on the opportunity for at least partial reconciliation and proper recognition for what he did for the club. Ah well.

The second initiative started about 18 months later, in February 2018, our first-team manager Neal Ardley forwarded an e-mail with the subject heading 'Malaysian investment'. It was an expression of interest in investing in the club which had come via a very circuitous route. Ananth Nathan, based in Malaysia, wanted to make contact. Having had no reply to a letter he'd sent me (which I never received) he approached a consultant based in Singapore who, in turn, approached Martin Leahy, a former colleague in Wales who might be able to help. It turned out that Martin's son had been at school with Jon Meades who was playing for us at the time. Jon passed the message on to Neal and finally contact was made.

We had a lot of similar approaches. They would start with 'we represent someone who'd like to invest in AFC Wimbledon'. Most of these were fishing expeditions from companies with no buyer behind them. Their aim was to identify football clubs that might be for sale so that they could hawk them around to potential buyers. I would send a standard reply saying that while we would welcome proposals to invest in areas such as naming rights for the new stadium, if by 'invest' they meant take control then that wasn't on the table. That was usually the end of the exchange.[71]

This time when I said control wasn't a possibility the answer was 'that might well be okay' so we agreed to meet. Football club director Mick Buckley and I met Dato[72] Ananth and his advisors at the Langham hotel in early March. The meeting went well and we came away cautiously optimistic.

Discussions continued for the next few months with hopes of an acceptable deal rising and then falling again, as is the way with many negotiations. Eventually in March 2019, nearly a year after our initial contact, Mick and I flew to Kuala Lumpur to meet Ananth and try to finalise a deal.

Despite all our efforts and genuine best intentions on the part of Ananth we were never able to agree anything on the scale we had originally envisaged. Nonetheless, our efforts were not in vain; Ananth is one of the largest investors in the club and is now an overseas vice-president. For once an e-mail out of the blue had led to a valuable investment for the club.

The third initiative arose because one of the ways I thought we should prepare for returning home to Merton was to improve our network of influential and wealthy local residents. I felt they could help us in all sorts

71 My favourite reply was from a Middle East-based man who represented 'a group' but who assured me that my place on the board would be secure after a takeover. After I rebuffed him a couple of times he wrote to tell me that we were unambitious and, 'The idea is to make money Erik. Why you think small? Why do you not think big?'

72 'Dato' is a title conferred by the ruler. We don't have a specific equivalent but a near approximation is 'Sir'.

of ways, from taking sponsorships at the club, to opening doors to people who could help us, and also, in the medium term, as possible investors when we launched the planned share issue later in the process.

In late 2017 I talked to Peter Miller about how best to do this. We agreed that we should hold a couple of dinners to which we could invite influential people and high net worth individuals. Peter is well connected but we also hit upon the idea of asking Robert Holmes to help. Robert was an obvious candidate because at one time or another his estate agency had sold most of the most valuable properties in Wimbledon, so he had excellent contacts.

One of Peter's first steps was to contact Nick Robertson, a successful businessman who lives in Wimbledon. Peter knew Nick's house because a friend had once lived in it. So he dropped Nick a note in January 2018 and, having met up, invited him to a game. Nick liked what he saw and he liked our story. They agreed that to get people round the table it would be better if the invitations came from him. He also offered to pay for the dinner which was held at the Ivy in Wimbledon. I immediately accepted! About 15 of us met for the meal.

I've always found that once people get to know us they get sucked into the ethos and spirit of the club, so there has never been a need to push ourselves forward; the club does the talking for us. Therefore my approach was low-key. I started by saying that I wasn't there to ask for money but instead I wanted to brief them about a major event, the new stadium, that was happening in the borough but also about the extensive community work that we had been doing for some years by means of our foundation, the charitable arm of the football club.

I was looking for feedback and ideas from round the table. I talked everyone through some of the latest designs for the stadium and our plans for widening our engagement in the community. Nick kept us broadly on track for a lively and very thoughtful evening.

We repeated the evening a little while later and I also met some of the participants separately to talk some more about their ideas and, simply, to build key relationships. And then, a few months later, it seemed like the right time to explain where we were with funding and seek support.

We held another two dinners which were a fascinating mix of challenge, scepticism and plain and simple offers of support. But in the end, the people we invited to those dinners, all hosted by Nick, invested a total of about £2.8m into the club. The majority of that was from Nick himself, who explained, 'I love football, I live in Wimbledon. I've not seen it first-hand but I understand enough to know that a football club in a community is a huge, huge asset and a major community benefit. And I'm in that lovely position where I can help the local community and I love football, so why wouldn't I? It's not a complex story.'

I started with the simple objective of widening our network and then broadening the agenda to seek investment. Nick saw and liked what we were doing and, literally, bought into the idea as did some of the other guests. None of the people who invested got anything in the way of influence in the club, over and above that they are the sort of people who have experience and ideas that can be on tap to those who wish to draw upon them.

I am absolutely certain that this idea is well worth continuing. There are many others who I am sure will support what we are doing when they see the fruits of our work over the last 19 years. I will watch with interest from the sidelines.

50

THAT'S NO WAY TO SAY GOODBYE

IN FEBRUARY 2016, two months after Merton's resolution to approve our planning application for the new stadium, I wrote to the Dons Trust board setting out my thoughts on succession planning. At the same time I gave notice of my intention to step down as CEO, a decision I said was non-negotiable. I set out a suggested timetable which envisaged starting to recruit in January 2017 with the successful candidate taking over from me the following July.

When I wrote to the DTB the target date for occupying the new stadium was the 2018/19 season. This proved to be over-optimistic, although nobody realised this at the time. My logic was simple. At Kingsmeadow the home stands were pretty much sold out for every game and Ivor had sold the naming rights for the stadium, as well as all four stands, the front and back of shirts, socks, almost anything that could take advertising. Ivor is so committed I think he would have had his forehead tattooed with an advert if the club benefitted!

We would be moving to a stadium with more than double the capacity of Kingsmeadow, with extensive conference and banqueting facilities. The market research we'd commissioned indicated there was substantial interest in using those facilities and in supporting the club after its return home. I thought it would be nonsense to hand over the stadium specification to a new CEO and say 'we designed this – now you need to make it work'. So my successor should have responsibility for creating the environment for the stadium to succeed commercially and be given enough time to do so.

It was clear a new CEO should bring experience of operating a bigger stadium and much stronger marketing and commercial skills than I could offer. I genuinely believed it was for the good of the club that I stood down and left my successor time in which to introduce their thoughts. But I was also looking after myself; after 14 years I was knackered!

Very soon we were dealing with London Mayor Boris Johnson calling in the planning decision, the sale of Kingsmeadow to Chelsea (Chapter 51), the increasing time needed to consider the stadium development, the design and implementation of a consolidated database to allow consistent communication with fans and would-be fans, the run-up to the play-offs, and a pile of other matters that were in danger of overwhelming the DT and football club boards. With the DTB entirely comprising volunteers, many with demanding jobs, it was disappointing but not surprising that they didn't consider a paper from its appointed succession planning group until November, nine months after I indicated my plans.

While all this was going on, there was still a club to run.

Promotion to League 1 meant we lost two of our promotion strike force. Bayo had played the second half of the promotion season as an impact substitute but he wanted to start games. Neal couldn't promise him that so there was a friendly parting of the ways.

We also lost Ade Azeez. Ade was in the final year of his contract and from January he could sign a deal for an overseas club for the following season. In this case 'overseas' was Scotland and Partick Thistle signed him. If he had transferred to an English club we would have been entitled to compensation because he was under 24. However, an international transfer meant we were due nothing. In came Tyrone Barnett and Dom Poleon, one a target man and the other a pacy striker, to try to replace Bayo and Ade.

Our first objective in League 1 was to consolidate. In a fairly uneventful league season we were comfortably safe from relegation by the end of March. We ended up 15th, and that was after a dreadful run at the end of the season when we took three points from the last six games. The excitement came in the FA Cup second round when we were drawn away to Curzon Ashton, three leagues below us in Conference North.

The game was chosen for TV, no doubt because of the possibility of an upset, and at half-time we were losing 2-0. Neal says, 'The lads were devastated and Bass was angry. I tried to turn it on its head and said, "You can either look at this as the worst time ever, or you could look at it as one of the greatest comebacks ever. I'm telling you, even if they score a third, I still think you'll have enough chances to score four."'

Sure enough Curzon did score a third goal and at 80 minutes we were 3-0 down. By 82 minutes it was 3-3 and then we scored an injury-time winner. Cue pandemonium among our fans and despair for Curzon Ashton. Once again Neal's immediate reaction was to make his way to the Curzon manager and players while Ivor and I made our way into the boardroom where the Curzon directors were in shock, but very gracious.

And so to the next round where we were drawn against Sutton United, long-time rivals in non-league days and our first opponents back in 2002. Most of our players didn't want to play on their artificial pitch and we were relieved to scrape a 0-0 draw. The winners of the replay would have a home tie against Leeds United. Sadly it was our turn to come off worse. We were 1-0 up when centre-back Paul Robinson was sent off after 15 minutes. We hung on for over an hour but conceded late goals to lose 3-1.

Much as we hated losing, we did our best to deal with it well. Club director Mick Buckley brought a bottle of champagne into the boardroom for the Sutton directors while Neal waited at the entrance to the tunnel to shake the hands of the Sutton players as they left the pitch. I was devastated to lose but genuinely pleased for Bruce Elliott, the Sutton chairman who had gone out of his way to host our first match. They went on to beat Leeds before losing to Arsenal at home in what was a very lucrative cup run for them.

The end of that season saw Tom Elliott leave. We'd tried everything we could to keep him but he had refused a contract extension after the play-off final and several other offers during the season. He was clearly determined to move on. I didn't blame him because Millwall were offering him double what we could afford to pay and a chance to play in the Championship. A small consolation was that the coaching and support he got from our management team had helped Tom to turn his career round. Sadly we'd been unable to achieve the same feat for injury-plagued Tyrone Barnett who also left that summer after scoring only two league goals in over 30 appearances.

The summer saw academy goalkeeper Joe Bursik play for England, who lost a penalty shoot-out in the final of the UEFA European Under-17 Championship. Nine of the England starting 11 were from Premier League academies, one was from Newcastle United in the Championship and then there was Joe, the odd one out, being from a Category 3 academy, League 1 club. It was obvious that a larger club would come for him and in fact three approached us: Crystal Palace, Stoke City and Derby County. The competition for his services helped to drive the fee up. There's no such thing as a holiday in football and I finalised Joe's £250,000[73] transfer to Stoke while standing in the rain outside our holiday home; there's no mobile signal in the house.

That summer also saw Jake Reeves and Dom Poleon transferred to Bradford City for £150,000 and £30,000 respectively. Dom, like Lyle Taylor, Tom Elliott and Jack Midson, is a striker who enjoyed his most successful league season while he was with us. I insisted that all the transfer documents were dated 1 July (the first day of our financial year) so that they were included in our 2017/18 season's income; this was a help when calculating our wages cap for that season (see Appendix 1 for an example of how the wage cap worked).

We went to strengthen our striker options and negotiated the recruitment of Michael Smith from Portsmouth. We could only afford Michael if one of our players was transferred out but at the 11th hour that deal broke down. So we were a striker short and it showed. In a lacklustre season we were the third-lowest scorers in the division and failed to score in 16 league games. We made up for the lack of striking power with a solid defence; 12 teams conceded more goals than us. It wasn't pretty to watch but needs must. In the January transfer window we signed Joe Pigott from Maidstone and his goals were a welcome boon in the second half of the season. We ended 18th which sounds a more comfortable position than it felt.

During 2017/18 the DTB had proceeded with the recruitment of a COO. In January 2018, nearly two years after I'd first said I wanted to step down, Joe Palmer arrived. He brought the marketing experience that I thought we needed, as well as having worked in a club with a much larger

---

73 Like most transfer deals, there was a sell-on clause. After making his first-team debut he had made about 15 starts at the time of writing. When an England under-21 keeper aged 20 is starting regularly in the Championship then many eyes will be upon him. I genuinely can't remember the terms of the transfer but I'm sure we will get a percentage of any profit if he should be sold. When I say 'here's hoping' I mean no disrespect to Stoke, who were courteous and professional throughout, or to Joe, who is a lovely lad and deserves to succeed.

stadium, namely Sheffield Wednesday. He was easily the best candidate we interviewed.

I had reluctantly agreed to continue to oversee the stadium development and in return the DT board agreed that I should retain responsibility for football. Joe took on everything else. To emphasise that everyone other than the staff at the training ground now reported to Joe, I vacated my office and gave it to him the day he arrived. From then on, and with a shortage of space in the club's office, I worked from home and grabbed whatever desk space I could find whenever I needed to come in.

The board were spooked by how close we had come to relegation and at one of our regular meetings we spent time discussing what to do. We were facing the loss of our top striker. Lyle Taylor's contract had expired and he had made it plain that he wanted to move on. That was hardly surprising as several clubs were hovering around him offering sums that were double our best offer. Discussions with his agent made it clear that he was set on leaving so Neal told his agent the best offer we could afford and made it clear that if Lyle changed his mind we'd make him our highest-paid player ever. He went to Charlton Athletic.

Our other main striker, Kwesi Appiah, had started the season well, including an outstanding display at Blackburn which had their directors asking who he was (he'd been playing abroad for some time). But in the next game, at home to Milton Keynes, he tore his hamstring badly and needed an operation. He was out for months and never really regained the early-season quality he'd shown. Simon Bassey says, 'Kwesi was a good trainer, the boys liked him and he was good in the group. Some time later I heard Michael Owen talk about how he had the same injury and couldn't play the way he used to so he tried to change his game. Kwesi never really trusted his leg after that and it affected him.'

With our top striker gone and our other key front man struggling to come back after injury we were facing a serious dilemma. The simple truth was that we couldn't generate enough income from Kingsmeadow to give Neal a reasonable budget for League 1. In the season that had just ended our financial results before interest, depreciation and tax were a loss of over £380,000 and that was after one-off transfer profits of £420,000. With a players' wages budget of £2.2m we'd been 21st in the wages league table, the equivalent of a relegation position. Replacing Lyle's goals would be well-nigh impossible within our budgetary constraints.

The football club board met to discuss what to do. We met weekly to cover operational issues and, since not all the directors were based on site, to keep everybody informed. Once a month we held a formal meeting with a review of financial results, commercial issues, etc. To keep the DTB closely in touch with the club's activities, we were usually joined at the formal meeting by Matt Breach, who by now was the Dons Trust chair.

In a long discussion we all agreed that our top priority was to ensure that we were still in League 1 when we opened the new stadium. But we faced a dilemma. The draft budget for 2018/19 showed we would lose about £500,000 despite almost certainly being the second lowest spenders in the league. If we decided we had to break even financially we would have to reduce the wages budget by £500,000 which would probably make us the equal lowest spenders in the league, nearly £500,000 behind the next lowest spenders and well under half the league average.

It was Hobson's choice. After a long discussion the idea emerged that we should increase the wages budget and take the financial hit. Matt Breach feels that if we hadn't done that, 'We would have got relegated immediately back into League 2. And if we'd been in League 2 we thought we wouldn't be able to do what we needed to be able to do to build the stadium. So effectively we took a calculated gamble.'

We added £450,000 to the budget and at Matt's request I prepared a cash flow that showed how the idea worked and submitted it to the next DTB meeting.

When the Football League analysis was published in the November it showed that without the increase we'd have been third-bottom of the wages table; with it we were equal 18th.

The season started slowly and by the end of September we were 16th. James Hanson had been signed to bring height and heading power to the squad, but he suffered an early-season injury. With Kwesi Appiah not back to his best after his operation we struggled to score goals. And in defence we'd tried to sign up-and-coming young goalkeeping star Aaron Ramsdale but he had broken a finger in training and so we missed out. He was to join us later in the season but a generally held view was that if we'd had him from day one we would have avoided at least some of the defeats we suffered in the first half of the season. On such small things are seasons determined and jobs kept or lost.

In October we went into a full-blown slump, losing six games in a row and scoring only one goal. By the end of the month we were second-bottom (remembering that four teams are relegated) and things were looking bleak. I'd say Wimbledon fans are, overall, more patient than most but this was too much for them.

November started with a home match against Shrewsbury. Despite dominating, we lost to a last-minute goal and were now six points from safety. At a board meeting early the following week Mick and Ivor proposed that we speak to Neal and set him a target for the next few games, starting with a televised FA Cup game away to Haringey Borough on the Friday night. We asked Neal to come to see Ivor and me at his house where I explained our proposal.

As I was doing so I found myself wondering what on earth I was doing. I've said many times that when you get to the point that you're setting a manager targets for, say, three games you've clearly lost faith in him and it would be more honest to sack him. Setting a target in that way simply undermines any relationship between you. And here I was, doing exactly that.

Some years later I talked to Neal about it. He said, 'The one thing I remember when I went in [to see Ivor and me] was, whatever is said, act the right way. Don't be disappointed or emotional, just act the right way. So I just sat there and the whole time I knew where this was heading, even though you were setting me a points target. I knew this was it, it was time. But I needed to go away and act the right way. So I said "okay, thank you" and left. I met up with the rest of the staff back at the ground to tell them the situation, and that was when Coxy said to me, "I know." I said, "What do you mean, you know?" He said, "Well, I went to get a ticket for the game and as I leaned over to get it I saw an e-mail with a new manager list."'

There is nothing to apologise for in having a list of potential next managers – indeed I think it is good practice to have such a list, regularly updated, in our back pockets. But I was appalled when I found out, years later, how Neal and Neil heard about it. That was very, very poor on our part. And, in retrospect, I wish I'd simply called it a day and shown Neal the respect he deserved instead of this half-arsed, rather shoddy route I took. If I could no longer stick to my principles, it was a red flag that I'd stayed too long.

We had a game that night in the Football League Trophy[74] but it says how we felt about the competition that it wasn't mentioned as part of any target. We won 4-0 but the focus quickly turned to the FA Cup tie. It was played on Haringey's artificial pitch in torrential rain, a horrible evening and an awful match, which we won 1-0 with a late deflected goal.

Neal says, 'While the game was going on, all I kept thinking was this is my last game in charge, I don't deserve to go out with a loss. I didn't enjoy one part of that game. It was the most horrendous hundred minutes in my life. After I went in and saw Coxy. I looked at him and he just shook his head at me as if to say "it's time". That was all I needed. I went home and I went out with Sarah and a friend on the Saturday and we spoke on the Sunday morning.'

Neal came to my house and we agreed it was time, shook hands and he left. He continues, 'It was tough, but I knew it was the right thing to do. I got a train there on my own, got a train back and I was quite emotional on the way home. You know, it was, that was it. I sent all the staff a message. Maybe in hindsight, now I look back at going unbeaten at the end of the season before and was it one season too many? You know, sometimes it's time, you know, and it was, it was time.'

Every manager who had joined us had taken us up a level from the previous one in terms of professionalism. Neal transformed the training centre and improved the way the backroom staff performed. Most of that isn't visible to fans so I thought it was important to acknowledge here.

What went wrong? I asked Neal and Simon Bassey to look back, with the benefit of hindsight. First Neal explains, 'If I had any regrets of what I did in my time at Wimbledon, it was trying to change too much too soon. We had money for Jake Reeves which helped us out, but losing Danny Bulman, losing Barry Fuller, losing Darius Charles, losing Bayo

---

74 The FL Trophy is a competition for Leagues 1 and 2 and is only really worthwhile if you reach the Wembley final. I thought it was of little interest and fans generally agreed – attendances were very low. In my eyes it was finally and completely undermined as a competition when the FL agreed to allow 16 Premier League and Championship clubs to enter under-21 teams in return for £1m of prize money. This idea is presumably of interest to those clubs because they hoover up all the brightest and best young talent for their academies then aren't in a position to give them experience of men's football. When the idea was first mooted it was seen as a foot in the door for such clubs to have B teams in the Football League. That idea went away but it resurfaced in 2020 when it was reportedly part of Greg Clarke's (the then-FA chairman) proposals to be considered for football reform.

Akinfenwa, all experienced players, people like that was too soon. I wanted to keep a really good team together, but the problem is that to keep them together in a higher league costs much more money than it originally did, so you end up paying more money for the same thing and that's the hard part. And it was getting harder and harder to find a new Lyle Taylor or a new Tom Elliott.'

Simon adds, 'It always seemed to me that we'd done great to get to League 1. Our job was to try to stay in League 1 until we got to the new stadium. A lot of the signings reflected that. Just get through it, get players who can do the job. Get to the new stadium, then we can start to build. We changed too soon.'

Just as when Terry Brown left, Simon took over as acting manager. He won us through to the next round of the FA Cup and took three points from the next three games, neither gaining nor losing ground on the pack of clubs above us.

But it was time to find a new manager.

51

HELLO, GOODBYE

WHEN YOU change manager mid-season no one is on holiday, so everyone who is interested knows that the job is available. For the previous few weeks they will all have been watching the situation like a hawk, ready to make the calls and send the CVs at the drop of a hat. So it wasn't surprising that within two days of Neal's departure being announced we had 62 applications for the role; eventually it rose to 81.

We started with our own list of three or four candidates we wanted to talk to, so we made calls to make sure they applied. One would-be contender who came to our attention late in the day was Steven Reid, the former Millwall, Blackburn and West Brom player, who was helping Simon Bassey in his caretaker role. Steven made it clear that he wasn't a candidate at that time but strongly recommended Simon, having seen his man-management and tactical skills close up. Despite Simon's obvious qualities there was a feeling we needed a change.

We quickly developed a longlist of ten applicants. It went down to nine when one candidate refused to submit a CV; if sending a CV is beneath you then you're almost certainly not going to fit into our culture. Nine days after we advertised the role we'd interviewed all nine and drawn up a shortlist of four. They were Shaun Derry, Wally Downes, Kevin Nolan and Russell Slade.

Wally played over 200 games for WFC and was much loved, and vociferously promoted, by a group of fans from that era. He told me, 'I've always felt there was unfinished business with the club because I left when I was 28. I left before the FA Cup Final although I wasn't getting a game.

All the jobs I'd had in coaching were all very good jobs but the club had had such success there was never really any call for me to be involved.'

But now there was an opportunity. Although he was coaching in India he could get out of it so he applied although, as he told us at the time, he'd never done an interview before.

Chief operating officer Joe Palmer, commercial director Ivor Heller and I did the first interviews. In every previous manager recruitment we'd involved a football expert; the previous time we'd used former Wimbledon manager Dave Bassett, but he was acting as Wally's agent so that ruled him out. This was something we'd not anticipated and we didn't have an alternative expert to turn to for an insider's view of the candidates. That was a mistake.

For the second interviews the panel was joined by board members Mick Buckley and David Charles. When we appointed Neal Ardley we'd used sports psychologist Steven Sylvester to give some insight into the candidates' personalities. Steve was unavailable, working in India with the West Indies cricket team, so we invited Nick Slade to join us.

We were all very impressed by Kevin Nolan's first interview and soon his agent was in my ear. I told him we'd like to see Kevin again but he had told us his salary in his previous role. That figure was £100,000 a year more than we could pay (and £50,000 more than my sources told me was the real figure). So I told his agent that if Kevin wanted more than the maximum salary we were able to offer then he shouldn't come to a second interview; he'd be wasting his time and ours. When he attended a second interview we assumed he understood our limits.

We had received unsolicited comments from one individual giving us a very negative view about him so during the interview I asked him how other people in football would describe him. He saw through the question instantly and replied, 'Well, if you asked [he named our source] he would tell you …' and almost word-perfectly repeated what we'd been told, before explaining why it wasn't fair. I liked that reply. But more importantly, we unanimously concluded that his plans for achieving our short-term objectives and his confident command of the dressing room made him the outstanding candidate.

I called his agent and said we were offering the job to Kevin. He immediately raised the salary question and I re-emphasised that we had an upper limit and we wouldn't be paying an agent's fee – after all, he'd done sod all (no, I didn't say that). He seemed to think that was merely a negotiating stance and said he would talk to Kevin. And then – silence. The job was never turned down, we simply didn't hear anything. We will never know why Kevin refused. Did his agent tell him the salary only after we offered the job? Was the lack of an agent's fee a key issue? Did he conclude that the players' wages budget wasn't enough? Were we too small a club for his ambitions? A few weeks later when everything had settled down I called Kevin and left a message asking for a chat, because feedback is always useful. Silence. After what had gone before that was disappointing but hardly a surprise.

Next in line were Shaun Derry, then at Oxford United, and Wally Downes, then coaching in India. We had to keep Shaun's name quiet since Oxford didn't know he had applied. The overall conclusion about Shaun was that he was probably the best candidate for the long term but we had thought Kevin was a better short-term bet to avoid relegation.

Wally's main advocate was Ivor plus a vocal group of fans who wrote in supporting his appointment. My personal view was that his track record in coaching made him a very strong candidate but he would be better as someone else's coach. But that option wasn't on offer.

We had long debates about what to do. In the end my reading was that Joe was marginally in favour of appointing Wally, Mick oscillated between support and being very uncertain, David was non-committal and Ivor was passionately in favour. Whether I wanted it or not, I was going to be the one who made the decision. My vote went to Wally.

We offered him the job and he accepted. And then some of his old tweets started to surface. Whatever his intention they were clearly offensive. They seemed to me to have been made in an attempt to be funny but they failed and were suddenly a serious problem for us. We needed to pause to take stock. Soon the e-mails started coming in.

To give a sense of the scale of the reaction, there were just under 30 e-mails telling us that we should have gone through his Twitter account with a fine-tooth comb before we appointed him (fair comment – we had done a cursory review and that wasn't enough). They also said that we should stop prevaricating and appoint him as he would bring back the true Wimbledon they felt had gone missing from the club. Some e-mails felt threatening, 'Ignore the consequences [of not appointing him] at your peril', while some were apocalyptic, 'Be prepared for a significant budget shortfall if Slade, Nolan or Derry come in. The repercussions will be far reaching, unfortunately…it is ugly out there. Really ugly.'

Conversely, there were about ten e-mails saying it was scandalous that we would even contemplate appointing someone who 'had tweeted homophobic and Islamophobic views'. Some felt we'd betrayed our ethos, 'By appointing Downes you will be condoning his views and will lose the credibility and respect across the footballing world you (and AFC) have built up over the years.'

With better processes we wouldn't have been in this position, but now that we were it seemed to me that this was a moral issue and the keepers of the club's conscience are the Dons Trust board. So we referred the issue to them. From a football point of view Wally was our choice. Was the DTB okay about the tweets?

They talked among themselves and then conducted an e-mail vote which confirmed that we should appoint Wally. They added that we should take follow-up actions, such as a re-education course, to make sure that similar issues didn't arise again. Wally was fine about the proposals, just relieved to get the job. No one from the DTB ever asked if we'd followed through with the education course.

The important thing for any manager in this sort of situation is to make an immediate impact. Wally says, 'I thought what I had to do was change whatever I could change quickly and that would be getting the fans back on board. I knew that Will Nightingale was well-liked so I made him captain straight away. I tried to get the players to realise that the only reason I was there was because what was happening wasn't working. So it had to change. I'd seen how they play and said that what we will start with will be very direct. We were letting in lots of goals at set plays, so we'd work on the set plays for the first ten days or so.

'Also the full-backs were playing far too many balls into midfield where the heaviest traffic was, so we'd lose the ball and it would be straight back down our end of the pitch. So I showed them some video examples and said to the full-backs when you get the ball slide it down the side of people to your wide man, don't go into the traffic.

'It needed someone to identify two or three changes that you can implement straight away. Get the fans on board, set plays, don't put balls into traffic. That was for the first ten days. Then you get the players on board.'

When Wally took over in early December we were seven points from safety. A string of good results meant we were only three points adrift on Boxing Day. Everything was looking rosy. In January we finally brought in Aaron Ramsdale, now recovered from his pre-season injury, on loan and with him in the team we won at Fleetwood in the FA Cup.

But then a disastrous run of one point from six games left us completely adrift and apparently doomed. We were bottom of the league, 11 points from safety and with the worst goal difference in the division.

In the middle of all of this, when we were at our lowest ebb, we played West Ham United at home in the FA Cup. They put out a strong team but, doing exactly what the TV cameras were hoping for, we put on a giant-killing performance and deservedly won 4-2. The final goal was scored by 19-year-old substitute Toby Sibbick. That was probably the trigger for his £265,000 transfer to Barnsley the following summer.

At half-time West Ham brought on Felipe Anderson as a substitute. This put the respective clubs' finances into context; Anderson's transfer fee of £36m was more than the cost of our new stadium and over 15 years' players wages for us. Three weeks later a team with five changes from the conquerors of West Ham lost 1-0 to Millwall in the next round.

Just over two weeks after the West Ham match we went on an extraordinary run. Wally says, 'I broke it down into single games – 15 cup finals – then broke those games into halves. Players at the lower level get very mixed thoughts – complexity is sometimes too much to cope with for them. I had to take the weight of responsibility from them and the best way to do that I thought was to put it into one game at a time.' He certainly kept it simple. Players told me that what they heard in half-time team talks was basically 'forward and wide' and 'do better'.

By now Aaron Ramsdale was showing the qualities that led to his £13m transfer from Bournemouth to Sheffield United a year or so later. Steve Seddon, who had been lined up by Simon Bassey even before Neal Ardley left, joined on loan and gave us width and energy plus a handful of crucial goals. Anthony Wordsworth and James Hanson were fit again and looking like the players we signed. They provided the support for Joe Pigott (who had nearly gone on loan in the transfer window) to score regularly. We were on a roll.

We won seven, drew five and lost only twice in what amounted to automatic promotion form. In what was to me the defining moment of that run, we picked up a crucial point at top-of-the-table Luton Town thanks to a late Seddon goal and a world-class save by Ramsdale, turning a deflected shot wide of the goal. At the full-time whistle he and goalkeeping coach Ashley Bayes had a huge hug; they had been practising deflected shots only the day before.

There were times that season where I felt that we had very little luck. But we did get one spectacular stroke of good fortune in the penultimate game of the season when Accrington beat Plymouth 5-1. As Accrington club secretary Mark Turner said, 'We played well but it was one of those games where every shot went in.' We won that day and so, thanks to Accrington's prolific goalscoring, our goal difference was now much better than Plymouth's. We went to our final game at Bradford knowing we only needed a draw to stay up, unless Plymouth won by four goals.

Plymouth did win, but only by one, so after grinding out a gratifyingly dull and very, very comfortable 0-0 draw at Bradford we survived on goal difference. The great escape indeed.

A month before the end of that season I finally retired, three years and two months after I first wrote to the DT board expressing my intention to do so. Eileen had just had the first of a series of serious (albeit not life-threatening) operations and I needed to be at home while she recovered. I also wanted Joe Palmer, my successor as CEO, to have time to make the big decisions about the following season, which needed to be made even before the current season ended. Joe was formally appointed shortly after I stepped down.

The other long-serving person who left at the end of that season was Simon Bassey. Marginalised all season, we (and that includes me) failed to treat him with the respect that his service and dedication to the club deserved. That's a matter of great regret to me; I hope it is to others as well.

The following campaign started very badly. The pre-season preparation included a four-day round trip to Ireland to play a friendly, a tour to Germany and several days in La Manga, Spain. Time was so squeezed that the sports science team struggled to fit in a proper fitness and conditioning schedule. That may well have been part of the reason for the results; we lost seven and drew three of the first ten league games. Wally says, 'I don't recall me having the arse-ache with the performances. We played well but we just couldn't get the win. I remember thinking that it was a confidence thing with these guys, get the first win and we will be fine.'

And then things got seriously worse. The FA charged Wally with misconduct for betting on football matches.[75] The charge was that he'd placed eight bets in two spells, five of them while he was at QPR in 2014 and three while he was with us.

As is normal for such issues, the club first heard about this by a letter from the FA which arrived two days before the season started. The club notified Wally the next day. There is then a standard process to go through. A couple of weeks later Wally took part in a phone call with FA representatives, to establish the facts. Wally confirmed that he had placed the bets in 2014 but had then stopped betting on football when he realised that it was no longer allowed. He also admitted the recent bets, which were for a reported £10 in total. The FA formally charged him on 19 September; a few days later the club announced the charge and suspended him. Assistant manager Glyn Hodges was appointed as acting manager.

The FA's wheels always seem to turn very slowly in these matters. As is usual in disciplinary cases, Wally requested a personal hearing. Accompanied by a League Managers' Association representative he attended the hearing on 17 October, nearly 11 weeks after we were first notified of the issue. He was found guilty, fined and banned from all football-related activities for 28 days. The club sacked him two days later.

On 23 October, following several wins while acting manager, Glyn was appointed on a permanent basis. Glyn appointed the club's recruitment manager, Nick Daws, as his assistant. Despite the winless start to the season, we weren't bottom when Glyn was first appointed. Bolton Wanderers had 12 points deducted for entering into a form of administration to alleviate their financial difficulties and in August Bury FC had been expelled from the Football League after failing to convince the authorities that they were in a position to fulfil their fixtures.

By the end of December Glyn had guided the team to 18th place, two points above the relegation zone, and everything was back on an upward path. But then the season fell apart again and when it ended early thanks to the Covid-19 pandemic, the club occupying the top relegation spot was gradually reeling us in. The Football League decided that relegation would be decided on the basis of points per game and on that measure

---

75 The rules about betting are very strict. Club employees are not allowed to bet on football in any shape or form, arguably not even on a kick-around in the park. The potential penalties are draconian.

we survived. Many of us drew a deep breath; one more bad result and we would have been in dire difficulty.

As I write, we are just over halfway through the 2020/21 season and, following a run of two points from 11 games, Glyn and Nick have been released, to use that tired phrase 'by mutual consent'. There is usually nothing mutual about it at all in my experience.

Just as this book goes to the publishers, it has been announced that Mark Robinson has been appointed as head coach and despite an initial win, a subsequent defeat has dropped us into the relegation places. I wish him well in his quest to keep us safe.

52

IF YOU BUILD IT

THE PROBLEM with trying to build a new stadium was that we had no money. When we started we were a brand new club operating at level eight of the football pyramid, with few assets and no business track record. If we wanted a stadium we had to remedy that so, over our first few years, we set out to build a reputation for reliability, financial prudence and community involvement. It had worked and here we were with the opportunity of a new stadium back in Wimbledon.

We still had no money but we owned Kingsmeadow, we were now in the Football League and we'd built a reputation for sustainability and reliability. Perhaps that's why some opportunities started coming our way.

In May 2013 we received an approach out of the blue from Fulbeck Land Limited. They had what seemed a quite eccentric suggestion, which was to build student flats on a raised platform above the Kingsmeadow car park. We told them that while their ideas were interesting the timing wasn't right. We didn't tell them that the car park wasn't ours to commit – it belongs to Kingston Council.

Later that year, when it became clear that a new stadium was a real prospect, we invited Fulbeck to return and we talked about what might be done with Kingsmeadow. There were two potentially major problems for anyone developing our site. The first was that a large proportion of the stadium and car park was designated as Metropolitan Open Land. In simple terms, MOL is the inner-city equivalent of the green belt and it is especially difficult to get permission to build on it.

The second issue, as anyone who visited the stadium might have noticed, was 'the odour problem'. This was the smell that sometimes emanated from the Thames Water sewage works, just beyond the adjacent athletics stadium. We'd been told that the existence of the odour problem could make a major development so close to the TW works very difficult indeed.

However, the proposal to build 1,500 student flats might be acceptable. The broad idea was to make the deal more attractive to Kingston Council by contributing to improvements in the adjacent athletics stadium. There would also be an artificial pitch to enable Kingstonian to play there. The athletics stadium would become a sporting hub, meeting one of the council's key objectives. Our planning advisor summarised our chances of success quite succinctly, 'It will be difficult, but the idea isn't bonkers.'

In early October 2013, Fulbeck made a formal written offer of a £10m payment, plus £2m to be paid towards the athletics stadium development. The offer was provisional on getting planning permission which they hoped could be done within 18 to 24 months. I went with Fulbeck to meet Kingston Council; they liked the concept so, with no other opportunities on the horizon, we entered into an exclusivity agreement.

As plans for a new stadium developed it became clear that the timescales for a deal with Fulbeck were a problem. Our planned timescale for returning to Merton meant that any funds we received from the development of Kingsmeadow would probably come too late to contribute to the new stadium. Nonetheless, at the time Fulbeck was the only option on the table, so we continued talking. In June 2014 they presented us with a much more detailed and well-worked proposition and, at about the same time, a much larger company, Development Securities, appeared on the scene.

Meanwhile, having got wind of what we were doing David Barnard, the former CEO of WFC and now a director at Chelsea (but very much an AFC Wimbledon fan), rang to say that if we were going ahead with Plough Lane, would we be interested in selling Kingsmeadow to Chelsea? I said 'yes' and within 48 hours I'd arranged with the Chelsea chairman, Bruce Buck, that he would have a look around the following week.

Buck arrived early and by the time I'd emerged from a meeting he'd already conducted his own tour of the stadium, which he described as 'tidy'. We discussed the price we were seeking and then the proposition was put on hold for several weeks until 'The Owner' (Roman Abramovich, although he was never referred to by name) was back in the country and able to see Kingsmeadow for himself. He never did come but in September Buck told us he had authority to negotiate a deal.

Meanwhile, talks with Fulbeck had been taken over by Development Securities and we were also now discussing the Kingsmeadow site with Newridge, who we'd originally partnered with over Plough Lane. The Chelsea deal was our preference because it wasn't dependent on getting planning permission and would provide immediate access to the funds we wanted. Nonetheless, to hedge our bets we kept talking to Development Securities and Newridge and in October 2014 they presented their respective proposals to the DT board.

In November 2014, shortly before we submitted the Plough Lane planning application to Merton, we received an offer from Chelsea. After some negotiation we got the bid up to £7.5m. This was over £2m less than the proposals from Development Services and Newridge but it was certain – the planning application for Kingsmeadow might fail and if that happened we'd be stranded. The deal with Chelsea felt like the real thing.

In December 2014 I sent a comprehensive report to the DTB setting out the three offers, a risk assessment, a commentary on the multiple steps to get from where we were to building a new stadium, the latest estimated stadium costs, the likely sources of finance, and an analysis of the timescales for getting planning permission. I ended by concluding, 'The direct sale of the stadium … [to Chelsea is] the only viable option for signing a s106 agreement that commits us to putting £7m into the stadium.' There was palpable excitement in the room. For years we'd been building towards this and now it was within our reach.

There were two other major considerations. One was that we would need an overwhelming vote by the DT members to authorise us to sell Kingsmeadow; it would be supremely ironic if the protections we'd put in place after the approach by Darragh MacAnthony made it impossible to sell Kingsmeadow and return to Wimbledon. The second was that Kingstonian would have to leave if we sold Kingsmeadow. For supporters who had seen our own club rendered homeless, that was a tough call to make.

We turned our thoughts to the design and construction of the new stadium. In January 2015, a month after we submitted our planning application to Merton Council, I arranged a one-off meeting on a Sunday for the DTB to be briefed. It was led by Andrew Williams, whom we'd appointed as our project leader, along with Barry Winterton of Mott MacDonald, who was to advise on the likely cost of the stadium, and Derek Wilson of Wilson Owens Owens, who was leading the design team.

The proposition was to spend £100,000 to enable the professional team to be briefed about our requirements in the new stadium. This briefing would form the basis of the design work that would be carried out once planning permission was granted. I reassured the DTB that the profit from the televised Liverpool game covered the cost and they agreed to proceed. We were on our way!

By the summer of 2015 we faced another financial challenge. The planning decision was being held up by wrangling with the GLA over their demands that we 'animate' the north/south street that ran alongside the east stand of the stadium. We either had to stand the stadium design team down or, if we wished to maintain momentum, invest a further £780,000 in developing a specification sufficient to go to tender once planning permission was granted. If we stood the design team down the opening date would be put back a season. The problem was that we still didn't have any money.

I suggested that I take up the issue with Chelsea, who had a vested interest in us vacating Kingsmeadow sooner rather than later. We had provisionally agreed that they would pay a £300,000 deposit on exchanging contracts on the sale of Kingsmeadow and I asked to double it to £600,000. The downside of this was that if we weren't able to go ahead with the stadium we would owe Chelsea £600,000 with no idea where we'd find it. But if we didn't go ahead the delay might cost us the Chelsea deal, which was essential to our funding.

Subject to getting agreement from Bruce Buck, the DTB authorised me to instruct the design team to go ahead. After some discussion he agreed to this on the understanding that the £600,000 was a deposit, that repayment (if it was ever needed) might take some time, and that we would move quickly to get the Kingsmeadow sale agreement finalised. I was happy to agree to that. The balance of the cost of £780,000 would be covered by asking the stadium design team to accept a share of the risk we were taking in commissioning the work; in other words they agreed to delay us paying them part of the cost and acknowledged that if everything fell through they might not be paid the final balance.

Things were moving on several fronts now. DTB chair Mark Davis was leading a team of volunteers to develop a briefing for DT members, asking them to vote to authorise the sale of Kingsmeadow. There were safeguards in the draft agreement with Chelsea to make sure we wouldn't finally complete the sale until we knew we could afford the new stadium. The members were being asked to authorise the DTB to instruct the football club board to complete the deal, so long as they were satisfied that all the necessary conditions had been met.

To allow the stadium to be sold we had to get 50 per cent of the DT membership to vote and 75 per cent of the members who voted had to be in favour of the resolution. A second vote with slightly lower thresholds would then have to be held within a month.

Mark and his team devised a campaign to get the deal approved. Its strap line was 'Back In Two Ticks'. After an intensive campaign to explain what we wanted to do, the vote took place at a special general meeting in September and another in October. The proposal sailed through, with only 23 votes against out of nearly 2,000 cast. We were one step closer to Plough Lane.

Things felt like they were going in our direction now. The GLA told us they were happy with our proposals to animate the north/south street and, off the record, added that the deputy mayor didn't think that the decision would go to the mayor; in other words they thought he wouldn't call it in. How wrong they were, as explained in Chapter 48.

By June 2015 the projected cost of the stadium had crept up to £25m, including some costs we'd already spent and a contingency. We would need a bank loan to complete the funding and, to my delight, we were told that a £5m loan would be available. And as back-up we had the potential for a share issue, so we felt we were covered.

At the beginning of every year the DTB elects a chair. This allows any newly elected board members a say in who it should be. In January 2015 Kris Stewart had put himself forward, as he was entitled to do, as an alternative to Matt Breach, who had been in the role for several years. Matt and Kris each got four votes and an e-mail vote was called so that the member who missed the meeting could vote. He voted for Matt.[76] This 5-4

—

76 As an executive of the football club I wasn't allowed to be a member of the DTB and so I had no vote.

split was reflected in many of the subsequent debates about the approach to getting ourselves a new stadium.

In the summer of 2015 the tensions around funding the new stadium surfaced with a bang. I submitted a paper to the DTB setting out how I believed we should go about it. This led to a major dispute because I disagreed with the 'fans funding first' approach which some board members had put forward; I thought it was premature. I argued, passionately (and, I came to realise, a little bit too vehemently), that if we got to a stage where we needed a specific sum to complete the stadium then the fans would deliver, almost irrespective of how much was needed. But if we'd already asked them to contribute we would be likely to be much less successful.

After I left the meeting there was a call for me to be disciplined for refusing to accept the DTB's proposed approach and a threat to call for me to go.[77] As chair of the DTB, Matt Breach acted as peacemaker and the immediate problems were smoothed over. But the underlying issues remained – the board was split 5-4 on many matters and Matt spent a significant amount of his time keeping everybody pointing in the same direction.

Meanwhile, to ease the pressure on me some DTB members took on the negotiations with Kingstonian. After extensive negotiations the DTB signed off a contractual requirement to pay £150,000 to buy out Ks' lease to play at Kingsmeadow and to pay off part of Ks' debts to their directors who were being asked to write off substantial loans. Most importantly, the deal included a proposal to offer Ks a £1m donation, either to help them to buy a share in an existing stadium or, in the worst case, to cover their likely ground-share costs for 40 years.

This was controversial. Some of our fans asked why we were paying them a donation at all. They argued that Ks had been the cause of their own demise and but for us they'd have gone bust long ago, plus we'd need every penny we could get to pay for the new stadium. Others, as well as some Ks supporters, argued that we shouldn't be making them homeless, however much we sugar-coated that particular pill with a donation. And they asked, 'Why couldn't Ks stay and share with Chelsea?' The answer was that the Ks board wanted to move and the £1m was a welcome contribution to help them to settle elsewhere.

---

77 I was completely unaware of this at the time, which is testament to how well Matt handled the situation.

Kedwell scores, 4-3. We're in the Football League

And relax. Stuart Cash and Terry Brown after the penalty shoot-out

Our first Football League game, August 2011. Jamie Stuart leads the team out in a replica of the shirt worn when Wimbledon FC played our first ever game in the Football League.

Neal Ardley, appointed as manager in October 2012

Jack Midson scores the penalty v Fleetwood to secure safety for the Dons, April 2013

The planning committee scrutinise the stadium plans, Merton Civic Centre, December 2015

The author at Merton planning committee

A 'resolution to approve' the application was passed unanimously. Commercial director Ivor Heller seems happy with the result

Danny Bulman (right) grabs goalscorer Tom Beere after a last-minute winner in the first leg of the play-off semi-final v Accrington Stanley, May 2016

Adebayo Akinfenwa (right) celebrates bringing the teams level on aggregate in the second leg of the play-off semi-final v Accrington Stanley, May 2016

League 2 play-off final, Wimbledon v Plymouth, May 2016

Left to right; Andy Barcham, Paul Robinson, Lyle Taylor and Tom Elliott take the pitch at Wembley, May 2016

'Thanks for getting me on TV, Barch' – Stuart Douglas tends to Andy Barcham

Lyle Taylor scores in play-off final: 1-0

Lyle Taylor and Neal Ardley are mobbed

The final score. We are promoted to League 1

Parading the play-off trophy

The scoreboard that got us into trouble with the Football League, March 2017

Left to right; Dan Norris of Hogan Lovells LLP, lawyer for AFC Wimbledon, Stephen Alambritis, Leader of Merton Council, and Merton Mayor Marsie Skeete, at the signing of planning permission for the new stadium, December 2017

Left to right: Galliard's Mike Watson, Council Leader Stephen Alambritis, former WFC captain Ian Cooke, Catalyst's Victor Clinton-Dove, CEO Erik Samuelson and Wimbledon legend Dave Bassett. Children from Smallwood Primary School and the AFC Wimbledon player development programme sounded a klaxon to start demolition work at the site of the new stadium, March 2018

Demolition work underway

Wally Downes and assistant manager Glyn Hodges at Fleetwood Town, January 2019

Scott Wagstaff scores against West Ham United in the FA Cup. We went on to win 4-2. January 2019

Wally Downes and goalkeeper Aaron Ramsdale celebrate avoiding relegation at Bradford, May 2019

Old Plough Lane in ruins, around 2000

May 2019, preparing the ground for the new stadium

November 2019, the west stand starts to emerge

March 2020, the west stand structure largely in place

With faint echoes of Feltham, the roof goes on

The new Plough Lane at night before the Doncaster game, 3 November 2020

The Dons' first goal in the new stadium

18 years, 5 months and 6 days after the FA Commission decision

LEAGUE 2 SALARY COST MANAGEMENT – PLAYER COSTS TO TURNOVER (INCL. FOOTBALL FORTUNE)

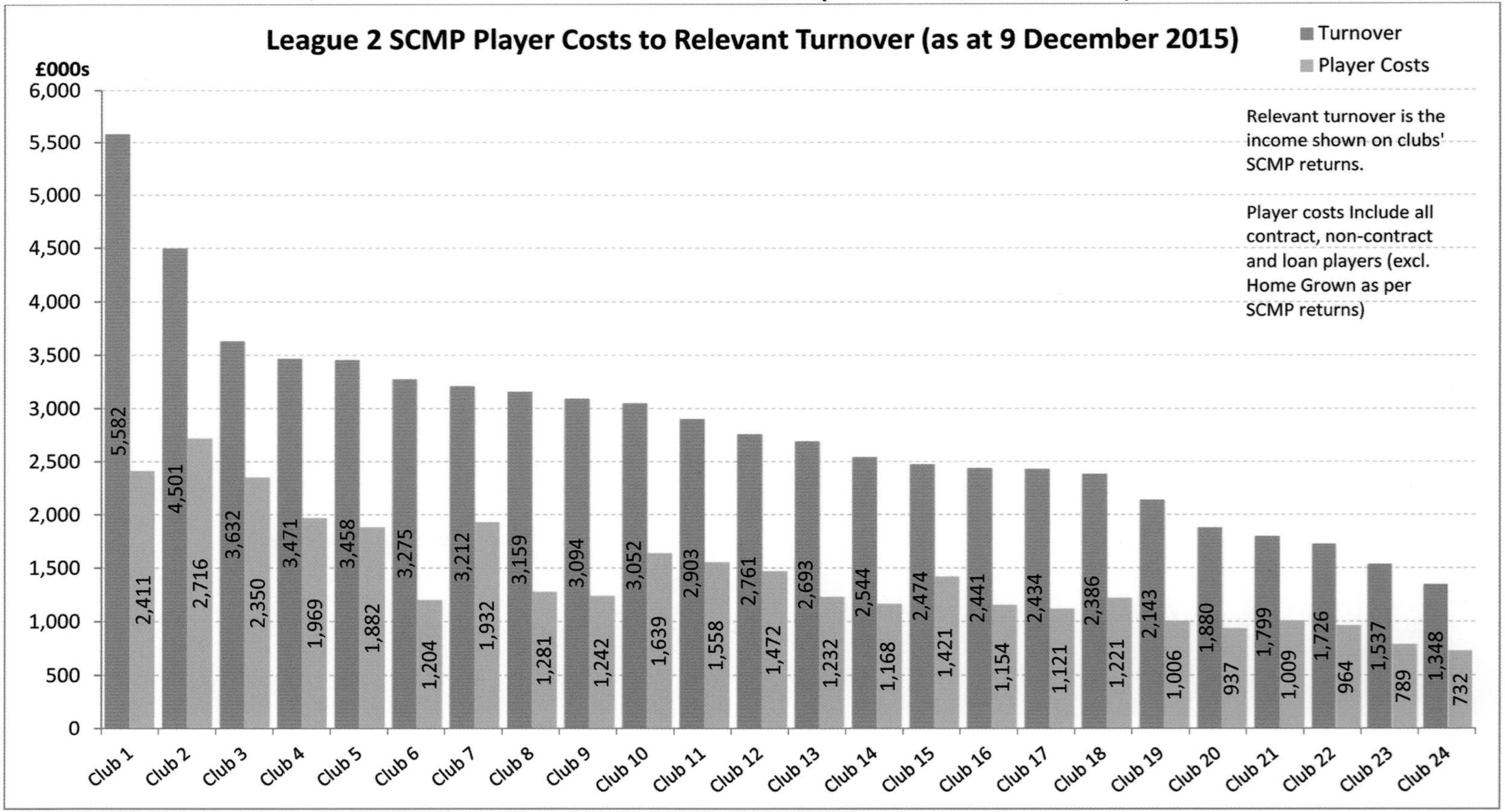

All 2015/2016 League 2 Clubs
Average Relevant Turnover - £2,813k (PY £2,815k)
Average Player Costs - £1,434k (PY £1,377k)

Comparison of the 18 Clubs in League 2 during 2013/14 and 2014/15
Average Relevant Turnover in 15/16 £2,806k (14/15 - £2,679k)
Average Player Costs in 15/16 - £1,385k (14/15 - £1,320k)

It was a constant battle to restrain the costs. By October they had crept up to £27.5m. We instructed Derek Wilson to make changes to the design to bring them down and he got them back to £25m, still including a contingency. But every time we did this it meant we would get a slightly lesser stadium.

Meanwhile, negotiations with Chelsea continued. On 17 December 2015 Dan Norris and I sat in their reception waiting to be taken to meet Bruce Buck, only to see him stride past and leave. We were taken up to meet the Chelsea in-house lawyer James Bonnington but without Buck we couldn't make progress. By then we'd concluded that when we saw him leave he'd been on his way to the Chelsea training ground to sack Jose Mourinho.

When Buck returned he told us we'd read about Mourinho on the news services and then we dived in to our agenda. That was a mistake. The best time to negotiate a good deal is not when someone is stressed after sacking the manager. The meeting wasn't a success and we ended up being pushed to give in on a couple of things we didn't like; we should have left and arranged an alternative date when I'm sure we'd have got a better result.

A few days before that meeting with Chelsea, Merton Council had passed a resolution to approve our planning application. This was great news but it was many months later than we had planned. The delay had two adverse effects. The first was to increase the cost of the stadium due to inflation in the construction industry. The second was that back in the summer of 2015 we had agreed with the DTB that we would invest £780,000 in developing the design ready to go to tender. This assumed that the Chelsea sale contract would be exchanged early enough for us to collect the deposit and pay for most of the fees. But the knock-on effect of delays in the planning application meant that we couldn't complete the Chelsea deal and now we faced a cash crisis.

It was now January 2016. If we instructed the team to complete the work and develop a document suitable for asking for tenders, then even with the £600,000 from Chelsea we would run out of cash by July. By the end of the calendar year we would be £350,000 overdrawn – but that was academic because we didn't have an overdraft facility. So we really had no option but to tell the stadium team to pause their work and that we would need to continue to delay paying some of their bills. If we did that then we would be okay for cash until the end of December 2016.

In the meantime we topped up our cash flow when Iain McNay's Cherry Red Records paid their 2016/17 sponsorship early and I loaned the club £120,000, interest free. The coming months were going to be a nervous ride.

In March 2016 we suffered a major blow when London Mayor Boris Johnson called in the planning application. This immediately put a 2018 opening in grave doubt. Better news was that we had obtained a letter of commitment for an interest-only loan of £5m at 3.75 per cent above base rate for 15 years. However, until we owned the land at Plough Lane we couldn't put up anything as security, so we weren't in a position to cement the offer. We had to assume the loan facility would still be available when we took ownership of the land.

By April 2016 we had reached agreement with Chelsea and signing was imminent. That would release the £600,000 and significantly ease our cash flow. Meanwhile, we had another issue to face. If for any reason the Chelsea deal fell through and we didn't sell Kingsmeadow to them, that would almost certainly kill the Plough Lane stadium. But as things stood, if that happened we would still be on the hook to pay Kingstonian the £1m donation.

That wasn't a risk we could take so we developed a separate agreement with Ks that if the Chelsea deal fell through they could return to Kingsmeadow on the same terms as before. This would release us from our obligation to pay them £1m. We thought it prudent not to tell Chelsea about this agreement.

Nerves were fraying as we continued to run very low on cash but on 27 May 2016 we finally exchanged contracts with Chelsea. On the same day we exchanged contracts with Kingstonian, in effect serving them notice to leave in the summer of 2017. And at last we had the £600,000 deposit from Chelsea. We could breathe again.

Further good news came in the summer when the new mayor, Sadiq Khan, returned the planning decision to Merton, followed by the Secretary of State and then Historic England refusing to intervene. Merton were, however, getting very edgy about Galliard's lack of energy to drive the deal forward and were wondering how committed they were to the project. It is difficult to hear such worries without a sinking heart, knowing what it might mean to our hopes of a new stadium. All we could do was look calm and deal with the things we could influence.

From my point of view, things didn't look as bleak as Merton feared. Negotiations with Galliard to secure the £14m contribution were continuing, albeit much more slowly than we'd like. The arm-wrestling continued over who was responsible for which costs; my stance was we couldn't afford anything over and above building the stadium.

Meanwhile, Merton and Galliard were at loggerheads over the amount of affordable housing. If that couldn't be resolved it was a show-stopper but I never really believed that would happen. In my opinion Galliard were simply pushing as hard as they possibly could to maximise their profits. I always believed they would come to a deal with Merton. What did concern me was that the negotiations were taking so long that we were now looking, at best, for a completion date in the middle of the 2018/19 season (and even that seemed optimistic). Thanks to Johnson's decision to call in the application and Wandsworth's lobbying, plus the snail's pace progress of the s106 agreement, we now had two years' worth of inflation to add to our costs. On top of that, as I said elsewhere, Kingsmeadow couldn't generate enough profit to support a League 1 team, and those losses would have to be funded for longer than we envisaged.

By March 2017 we were still miles away from getting a signed s106 agreement and I was getting increasingly nervous about the cost of the stadium. After consulting Andrew Williams and Barry Winterton, we agreed that the best way to get some reassurance about costs was to test our assumptions by carrying out a two-stage tender. This meant going to three selected companies and asking them for their best estimate of the costs based on the design to date. If they came out too high then we could take steps early enough to reduce them.

From the three tenders we would then select one to take us to the second more detailed costing, but we would be starting with a lot of comfort that we were likely to end up with an acceptable cost. While this isn't the most common way of tendering it's not unusual – and I wanted some assurance that we really could afford the stadium. I took the proposal to the DTB and they authorised us to go ahead.

Andrew Williams reported the results of the tenders to the May DTB meeting. The results were very reassuring. Even after allowing an extra £3m for subsequent inflation, possible errors in the tenders and uncertainty (since the tenders were based on high-level design assumptions), the average construction cost of the two lower bids was £21m. After adding in, say,

£5m for items such as fixtures and fittings, and the pitch, we were within the range of funds we were confident we could raise.

Things were looking up, but not for long. After further meetings with the tenderers the figure for building the stadium rose by £2m, eating into the contingency. Nonetheless, we were still within the range we were confident we could finance so we appointed Andrew Scott Limited to develop the second stage of the tender to arrive at a detailed cost to build the stadium. While it wasn't a deciding factor in our choice, we particularly welcomed their offer to defer payment of the approximately £750,000 of fees for the next stage of the project.

Meanwhile, Dan Norris and I (but mainly Dan) continued to negotiate the agreements. This was no small task.[78]

By now we were looking at a 2019 opening date for the stadium but at last a signing date for the s106 was being proposed. It was targeted for 22 September which, by chance, was the day we were due to be playing the franchised club at Kingsmeadow. I rather liked the idea that we'd be celebrating that night, come what may. Unfortunately the date slipped again – and we lost the game. It wasn't a great day.

It was at this point that we also realised that a recent change in the wording of the Development Agreement by Galliard's lawyers meant

---

78 To illustrate the scale and complexity of the negotiations, here's a list of the documents with a one-sentence summary for each:

1. s106 agreement – The 'master document', pulling everything together
2. Planning conditions – specific requirements setting out various responsibilities imposed on Galliard and us within the s106 agreement
3. s278 – the agreement that covers works to be done to local roads and pavements etc.
4. Development Agreement – the commercial agreement between us and Galliard
5. Transfer document – this set out how the land would be transferred to us and access rights for Galliard and the club across each other's land, during construction but also in perpetuity
6. Viability assessment – produced by the developer to determine the amount of affordable housing that might be provided and assess the profitability of the deal for the developer

There were also important appendices to these documents, including:

7. The phasing plan – what would be built and when
8. Development construction and environmental management plan – responsibilities of the construction companies
9. Site plan – Setting out the site boundaries and who owns what
10. Site clearance – what needed to be done to prepare the land for building
11. Crèche cost and specification – this is self-explanatory (the requirement for a crèche was later dropped, long after this document had been drafted)

And finally – once all the documents were completed they had to be cross-referenced to ensure they were consistent.

that the £14m to be paid to us was inclusive of VAT, if it turned out to be chargeable. So if the £14m was subject to VAT (which, admittedly, we thought was unlikely) we would only get £11.7m, because £2.3m would have to be paid to HMRC. This seemed obtuse to us. Galliard were claiming that if VAT was payable they couldn't recover it. However, they intended (which we were happy about) to transfer the land and the development obligations to another entity which we were sure they could register for VAT and then recover it.

Setting aside the technicalities, a suspicious person would say that Galliard were putting themselves in a position whereby if VAT was chargeable they could end up reducing their payment to us to £11.7m.

While we were still arguing about the VAT, in October we hit another road block. Galliard called me to say that they had discovered a mistake in calculating the Community Infrastructure Levy (a tax payable by developers) and, taken together with the effect of inflation over the period in which we had been negotiating the deal, there were further costs to add to their liabilities.

A few minutes later I got another call in which they ran through the various outlays they faced. As a result, they proposed that they reduce the payment to us from £14m to £10m, plus a £4m interest-free bank loan for ten years. I'd been warned to expect something like this; a late approach trying to change the deal is apparently quite normal in the industry.

From a £14m contribution, we were now facing possibly getting a £10m contribution, a £4m loan repayable after ten years and a potential £2.3m VAT debt. And this arrangement would cast doubt on our overall financing because no doubt Galliard would demand security against the £4m and that would screw up our chances of a substantial loan. This wasn't viable.

I was on a brief holiday but these things can't wait, so I put in the necessary calls to collate views from the football club board, Andrew Williams and Dan Norris. The feedback from Merton was that they had been presented with a similar case and had requested supporting documentation. Their instinct was, like mine, that this was a negotiating stance and we should resist it. If we didn't, Galliard would be back later asking for more and, as they put it, we'd both be facing 'death by a thousand lashes'.

Even more concerning was that if we agreed a lower sum than £14m or if Merton agreed a change to the viability assessment then we would probably need to re-open the planning permission, which would involve a new consultation process. This would take weeks, possibly months to achieve. We agreed to meet Galliard early the next week to make sure we understood where we were and what the issues were.

In some ways, it's quite helpful when something is so extreme because it takes away any choice. If we agreed to Galliard's proposal we couldn't afford the stadium. If we said 'no' they *might* pull out of the deal and we would lose the stadium. The other risk we were facing, whichever approach we chose, was that if the deal fell apart we'd owe Chelsea £600,000 and various members of the stadium design team about £300,000 in total. So my recommendation was to tell Galliard 'we can't do this' and see if Merton were willing to concede enough to keep the deal on track. The back-up plan, if Galliard did pull out – although I never really thought they would – was to approach NAMA ourselves, possibly in partnership with Newridge.

There was never a dull moment on my holidays!

The debate about the VAT was a real low point, as Dan recalls, 'I walked away from that meeting thinking the deal could well break down because I didn't think I could recommend to you – the club – that you should take the risk. It came up on the day we were playing Milton Keynes at home and I was so despondent I didn't want to go behind the goal with my mates. Instead you arranged a seat in the main stand for me.'

I reported this stand-off to the DTB and said that while I was confident there was no VAT to pay, I couldn't promise I was right and so I was concerned that we would be taking a mighty risk if we went ahead. To my absolute surprise their view was we should proceed anyway; by then Plough Lane was such a tangible prospect that any idea of giving up on it seemed impossible for anyone to entertain.

In one of the very few times I ignored the DTB, I agreed with Dan that we should hold out on the issue. Eventually we arranged for one of his partners to write to HMRC about the issue and the reply put our fears to rest. But what a waste of time, energy and money.

On 13 December 2017 we finally signed the s106 agreement and the DA.[79] By now I'd concluded that we'd lost a 2019 stadium opening.

—

79 Kingsmeadow had been held in a subsidiary called AFCW Stadium Limited, controlled by the Dons Trust. After some debate we decided to put the Plough Lane land and stadium into a new company, also controlled by the DT, called The Wider Interests of Football Limited.

In January 2017, with the s106 and DA now signed, we met Merton Council to try to unravel some of the problematical conditions that were attached to the planning agreement. It was essential that we got these conditions changed because, for example, one about opening times meant that we would need to kick-off at 7pm if we were playing a cup game that might go to extra time and penalties.

The meeting went through our proposed changes to the planning permission and to see whether Merton's officials could agree them without further consultation, or whether it required a more formal approach, known as an s73 application. We'd rather avoid an s73 application if we could but if it proved necessary it would still be a much less onerous process than a full application. A couple of very welcome changes were that Merton had agreed with the GLA that there was no longer any need for a crèche or a café.

We also asked about the possibility of a rugby club playing at Plough Lane. We'd first spoken to London Irish in 2013 but they had decided to focus on sharing with Brentford and everything went quiet. However, they had recently resurrected their interest and we were now in serious talks with them, to the extent that we were looking at the design changes necessary to accommodate a rugby team in the stadium.

We had made it clear that they couldn't take a significant shareholding in the club and that DT members would need to approve any deal. We thought many fans would have misgivings about the idea so we were proceeding with caution. However, aspects of their interest sounded very attractive. They were willing to make a one-off payment that would allow us to fit out the top tier of the west stand, which we weren't planning to do in the first phase. They were also interested in building the permanent east stand during the first phase of construction; we were less keen about that because it might make the stadium bigger before we would have crowds large enough to fill it.

Soon after Joe Palmer arrived as chief operating officer (COO), I involved him and football club director Mick Buckley in the talks. The proposition was that London Irish would put in about £7m of cash. I wanted some of that money to help fulfil our funding needs while they wanted to use it for expanding the west stand and building the final version of the east stand. Mick and Joe did some analysis of what they thought London Irish could afford as rent on top of the £7m lump sum and we made them an offer.

London Irish had been playing in Reading and struggling to draw crowds to travel to the Madejski Stadium. Mark Bensted, now the CEO of London Irish, explained their interest, 'There was some doubt whether Brentford would get going so our discussions with you were honest, although we did say that Brentford was our preference. We also said there was a strong case for Wimbledon. We loved your story and it would have been two groups of people coming home – us coming home to London, you coming back to your spiritual home. There would have been a good story there, it would have worked. We'd have made it work.

'We were very impressed with everything that you were doing. You had a small team but you'd done it all yourselves and the stadium plans looked really good. There were no downsides at all … we could see that Brentford were going to lose another year and [it seemed] that their new stadium was probably therefore going to be delivered two years later than we had both first thought.'[80]

We got very close to a deal but couldn't agree terms. Mark says, 'You just thought we had deeper pockets than we actually did … we thought we are on the wrong page here. We were hoping for a rent-free period to take account of the fact that we were putting in a big chunk of capital.'

It is easy to have hindsight but I think we asked for too much. I would have been willing to ask for less because I thought we'd have done well out of a deal with them. But I can't complain because I didn't say so at the time, or at least not forcefully enough. So we will never know how it might have turned out. London Irish subsequently did a ground-share deal with Brentford and we wish them well.

Scotts were now working on the detailed tender to tell us the cost of building the stadium. The report was delivered in August 2018 and it was a shock; the costs were substantially higher than the estimates we'd been working with and were unaffordable. After extensive discussions we came to the conclusion that we should exercise our right to terminate the contract and look elsewhere.

Having made that change we approached Buckingham Group in September to ask if this was a project they wanted to be involved in. The brief was basically, 'This is our budgeted cost, can you build a stadium to this broad specification for that price?' They were keen to take on

—

80 Ironically, both clubs ended up opening their stadiums in 2020/21.

the project and over the next few weeks we worked with them. In early November they presented us with their proposed changes to the stadium design and the associated costs. The work had been done at some speed so we asked Mott MacDonald to audit the figures. Nonetheless, at first glance they had come in £3m cheaper, albeit at the cost of giving up some of the features we'd ideally like to have had.

As always we were operating on the edge when it came to cash and we urgently needed to complete the deal with Chelsea. To do that we had to take over the land from Galliard and our agreement was that we couldn't do that until they'd finished work on a new culvert on the site.

The only option to bring in cash before we ran out was to vary our agreement with Galliard and remove that requirement. And this is why Dan Norris spent Christmas Eve at home, doing the necessary legal work to complete the deal. This released all the pressure on finances. And I finally got my loan repaid.

Life wasn't getting any simpler. In December 2018 we submitted an s73 application to make various changes to the planning agreement. True to form, the Wimbledon Park Residents' Association raged about it and threatened a judicial review. The application was due to be considered in February 2019 and then there would be a six-week period before we could be sure that we were finally clear to go ahead.

Meanwhile, Buckingham's proposed design alterations would need yet more planning changes. These would require an application which could be signed off by officers within their delegated authority. But we couldn't apply for these further changes until the s73 permission was final. It meant that to keep anywhere near to our schedule we would need to start work on the stadium knowing that we didn't have permission for some of the design changes we were implementing – we needed to assess the risk and decide if it was acceptable.

By now Joe had been with us for nearly a year and, as had been planned, he had taken over working with Buckingham on the stadium design, principally to introduce changes that would enable us to maximise the commercial income.

In February 2016 I had given notice of my intention to stand down from my role as CEO within a year or so, and it was now the spring of 2019. It was time to go. That might seem a strange time but I thought I shouldn't be overseeing the development of the following year's football club budget when I wouldn't be there. Joe would have to deliver the budget so he should be given the time and authority to set it.

Of course the world didn't stop just because I was no longer involved. There was more drama to come.

53

THE END

IN LATE 2018, knowing that I was planning to leave and realising that we needed a different structure, DT chair Mark Davis expanded the existing stadium oversight group. He widened the membership to include club directors Joe Palmer and Mick Buckley, along with Edward Leek, Colin Dipple, Rob Crane, Roger Evans and Luke Mackenzie from the DTB. Andrew Williams had been unwell and he was succeeded as project manager by Joe Giordano while Financial Controller Tom Rawcliffe was on hand to provide financial updates. The group met every Monday morning to appraise progress.

To reduce the risk of delay and further inflation, the club issued a series of Letters of Intent to allow work to start. Each letter instructed Buckingham to carry out specific work which we knew we could afford from the finances available to us at the time, while deferring signing up to the full contract until we knew we had the necessary funds.

Design changes were made to make the stadium easier and cheaper to build. Nonetheless, costs continued to rise with increases for kitchens, higher specification IT systems, additional ground preparation, a better quality pitch and some general cost creep.

To exacerbate the problems the changed financial background, including the highly publicised expulsion of Bury from the Football League, the financial difficulties at Bolton Wanderers and uncertainty around Brexit, meant that the expected loan didn't materialise. This left a huge hole in the financing. Furthermore, the decision to try to ensure we stayed in League 1 by continuing to subsidise the wages budget for a further two seasons was also eating into funds.

Despite tireless efforts by Mark Davis and Edward Leek in particular, by December there was no obvious way to fund the shortfall. Meanwhile, some would-be external investors had appeared on the scene and were willing to bridge a large part of the gap. However, accepting their proposal would have meant a significantly increased risk of losing control of the club in the medium term.[81]

A decision needed to be made soon if construction work was to be able to continue. Stopping and starting again would add a lot more cost – so a Special General Meeting was called. Mark Davis chaired it. He explained the financial shortfall and the proposed share issue that would mean eventual loss of control of the club and stadium. Based on the evidence Mark presented, I could see no other option. It certainly seemed very bleak.

A group of DT members argued that there were other avenues to raise finance that hadn't been looked at and that we could cover a hefty chunk of the shortfall by issuing a bond.

The prime movers for the idea of a bond were Charlie Talbot, Graeme Price, Damian Woodward and Xavier Wiggins. Charlie recalls, 'I was sitting with Xav and Graeme and we said we thought a bond could work and Mark actually said, "It's not likely to be a game-changer; we might raise £1m or so." So we said let's just take a quick straw poll in the room.' That poll showed a lot of support for exploring the idea and it was agreed that a small group would look at it early the following week.

Charlie says, 'What happened next very much showed the very best of our club again and how we've always been at our best in either a genuine or perceived crisis. It was a fairly fractious meeting where the floor basically said "we think we could bring more money in" and Mark, the chair of the meeting, sort of went "really?" And then three days later Mark, Graeme, Xav and I were all working together to put the thing together and working really well.' They were joined by Edward Leek, a DTB member with a

81 Initially we would retain over 50 per cent of the shares in AFCW PLC (which owns the club and stadium companies) but the external investors would have the ability to insist on a further share issue if there was a financing requirement. If we couldn't afford to participate on a pro rata basis we would almost certainly end up with less than 50 per cent of the shares and consequent loss of control.

corporate finance background, and Luke Mackenzie, who had recently been re-elected to the DTB after an absence of several years.

Charlie continues, 'Xav, Damian and I were very sure that we wanted a solution that worked for the whole club to come together. There were, as always in these situations, some slightly more conspiratorial theories about the situation which I didn't buy in to then and I don't buy in to now. I mean, people not seeing other ways out does not mean they want to sell the club.

'Mark and Edward in particular did loads of legwork on it from the Dons Trust side. So they put a load of hours in almost immediately on something which they hadn't thought would work. I feel that the very Wimbledon thing about it is we went from a fractious meeting on Friday evening and by Tuesday lunchtime everyone was working hard on making it happen.

'We put it together with the DTB. I think they suspected that it wouldn't go very far and Mark and Edward would probably admit that at the time they were thinking that this might raise a million or two and that wouldn't do any harm.

'We put the bond together over Christmas and New Year. The offer was that you could choose your own interest rate up to four per cent, for five, ten or 20 years. When we launched the bond the initial deadline was 14 February but behind the scenes we always knew we could extend it if we wanted to. But we set a fixed date because obviously it focuses the mind and we wanted money coming in.

'Like a lot of these things the first £1m took a couple of weeks to come in and then after that it really started to acquire a life of its own. I think we were somewhere between £1m and £2m before we went to the official launch event. Because of the timescales of everything else we did the official launch event long after the bond had been launched. That's when we got loads more press coverage and it got featured on Sky Sports News and all over the media.

'By that time some other people had come on board. I ran all the infrastructure side while Graeme oversaw the finance side and talking to the regulators. Damian was dealing with me on incoming enquiries and administration. And this was the point at which Xavier acquired this volunteer army of fans on the street as part of the response to the Covid lockdown. We had all these people who said "how can we help?" So we had an army of people going out to the local community and telling them what we were doing and leafleting and promoting it. We had volunteers outside train stations which became quite interesting because that's when we had conversations with people who were saying they didn't realise the football team were coming back.

'The big success of the bond was not only the money. In a very Wimbledon way it took an awful story and an awful problem and made it a feelgood story. Once it hit £2.5m the momentum went crazy.'

Eventually the bond raised £5.6m (and the offer has never closed). Taken with the one-off lump sum investment by Nick Robertson and the offer of a £4m loan in the financial market, the funding gap was largely covered. The DT board was now sufficiently confident to sign the final contract with Buckingham and building went ahead although, even then, we suffered more delays thanks to the Covid pandemic. However, on 29 January 2021, 18 years and eight months after the FA Commission's decision, Buckingham handed over the keys and the stadium was ours.

This book ends as it began, with everyone facing an awful story and an awful problem – and then a group of dedicated fans said 'we're not accepting that', took hold of it, made things happen against the odds, and turned it into a feelgood story.

54

PRESERVE YOUR MEMORIES

AS I finish writing this book it is February 2021, nearly two years since I retired.

On 3 November 2020 the stadium was sufficiently finished to allow the club to stage its first home game even though, due to lockdown rules, no fans were allowed to attend. Nonetheless, it was a momentous event. A small number of guests were allowed and I was pleased to be one of them.

We've been playing at Plough Lane for three months. Sooner or later the stadium will be licensed to allow fans to attend, even if the pandemic means that date is still uncertain. On a limited budget the team is struggling and near the relegation zone but there is plenty of time to put that right before the end of the season. And if we don't, well we've overcome much bigger setbacks, so we'll recover.

I've re-read what I've written and I marvel at the range of skills that we brought to bear to make it all happen. It's a cliché but nonetheless still true that we could not have succeeded without the combined efforts of the fans and a lot of goodwill in the wider community, not least Merton Council, whose support has been unwavering. All too often individuals in high-profile positions, people such as me, get the credit for what was really a team effort; I wanted to put that right as much as possible in this book. Nonetheless, I am sure I've not mentioned a number of good people whose contributions deserve to be recognised. I can only apologise to them.

As for my part in all this, I'm not looking for any thanks. That isn't why I did what became a vocation. I know what I did well and that is enough for me. Conversely, I know what mistakes I made and continue to beat myself up over them; I don't need any assistance to do so from posts on social media and chat sites.

Although the CEO role required a high public profile, that part of the job was never something I sought and since I retired I've consciously stepped into the background. Indeed, when I retired one of my few requests to the DT board was 'NO FUSS'. With no irony intended, I am grateful to them for honouring my wishes. To put it another way, and to borrow Kris Stewart's life-changing phrase, I just want to watch some football.

I am optimistic about the future. There is a renewed energy around the place which reminds me of when we started back in 2002. And with the AFC Wimbledon Foundation soon to be based at Plough Lane, we are perfectly placed to expand our community activities.

We've now achieved our long-term aim of a stadium back in Wimbledon, we are in League 1 and we've retained our fans-owned status. A strategy review is under way to clarify 'what next?'. Whatever it is, it won't be ordinary. The last 19 years have shown that.

APPENDIX 1

SALARY CONTROL IN THE FOOTBALL LEAGUE

There's a lot of talk about wage caps in football. The subject is not well understood and while it is of interest to a limited audience I thought I'd explain it, with reference to a specific season, namely 2015/16. I chose that because it is sufficiently long ago that it can't be disclosing any great secrets, and also because it was a particularly relevant season for us.

Each division of the Football League has different salary control rules. The Championship's rules are much less demanding than Leagues 1 and 2 and are designed to take into account the imbalance caused by recently relegated Premier League clubs having massive parachute payments, which dwarf the income of the other clubs in the Championship. Until relatively recently, Championship clubs were allowed to make losses of £39m over a three-year period so long as the losses were covered by the owner.

The rules for League 1 and League 2 clubs are very different. They have also changed very recently. In 2020/21 total spending caps of £2.5m for League 1 and £1.5m for League 2 were introduced. However, in February 2021 the Professional Footballers' Association won an independent arbitration ruling and the caps were immediately suspended. So far as I understand it, clubs are now being assessed in the light of the rules that operated until the summer of 2020.

This appendix sets out an example of how the wages cap is calculated under the rules which applied prior to this season and which appear to apply again following the recent ruling.

EXAMPLE

The figures are taken from the AFC Wimbledon report in 2015/16. That is long enough ago that they are of little commercial value to anyone. The report is submitted in the June before the season starts. Each player's annual wages are listed, along with any signing-on fee, match and appearance bonuses and relocation costs if any. In June we wouldn't have completed our recruitment so some players' names are 'A left-back' with a planned wage next to it. As contracts are signed the FL gets copies and updates the report. They include their estimate of bonuses if ours looks unrealistic.

Wages costs:	
Senior squad	
Total wages **	£1,054,300
Signing-on fees, bonuses etc.	53,600
Total	1,107,900
National insurance	142,831
Agents' fees	13,700
Medical and insurance costs	32,000
Total wage costs	£1,296,431

** There were also nine under-20 players whose costs are ignored for wage cap purposes.

Turnover:	
FL distribution	£474,000
Solidarity	240,000
Gate money (including season tickets)	965,489
Gross profit from bars, sponsorship etc.	578,347
Total turnover	2,257,836
Football fortune income (donations etc.)	435,200
Total turnover	£2,693,036

The calculation is then:

Allowed spending is:	
Turnover of £2,257,836 x 55%	£1,241,810
Football fortune income x 100%	435,200
Maximum allowed spending	1,677,010
Total planned spending (from above)	1,296,431
Headroom (i.e. extra we could spend)	£380,579

These figures are then used for several reports.

The first is a table of budgeted spending as a percentage of allowed spending. Before adding to the wage bill, any club with a result above 95 per cent must first certify to the FL that the extra spending will not take them above 100 per cent.

The second report is a histogram of each club's spending and turnover which allows clubs on an anonymised basis to see what competitors are doing.

In the attached example, we are club 13. In the table you can see the turnover of £2,693,000 and spending of £1,232,000. The turnover agrees with the total shown on page 405. The spending total has presumably been adjusted for the actual wages of signings after we submitted our estimates.

For those who are interested the table also shows where our spending fits relative to other clubs – we were 13th in the wages table.

NOTES:

The report is submitted in June. A second report is submitted after the January transfer window closes.

For the purposes of this report, commercial turnover is the gross profit. So, for example, it includes the profit on merchandise before taking shop staff wages into account.

Football fortune income must be guaranteed. So, for example, if we include donations in our report they must be committed, not a hoped-for figure. The January report can include TV facility fees and cup prize money in this category; in June these can't be known so they are excluded.

I always found the January report interesting because it indicated how much extra spending was being pumped into wages. Unfortunately, the club numbers changed so it was only possible to draw conclusions at the consolidated level.

APPENDIX 2

CUP PROFITS AND HOW THEY WORK

I used to get disproportionately irritated when fans and the media talked about bumper pay-days from an FA Cup home draw. So this appendix, I suspect for a fairly narrow audience, is to illustrate how much we would earn from a sell-out game against a Premier League club.

Before a tie like this we are required to agree the ticket pricing with the opponents. Our policy was always to charge our usual matchday prices. We're a fans' club and so we couldn't go price-gouging just because we had a big home match.

The example here is of a game against 'A Club FC', which is a Premier League club. The numbers are fictitious but credible. They are reported on two standard forms, reproduced here. The first is the snappily titled Statement of Receipts and Payments – Analysis of Ticket Sales and Paid Admissions.

The form is largely self-explanatory but here's a few notes:

- The form shows a total of 4,650 people attended and receipts of £70,870
- We list ticket sales by stand, then by price range. Our price structure is fairly simple!
- For ease of presentation I've grouped our two terraces together under one heading
- If we sell an executive package, which usually means a decent ticket to the game plus a meal, programme, etc., let's say for £100, we don't have to share the receipts. Instead we have to account to the other club for the cost of the seat alone. In this example, we sold 100 executive packages for £10,000 of income

APPENDIX 2

SHEET DISTRIBUTION
1 x The FA
1 x Opponents
1 x Retained

STATEMENT OF RECEIPTS & PAYMENTS FORM

TheFA

PLEASE COMPLETE IN BLOCK LETTERS
(Please write in ink)

CLUB: AFC WIMBLEDON			
COMPETITION: THE FA CUP ✓	THE FA TROPHY ☐	THE FA VASE ☐	THE FA YOUTH CUP ☐
DATE OF MATCH: 24/02/18	ROUND: 3	MATCH No: 10	

MATCH (Home Team) AFC WIMBLEDON
(Away Team) A CLUB FC

VENUE KINGSMEADOW

ATTENDANCE *Paying* 4,400 + *Complimentary* 250 = *Total* 4,650

RECEIPTS	£	P
Receipts from Terraces, Stands Enclosures	70,870	–
The analysis of Tickets Sales and Paid Admission Form must be sent with this form, detailing all receipts for FA Cup and FA Trophy ties	11,811	67
LESS: VAT		
TOTAL RECEIPTS	59,058	33
PAYMENTS *(Exclusive of VAT)	£	p
Police Charges	6,400	–
Gatemen/Stewards	5,800	–
Fee and Expenses of Match Officials	900	–
Travelling Expenses of Visiting Club	2,000	–
Hotel Expenses of Visiting Club *(Where necessary)*	2,500	–
Floodlighting	200	–
Medical	950	–
Water/Snow Clearing		
TOTAL PAYMENTS	18,750	–
BALANCE FOR DISTRIBUTION	£	p
Profit	40,308	33
Loss (Shared)		
Loss: Visiting Club receive travelling expenses less their $1/2$ (half) of loss		

For FA Cup and Trophy ties the Analysis of Ticket Sales and Paid Admission Form must be sent with this form.

PROFIT Please complete appropriate section	£	P
45% HOME CLUB	18,138	75
45% VISITNG CLUB	18,138	75
10% FA POOL	4,030	83

TROPHY / VASE / YOUTH CUP	£	P
All Rounds 50% Home Club 50% Visiting Club		

Date............

but A Club FC is only entitled to share in the value of the seats included in the package, i.e. 100 adult seats at £25 each
- Complimentary tickets (comps) total 250 in this example. Under this heading we included everyone who had a seat or a place on the terrace but didn't pay. Each club is entitled to 50 comps and in this example a further 100 would typically be for press, scouts, medical staff, etc. So that's 200 in total
- That leaves 50 to be accounted for because, for example, we gave extra seats for players' families for such a big game (in practice the demand is much higher than we could ever accommodate). We have to account to the other club for these tickets at the going rate. I've assumed there were comps comprising 30 adults, ten concessions and ten under-18s in the North Stand, where we tended to have more seats available

The total receipts from this form are transferred on to the Statement of Receipts and Payments Form.

First, VAT is deducted, then match-related expenses. The ones shown here are fairly typical costs for a major home cup game. Just a few notes:

- In general we don't incur police costs for league games. The requirement for a police presence for a game like this would be the outcome of a Safety Advisory Group meeting specially convened for this game
- The travel and accommodation costs for the visiting club are limited by laid-down rules but these look reasonable for a club which had to stay overnight. For a league game they are entirely the responsibility of the visiting club
- The match officials' costs include travel expenses
- The floodlight deduction is a standard sum
- 'Medical' is St John Ambulance, etc.

The profit of £40,308.33p is split three ways: 45 per cent each to the clubs and ten per cent to the FA. We would also reimburse the visitors with their travel and hotel costs. By deducting those costs from the profit calculation and then reimbursing them with the full amount, we both end up suffering half the costs.

APPENDIX 2

SHEET DISTRIBUTION
1 x The FA
1 x Opponents
1 x Retained

STATEMENT OF RECEIPTS & PAYMENTS ANALYSIS OF TICKET SALES AND PAID ADMISSIONS

The FA

PLEASE NOTE: THIS FORM APPLIES TO FA CUP AND FA TROPHY MATCHES ONLY

PLEASE COMPLETE IN BLOCK LETTERS (Please write in ink)

CLUB: AFC WIMBLEDON		THE FA CUP ■	THE FA TROPHY ☐
DATE OF MATCH: 24/02/18	ROUND: 3	MATCH No: 10	VENUE: KINGSMEADOW
HOME TEAM: AFC WIMBLEDON		v AWAY TEAM: A CLUB FC	

TICKET SALES AND PAID ADMISSIONS AT EACH PRICE		Number [1]	Price (£) [2]		Receipts (£) [1+2]
MAIN STAND ADULTS		500	25		12,500
MAIN STAND CONCESSIONS		250	15		3,750
MAIN STAND u18s		50	11		550
NORTH STAND ADULTS		450	20		9,000
NORTH STAND CONCESSIONS		200	13		2,600
NORTH STAND u18s		150	9		1,350
TERRACE ADULTS		2,000	16		32,000
TERRACE CONCESSIONS		500	10		5,000
TERRACE u18s		200	4		800
ACTUAL SALES / RECEIPTS DUE	[A]	4,300		[V]	67,550
SEASON TICKETS SOLD FOR FA CUP/TROPHY MATCH (SEE RULE 20(c)(iv) in Cup and Rule 20(a) in Trophy)					
	[B]	0		[W]	0
EXECUTIVE PACKAGES(SEE Rule 20(c)(v) in Cup and Rule 20(b)(iv) in Trophy)					
ADULT		100	25		2,500
TOTAL EXECUTIVE PACKAGES	[C]	100		[X]	2,500
COMPLIMENTARY TICKETS					
Issued	[D]	250			
Less: Allowance per Rule 20(a)	[E]	200			
Excess over allowance	[D]–[E]=[F]	50			
Any excess to be stated at sales price					
NORTH STAND ADULTS		30	20		600
NORTH STAND CONCESSIONS		10	13		130
NORTH STAND u18s		10	9		90
SUB TOTAL	[F]	50		[Y]	820
TOTAL MAXIMUM ATTENDANCE/RECEIPTS	[A]+[B]+[C]+[D]=[G]	4,650		[V]+[W]+[X]+[Y]=[Z]	70,870
TICKETS SOLD BUT NOT USED	[H]	0			
TOTAL ATTENDANCE AND RECEIPTS	[G]–[H]=[I]	4,650	TO STATEMENT	[Z]	70,870 TO STATEMENT

Date.. Signed Director/Football Secretary ....

So from a 'pay-day' home draw we would make just over £18,000 from the gate money. We would also, of course, make money from the bars, the premium ticket sales (although we had so few seats available this income was limited), sponsorships, programme sales and merchandise. But the real financial benefit is if the game is televised. At that point the facility fee might be £75,000 per club and the commercial income from sponsorships would increase due to the extra exposure.

The example given is for an FA Cup third round tie for which the prize money was £135,000 until 2020/21, when it was reduced to £82,000, due to cost constraints at the FA caused by the Covid pandemic. Because our players weren't high earners we had a generous bonus scheme in the FA Cup. A substantial share of the accumulated prize money was split between them in proportion to the number of appearances they made in the competition.

If, for example, we were drawn away to Manchester United we would get an enormous boost from our share of the gate money but the players would get nothing if we lost. So we instigated a scheme whereby players were paid a proportion of our share of the profits from the attendance from the third round onwards, with a higher proportion if we won.

There is no prize money from the EFL Cup, currently branded as the Carabao Cup.

Clubs are not allowed to include a proportion of TV facility fees in their bonus schemes. So when you see a small club with a limited capacity, like us, get a home tie against a big club rest assured we aren't making a lot of money unless the TV cameras are there.

ACKNOWLEDGEMENTS

THIS BOOK, like the club, reflects the combined efforts of a great many people. I will try to acknowledge everyone who has contributed but I can say with reasonable certainty that I will omit one or more people. That is not intentional and I apologise now.

To start at the beginning, I was encouraged and given very helpful guidance as I set off on this project by David Conn of *The Guardian*, Ardella Jones of Chalk The Sun, and Toby Porter of the *South London Press*. My grateful thanks to you all.

My wife Eileen, Stephen Crabtree and Chris Heald kindly read every word (Eileen read many of them at least twice) and gave me a combination of support, constructive criticism and encouragement. Doug Yarrow read selected chapters to give me an independent football fan's view. Special thanks to you all for giving up your time to do this.

My thanks also to Ciara Lloyd, who very kindly gave me advice and did the ground work that led me to Pitch Publishing who have turned my words into this book. And of course to Paul and Jane Camillin, who published this book and offered wise advice.

Over a period of 16 months I inveigled 80 people into helping me to relive their involvement in the club. Some had so much to say that we needed more than one session, making 96 conversations in all. They are all listed at the end of this section, with grateful thanks. Almost all of them are quoted in the book; those who aren't quoted nonetheless provided colour and detail about the events I describe. Not only did they add flesh to the bones of this story but those conversations were easily the most enjoyable part of the project. And I found out some things that were kept from me at the time, which was just as well!

Clair Richardson transcribed many of the conversations, saving me huge amounts of time and improving the accuracy dramatically.

I spent an age at Wandsworth Library going through old copies of local newspapers; my thanks to them. Thanks too, to Matt Badcock of the *Non-League Paper* for opening up their archives to me and to Stuart Hammonds for digging out some of the articles he wrote while working there.

I am also incredibly grateful to John Lynch at Wimbledon in Sporting History (WiSH), Bert Dale, Dave McKnight and Stephen Crabtree for digging out the most arcane facts I requested with consummate ease. John also allowed me to borrow Ray Armfield's 41 scrapbooks chronicling the club's rise from the Combined Counties League to the Football League. My thanks to Ray – but next time please leave the dates on the cuttings! Also, my thanks to Niall Couper for allowing me to quote extracts from *This Is Our Time* and Herbie Knott for allowing me access to interviews he conducted shortly after the club was formed.

Over the years the club has also been consistently and generously supported by its major sponsors, Cherry Red Records, Paul Strank Roofing, Chemflow, John Green, Ryan O'Sullivan and Moorad Choudhry. Without them there may well not have been a club to write about. This seems the right place to mention Terry's Badges, who gave the club half their profits from their Kingsmeadow stall every year.

And finally, and most importantly, the support and love of Eileen and our children and their families, namely, Pieter, Charlotte, Alexandra and Elisabeth; John, Sarah and Mabel.

* * *

The book draws extensively on conversations with the following people, for which many thanks to:

Tom Adam, Stephen Alambritis, Gary Alexander, Dave Anderson, Neal Ardley, Bruce Badcock, Simon Bassey, Alan Bennett, Mark Bensted, Gary Brabin, Matthew Breach, Seb Brown, Terry Brown, Steve Butler, Tara Butler, Lou Carton-Kelly, Malcolm Clarke, Alan Constable, Bert Dale, Mark Davis, Ben Dawson, Roger Dennis, Stuart Douglas, Wally Downes, Lee Earl, John East, Bruce Elliott, Sam Elliott, Nicky English, Matt Everard, David Fowkes, Sean Fox, Daniel Francis, Phil French, Jason Goodliffe, Gareth Graham, David Growns, Ivor Heller, Nigel Higgs, Tim Hillyer, Roger Hobkinson, Andy Holt, Alan Inns, Andrew Judge, Ben

Judge, Danny Kedwell, Linda Kirby, Gordon Law, Dennis Lowndes, Luke Mackenzie, Jon Main, Iain McNay, Neil Messenbird, Peter Miller, Lee Minshull, Daniel Norris, Steven Powell, Clair Richardson, Mike Richardson, Nick Robertson, Mark Robinson, Nick Robinson, Paul Robinson, Kevin Rye, Eileen Samuelson, Jeremy Sauer, Hugh Scanlon, Paul Scott, Stephen Sexton, Joe Sheerin, Jim Sturman, Nick Sullivan, Steven Sylvester, Charlie Talbot, Mark Turner, Simon Wheeler, David Wilkinson, Andrew Williams, Trevor Williams, Malcolm Winwright.

PHOTO CREDITS

Photographs were provided by:

Getty Images, Andy Nunn, Alamy, ProSports, ColorSports, The Air People, Rex/Shutterstock.

Particular thanks are due to:

Paul Willatts, for most of the photos from the early days.
Adrian Spink, for the demolition photo.
Kirk Pritchard for the photo with the new stadium roof.
And Wimbledon in Sporting History (WiSH) for some photos and their overall support during the writing of this book.

WIMBLEDON
WIMBLEDON